Praise for *Dalit Journeys for Dignity*

"This book expands the remit of Dalit Studies in significant and exciting ways by its focus on the relationship between caste, space, embodiment, and religious belonging. It also reconfigures older knowledge about caste, land, and labour through a feminist lens, enabling a productive critique of caste conjugality, family, and kin."

— V. Geetha, author of *Bhimrao Ramji Ambedkar and the Question of Socialism in India*

"In this richly textured volume, each essay focuses on different aspects of the striving for dignity and ethical life among Dalit communities. This is a decisive and timely contribution to the flourishing body of scholarship on Dalit life, aspiration, and horizons that have emerged in the past decades."

— Thomas Blom Hansen, author of *Wages of Violence: Naming and Identity in Postcolonial Bombay*

DALIT JOURNEYS FOR DIGNITY

⁓

Dalit Studies Volume Two

SUNY series in Hindu Studies
Brian Collins, editor

Dalit Journeys *for* Dignity

RELIGION, FREEDOM, AND CASTE

edited by

RAMNARAYAN S. RAWAT

K. SATYANARAYANA

P. SANAL MOHAN

First published by Permanent Black D-28 Oxford Apts, 11 IP Extension, Delhi 110092
INDIA, for the territory of SOUTH ASIA.
First SUNY Press edition 2025.
Not for sale in South Asia.

Cover credit: The cover, courtesy of artist-activist Siddesh Gautam, imagines Dr. B. R.
Ambedkar and his followers during the Mahad Satyagraha.
Cover design by Anuradha Roy.

Published by State University of New York Press, Albany
© 2025 Ramnarayan S. Rawat, K. Satyanarayana, P. Sanal Mohan
All rights reserved
Printed in the United States of America

EU GPSR Authorised Representative:
Logos Europe, 9 rue Nicolas Poussin, 17000, La Rochelle, France
contact@logoseurope.eu

For information, contact State University of New York Press, Albany, NY
www.sunypress.edu

Library of Congress Cataloging-in-Publication Data

Names: Rawat, Ramnarayan S., Satyanarayana, K., Mohan, P. Sanal, editors.
Title: Dalit journeys for dignity: religion, freedom, and caste / Ramnarayan S.
    Rawat, K. Satyanarayana, P. Sanal Mohan.
Description: [Albany] : [State University of New York Press], [2025] |
Series: SUNY series in Hindu Studies | Includes bibliographical references.
Identifiers: ISBN 9798855802627 (hardcover) | ISBN 9798855802634
  (ebook) | ISBN 9798855802610 (paperback)
More information available at https://lccn.loc.gov/2024000343.

For a Fistful of Self-Respect

I do not know when I was born,
but I was killed on this very land thousands of years ago
"The endless cycle of birth and death"
I do not know the theory of Karma,
but I am being born, again and again, in the very place I died.
I was Shambuka in the Treta yuga.
Twenty-two years ago, I was Kanchikacherala Kotesu.
My birthplace is Kilvenmani, Karamchedu, Neerukonda.
Now, "Chunduru" is the name of the cold-blooded cruelty of landlords
tattooed on my heart with their ploughs.
Chunduru is not a noun any longer; it's a pronoun.
Each heart is now a Chunduru, a fiery tumour.
I'm the wound of the people, a communion of wounds.
For ages, a slave in a free country,
subject to insult, atrocity, rape, torture,
someone raising his head for a fistful of self-respect.
My very existence in this nation, drunk on caste and wealth, is a protest.
I am someone who dies, time and again, to remain alive.
Don't call me a victim.
I'm a martyr, I'm a martyr, I'm immortal.
An immortal banner of defiance.
Don't shed tears for me.
If you can,
bury me in the town centre.
I will sprout into a bamboo grove that gives out the music of life.
Print my corpse as the cover picture for the nation,
I will glow as a beautiful future in the pages of history.

– Kalekuri Prasad[1]

[1] Kalekuri Prasad, "For a Fistful of Self-Respect" (1990), trans. N. Bhanutej, in K. Satyanarayana and Susie Tharu, eds, *Steel Nibs are Sprouting: New Dalit Writing from South India. Dossier II Kannada and Telugu* (Noida: HarperCollins, 2013), pp. 602–3.

Contents

CASTE AND THE SECULAR

Preface and Acknowledgements

WE ARE DELIGHTED that this Dalit Studies volume, *Dalit Journeys for Dignity*, is now being published. While autonomous, it is the second volume within an ongoing project. Despite disruptions caused by Covid-19, and a number of distractions in our personal and professional lives, we are happy to have reached this significant milestone.

The second International Dalit Studies Conference was jointly organised by the Dalit Studies Collective (DSC) and the Centre for the Study of Developing Societies (CSDS), Delhi. A three-day conference, "Human Dignity, Equality, and Democracy", was held over 22–24 January 2018 at the CSDS. K. Satyanarayana and Sanal Mohan (DSC), and Aditya Nigam and Prathama Banerjee (CSDS), acted as its planners and co-ordinators: Aditya and Prathama were incredibly generous and supportive throughout the entire process. The conference could not have taken place without the support of the Director of the CSDS, Dr Sanjay Kumar. We are grateful to colleagues, friends, and the staff at the CSDS for its success.

We are very grateful to Gopal Guru for his keynote address on the theme of dignity, which set the right tone for the conference proceedings. We convey our gratitude to the conference participants: Anupama, Awanish Kumar, Chinnaiah Jangam, Dickens Leonard, Dwaipayan Sen, Jayaseelan Raj, Jestin T. Varghese, Koonal Duggal, Lucinda Ramberg, Parthasarathi Muthukkaruppan, Prameela K.P., Ramnarayan Rawat, Sharika Thiranagama, Sumeet Mhaskar, Varsha Ayyar, and Yasser Arafath. We are very grateful to the conference discussants and chairs: Aditya Nigam, Aniket Jaaware, G. Arunima, Janaki Nair, Joy Pachuau, Mary John, Nivedita Menon, Prathama Banerjee, Priyadarshini Vijaisri, Satish Deshpande, K. Satyanarayana, Shail Mayaram, and Simona Sawhney.

The conference created new friendships and opportunities and we were honoured by Isabel Wilkerson's participation. A prominent African-American author and journalist, she had come to do research for her book, *Caste: The Origins of Our Discontents* (2020).

The Dalit Studies Collective is an open collaborative forum that serves as a platform to introduce the new scholarship of younger Dalit Studies scholars based primarily in India. Three of its members – K. Satyanarayana, Ramnarayan Rawat, and Sanal Mohan – first discussed plans to organise a second symposium on the theme of dignity during a three-day meeting over 8–10 July 2015 at the Indian Council of Social Science Research (ICSSR) Guest House in Delhi. We are grateful to Gopal Guru for his encouragement and discussions on the subject.

Since our meeting in 2015 and the publication of the first Dalit Studies volume in 2016, the landscape of Caste and Dalit Studies has expanded considerably. This collection of essays will contribute to and enrich the stakes of the vibrant debates on caste inequality and struggles for self-respect. The several fresh Dalit voices in this volume expand the scope of Dalit Studies by engaging with musical traditions, sartorial practices, emancipatory possibilities of faith, modern industry, and the role of caste in colonial and contemporary society.

The volume's thematic focus on dignity – with particular emphasis on religious conversion, new devotional traditions, and occupational and spatial secular practices – emerged during the conference proceedings and in conversations after the meeting. As the direction of the volume became clearer, we invited Chandra Sekhar to contribute a paper on Dalit conversion to Christianity, and Ramnarayan Rawat wrote a new paper on the features of the Sant-Mat religion and its entanglements with the political. Five chapters (2–6) examine the investments and challenges of conversion to Christianity, Buddhism, and the Sant-mat religion centred on Raidas and Kabir. The next four chapters (7–10) investigate Dalit sartorial and occupational innovations and initiatives to transform ideas of home and reimagine history. Collectively, the essays signal the emergence of new themes in the study of caste and untouchability in South Asia.

Ramnarayan Rawat and K. Satyanarayana had initially planned to write a shorter introduction. However, explorations into the history of dignity, particularly in the works of Dr B.R. Ambedkar, and engagement with the articles in this volume soon transformed the introduction into a full-fledged article. While tracing the genealogy of dignity in Ambedkar's writings we discovered that ideas of self-respect were foundational in shaping the evolution of his intellectual thought and interventions in Indian society. Ambedkar's decision to include "dignity" as one of the defining values in the Preamble of India's Constitution comes not just from constitutional theory. We introduce two critical concepts of Ambedkar's thought – his notion of the "social" and of "moral stamina" – both of which emerged from his participation in Dalit movements in the 1920s and 1930s. They serve as a framework for building a politics of self-respect and human dignity.

Friends and colleagues in the University of Pennsylvania's Department of South Asia Studies, South Asia Center, and the Center for the Advanced Study of India have been solid supporters of the Dalit Studies initiative. Over the last decade these three programmes have created space for members and participants of our two Dalit Studies conferences to engage with the wider intellectual community at Penn, and with the South Asia Studies Department's Caste and Race Initiative. Mark Lycett, director of Penn's South Asia Center, has been very generous in supporting the Caste and Dalit Studies initiatives. We are indebted to the South Asia Center for assisting in the production of this volume.

In large measure, we owe this book to the contributors who remained steadfast in their commitment. We thank each of them from the bottom of our hearts. Siddhesh Gautam, artist and activist, graciously agreed to share one of the paintings from his series, "the Mahad Satyagraha", for which we are immensely grateful. We take this opportunity to pay our tributes to Aniket Jaaware (1960–2018), a scholar, novelist, and teacher. A fellow traveller, Jaaware was closely associated with the Dalit Studies project.

We want to express our sincere thanks to Rukun Advani for agreeing to publish the second Dalit Studies volume and copyediting the essays in it. The manuscript benefited greatly from his superb editorial skills, adding clarity to the arguments. Anonymous feedback from readers solicited by Permanent Black helped us considerably in fine-tuning our Introduction as well as several of the contributions.

We are grateful to Rudrangshu Mukherjee for accepting this book in Ashoka University's prestigious "Hedgehog and Fox" series, and to Wendy Doniger and James Peltz at SUNY Press for so promptly responding to Permanent Black's offer and agreeing to copublish this book in their reputed "Hindu Studies" series.

We could not have reached this stage without the loving support of our family members. Sanal Mohan wishes to thank editors and contributors who patiently awaited his responses while he had health issues and was undergoing treatment. With great love, he acknowledges the unflinching support and care of his family – his wife Raina, and sons Nikhil and Emil – who made it possible for him to return to academic work.

Satyanarayana would like to thank his family, Pavana and Taara, for their loving support. His colleagues – Madhav, Satish, Uma, and Parthasarathi at the English and Foreign Language University, Hyderabad – have played a critical role in shaping the Dalit Studies research agenda over the years.

The love and affection of Lisa, Leela, and Rohan have made the long journey of putting together this volume a pleasure for Ramnarayan Rawat. He feels fortunate to have the support of extended families in Delhi and Iowa, and friends and neighbours on Beaumont Avenue in Philadelphia. He was supported by the European Union's Horizon 2020 research and innovation programme under grant agreement No 853051 for the project on "India's Politics in Its Vernacular". He thanks colleagues in History and Asian Studies at the University of Delaware who have also always been terrific supporters of his research projects.

RAMNARAYAN S. RAWAT

K. SATYANARAYANA

P. SANAL MOHAN

(ON BEHALF OF THE DALIT STUDIES COLLECTIVE)
Clare Hall, University of Cambridge; Hyderabad;
and Kottayam, July 2024

1

Introduction

On Dignity: A History of the Dalit
Social and the Struggle Against Caste

RAMNARAYAN S. RAWAT AND
K. SATYANARAYANA*

IN 1838 A DALIT weaver and itinerant cotton seller, Nanchari, converted to Christianity. Hailing from the untouchable village of Rudravaram in Kurnool District in the southern Indian state of Andhra Pradesh, he first encountered missionaries during his travels selling yarn. Nanchari had a series of conversations on Christianity with an English missionary, William Howell, in a prison where he, Nanchari, was serving a five-year sentence, 1837–42, for entering a temple and thus transgressing the boundaries of caste. Soon after his release, Nanchari spent several months living in a missionary settlement learning about the new religion and then led a mass conversion in his village. In Dalit vernacular sources Nanchari appears as a leader whose engagement with missionary groups was motivated by his quest for self-respect, enriched by the new experience of living for the first time in a community of non-Dalits.[1]

Dalit aspirations for self-worth and their search for a more just religious system have taken several forms in modern India. In the early twentieth century, in Punjab and Uttar Pradesh, Dalit groups fostered a new

---

*We are grateful for Sanal Mohan's comments and suggestions.
[1] Chandra Sekhar, "A Dalit Convert".

1

public relationship with the medieval untouchable poet-saint Raidas and the low-caste poet-saint Kabir to promote the Sant-mat religion which believed in divinity as aniconic. Dalit Hindi writers from the 1920s to the present have emphasised the notion of *atam-anubhav gyan* to highlight a person's self-experience in acquiring knowledge and a critical path to self-respect. They have argued that this concept, *atam-anubhav gyan*, played a critical role in the personal growth of medieval poet-saints Raidas and Kabir, and therefore occupied an important place in their teachings.[2] Whereas, in Punjab in the twentieth century, the Chamar Dalits had generated an autonomous religious identity centred on the poet-saint Raidas and created alternative religious spaces despite shared liturgical ties with Sikhism. The emergence of a distinctive Raidas religion (Ravidassia in the Punjabi language) gained structural traction after the 1970s, and in this the Punjabi Dalit diaspora of the West played a significant role. The martyrdom of Guru Ramanand, the religious head of the Raidas temple at Dera Sachkhand Ballan in Punjab, in May 2009 in Vienna contributed singularly to the Ravidassia religion's permanent severance from Sikhism – marked by the consecration of a separate book and liturgy.[3]

A desire for self-respect found expression through the exploration of new relationships with clothing, occupations, and homesteads. Institutional changes in British India energised Dalit groups who embraced new opportunities to challenge caste-enforced sartorial practices, vocations, and segregated living quarters. Dalit groups in northern India regarded dressing in clean clothes and wearing Western clothes as markers of collective ambition to assert a new sense of their self.[4] In the early twentieth century Dalit groups in Mumbai associated labour in the textile industry with a new, secular, and casteless form of work that was unconnected to caste notions of purity and pollution. Yet, as the demand for workers increased during and after World War I, caste intervened via a reconstitution, along purity–pollution lines, of the various mill departments in the textile industry. This effectively restricted Dalit

---

[2] Rawat, "An Ethical Community of Equals".
[3] Duggal, "Between Blasphemy and Martyrdom".
[4] Prasad, "Caste and Sartorial Dignity".

labour from well-paid jobs, these having been cornered by the dominant Maratha caste.[5]

In the Palakkad District of Kerala, families of former Dalit slave castes had to cultivate previously unexperienced emotions around the notion of the homestead when they acquired legal rights to their "workplace". After independence the Indian government, responding to the long-standing demand of Dalits in British India, granted former Dalit slaves titles over their places of residence. Owning a house with separate rooms and building new ideas around generational wealth nourished new conceptions of self-respect for these former slave-caste families.[6] In another part of northern Kerala, in Kannur District, Dalit Catholics led a resistance movement between 1958 and 1962 to establish a separate congregation: they wished to escape from the violence and stigma they had experienced from the dominant Syrian Christians of the St Thomas Syrian Church. Their shared social suffering had produced a "spirit of belovedness" among Dalit Christians; they organised prayers and meetings in Dalit houses, developed strategies for creating an untouchable church, and invited an Italian missionary, Fr. Taffarel, to lead their congregation.[7]

In northern Karnataka a commitment toward the "emancipated rational" among a new generation of educated Dalit men with salaried jobs was linked with conversion into the enlightened religion of Buddhism. At the same time, Dalit wives held on to another kind of ethical dignity by insisting on a devotional relationship with non-Buddhist religious deities that they had inherited from their mothers' families.[8] In Tamil Nadu, Buddhism played a seminal role in Iyothee Thassar's recovery of the anti-caste history of India. Thassar published a 65-part history of India (*Sarithiram*; 1910–12) in the Tamil language to narrate a casteless history of India by reinterpreting caste categories – such as Varna jatis, names of places, and religious figures – deploying an anti-caste perspective and an interpretive model of terms that borrowed creatively from the Pali and Tamil languages. Using the hermeneutics of the historical

[5] Mhaskar, "Caste and Occupational Choices".
[6] Thiranagama, "Inheritance and Caste".
[7] Varghese, "Oppression, Resistance".
[8] Ramberg, "Dalit Futures".

discipline, Thassar was making Dalit civilisation claims not evident in Indic histories. Later, Swami Achutanand and Dr Ambedkar would also contribute to writing anti-caste histories.

The articles in this volume illustrate that the struggle for self-worth and self-respect emerged from the very beginning of Dalit activism, and we use the "social" to define the struggle against caste. This definition of the Dalit social resonates with the use of this term by Ambedkar, who argued that a candid public discussion of caste is vital to creating a democratic India. The essays in this volume explore the history of the Dalit social and the concomitant search for dignity that emerged through engagements with religious ideas and the exploring of opportunities in the secular domain. These encounters produced new sources to define the self and inevitably involved contesting the existing hierarchical restrictions that had long governed employment opportunities, access to space, and sartorial practices. The histories recorded here of the Dalit social show an evolution in struggles against caste, against religious prescriptions found in Hindu religious texts such as the *Manusmriti*, and against practices restricting access to secular spaces in urban and rural areas.

The Dalit social was also increasingly defined by its struggles for dignity, which became a foundational principle of Dalit movements. Dalit engagements with questions of self-worth and self-respect have expanded historical and theoretical definitions of dignity in critical and novel ways. Struggles for self-worth became visible over the nineteenth and twentieth centuries within the contexts shaped by British-Indian institutions and practices. As members of historically marginalised and oppressed communities, Dalit activists appropriated new practices and institutions to advance the cause of self-worth. The Dalit social emerged by exploring religious alternatives (through acts of conversion), by reinventing opportunities in the secular domain (occupations), and by cementing a commitment to constitutional democracy as well as to the institutions of the democratic state.

In the first section of this introduction we will explore the critical role of religion in constituting the Dalit social, revealing how this relationship took many forms – such as conversion to Christianity or Buddhism or an appropriation of the Sant-mat religion. Dr Bhimrao Ramji Ambedkar concluded in 1935 that Dalits must find a new religion: this was because he had been unsuccessful in persuading Hindus to treat untouchables as fellow human beings despite the three non-violent demonstrations (satyagrahas) he had led in Maharashtra between 1927 and 1930.[9]

In the second section we argue that in his book, *Ranade, Gandhi, and Jinnah* (1943), Ambedkar outlined a new conceptual framework for the study of modern India by distinguishing the social from the political. He argued that without addressing the social question characterised by caste – the sphere where "tyranny and oppression" occur in society – a true democratic society is beyond reach.

In the third section we propose that this unique history of Dalit struggle for self-respect and concern with the social informed Ambedkar's decision to include dignity in the Preamble of India's Constitution (1950). The "fraternity-dignity values" defined in the Indian Constitution sought to protect the ethical treatment and social welfare of Dalits, Adivasis, and other minorities.

In the final section we introduce Ambedkar's notion of "moral stamina" as a critical methodological concept for excavating and recovering Dalit agency within everyday struggles against atrocities to achieve meaningful constitutional and social changes.

Religion is Social: A Fraternity of Equals

"Does Hinduism recognize [untouchables'] worth as human beings? Does it stand for their equality? Does it extend them the benefit of liberty?"[10] Ambedkar raised these questions in his 1936 speech at a Dalit (Mahar) meeting and subsequently published a book on this subject. His collected writings on democracy, law, caste, and religion are permeated with probing questions on the self-worth of Dalits as human beings. He argued that untouchables would benefit by leaving Hinduism and

[9] He was also unsuccessful in persuading the leaders of the Indian National Congress and Hindu organisations to safeguard untouchables' rights of representation within the political negotiations surrounding the new constitutional measures that were discussed in 1930–1 in London.

[10] "Conversion", in Rodrigues, *The Essential Writings of B.R. Ambedkar*, p. 228.

converting to Christianity, Islam, or Buddhism, whose ethics have "universalized and equalized all values of life."[11] He explained in great detail that "Hinduism is inconsistent with the self-respect and honour of the Untouchables," and that therefore they need a new religion.[12] For Ambedkar questions of religion and the moral order were intimately tied to the successful transformation of India into a democratic society. He came increasingly to believe that "there were no rights in the Hindu Society which the moral sense of man could recognize," and therefore argued that Hinduism represents a major barrier to creating "a real social democracy".[13] He insisted that political democracy cannot be created by individuals who adhere to a religious orthodoxy committed to the caste and varna hierarchy.[14]

We need to locate Ambedkar within this genealogy of the Dalit social led by leaders and organisations in late colonial India who envisioned non-Hindu religions that promised and promoted self-worth and self-respect. Conversion to Christianity, Buddhism, Islam, and the appropriation of Raidas and the Sant-mat religion emerged as constitutive features of the Dalit social. Nanchari in the 1830s, and Swami Achutanand and Mangoo Ram in the 1920s, recognised this relationship between religion and the Dalit social. Ambedkar's questions resonated, and continue resonating, with an already existing Dalit motivation to convert. Converting to a new religion represents an ethical desire for self-respect, a commitment to the creation of a community of equals, and to build a dignified social life. In this modernist reading, religion functions as a vital ancillary to a democratic society grounded in the dignity of Dalits, women, and other minorities, with Ambedkar as the leading theorist of this uniquely Dalit position.

In the 1920s Ambedkar adopted his strategy of reforming Hinduism by inviting its leaders to consider Dalits as their equals. Between 1926 and 1932, with this goal in mind, he led several campaigns in Maharashtra to engage orthodox Hindu groups and leaders in public discussion. The Mahad satyagraha in March 1927 was Ambedkar's first such public

[11] Ibid., p. 230.
[12] Ibid., p. 229.
[13] Ambedkar, *Ranade, Gandhi, and Jinnah*, p. 37.
[14] Ibid., pp. 37–8.

protest, the demand being that Dalits be allowed to drink water from the Chavdar public tank in the town of Mahad. Caste-Hindu groups in Mahad reacted with violent opposition to the Dalit campaign and refused to treat Dalits as human beings. Responding with hostility to the Dalit procession, in August 1927 the Mahad municipality rescinded its 1924 civic order which had opened public spaces to all citizens. In December the same year, as part of the campaign, Ambedkar publicly burnt the *Manusmriti*, the sacred Hindu law book which prescribed the humiliation of Dalits and advocated treating them as filth.[15] Over the next few years Ambedkar led several Hindu temple entry campaigns, including two well-known struggles – the October 1929 Parvati temple movement in Pune, and the March 1930 Kalaram temple movement in Nasik. The second of these turned into a strong Dalit movement. The organisers of the Nasik satyagraha spent considerable time and resources orchestrating a powerful and visible intervention. Explaining the motivation behind the campaign, Ambedkar argued that "this Satyagraha movement is going to prove whether [the] Hindu mind treats human beings as human beings. This Satyagraha is to change the heart of Hindus. This movement will decide whether [the] Hindu mind regards humanity in the new age."[16] In response, caste-Hindus closed the Kalaram temple in Nasik for a year and refused to accept Dalits as either human or their equals. A thoroughly disillusioned Ambedkar declared, "[W]hen the Untouchables lost all hope for their salvation through social reform, they were forced to seek political means for protecting themselves."[17] These movements fostered self-confidence among Dalits for legal equality as a source of anti-caste social equality.

Ambedkar's experience in these temple-entry movements shaped his recognition of religion as a vital medium for producing self-worth. It had become clear to him that the reform and reorganisation of Hinduism was

---

[15] According to Ambedkar, the *Manusmriti* prescribed a "penal sanction" to maintain caste. He cites the famous killing of Shambuka, an untouchable saint, by Lord Rama. It authorised "cutting off the tongue or pouring of molten lead in the ears of the Shudra," among other harsh measures against untouchables. Ambedkar, *Annihilation of Caste*, p. 61.

[16] Ambedkar, "Kalaram Temple Entry Satyagraha", p. 182.

[17] Ambedkar, *What Congress and Gandhi*, p. 190.

impossible. Having arrived at a critical assessment of this religion, he declared that its theological beliefs and institutional practices were inconsistent with the values of social equality and dignity. In his presidential address at the Depressed Classes conference in Nasik on 13 October 1935 he said, "[U]fortunately, I was born in Hinduism but I will not die as a Hindu."[18] In this address Ambedkar defined in categorical terms the objectives of a new Dalit movement which was to achieve "social freedom for the Untouchables" but not the reform of Hindu society. A year later in his famous presidential address, "The Annihilation of Caste", he called for the building of a democratic society in India, which would entail destroying the Hindu religious texts that had sustained the caste system. As is well known, Ambedkar was unable to actually deliver the speech because the Hindu social reform organisation based in Lahore, Punjab, withdrew its invitation to him after its top personnel saw an advance copy of his speech in May 1936.[19]

These campaigns by Dalit groups motivated Ambedkar to seek religious alternatives and by 1936 he had concluded that eradicating caste discrimination required a fundamental rupture with the Hindu religion. Describing Hinduism as a "living example of inequality," he argued that orthodox Hindu society's commitment to its religion had sustained untouchability.[20] In the Hindu religion certain people were regarded as so low and so unclean that even their touch was thought the cause of a caste-Hindu having become impure. The touch of an "untouchable" person – a human being – was believed to pollute water, food, and even a sacralised location such as a temple; it supposedly made a holy and pure God unworthy of worship. The "untouchables" were was equated with filth, their body and words reduced to an equivalence with stigma and pollution. It was obvious to Ambedkar that Hinduism was "a religion of rules, a compendium of ritual regulations which are based on [the] caste ideology of hierarchy and untouchability," and that these beliefs were so fundamentally embedded within it that untouchables could never be seen as human beings.[21] In his famous 1936 lecture,

[18] Ambedkar, "Unfortunately, I was Born a Hindu Untouchable", p. 95.
[19] "Prologue", in Ambedkar, "Annihilation of Caste", p. 28.
[20] Ambedkar, "What Way Emancipation", p. 124.
[21] Ambedkar, "Annihilation of Caste", pp. 74–5.

which he published as the *Annihilation of Caste*, he argued that social and religious reform in the colonial period had mainly focused on reforming orthodoxies that structured the Hindu family, but not the removal of caste. This kind of reform was, in his view, insufficient and indeed a failure to grapple with the framework of tenets that sustained Hinduism. Acknowledging that his efforts at reform had failed, Ambedkar decided to find solutions in a new religion as a personal and social quest for dignity. He argued that it was time to leave Hinduism because it was a religion that did not contribute to "the spiritual development of an individual."[22]

Ambedkar turned his attention to building self-confidence and dignity among untouchables, and at the heart of this trajectory was conversion to a religion which valued compassion. In his 1936 lecture he spelled out that the religious conversion movement was aimed at achieving "a life of self-respect and equality for all untouchables."[23] Accordingly, the ideal religion should comprise rules and values that bind its adherents to ensuring equal access to individual welfare and progress. The social value of religion was key: Ambedkar disagreed with the conventional Marxist definition that regarded religion as a feature of the superstructure, unrelated to the more important material foundations of a society. His ideal religion would promote the "value of life without distinction" and emphasise universal moral values.[24] He aligned this ideal religion with ecumenical principles (a) recognising one's worth as a human being; (b) forging bonds of fraternity, liberty, love, respect; and (c) fostering a sense of kindred spirit.

Conversion would offer Dalits membership in a community. Invoking anthropological notions of kinship, Ambedkar observed that conversion to a preferred religion should ideally play a vital role in nurturing a relationship between Dalits and members of other religions which would foster social equality in the community – "equal position, equal protection, and equal justice."[25] Conversion would end social isolation and the inferiority complex of Dalits; they would

---

[22] Ambedkar, "What Way Emancipation", p. 123.

[23] Ibid., p. 119.

[24] Ambedkar, "Away from the Hindus", p. 411.

[25] Ibid., p. 412.

acquire a new religious identity which would pave the way for social emancipation.

Caste and the Curse of the Political

> Most people do not realize Society can practice tyranny and oppression against an individual in a far greater degree than a Government can. The means and scope that are open to society for oppression are more extensive than those that are open to Government, also they are far more effective.
>
> – Dr B.R. Ambedkar (1943)[26]

In his collective writings and activism Ambedkar consistently demanded that Hindu nationalist groups address caste's creation of graded inequality, exclusion, and humiliation of lower castes and Dalits. In *Ranade, Gandhi, and Jinnah* (1943) Ambedkar contended that Justice M.G. Ranade (1842–1901) was one of the few caste-Hindu leaders who had asserted that social change must precede the demand for political power by Indian nationalists. His argument was that Justice Ranade possessed a "correct understanding of the inter-relation between the 'social' and the 'political'" because he addressed the foundational problem of caste and untouchability which Hindu religious practices had actively sustained.[27] Ranade had aimed at building a moral conscience in Hindu society to combat the fact that its religious ideology promoted selective privileges and disadvantages.[28] The greatest strength of Ranade's ideological agenda was to have recognised the undemocratic character of the social in India. Around the same time, in the 1890s and 1900s, Pandit Iyothee Thass' engagement with Buddhism in Tamil Nadu had followed his earlier failed efforts to participate in the activities of caste-Hindu reform organisations because of his caste. Ranade, Thass, and Ambedkar demanded that Indian groups critically debate caste, the core concept which monitors the quotidian rhythm of secular and religious life – and the essays in this collection explore these themes. The contributors here engage and advance one of Ambedkar's theoretically insightful formulations, namely the distinction between the

[26] Ambedkar, *Ranade, Gandhi, and Jinnah*, p. 21.
[27] Ibid., p. 33.
[28] Ibid., pp. 36–8.

social and the political at the high noon of the Indian national movement, which he developed in his writings and speeches between 1927 and 1948. His overriding concern in aligning the social with caste illustrates the centrality of the concept of dignity in Dalit political thought.

Ambedkar's 1943 historical study offers an alternative genealogy of the social and the political; his perspective is at variance with the study of modern India from that of nationalists and Hindu reform groups who prioritised self-governance – this is "the curse of the political" inasmuch as it obscures and sidelines the social. The competing claims of the social and the political emerged in late British India, representing the interests of the colonial state and the nationalists. Recent writings on the social have highlighted the singular role of the colonial state in producing "a politics of community-based claims" created by practices of government-ality, such as the census.[29] Consequent upon his considerable historical discussion of events in the nineteenth century, Ambedkar argued that Indian political organisations had reached a general consensus that they should avoid discussing the contentious caste question. They thereby failed to recognise that Hindu society's beliefs and practices contained tools of tyranny and oppression more effective than those possessed by the government. Ambedkar described Justice Ranade as a titan among Hindu reformers and among the very few who had addressed the question of the social. As the founder of several reform organisations, the well-known Indian National Social Conference in 1887, Ranade's intellectual agenda and social activism had centred on fighting Hindu society's oppression against the individual, especially in relation to caste and gender.[30] Such was his reputation that in 1892 Dalit leaders of the Mahar community had approached Ranade to draft a petition against the government order banning recruitment of Mahars into the army. Ranade, said Ambedkar, had also defended the right to liberty of Indians

[29] A comprehensive discussion on the social and political appears in the introduction by Sinha, *Specters of Mother India*, p. 8. A good discussion on the relationship between colonial sociology and the social appears in Prakash, "The Colonial Genealogy of Society".

[30] Ambedkar makes a passing reference to the role of Jotiba Phule, the social reformer who also addressed questions of caste and gender reform: Ambedkar, *Ranade, Gandhi, and Jinnah*, p. 44.

to travel to foreign lands: he had challenged the claim of orthodox Hindu groups that such journeys violated religious and caste purity. Ranade had in fact led reforms in four critical areas – marriage, remarriage, property, and education.[31]

Feminist historians have documented Ranade's role as the sole reformer supporting women's rights in the face of opposition by nationalist groups.[32] In the spring of 1891 the British Indian government in Calcutta signed the Age of Consent Act whereby the legal minimum age for a girl's marriage was raised from ten to twelve years. The Bill generated intense opposition from liberal and orthodox Indian groups in the major presidency capitals. In Bombay, the public show of support from women's groups met the active criticism of orthodox Hindu groups. Ranade was the only leading Indian leader to support women activists in Bombay and defend the British government's action. Alongside his associates, he challenged submission by educated Indian groups to the diktats of the Hindu shastras. Ambedkar expressed his appreciation of Ranade's commitment to modernity, his willingness to confront the failure of Hindu nationalist leaders to address inequality and unequal access to education – the issues that had been raised by women activists.[33]

By the twentieth century, Ambedkar said, Indian political organisations had decided to focus exclusively on political power and representation. "The politician triumphed over the Social Reformers," he wrote in 1943.[34] Ambedkar had found an ally in Ranade. It needs to be recalled that in *Annihilation of Caste* (1936), a full seven years earlier, Ambedkar had anticipated what he valued in Ranade because he had underlined the centrality of reforming Hindu society to challenge caste

[31] Ibid., pp. 41–2.

[32] "Potent Protests: The Age of Consent Controversy, 1891", ch. 4 in Sinha, *Colonial Masculinity*, p. 141; and Anagol, "Rebellious Wives and Dysfunctional Marriages", pp. 420–65.

[33] Ambedkar, *Ranade, Gandhi, and Jinnah*, pp. 41–2. Ambedkar chose to ignore Ranade's views on the ancient Indian past, especially regarding Aryan society, which he regarded as possessing some redeemable features. Similarly, Ranade's second marriage to a young teenage bride following the death of his first wife illustrates a complicated relationship with the question of women's reform.

[34] Ibid., p. 43.

hierarchy and practices of humiliation as a vital precondition for achieving real social democracy.[35] The nationalist leadership had concluded that political change in the government could be achieved without engaging the social: Ambedkar suggested that Congress had reached this conclusion even as far back as 1892, when its president had declared in the annual meeting that changes in the social were not a prerequisite for the cause of political reform. The Congress leadership and Hindu elites had, in effect, refused to confront those of their shastras which justified a caste and gender hierarchy. Indeed, in the twentieth century the Congress leadership, first led by B.G. Tilak (1856–1920), and later by M.K. Gandhi (1869–1948) and Jawaharlal Nehru (1889–1964), had decisively moved in favour of self-governance. A deeply conservative politician, Tilak set the tone for the Congress by appealing to caste purity as sanctioned by the Hindu shastras as a key element for Indian rejuvenation. Nehru, a socialist-nationalist leader, regarded caste as an anachronistic institution and therefore viewed both social and political struggles in casteless terms. Nehru and the Left in general sincerely believed that economic transformations in the twentieth century would eventually lead to the decline of caste identities.

It was ultimately Gandhi, a constitutionalist and a moderate, who forced the Congress to engage with the question of caste after he took over the Congress leadership. Indeed, the Congress' 1920 resolution on the Non-Cooperation movement committed it to removing the disabilities faced by untouchables.[36] Gandhi and liberal members of the Congress offered a religious accommodation to untouchables within Hinduism – for instance by offering public support on the temple-entry satyagrahas without actively participating in them, but nevertheless generating extensive discussions on the subject within the Hindu community. In addition, they promoted Hindu purity habits among the untouchable community by establishing organisations such as the Harijan Seva Sangh, founded in 1932. Chinnaiah Jangam documents the activism of "Dalit leaders and organisers who were followers of Gandhi" and his substantial intervention on the question of caste inspired a number

---

[35] Ambedkar, *Annihilation of Caste*, pp. 38–41.
[36] Ambedkar, *What Congress and Gandhi*, p. 55.

of activists in the city of Hyderabad.[37] Gandhi acknowledged that the caste system is coeval with the principles of modern economic activities whereby people can belong to any of the four varna professions (or occupations) of their own free will. His view convinced large numbers of Hindus, including prominent leading vernacular writers, to raise this subject, which forced a lively public debate on caste.[38]

The constitutional discussion over representation in the legislative assemblies during the interwar years offered a radical opportunity for Dalit groups to renew discussions on caste and representation. They demanded social democracy rather than just a mere replication of Westminster democracy, arguing that a simple representative democracy would further strengthen the control of caste-Hindus in the legislative, administrative, and judicial branches of government. The Government of India Act of 1919 had introduced the principle of limited representative government in provincial assemblies and allowed for separate and proportional representation for Sikhs in Punjab and the Dravidian community in Tamil Nadu. In the 1920s Dalit groups all over India organised campaigns to limit the expansion of caste domination in the legislative assemblies. They sent large numbers of telegrams in support of B.R. Ambedkar, as well as in support of their collective demand for separate communal electorates and proportional representation as subjects needing discussion at the London round table negotiations in preparation for India's a new constitution in 1931–2. In 1932 the British government granted separate representation to Dalits as part of the constitutional changes that would eventually expand suffrage to 16 per cent of the adult population in the Government of India Act of 1935. However, following large-scale opposition by the Congress, led by Mahatma Gandhi, the British government withdrew this provision. Nationalist politicians blamed the British government for promoting Dalit politics but refusing to discuss the ways by which caste practices condemned nearly a fifth of the subcontinent's population to sub-human status. According to Ambedkar and other provincial Dalit leaders, separate representation would have provided a meaningful partial resolution to the "wrong

[37] Jangam, *Dalits and the Making of Modern India*, p. 13.
[38] Zelliot, "The Congress and the Untouchables".

social system, which is too undemocratic."[39] Hence, by 1930 most Dalit groups had realised that meaningful engagement – by both Hindu orthodoxy and the nationalists – with the social continued to be an insurmountable barrier because the curse of the political is to prioritise self-governance and prevent meaningful debate on the social.

Therefore, it is important to recognise that Ambedkar's *Annihilation of Caste* (1936) and *Ranade, Gandhi, and Jinnah* (1943) represent original theoretical interventions explaining the persistent overriding commitment to the political in South Asian history, and a corresponding refusal by entrenched orthodoxy to acknowledge the foundational relevance of the social for a sincere discussion on eradicating caste hierarchy. This was how it was on the eve of Indian independence, when Ambedkar and other Dalit leaders were clear that the Indian leadership had chosen to ignore any substantive engagement with caste and simultaneously restricted the representational rights of Dalits. Both of these books illuminate the reason Dalit actors emphasised the social, as against the Congress and other nationalist organisations who upheld the political. At the core of the nationalist view is the belief that caste is a problem peripheral or even external to Hinduism, an accretion that with noble effort can be alleviated and in the end exterminated. By contrast Ambedkar's experience of life and his analysis of the real-life situation of Dalits show the view that the core problem of caste besetting Hinduism is internal to Hinduism – that the problem is structural and foundational. This being so, his commitment is to the critical Dalit investment in the struggle for dignity in order to unravel the practices of humiliation woven deeply within the Hindu social matrix.

Dignity Enters the Indian Constitution

"FRATERNITY assuring the dignity of the individual and the unity of the Nation . . .", declared the Preamble to the Indian Constitution of 1950.[40] There is no doubt that Ambedkar's insistence on incorporating the term "dignity" into the Preamble of the Indian Constitution drew from his participation in Dalit struggles and acute awareness that only a

[39] Ambedkar, *Ranade, Gandhi, and Jinnah*, p. 39.
[40] Preamble to the *Constitution of India*.

liberal constitution can challenge caste. His four decades of public discussion on self-worth and commitment to the innate humanity that inspired everyday Dalit battles reached a milestone when he, as a legal
scholar and drafting chairman of the Indian Constitution (1948–50),
incorporated this term as one of the four elements of the Preamble.[41] This
section of the Indian Constitution promises its rights-bearing citizens
Justice, Liberty, Equality, and Fraternity to assure "the dignity of the individual".[42] Provisions in the Constitution, such as Article 17, abolished
the practice of untouchability; Article 21 guaranteed the right to life;
and Article 25 promised freedom of conscience and religion to protect
the dignity and fraternity of discriminated groups. Using published and
unpublished sources of the Constituent Assembly (1947–50), Aakash
Singh Rathore has argued that "the appearance of the term 'dignity' in
the preamble to our Constitution stemmed" from Ambedkar's conviction that it was important to protect the dignity of every individual.[43]
Ambedkar's prolific use of the word in this sense "appeared 150 times in
his writings and speeches," showing his insistence that the term be con-
stitutionally enshrined.[44]

The eminent legal scholar Upendra Baxi has argued that even
though dignity appears as "the last of the four values enunciated by Preamble to the Indian Constitution," it has played an extremely active role
in judicial activism: barring "two exceptions, the Indian Constitution
(with a hundred amendments) does not further elucidate this sense of
dignity as a subset of the virtue or value of 'fraternity'."[45] It is not a mere
appendage to fraternity. Baxi demonstrates that the "dignity values re-

---

[41] I (Ramnarayan Rawat) gratefully acknowledge a wonderful conversation
with Ajay Skaria on moral stamina in Cambridge at the "Politics in Vernaculars"
annual meeting in June 2022. He also alerted us to Rathore's book, *Ambedkar's
Preamble.*

[42] The *Constitution of India.*

[43] Rathore, *Ambedkar's Preamble*, p. 119.

[44] Ch. 5, "Dignity: Not Bread but Honour", in Rathore, *Ambedkar's Preamble*, p. 120.

[45] The Forty-second Amendment to the Constitution in the Emergency
years of 1975–6 added two exceptions: (a) "the phrase 'the unity and integrity of
the Nation' was added to the preamble's reference to fraternity, and (b) Part-
IV-A, 'The Fundamental Duties of the Citizen'." Baxi, "The Place of Dignity",
p. 429.

main more suited to the language of rights" which have empowered the "emergency judicial activism" of the Supreme Court and emboldened the Indian parliament to create legal rights to address the question of caste discrimination.[46] He says the "Indian constitutional combination of fraternity and dignity wages a war against the indignity of caste-based apartheid via a manifold action enabling access to the rights to literacy and public services, and even legislative representation."[47] The Indian parliament has used the value of dignity in the Preamble to create a "constitutional arrangement by enacting a code of constitutional criminal law" that makes possible the articulation of fundamental human rights. For instance, the remarkable Scheduled Castes and the Scheduled Tribes (Prevention of Atrocities) Act, 1989, makes practices of exclusion and violence against these communities a criminal offence, and provides for an administrative structure to protect Dalits and Adivasis.[48] The recognition of dignity in the Constitution has, clearly, played a singular role in protecting discriminated groups against caste racism.

The intellectual genealogy of dignity in the Indian context suggests its origins in the moral and social struggles of Dalit groups. Baxi argues that this unique trajectory of dignity provides an alternative explanation to the "Euro-American incarnations of the idea."[49] The discussion of dignity in legal histories in the contexts of the United Kingdom, France, and the United States indicates that it originated in the 1940s, closely tied to an already existing notion of rights-bearing citizens who were guaranteed dignity in their respective constitutions. However, it was only after 1945, following the establishment of the United Nations, that national constitutions began to adopt the term in their preambles and proclamations.[50] The preamble of the Charter of the United Nations (1945) adopted the term "human dignity" as an ideal that "we the peoples of the United Nations" are committed to achieving.[51] Legal and constitutional scholars have argued that the term represents a compromise among

[46] Ibid., p. 430.
[47] Ibid., p. 431.
[48] Ibid., p. 433.
[49] Ibid., p. 429.
[50] Article 1 of the German Federal Constitution, cited in Schachter, "Human Dignity", p. 848.
[51] Ibid.

countries belonging to the various ideological camps that emerged after World War II and decolonisation, and that it carried a shared core belief present in the post-war order.[52] In the 1950s and 1960s the term "human dignity" appeared as a legal category and informed the efforts of courts to defend the fundamental rights of citizens, especially minorities and women, and uphold social justice policies. In the case of India, the inclusion of the term created a substantive constitutional mandate for the state and its institutions. Courts in India have used this provision, along with others relating to the abolition of the practice of untouchability, to defend the dignity of Dalits against humiliation.[53]

Our objective here is to demonstrate that there are several historical trajectories of dignity and that the critical role of Dalit struggles in late British India adds a new dimension to accounts in the European context. The history of Dalit activism demonstrates that the question of self-worth and the politics of self-respect were foundational to Dalit engagements with liberal democracy. In the European context a large body of writings in the fields of philosophy, political theory, and law have argued that the unique origins of European liberal democracy stem from debates over rights and the state.[54] Kant's writings, especially those on metaphysics and morals, along with the works of Rousseau and Hegel, have resulted in sustained discussions on the subject. In Kant's writings the subject received a systematic theoretical treatment by his emphasis on the self-worth of a human being as a rational thinking person with an innate capacity to possess these attributes.[55] Despite class and gender inequities in the West, a shared Christian religious discourse and access to built spaces such as churches provided non-elite groups recognition within the whole. Indeed, in Europe religious and political leaders both engaged in discussions on this subject.

By contrast, Dalit groups were considered outcastes from Hindu society and therefore most of the mainstream nationalist and reform groups elided this question – except for a few noted leaders and organisations.

---

[52] Shultziner and Rabinovici, "Human Dignity", p. 108.

[53] Sharma, "Law as an Instrument".

[54] Schachter, "Human Dignity"; Shultziner and Rabinovici, "Human Dignity".

[55] Shultziner and Rabinovici, "Human Dignity", pp. 107–9.

Ranade, as discussed above, was one of these rare exceptions who questioned the Hindu positioning of Dalits and women. Mahatma Gandhi was another, though, as mentioned, while he raised untouchability as an ethical issue and persuaded the Congress leadership to address it, he resisted efforts to engage with untouchability as a social question. He argued instead that issues such as Dalit entry into Hindu temples should be resolved ethically, not politically. In a seminal essay, "Humiliation", Gopal Guru argues that the "colonial configuration of power produced by western modernity" motivated the caste-Hindu elite in British India to demand racial parity, but this produced little or no empathy for caste exclusion and violence.[56] Rather, it was Dalit activists, such as the weaver Nanchari, Swami Achutanand, and others discussed in this volume, who raised questions of self-worth and dignity.

Moral Stamina: The Dalit Relationship with Democratic Politics

In August 1985 Thella Judson and Laban of Karamchedu village in Prakasam District began a fast-unto-death to demand that the Andhra Pradesh government uphold the rule of law and file charges against the perpetrators of the Karamchedu massacre.[57] They had survived a violent attack on the Dalit community in July 1985 by a 3000-strong crowd of farmers and landlords of the dominant Kamma caste. Armed with javelins, axes, crowbars, and sticks, and using tractors as assault vehicles, the powerful Kamma farmers hacked, killed, and maimed unarmed Dalit residents who had to run and hide in mounds of hay nearby or in the woods. The Kammas lynched eight Dalit men, raped three women, and left scores of people injured. The atrocity was meant to "teach Dalits a lesson" for challenging caste hierarchy. Dalit groups in Karamchedu village had refused to support a Kamma leader in local elections; they had refused to bow to humiliations heaped on them by Kammas, and this had irked the dominant Hindu community.[58]

[56] Guru, "Introduction: Theorizing Humiliation", p. 3.
[57] Rao, "Karamchedu", pp. 520–7. This paragraph is based on Rao's article.
[58] Srinivasulu, "Caste, Class and Social Articulation".

The lynching of Dalits, the rape of women, and a fast by two of the Dalit victims demanding that the state implement the rule of law mobilised civil rights groups in Andhra Pradesh to question the social conditions that enabled such caste atrocities.[59] A collective moral outrage created a new spirit of solidarity within the community. A few weeks after the massacre, Katti Padma Rao, a Sanskrit lecturer, and Bhojja Tharakam, the leader of the Left-leaning civil rights group – the Andhra Pradesh Civil Liberties Committee – founded the Dalit Mahasabha in August 1985.[60] The Dalit Mahasabha, various civil rights groups, and the Dalit victims of Karamchedu village led a sustained agitation, which included a demonstration of nearly 300,000 Dalits in Chirala town near Karamchedu, a series of rallies outside the state legislature and the chief minister's house, and marches and processions throughout the state. They demanded that the state file criminal charges to prosecute the Karamchedu perpetrators. The Dalit Mahasabha outlined a rehabilitation programme for the victims of this caste-Hindu violence.[61] The political agitation eventually forced the state government, led by Chief Minister N.T. Rama Rao, to file criminal charges. The dominant agrarian and business caste of Kammas had close ties with N.T. Rama Rao, who himself belonged to this community and had resisted taking legal action against the Kammas.

The Dalit satyagrahas led by Ambedkar in the 1920s and the Karamchedu movement led by the Dalit Mahasabha in 1985 demanded that the state implement its rules and regulations to protect Dalit dignity and Dalit

[59] This paragraph draws from K. Balagopal's two reports. First, on the rise of the Telugu Desam Party led by N.T. Rama Rao, https://balagopal.org/the-karamchedu-killings-the-essence-of-ntr-phenomenon/. Second, the report on the Karamchedu massacre, https://balagopal.org/the-karamchedu-massacre-a-report/.

[60] Several Dalit organisations were founded to strengthen the Dalit community and to mobilise public support, such as the Dalit Sangarsh Samiti, 1974, in Karnataka; the Dalit Mahasabha, 1985, in Andhra Pradesh; and the Viduthalai Chirutaigal Katchi, 1982, as well as the Devendra Kula Vellalar Federation, 1995, in Tamil Nadu.

[61] https://balagopal.org/the-karamchedu-killings-the-essence-of-ntr-phenomenon/ https://balagopal.org/the-karamchedu-massacre-a-report/. See also People's Union for Democratic Rights, *Agrarian Conflict in Bihar*.

lives. Dalit civil rights movements, we seek to show, are examples of the "moral stamina" which promotes strategies such as processions for "hailing the state". This method, it has been pointed out, is an important quotidian feature of politics in India to demand that the state enforce the rule of law, protect citizens, and cultivate a spirit of continuous civic engagement.[62] In *Ranade, Gandhi, and Jinnah* Ambedkar uses the phrase "moral stamina" to define the critical role of Dalit activism in establishing "real social democracy" based on the Constitution; he deemed this necessary to create a "strong moral fibre" in the community.[63] Moral stamina was necessary if Dalit activism was to succeed, since their struggles were likely to be prolonged; it was, moreover, also critical in reformulating the "moral tone of Hindu society". Moral stamina is thus a useful analytical category on account of its focus on the critical role in the constitution of Dalit life as well as a critical method to transform the social.[64] The term illustrates a core theme of the present volume – the relationship between self-respect and activism – and draws from Ambedkar's philosophy and approach to modern social life. We argue that Dalit groups in modern India have recognised and internalised the vital value of moral stamina in negotiating modern India.

Another feature of moral stamina is religious conversion to Buddhism, Christianity, and Islam to assert civic rights. Islam has appealed to sections of Dalit groups wanting escape from oppressive social conditions. In February 1981 nearly 180 untouchable families from the Pallar untouchable caste converted to Islam in Meenakshipuram, a village in Tirunelveli District, Tamil Nadu. This incident garnered attention in the national media, especially from right-wing Hindutva groups. Over the previous decade the Pallars had experienced accelerated cases of economic and social oppression from the dominant landed community of Thevars, a non-Brahmin Shudra caste.[65] Omar Shariff, the local Dalit activist who led this conversion movement, also explained that "our

---

[62] Chs 3, 4, and 7 in Mitchell, *Hailing the State*.

[63] Ambedkar, *Ranade, Gandhi, and Jinnah*, p. 40.

[64] We have borrowed this term from ibid., p. 37.

[65] Mathew, "Politicisation of Religion".

feeling of self-respect encouraged us to convert religion."[66] Local Dalits traced their genealogy to the leader of Dravidian politics, E.V. Ramasami Naicker, who had encouraged lower-caste conversion between 1928 and 1931.[67] Similarly, historians have argued that in colonial northern India sections of the Chuhra untouchable castes had a unique relationship with Islam.[68] The religion of the Chuhra castes had prominent Islamic features and was centred on the worship of their spiritual leader, Lal Beg, who was regarded as a prophet. By the middle of the twentieth century Chuhra religious heads (*bhagats*) began to incorporate elements from the Hindu religion, especially the devotion to the saint Valmiki, author of the Ramayana.[69]

The analytical framework of moral stamina which is deployed here to explain a century of Dalit activism seeking "real social democracy" has taken several forms: (a) social and political activism; (b) the genre of the Dalit autobiography; and (c) an expansion of Dalit vernacular literature into a distinctive body of protest writing. In an earlier volume, *Dalit Studies* (2016), discussion had focused on the visibility of Dalit actors in the 1990s. This visible activism had been propelled by the interventions of Dalit political parties in the states, Dalit student bodies in university campuses, and non-political social organisations that had contributed most in bringing the question of caste into Indian academia – including its shape as the rising field of Dalit Studies.[70] The example of the Dalit Mahasabha illustrates the role of transitional organisations in sustaining Dalit moral stamina. In the past decade there has been considerable discussion of Dalit literary writings in the vernacular, and of Dalit life narratives as examples of the struggle for dignity and the individual's dissent against caste oppression.[71] There seems little doubt that Dalit writings have served as a collective statement to strengthen what Ambedkar called

[66] Baxter, "Two Concepts of Conversion at Meenakshipuram", p. 265.

[67] Ibid., p. 275.

[68] Chs 1 and 2 in Prashad, *Untouchable Freedom*. Ch. 1 in Lee, *Deceptive Majority*.

[69] Ch. 7 in Lee, *Deceptive Majority*.

[70] "The Contemporary Context", in Rawat and Satyanarayana, eds, "Introduction", in *Dalit Studies*, pp. 1–8.

[71] Vasant Moon's autobiography, *Growing up Untouchable*, does a fantastic job of capturing Ambedkar's popularity in the period between 1930 and 1950: Moon, chs 6–18.

the "strong moral fibre" of the community, enabling the stamina required to sustain struggle.

Dalit autobiographies in the vernacular have emerged as a unique genre to narrate personal stories of moral stamina. These illustrate a commitment to education, activism, secular occupations, democratic practices, and the building of alternative religious models. Though available in several Indian languages, this field is particularly visible in Marathi, Telugu, Hindi, and Tamil. Dalit autobiographies have nourished Dalit moral stamina, of course, but they are also texts that have created new models and new expectations. Early Dalit autobiographies in the 1970s and 1980s frequently reflected on Ambedkar's view of modern life. In Baby Kamble's autobiography, *The Prisons We Broke* (1986), Ambedkar appears as a historical person at a meeting of Mahars where he declares "We are humans. We, too, have the right to live as human beings." He addresses his community: "[M]y poor dear brothers and sisters, do not eat carcasses any more. Don't clean the filth of the village. Let those who make the filth clean it up themselves . . . Let three-fourths of our people die in this endeavour, then, at least the remaining one-fourth will be able to live their lives with dignity."[72]

In the pedagogic mode of such memoirs and self-writing Ambedkar's very presence is often invoked to remind Dalits of their right to live as human beings. Daya Pawar's autobiography *Baluta* (1978), along with Baby Kamble's, reflects a new field of vernacular writing focusing on the wretched conditions of humiliated protagonists. This early Dalit Marathi literature represents anger and the assertions of a younger generation of Ambedkarite Dalits, a sample of which appeared in the classic English collection *Poisoned Bread* (1992). That collection contains essays closer in style to memoirs, and documents in graphic detail stories of hunger and suffering, violence and caste discrimination, destitution and dehumanisation. First-hand Dalit experiences are presented with a fresh and direct approach. Marathi Dalit literature has come to be defined by the emergence of "the Ambedkarite hero", an angry and assertive Dalit character. It challenges the myth of caste as a remnant of the past and reveals the continuing presence of caste's perpetuation of inequality, exclusion, and stigma.

[72] Kamble, *The Prisons We Broke*, p. 65.

By the end of the twentieth century it was clear that concerns with "strong moral fibre" and self-respect had considerably shaped Dalit vernacular literature. Telugu literature too has highlighted the subjective sense of human worth. In his famous 1985 song "Dalita Pululu", the people's poet and balladeer Gaddar describes dignity by illustrating a new set of expectations and markers of Dalit life, including access to education, houses, jobs, and clean "sparkling clothes".[73] Gaddar wrote this song in response to the Karamchedu massacre and in it refers to Dalit youth as tigers:

> Youngsters buil\t like weightlifters
> Well-versed in martial arts
> As well as education
> Ask those who belittle and denigrate them
> To mind their language.
> They wear sparkling white clothes
> Move in their hamlet like Jasmines.
> "We may not own property
> But we have self-respect," they say
> When we sip coffee sitting on a chair
> A rich lord seethes with anger.
> We are not living off someone else's father
> We are spending our own money
> It is our right, they say.

Gaddar represents educated Dalit youth as assertive, confident, and conscious of their clothing and appearance. Kalekuri Prasad's poignant poem "A Fistful of Respect", written in response to the Dalit massacres of the 1980s and used as the epigraph of this book, similarly highlights this commitment of Dalit activism to self-worth and self-respect. Victims of atrocities are represented as martyrs who died for "a fistful of respect". Such poems and autobiographies have provided Dalit activists an arena for engaging with civil society and confronting the atrocities against their community that were manifest in the 1980s and 1990s.

What is new in independent India is that minor altercations between Dalits and caste-Hindus have turned into massacres of Dalits in untouchable neighbourhoods and generally resulted in the destruction of their

---

[73] Satyanarayana, "Social Inequality and Human Dignity", pp. 41–5.

property. Altercations in the social leading to lynching are quite obviously the products of a changed context. There are two key visible elements of this changed context. First, the improved socio-economic conditions and new economic mobility of Dalits, the result of greater access to educational and employment opportunities. Second, Dalit groups in the various parts of India have become active and savvy participants in electoral politics and have even established political organisations to intervene effectively within political debates.[74] Consequently, the backlash against Dalits has been correspondingly severe. Fact-finding reports by civil rights groups have noted that massacres have been planned and executed with the clear objective of reasserting the authority of dominant agrarian castes and reminding Dalit communities of their subordination.[75] The most notorious of these Dalit massacres occurred in Kilvenmani village in Nagapattinam District, Tamil Nadu, in 1968; in Belchi village in Patna District, Bihar, in 1977; and in Karamchedu and Chundur villages in Andhra Pradesh in 1985 and 1991, respectively. These contributed dramatically to new alignments within caste and Dalit politics.

The massacres of Dalit working families, including of children and senior citizens, and the rape of women have emerged as the most visible of the new phenomena in postcolonial India. The violence has included several forms of atrocities, including the burning of hamlets, attacks with axes on Dalits in broad daylight in public places, the raping of Dalit women in public spaces, and the destruction of crops, food, property, and natural resources like water tanks. In the central districts of Bihar, dominant Hindu agrarian caste groups have organised caste militias, such as the Ranbir Sena, founded in 1994 to discipline Dalits who were demanding better wages for their labour.[76] The 1999 *Human Rights*

---

[74] This specific point is made in K. Balagopal's report on the Karamchedu massacre, https://balagopal.org/the-karamchedu-massacre-a-report/. For a historical outline on this theme, see ch. 5 in Srinivasulu, "Caste, Class and Social Articulation".

[75] People's Union for Democratic Rights, *Agrarian Conflict*; Balagopal, https://balagopal.org/the-karamchedu-massacre-a-report/.

[76] Accessed on 28 October 2022. See also People's Union for Democratic Rights, *Agrarian Conflict*.

Watch Report says massacres of Dalits "frequently take place at night; in many cases, the victims, including women and children, have been shot in their beds while they were sleeping."[77] Between 1995 and 1997 more than 300 Dalits were killed in central Bihar alone. K. Balagopal has argued that surviving Dalit victims of massacres and violence have often rediscovered their own worth and dignity.[78]

The unique relief measures employed for the victims of the Karamchedu massacres in 1985 are critical to the drafting and subsequent passing of the Scheduled Castes and the Scheduled Tribes (Prevention of Atrocities) Act, 1989. This Act mandated that state governments provide administrative assistance for obtaining legal, social, and economic relief to victims. The Act made the state government machinery accountable for complaints lodged by victims. The Dalit Mahasabha leaders Katti Padma Rao and Bhojja Tharakam, and a government relief committee led by the senior officer Sri Sankaran, adopted these targeted measures: (a) the families of victims received a cash grant of Rs 100,000 and employment in government offices; (b) all of the 430 victimised families were provided with new houses built by the state; (c) each family was given nearly an acre of land for cultivation; (d) additional government jobs were provided for families that had not suffered direct harm; and (e) those families that had relocated to the nearby town of Chirala were offered employment opportunities in private industries. Most of these relief measures were incorporated in the 1989 SC and ST Act.[79] Katti Padma Rao writes that the safety and security found in the new Dalit colony in Chirala town provided a new generation of families and children safe access to education and dignity of life. Within just two decades after 1985, the community had produced doctors, engineers, and government officers.

The moral stamina of victims in Karamchedu spurred Dalit activists to demand that the state uphold the rule of law and advocate constitutional changes that would better protect and support those affected by

[77] Human Rights Watch, "The Pattern of Abuse".

[78] Balagopal, *Ear to the Ground*, p. 373.

[79] For a detailed discussion of the SC/ST (Prevention of Atrocities) Act, 1989, see Satyanarayana, "Caste Violence", pp. 37–51; and Rao, "Legislating Caste Atrocity", in Rao, *The Caste Question*, pp. 167–78.

the violence of massacres. Katti Padma Rao and Bhojja Tharakam realised that the existing laws, such as the Protection of Civil Rights (PCR)
Act of 1955, did not provide effective protection to Dalit families, children, women, and senior citizens – those impacted by the violence. They
successfully enlisted the support of national Dalit leaders and members
of the Indian parliament based in Delhi, with two parliamentarians in
particular, Ram Vilas Paswan and Buta Singh, playing an active role.[80]
This group of regional and national Dalit leaders became deeply involved
in drafting the new 1989 Act that would guarantee security and dignity
to Dalit communities across the country. A critical issue that this group
addressed was the incorporation of measures into the Act that could protect witnesses of the massacres – whereby such witnesses would be willing to provide evidence to the police and the courts. Their efforts resulted in the 1989 Act containing "stringent provisions for punishing
the accused" – those who perpetrated atrocities on Dalits.[81]

❧

Ambedkar's ideas of "the social" and "moral stamina" define the core
concepts of Dalit activism and its engagement with the question of caste.
Conjointly they offer a conceptual framework enabling fresh study of
the initiatives of Dalit groups in finding institutional alternatives to caste
inequality – and in this quest discovering religious choices and probing
new opportunities in the secular domain form a vital part. Discussion
on religion and on the secular was built on practices that would nourish
a sense of self-worth within the Dalit community and promote social
equality – in Ambedkar's words, "equal position, equal protection, and
equal justice." The politics of self-respect was morally tethered to Dalit
opposition to the conditions of humiliation and stigma defined by orthodox Hinduism, especially in the *Manusmriti*. In this genealogy of
activism, the collective self of the Dalit social captured by Ambedkar
in *Ranade, Gandhi, and Jinnah* was a crucial step toward the moral reform of society for the establishment of true democracy. It is thus clear

---

[80] The leaders benefited from support extended by the Congress government
led by Rajiv Gandhi in 1989.

[81] Rao, "Karamchedu", p. 523.

that a new approach to religion was a necessary step in defining Dalit assertions of self-worth and a politics of self-respect. Creating new opportunities in the secular arenas, guaranteed by constitutional changes, ensured that Dalit groups secured the economic resources required to strengthen their ethical struggle. Dignity appears today in the Preamble of the Indian Constitution because of a century of Dalit resistance against caste. Ambedkar insisted on using the term and persuaded his colleagues in the constitution drafting committee to include it.

The objective of this volume is to provide a distinctive history of the Dalit social as constituted centrally by the struggle against caste which inaugurated the politics of dignity located in modern ideas and practices. That several essays deal with religion is an outcome of the second Dalit Studies conference on "Human dignity, equality, and democracy" held in Delhi in January 2018. Five essays out of the nine, chapters 2–6, in the volume, examine diverse trajectories taken by Dalit groups towards religion. The essays by Chandra Sekhar, Rawat, Ramberg, Duggal, and Varghese explore Dalit personal investment in religious alternatives and investigate the relationship between conversion and the formation of the Dalit social. These articles also explore the role of religion in enabling the first step in a politics of self-respect.

The articles by Anupama, Thiranagama, Mhaskar, and Leonard, chapters 7–10, highlight the vital new dimensions of the Dalit social as they relate to clothing, homesteads, occupations, and the discipline of historical interpretation. Yet some of these articles, such as those by Ramberg, Varghese, Thiranagama, and Mhaskar, also highlight the contentious role of spaces – institutional (church), familial, and personal – mediated by religious alternatives and secular opportunities.

Readers will discover in this collection that two of Ambedkar's concepts – the social and moral stamina – offer, first, a new perspective on Dalit investments in the domains of religion and the secular, and second, their extension into values enshrined in the Indian Constitution which provide the most stable institutional structure for protecting the dignity of individuals and communities. The time Nanchari spent living with Anglican missionaries to learn about Christianity around 1842–5, the Dalit satyagrahas in the 1920s for equal treatment, and the fast by Thella Judson and Laban in August 1985 to demand that the state uphold the rule of law, are a few examples among the many others discussed in this volume. Collectively, they illustrate two centuries of tenacious Dalit activism to demand "a fistful of respect".

References

Ambedkar, B.R., *Annihilation of Caste* (1936), in *Dr. Babasaheb Ambedkar Writings and Speeches, Vol. 1* (Bombay: Education Department, Government of Maharashtra, 1989).

Ambedkar, B.R., "Away from the Hindus", in *Dr. Babasaheb Ambedkar Writings and Speeches, Vol. 5* (Bombay: Education Department, Government of Maharashtra, 1989).

Ambedkar, B.R., "Kalaram Temple Entry Satyagraha, Nasik and Temple Entry Movement", in *Dr. Babasaheb Ambedkar Writings and Speeches, Vol. 17, Part I* (Bombay: Education Department, Government of Maharashtra, 1979).

Ambedkar, B.R., "Unfortunately, I was Born a Hindu Untouchable but I will Not Die a Hindu", in *Dr. Babasaheb Ambedkar Writings and Speeches Vol. 17, Part III* (Bombay: Education Department, Government of Maharashtra, 1979).

Ambedkar, B.R., "What Way Emancipation", in *Dr. Babasaheb Ambedkar Writings and Speeches Vol. 17, Part III* (Bombay: Education Department, Government of Maharashtra, 1979).

Ambedkar, B.R., *Ranade, Gandhi, and Jinnah* (Bombay: Thacker and Co., Ltd, 1943).

Ambedkar, B.R., *What Congress and Gandhi Have Done to the Untouchables* (Bombay: Thacker & Co., 1946).

Anagol, Padma, "Rebellious Wives and Dysfunctional Marriages: Indian Women's Discourses and Participation in the Debates over Restitution of Conjugal Rights and the Child Marriage Controversy in the 1880s and 1890s", in Sumit Sarkar and Tanika Sarkar, eds, *Women and Social Reform in Modern India*, vol. 1 (Ranikhet: Permanent Black, 2007).

Anupama, "Presenting the Dalit Body: Caste and Sartorial Dignity in North India", in Ramnarayan S. Rawat, K. Satyanarayana, and P. Sanal Mohan, eds, *Dalit Journeys of Dignity: Religion, Freedom and Caste* (Ranikhet: Permanent Black, 2025).

Balagopal, K., *Ear to the Ground: Writings on Class and Caste* (New Delhi: Navayana Publishing, 2011).

Balagopal, K., https://balagopal.org/the-karamchedu-killings-the-essence-of-ntr-phenomenon/, accessed 28 October 2022.

Balagopal, K., https://balagopal.org/the-karamchedu-massacre-a-report/, accessed 28 October 2022.

Baxi, Upendra, "The Place of Dignity in the Indian Constitution", in Marcus Düwell, *et al.*, *Human Dignity: Interdisciplinary Perspectives* (Cambridge: Cambridge University Press, 2014).

Baxter, Matthew H., "Two Concepts of Conversion at Meenakshipuram: Seeing through Ambedkar's Buddhism and Being Seen in EVR's Islam", *Comparative Studies of South Asia, Africa and the Middle East*, vol. 34, no. 2, 2019.

Chandra Sekhar, "A Dalit Convert in the Nineteenth Century South India: Recovering the Legacy of Nanchari among Telugu-speaking Christians", in Ramnarayan S. Rawat, K. Satyanarayana, and P. Sanal Mohan, eds, *Dalit Journeys of Dignity: Religion, Freedom and Caste* (Ranikhet: Permanent Black, 2025).

Constitution of India, The, New Delhi, 1950, https://legislative.gov.in/constitution-of-india, accessed August 2022.

Duggal, Koonal, "Between Blasphemy and Martyrdom: The Formation of the Ravidassia Religion", in Ramnarayan S. Rawat, K. Satyanarayana, and P. Sanal Mohan, eds, *Dalit Journeys of Dignity: Religion, Freedom and Caste* (Ranikhet: Permanent Black, 2025).

Guru, Gopal, "Introduction: Theorizing Humiliation", in Gopal Guru, ed., *Humiliation: Claims and Contexts* (New Delhi: Oxford University Press, 2009).

Human Rights Watch, "The Pattern of Abuse: Rural Violence in Bihar and the State's Response," in https://www.hrw.org/report/1999/03/01/broken-people, accessed 28 October 2022.

Jangam, Chinnaiah, *Dalits and the Making of Modern India* (New Delhi: Oxford University Press, 2017).

Kamble, Baby, *The Prisons We Broke*, trans. Maya Pandit (Chennai: Orient Longman, 2008).

Lee, Joel, *Deceptive Majority: Dalit, Hinduism, and Underground Religion* (New Delhi: Cambridge University Press, 2021).

Mathew, George, "Politicisation of Religion: Conversions to Islam In Tamil Nadu", *Economic and Political Weekly*, vol. 17, no. 26, 26 June 1982.

Mhaskar, Sumeet, "Caste and Occupational Choices in Modern Indian Industry, 1870–2009", in Ramnarayan S. Rawat, K. Satyanarayana, and P. Sanal Mohan, eds, *Dalit Journeys of Dignity: Religion, Freedom and Caste* (Ranikhet: Permanent Black, 2025).

Mitchell, Lisa, *Hailing the State: Indian Democracy Between Elections* (Durham, NC: Duke University Press, 2023).

Moon, Vasant, *Growing Up Untouchable in India: A Dalit Autobiography* (New York: Rowman & Littlefield Publishers, Inc., 2000).

People's Union for Democratic Rights, *Agrarian Conflict in Bihar and the Ranbir Sena* (Delhi, October 1997).

Prakash, Gyan, "The Colonial Genealogy of Society: Community and Political Modernity in India", in Patrick Joyce, ed., *The Social in Question: New Bearings in History and the Social Sciences* (New York: Routledge, 2002).

Prasad, Kalekuri, "For a Fistful of Self-respect", trans. N. Bhanutej, in K. Satyanarayana and Susie Tharu, eds, *Steel Nibs are Sprouting: New Dalit Writing from South India* (Noida: HarperCollins, 2013).

Prashad, Vijay, *Untouchable Freedom: A Social History of Dalit Community* (New Delhi: Oxford University Press, 2000).

Ramberg, Lucinda, "Dalit Futures and Sexual Modernity in South India", in Ramnarayan S. Rawat, K. Satyanarayana, and P. Sanal Mohan, eds, *Dalit Journeys of Dignity: Religion, Freedom and Caste* (Ranikhet: Permanent Black, 2025).

Rao, Anupama, *The Caste Question: Dalits and the Politics of Modern India* (Berkeley: University of California Press, 2009).

Rao, Katti Padma, "Karamchedu: A Turning Point in Dalit History", trans. Kaki Madhava Rao, in K. Satyanarayana and Susie Tharu, eds, *Steel Nibs are Sprouting: New Dalit Writing from South India* (Noida: HarperCollins, 2013).

Rathore, Aakash Singh, *Ambedkar's Preamble: A Secret History of the Constitution of India* (Gurgaon: Vintage, Penguin Random House, 2020).

Rawat, Ramnarayan S., "An Ethical Community of Equals: A Dalit History of Sant-Mat Religion in Late-Colonial India", in Ramnarayan S. Rawat, K. Satyanarayana, and P. Sanal Mohan, eds, *Dalit Journeys of Dignity: Religion, Freedom and Caste* (Ranikhet: Permanent Black, 2025).

Rawat, Ramnarayan S., and K. Satyanarayana, eds, *Dalit Studies* (Durham, NC: Duke University Press, 2016).

Rodrigues, Valerian, ed., *The Essential Writings of B.R. Ambedkar* (Delhi: Oxford University Press, 2002).

Satyanarayana, K., "Caste Violence: Free Speech or Atrocity?" in Pavan Kumar Malreddy, Anindya S. Purakayastha, and Birt Heidemann, eds, *Violence in South Asia: Contemporary Perspectives* (New Delhi: Routledge, 2020).

Satyanarayana, K., "Social Inequality and Human Dignity", *Seminar*, vol. 672, August 2015.

Schachter, Oscar, "Human Dignity as a Normative Concept", *The American Journal of International Law*, vol. 77, no. 44, 1983.

Sharma, Girdhar Behari, "Law as an Instrument for Abolition of Untouchability: Case of Rajasthan", *Economic and Political Weekly*, vol. 10, no. 15, 1975.

Shultziner, Doron, and Itai Rabinovici, "Human Dignity, Self-Worth, and Humiliation: A Comparative Legal-Psychological Approach", *Psychology, Public Policy, and Law*, vol. 18, no. 1, 2012.

Sinha, Mrinalini, *Colonial Masculinity: The 'Manly Englishman' and the 'Effeminate Bengali' in the Late Nineteenth Century* (Manchester: Manchester University Press, 1995).

Sinha, Mrinalini, *Specters of Mother India: The Global Restructuring of an Empire* (Durham: NC, Duke University Press, 2006).

Srinivasulu, K., "Caste, Class and Social Articulation in Andhra Pradesh: Mapping Differential Regional Trajectories" (London: Overseas Development Institute, September 2002).

Thiranagama, Sharika, "Inheritance and Caste Formations in Kerala", in Ramnarayan S. Rawat, K. Satyanarayana, and P. Sanal Mohan, eds, *Dalit Journeys of Dignity: Religion, Freedom and Caste* (Ranikhet: Permanent Black, 2025).

Varghese, Jestin T., "Oppression, Resistance, and Formation of Faith Community among Dalit Christians of Kerala", in Ramnarayan S. Rawat, K. Satyanarayana, and P. Sanal Mohan, eds, *Dalit Journeys of Dignity: Religion, Freedom and Caste* (Ranikhet: Permanent Black, 2025).

Zelliot, Eleanor, "Congress and the Untouchables, 1917–1950", in Stanley Wolpert, ed., *Congress and Indian Nationalism: The Pre-independence Phase* (Berkeley: University of California Press, 1988).

2

Recovering the Legacy of Nanchari, 1830–2018

Dalits, Conversion, and Christianity in South India

CHAKALI CHANDRA SEKHAR

A N UNTOUCHABLE (Mala) weaver and itinerant trader of cotton cloth, Aguta Nanchari was also the headman of his community in Rudravaram village of Kurnool District. He was among the first to convert to Christianity in 1838 in Rayalaseema. A well-known figure among the untouchable community in the Rayalaseema region, his story is unknown to the outside world though he occupied an important place in the history of Christian missions for initiating Dalit conversion movements in Rayalaseema in the third decade of the nineteenth century. The reason is that there is hardly any information available about him in mission accounts. As a weaver-trader, Nanchari travelled extensively in the region and experienced first-hand the existence of missionary propaganda. I started my search of the historical Nanchari with one paragraph in vernacular material to recover his story from the archives of the London Mission Society (hereafter LMS), the Society for the Propagation of the Gospel (hereafter SPG), and additional field-work from his village. In the process I managed to learn more about him.

By examining his life experiences, including imprisonment on account of his temple entry attempt and embrace of Christianity in prison, this article provides the first substantive life story of Nanchari as well as new insights into the history of Dalit conversion movements in South India. Studying individuals is important because it sheds light on motivations for the conversion of entire Dalit communities and mass movements. Leaders like Nanchari inspired and provided leadership to those active in Christian conversion movements. I explore issues around Nanchari's temple entry, reasons for his imprisonment, dialogue with missionaries, and motivations for conversion. And the article brings the Rayalaseema region into the map of conversion studies in history and anthropology.

I first read about Nanchari's conversion story in Busamella Benjamin's book, *Andhra Pradesh Christava Sangha Charitra* (1976; History of the Christian Church in Andhra Pradesh). From this I discovered Nanchari had first heard Christian messages in the Cuddapah jail and soon converted while incarcerated: he was completing a term for attempting to enter a Hindu temple. Upon his release from jail he encouraged his community to embrace Christianity, which led to a mass conversion movement. The episode relating to Nanchari's attempt to enter the Hindu temple attracted my attention because, as I know from my own experiences in a village, no one from the Dalit community is allowed to enter Hindu temples. Over my childhood I was denied entry to the innermost sanctuary of the Hindu temple on account of my (Dhobi) caste identity. I thus felt it was imperative to know more about Nanchari's rebellion and started to search for him in archival and vernacular material. Soon I realised there are different narratives on his conversion in the LMS, SPG, and local language materials.

Historically, caste and Christianity in South Asia have been studied from various perspectives – the history of Protestant missions, the social background of the missionaries, similarities between Christianisation and Sanskritisation, and the relationship between missionaries, the state, and colonial officials. Several studies have looked at the mass conversion movements of the lower castes, the dynamics and impact of these movements, their motives, and the agency of the converts. Scholars have also discussed the interaction of lower-caste communities with European missionaries, social changes that religious conversion brought for and within Dalit men and women, the enabling of struggles against local caste oppressors, the lived and everyday religion of converts, and the imagining and articulation of a life of equality through conversion.[1] A few have focused on the conversion of individuals who led their entire communities to embrace Christianity. Historians such as Robert Frykenberg, Jarrell Pickett Geoffrey Oddie, James Taneti, and John Webster are among these.

Five prominent individuals and areas studied can be listed: Vedamanickam in the Tamil-speaking districts of Travancore (1805) from the Sambavar, an outcaste community; Venkaiah from Mala (1859) and Peraiah (1866) from the Madiga communities in Telugu-speaking regions; Ditt from the Chuhra community of Punjab (1873); and Alagan from the Adi-Dravida community in Trichinopoly District of Kerala (1913). These people led mass conversion movements and contributed to the spread of Christianity. Studies of their activity in the contexts of Kerala, Tamil Nadu, Punjab, and Andhra Pradesh have discussed the background of these individuals, their encounters with missionaries, the circumstances of their conversion to Christianity, and what led them to make their communities embrace Christianity *en masse*.[2]

Nanchari, who embraced Christianity and was the leader of the conversion movements of the Dalits in Rayalaseema, stands apart from his peers in this domain because the missionary archive is mostly silent about

[1] Balasundaram, *Dalits and Christian Mission*; Bugge, *Mission and Tamil Society*; Christhu Doss, "Repainting Religious Landscape"; Forrester, *Caste and Christianity*; Frykenberg, "On the Study of Conversion Movements"; idem, "The Impact of Conversion"; Gladstone, *Protestant Christianity*; Kawashima, *Missionaries and a Hindu State*; Kent, *Converting Women*; Kooiman, "Mass Movement, Famine"; idem, *Conversion and Social Equality*; Luke and Carman, *Village Christians*; Mallampalli, *South Asia's Christians*; Mohan, *Modernity of Slavery*; Mosse, *The Saint in the Banyan Tree*; Oddie, *Religious Conversion Movements*; Paul, "Dalit Conversion Memories" Viswanath, "The Emergence of Authenticity"; idem, *The Pariah Problem*.

[2] Pickett, *Christian Mass Movements*, pp. 38–50; Forrester, "The Depressed Classes"; Frykenberg, *Christianity in India*, pp. 226–30, 234–9; Manickam, *The Social Setting of Christian Conversion*, pp. 80–98; Oddie, "Christian Conversion in the Telugu Country"; Taneti *Caste, Gender and Christianity*, pp. 53–5; Webster, *Dalit Christians*, pp. 51–63; idem, *Historiography of Christianity*, pp. 98–114.

him, whereas the missionaries wrote detailed accounts of conversion by the five listed individuals in their annual reports and mission histories. They were also useful as propaganda: missionaries wrote up hagiographies of these converts as part of their promotional literature. Nanchari, by contrast, was restricted to one paragraph in this literature.

A reason for his absence in the record is that Rayalaseema, one of the Telugu-speaking regions of the Madras Presidency rife with Dalit conversions, is virtually absent in social science and historical studies. The area has not been recognised as a specific case of conversion movements and been subsumed within the Telugu-speaking and Andhra coastal regions.[3] This subsumption has meant that the specificity of the caste domination it manifests – which provided the context for socio-economic and religious difficulties in the lives of Dalits and their mass conversions – has been missed out. My effort here is to put the Rayalaseema region into the map of conversion studies.

I seek to do this by combining archival research with ethnographic fieldwork. The LMS and SPG archival material from which I draw includes monthly reports, annual reports, and the handwritten reports of missionaries, as well as magazines and missionary conference proceedings. The anuals and gazetteers of the Ceded Districts, and vernacular material in Telugu have also been used. These are supplemented with oral narratives collected during fieldwork in Nanchari's village, Rudravaram, in November 2016 and January 2017. How did Nanchari manage to mobilise an entire community to embrace Christianity in Rayalaseema? This is the core question I set out to answer.

Nanchari's Story: A Tapestry of Mission Archives and Vernacular Texts

While drawing Nanchari out from the archives of the LMS, SPG, and Telugu vernacular sources, I will here provide historical context to the Rayalaseema region, tracing the establishment of mission organisations

[3] For studies of Dalit conversions and Christianity in Andhra Pradesh, see Carman and Rao, *Christians in South Indian Villages*; Harper, *In the Shadow*; Luke and Carman, *Village Christians*; Oddie, "Christian Conversion"; Taneti, *Caste, Gender and Christianity*; idem, *Telugu Christians*; Chandra Sekhar, "In Search of a Touchable Body"; Mocherla, *Dalit Christians*.

and examining the socio-economic conditions of Dalit communities like the Malas and Madigas during the colonial period.

Nanchari in the LMS Archives

The districts of Bellary, Cuddapah, and Kurnool, which correspond to the modern Rayalaseema region, were ceded to the British by the Nizam in 1800 and came to be known as Datta Mandalalu (in English: the Ceded Districts). They were thereafter part of the Madras Presidency.[4] The region had seen substantial transitions with the arrival of the colonial administration, one of which was the influx of Protestant missions. One Protestant mission group, the LMS, commenced its operation in Cuddapah town in 1822, with William Howell, a Eurasian, appointed as its first missionary. Before joining the mission he had worked as a surveyor under the famous British survey general of Madras and collector of antiquities Major Colin Mackenzie. His work had involved surveying Mysore and other parts of South India. From 1809 to 1813 Howell had worked on a survey of the Ceded Districts.[5]

In Rayalaseema, after the Reddys, the Malas and Madigas constituted the largest caste groups of the region, numbering 181,164 in Cuddapah District and 149,024 in Kurnool.[6] When British rule began here, the Malas and the Madigas lived a wretched existence in servile conditions, occupying the lowest stratum of society. They were socially discriminated against, subjected to untouchability, and performed the lowest kinds of services – sweeping, scavenging, coolie labour, gravedigging, skinning animals, tanning leather, and removing the carcasses of dead animals. These menial activities, alongside their willingness to eat beef, constituted the reason for the impure status and stigma of untouchability attached to them.[7] Not considered part of the *ooru* (village), they lived on

---

[4] Ranga Reddy, *The State of Rayalaseema*, pp. 3–4. Rayalaseema is the contemporary name for a regions which consists of Anantapuram, Annamayya, Chittoor, Kurnool, Nandyal, Sri Satya Sai, Tirupati, and YSR districts. During colonial times the region was known as the Ceded Districts.

[5] West, *William Howell*, pp. 6–7.

[6] Cornish, *Census Report of Madras Presidency*, pp. 256, 271.

[7] Thurston, *Caste and Tribes*, vol. 4, pp. 308, 330, 348–50; *Mission Field*, 1859, 204.

the fringes of villages, which in Telugu were called *palem* (Dalit settle-ment). As Ramnarayan Rawat has remarked, degraded spatial location was an aspect of the upper-caste varna ideology.[8] The justification given for segregating village and palem was pollution – even their proximity with caste-Hindus was considered intolerable. While other castes lived in mud-roofed houses within the village, the dwelling units of the Malas and Madigas were made of mud-stone walls with thatched roofs of pal-myra. The palem was out of bounds, being thought too impure to be visited. Temples and drinking-water wells in the village were out of bounds for Malas and Madigas.[9] The hallmark of caste-Hindu perversity is to first compel a group to perform vital but degrading tasks associated with waste and its removal, and then to condemn the group for perform-ing them. This applied squarely to the Malas and Madigas, who per-formed socially necessary and valuable tasks and in return were treated as less than human. As Rupa Viswanath puts it, the marks of positive social status were forbidden to them.[10]

From the beginning of his missionary work, Howell was focused on converting individuals from the dominant and upper castes. Even though there were converts from the Pariah community, he does not men-tion who they were nor how and when they converted. The LMS annual reports from 1822 to 1842 record only the conversion stories of Reddys and Brahmins.[11] To understand why Howell employed this strategy in his work, we need to engage with the top-down model of conversion which Protestant missionaries practised in the early years of their activi-ties in South India. Scholars have illuminated the reasoning behind this model: if the upper castes at the top of the social hierarchy converted first, they would work as agents and motivate those lower down to fol-low suit.[12] The problem was that missionaries often faced difficulties

---

[8] Rawat, "Occupation, Dignity and Space", p. 1064.

[9] Cole, *Indiana*, p. 4; Cornish, *Census Report*, p. 168; Phillip, *The Outcastes' Hope*, pp. 1–2.

[10] Viswanath, "Authenticity Talk", p. 128.

[11] *ARLMS*, 1838, p. 54; Lewis, *History of the Telugu Mission*, p. 2; Simmons, *A Hundred Years*, p. 8.

[12] Forrester, *Caste and Christianity*, p. 69; Jenkins, *Religious Freedom*, p. 35; Kent, *Converting Women*, p. 43; Viswanath, *Pariah Problem*, p. 41; Webster, *Dalit Christians*, p. 43.

implementing this top-down model of conversion. Potential converts, especially Brahmins, responded with indifference to the prospect of conversion, evading the issue with the argument that all gods were ultimately one despite their different names. Many in the upper castes also viewed conversion to Christianity as the route to a spoiling of their caste status.[13] Some who converted did not admit it publicly and were even unwilling to be baptised or attend church. Converts were often proscribed by the unconverted within their caste while others faced hostility or ostracism in their own families.[14] When an individual called Veerappa from the Brahmin community converted, his caste-men hired assassins to murder him.[15] By the end of 1850, those who professed Christianity in Cuddapah station were 150, while church members were only thirty-two.[16]

In Rayalaseema, Dalit subjectivity entered the mission archive with the beginning of mass conversion movements in 1852. Nanchari was in the forefront of these movements. The earliest reference to him is in Gribble's manual of Cuddapah District. Gribble provides the details of the LMS, which he collected from an LMS missionary, W.G. Mawbey.[17] He mentions visits by missionaries to the Cuddapah prison, the presence there of a prisoner from the Mala caste, his interaction with missionaries, his "joyful tidings" and conversion, and his leading role in converting untouchable families of his village.[18]

Mawbey, a missionary active in Cuddapah from 1865 to 1875, thus provided what went into the earliest published account of Nanchari's conversion, despite not himself being a missionary at the time of Nanchari's conversion. The source of Mawbey's account remains unclear as there are no references to Nanchari in Howell's reports from 1824 to 1842. It is likely that Mawbey relied for his account on oral tellings passed down from earlier missionaries. He portrayed Nanchari as a pivotal figure whose conversion initiated a movement among Dalits, yet omitted key details – such as the name "Nanchari", his imprisonment,

---

[13] *MMCLMS*, Nov. 1845, p. 167; Jan. 1849, p. 9.

[14] *MMCLMS*, April 1846, p. 54.

[15] Simmons, *Hundred Years*, p. 8.

[16] *ARLMS*, 1850, p. 58; *Proceedings of the Missionary Conference*, p. 118.

[17] Gribble, *A Manual*, p. 278.

[18] Ibid., p. 279.

the nature of his crime, his motivations for conversion, and the time of his release. Subsequent LMS literature supplemented Mawbey's account with additional information, revealing that Nanchari was a headman of his community.[19]

Mawbey's narrative underscores Howell's evangelistic efforts in the Cuddapah prison, highlighting Nanchari's pivotal conversion experience therein, which was deployed subsequently to catalyse mass conversion movements. With British rule established in Rayalaseema, a prison had been erected in Cuddapah town in 1813, and Howell had commenced visits and preaching there in 1823. His engagement with prisoners had elicited gratitude among them: many had prostrated themselves before him and offered contributions.[20] Regular Sunday visits facilitated the distribution of scriptural excerpts and tracts, which prisoners consumed avidly during nightly readings and group discussions.[21] Howell's sermons, focusing on themes of human fallibility, Christ's life, crucifixion, and salvation resonated with the inmates, although some perceived the missionary's visits as attempts to undermine caste affiliations.[22] In 1829 a school was inaugurated within the jail, employing Veerappa, a Brahmin convert, as a teacher.[23] LMS reports show prisoners embracing Christianity under Howell's influence, emerging as mission workers and evangelists upon their release.[24] Nanchari's conversion, as recounted by a missionary called Simmons, occurred during one of Howell's prison visits, culminating in Nanchari's baptism in 1838 and the adoption by him of the name Abraham.[25] Within LMS accounts Howell assumes a central role in

[19] Gopalakristnamah Chetty, *Manual of the Kurnool District*; Lewis, *History of the Telugu Mission*; *Proceedings of the Missionary Conference*, 1879; Simmons, *Hundred Years*, pp. 9, 11; Marler, *A Century of Missionary Work*, pp. 20, 88; *ARLMS*, 1924, p. 47.

[20] *QCTLMS*, 1824, p. 116; *ARLMS*, 1824, p. 74.

[21] *ARLMS*, 1828, 368; 1830, pp. 44–5.

[22] *QCTLMS*, 1824, pp. 119, 121–2; ibid., 1827, p. 399; ibid., 1830, p. 501; *ARLMS*, 1835, pp. 434–5.

[23] *ARLMS*, 1830, p. 45.

[24] *QCTLMS*, 1831, 431; *ARLMS*, 1835, pp. 434–5.

[25] Simmons, *Hundred Years*, p. 11.

Nanchari's conversion journey by actively visiting, preaching, and administering baptism within the prison environment. His agency in Nanchari's conversion is emphasised, demonstrating the profound impact of missionary outreach within prison settings.

Nanchari in the SPG Archives

The SPG Telugu Mission started in Cuddapah with a few families separating from the LMS Telugu Mission when Howell joined the SPG in 1842. After Howell had severed his connection with the LMS, some forty-six of the converts formed a separate Anglican community.[26] Soon after Howell joined the SPG he was reordained and moved to work among Telugu-speaking converts at Vallaveram near Madras. Howell was replaced in Cuddapah by the Rev. W.W. Whitford, who took charge of the congregation for seven years. In 1849 the Additional Clergy Society sent the Rev. Uriah Davies to minister to the English and Telugu congregations of Cuddapah. With the help of Alfred Wood as his interpreter, Davies went out to preach and undertook evangelistic work until he left the SPG in 1854 on account of an illness.[27]

According to the SPG records it was during the time of Uriah Davies that Nanchari embraced Christianity. In 1881 the Rev. Samuel Morley, domestic chaplain, and Frederick Gell, Bishop of Madras, visited various SPG Telugu Mission stations. During their visit to Rudravaram they met Nanchari: about this Morley writes: "At Rudravaram we saw Moses . . . now an old man. He sat down on the ground, gave us an animated account of his conversion, and spoke with great energy and fire respecting the spread of Christianity." Based on his conversation, Morley also provides the following details:

> A man at Rudravaram, about sixty miles from Cuddapah, heard (as he went about selling thread which he had spun) of Christianity and wished to know more. One day, he suddenly conceived the idea of going to Cuddapah to inquire about Christianity. The London Mission agents to whom he went thought him mad and would have nothing to say to him. At last, he found

[26] Marler, A Century of Missionary Work, p. 21.

[27] Hibbert-Ware, Missions in the Telugu Country, p. 53; Hosea, Saga of the Humble, pp. 2, 50.

his way to Alfred Wood, who brought him to Mr Davies, and in due time, he was baptised and called Moses. He took Mr Davies to Rudravaram, and here the first converts in the District were made.[28]

Morley's account is the earliest reference to Nanchari in the SPG material. It does not speak of Nanchari's imprisonment and his connection with the LMS. Instead it combines five incidents that occurred at differing time periods. The first pertains to Nanchari hearing of Christianity – Morley talks of how he heard of Christianity but not when. It is possible that he was referring to Nanchari's encounter with Christianity in prison. The second incident is Nanchari's visit to Cuddapah and encounters with LMS agents. This gives us a clue to establishing Nanchari's connection with the LMS, which may have happened between 1842 and 1844, as this was the period when Howell departed and local agents carried out LMS work until another missionary, Edward Porter, was appointed in 1844.[29] During this time the SPG Mission was very much present in Cuddapah town. But Nanchari went directly to LMS agents in Cuddapah as he wished to seek out Howell; since Howell was no longer around, the LMS agents were not overly welcoming with him. This also helps us understand that Nanchari was perhaps released between 1842 and 1844, after Howell had left Cuddapah.

The third incident is Nanchari's meeting in Cuddapah with Alfred Wood, who took him to the missionary Davies. This possibly took place between 1849 and 1854, which was when Wood and Davies worked together. The fourth incident is what Morley mentions: "in due time, he was baptised." Nanchari's baptism did not happen immediately after he met Davies. This was because converts in the SPG Mission had to learn the Lord's Prayer and Ten Commandments before they were baptised. Their conduct was carefully tested. No convert was baptised until he had been under instruction for two years.[30] According to Hibbert-Ware, who served as SPG missionary in the Kurnool District, Moses (Nanchari) asked questions about the new religion at Cuddapah where he met Alfred Wood; the latter "took him to Mr Davies, with whom he stayed as an inquirer

[28] *The Mission Field*, 1882, p. 12.
[29] Marler, *A Century of Mission Work*, p. 21.
[30] Higgens, *Here and There*, p. 70.

for many months."[31] This suggests Nanchari stayed for several months with the Rev. Davies to learn more about the new religion and the new god.

The fifth incident is the visit by Davies to Rudravaram, followed by the group conversion – which did not happen immediately after Nanchari's baptism. Again, Hibbert-Ware helps us understand why. He observes that there had been a conflict between the Malas on the one hand and the dominant castes as well as the officials of Rudravaram on the other. The Malas went to Cuddapah to settle their case in court. There Alfred Wood, one of the catechists in the SPG Mission, helped them win their case and taught them the Christian religion. They returned to their village, where Wood followed them. Consequently the whole community of Malas in the village was placed under his instruction. Later Davies visited, preached to them, and baptised thirty people on 22 July 1852.[32]

Morley and Hibbert-Ware's accounts provide further information on the untouchable occupations, especially Nanchari's profession. The Malas and Madigas in Rayalaseema not only lived lives of degradation and poverty, they were slaves in all but name since their livelihood was tied to their work as subservient agricultural labourers under dominant-caste landlords such as the Reddys.[33] Malas also eked out a living by weaving and spinning; men, women, and children were all involved in these activities. Each weaver had his own customers; one family of the Malas would weave for one family of Sudras for generations. Often, Mala men travelled to villages and towns to buy raw cotton and sell woven clothes, particularly in the regular marketplaces. Nanchari was a trader in thread, buying cotton and selling thread that had been spun in his village.[34] Their artisanal occupation made some Malas mobile, and Nanchari travelled around the region. The culture of travel and mobility signifies some element of freedom.[35] While touring the villages, towns, and markets of his

---

[31] Hibbert-Ware, *Missions in the Telugu Country*, p. 53.

[32] Ibid., pp. 53–4.

[33] Thurston, *Castes and Tribes*, vol. 4, p. 351.

[34] Hibbert-Ware, *Missions in the Telugu Country*, pp. 81–2; Oddie, "Christian Conversion", p. 66; Thurston, *Castes and Tribes*, vol. 4, pp. 309, 351; *ARLMS*, 1853, p. 87; *The Mission Field*, 1859, p. 202.

[35] Grewal, *Home and Harem*, p. 136.

area, Nanchari seems to have enjoyed freedom from the traditional caste roles that confined Malas to agrarian work.

The SPG annual report of 1952 provides details of Nanchari's conversion and centenary celebrations. It says that the "Spirit of God so worked in the heart of a man called Nanchary (later Moses) of Rudravaram, that he and his fellow villagers accepted the new faith and were baptised on July 22, 1852." The report also records the centenary celebrations of 1952, which commenced on Sunday the 27th at Rudravaram church, with the Rev. C.J.G. Robinson, Bishop of Lucknow, delivering a sermon, after which he visited the tomb of "Nanchary" (the first convert) and the house where Nanchary's grandson now lived.[36]

So here, for the first time, we have Nanchari's name appearing in the mission report. This was because the Rev. B.E. Devaraju had sent a report from Nandyal Church to the office compiling information for their report. In the SPG archival material the focus is on the missionary Davies who played a prominent role in Nanchari's conversion. Agency is attributed to Davies as the person who interacted with, instructed, and baptised Nanchari and his fellow villagers. We get confirmation here that Nanchari was baptised and christened as "Moses".

Nanchari in Vernacular Material

The third source of material is Church history books, souvenirs of centenary celebrations, and hagiographies of local workers written in Telugu. The writers of the vernacular material are from SPG Mission-related church backgrounds. While writing the history of the SPG Telugu Mission the theologian B.E. Devaraju provides the following information about Nanchari in his book published in 1969:

> During the time of missionary Whitford in Cuddapah, there was a Mala person named Nanchari in Rudravaram village of Kurnool District. He was a trader in a thread [sic]. Having a desire to know God, he visited some Hindu pilgrimage places, and one of those was Ahobilam, where he entered the temple to have a *darshan* of god Narasimha. When Brahman priests identified him as an untouchable, they created a nuisance, and Nanchari was arrested. The judge punished him with imprisonment and sent him off to jail.

[36] *To All Men*, pp. 50–2.

During the same time, the missionary visited him in jail and preached the Gospel. He embraced Christianity in jail, and after his release, he shared with his relatives about Christianity.[37]

Devaraju himself was from the Dalit community of Cuddapah District. Between 1950 and 1951 he worked as Acting Commissary and Vicar General of Nandyal and was part of the SPG centenary celebrations in 1952.[38] He had sent his centenary celebrations report to the compilers of the SPG magazine and is the first to provide this detailed information about Nanchari – the kind unavailable in other sources.

Subsequent writers reiterated Devaraju's narrative of Nanchari.[39] The vernacular material informs us that Nanchari was converted during Whitford's tenure, this Whitford having been a chaplain at Poonamalle, Madras. In the absence of a missionary in the SPG Mission after Howell left, Whitford ministered to Cuddapah by visiting it occasionally from 1842 to 1849. Apart from Devaraju, all the other writers say Alfred Wood was involved in the process of Nanchari's conversion. Bunyan Hosea records it this way: "A Mala by name Nanchar from Rudravaram village was in Cuddapah jail, for having entered a Hindu temple in his village. The Wood Brothers, who used to visit the jail to preach the gospel, heard his story and released him. Nanchari, who accepted Christ as his Saviour, took the Wood Brothers to Rudravaram, and in the days following, Rev. U. Davies visited the village and baptised thirty people."[40]

Basil Wood and Alfred Wood, siblings from Tamil Nadu, migrated from Tanjore to Cuddapah for their evangelical purposes. Collaborating with Howell, they preached the gospel at the British cantonment and prison in Cuddapah town. Upon Howell's transition to the SPG, the Wood brothers followed suit, leaving the LMS to join the SPG. They played pivotal roles in the SPG's early history, particularly during 1842–9 when they assumed leadership of the mission in the absence of a missionary.[41]

[37] Devaraju, *Bharatadesa*, pp. 149–50.
[38] Sundara Rao, *Telugulo*, pp. 184–5.
[39] Benjamin, *Andhra Pradesh*, pp. 4–5; Hosea, *Saga of the Humble*, pp. 50–1; Satya Murthy, *A Brief History*, p. 65.
[40] Hosea, *Saga of the Humble*, pp. 50–1.
[41] Ibid., p. 86.

Vernacular sources illuminate Nanchari's spiritual quest. In religious matters, the Malas and Madigas had their own separate religious organisation. The chief objects of their worship were village deities named Sunkulamma, Gangamma, Peddamma, Yellamma, and Maramma.[42] For generations, despite being devotees of Hindu gods and worshipping them, these two communities had been barred from entering temples because of their caste status. In fact, all untouchable communities were prohibited even from coming near temples and had to offer prayers from a distance to avoid contaminating Hindu sacred space. Caste-Hindus who encountered an untouchable in the temple reacted with the violence of a snake whose tail has been trod on.[43] As Jesús Cháirez-Garza puts it, the temple was not inaccessible to untouchables, being deemed inherently untouchable by them.[44]

From historical accounts it is evident that many elders of the Dalit community who spearheaded mass conversion movements were deeply devout individuals even before embracing Christianity. Vedamanickam, who led the conversion movement in Travancore, yearned for spiritual enlightenment. Denied access to Hindu temples, he sought solace by visiting pilgrimage sites.[45] Similarly, Venkaiah and Peraiah, instrumental in conversion movements in Andhra, were driven by strong religious fervour. Venkaiah, initially devoted to village-goddess worship, embarked on a quest for deeper spiritual understanding when learning about Christianity.[46] Peraiah, initially associated with the Rajayoga sect, eventually transitioned into becoming a religious teacher after years of dedicated meditation and spiritual practice under the guidance of his guru, Veeramma.[47]

Like Vedamanickam, Venkaiah, and Peraiah, Nanchari sought a divine encounter and tried entering the Ahobilam temple near his village despite the caste prohibition. He was apprehended and imprisoned

---

[42] Gopalakristnamah Chetty, *A Manual*, p. 142; Nicholson, "Social Organisation of the Malas", p. 99.

[43] Jangam, *Dalits*, pp. 74, 79, 174.

[44] Cháirez-Garza, "Touching Space", p. 7.

[45] Pickett, *Christian Mass Movements*, p. 39.

[46] Darling, *Telugu Convert*, p. 9.

[47] Taneti, *Caste, Gender and Christianity*, pp. 53–5.

by the temple priests and the village Karunam.[48] Karunams, primarily Brahmins, held authority over village lands and records.[49] The historian Chinnaiah Jangam notes that their power derived from managing land documentation and serving as intermediaries between the government and the village. Additionally, they upheld caste traditions as custodians of caste dharma.[50] This partnership between temple priests and Karunams was the reason for Nanchari's incarceration.

Constance Millington's *An Ecumenical Venture* (1993) provides a different explanation: "A Mala named Nanchari from Rudravaram . . . was caught stealing and jailed. He had lived by selling thread in the daytime and stolen timber at night. In jail, he heard the Gospel preached, and on his release from prison, he met the evangelist Alfred Wood, who took him to Uriah Davies for Christian instruction."[51] Timber theft is the new dimension, there being no mention of it earlier. During my fieldwork in 2017 I learnt through Kanakamma – a descendant of Nanchari's who was one of my interviewees – that in the nearby villages of Ahobilam, including Rudravaram, the Madigas and Malas cut trees from the nearby forest and sell them in local markets to earn a livelihood.[52] This activity may well have led to accusations of timber theft against Malas and Madigas. It is equally plausible to assert that the accusation of timber theft against Nanchari served as a convenient pretext: the Brahmins and Karunams needed a credible accusation to imprison a Dalit, and timber theft served their purpose.

Nanchari through Oral Narratives: Unveiling Historical Memory

Oral traditions have been crucial in preserving the memory of Nanchari and providing an alternative perspective even after nearly two centuries. The ethnologist Jan Vansina observes that oral traditions are unwritten historical memories extracted orally from people. He argues that

---

[48] Benjamin, *Andhra Pradesh*, pp. 4–5.
[49] Gribble, *Manual*, p. 34.
[50] Jangam, *Dalits*, p. 201.
[51] Millington, *An Ecumenical Venture*, pp. 6–7.
[52] Kanakamma, personal interview, 3 Jan. 2017.

there is a difference between oral histories and oral traditions. The sources for oral history are recent events and situations that have occurred during the participants' lifetime. Oral traditions, on the other hand, are not contemporary but are handed down from generation to generation beyond the participants' lifetime; they represent the past in the present.[53] The interviews I conducted offer insights into Nanchari's conversion, his experience, and how his memory persists today. The narratives that emerge in them contrast with the impersonal and superficial missionary accounts of the same events. To deepen my understanding of Nanchari I employed an ethnographic-historical approach. By examining missionary writings and vernacular materials I identified three key locations in Nanchari's narrative: his village Rudravaram, the Ahobilam temple, and the prison in Cuddapah. A geographical exploration revealed that Rudravaram and Ahobilam are closer to Nandyal, a major town in the Kurnool District – from where I myself come.

Through a friend, in October 2016 I contacted Sudhakar, a 45-year-old pastor resident in Rudravaram. Subsequently, from 5 to 11 November 2016 I conducted fieldwork in Rudravaram, the Ahobilam temple, and Cuddapah. Before my arrival, Sudhakar had arranged meetings with several elderly villagers, facilitating interview trust-building. During my fieldwork I interviewed individuals named Bala Krupanandam, Bhagyamma, Jameena, Jeevamma, Leelamma, Madhu, Manikyamma, Moses, Premamma, and Yakobu. All these interviewees were Christians of the Mala community. Most were daily-wage labourers born and raised in their village. Our conversations were in Telugu and in the nature of informal discussions. My effort was to steer the conversation towards topics such as the introduction of Christianity in their village, recollections of Nanchari, and occasions commemorating him.

During my initial visit I learned of Kanakamma, Nanchari's great-granddaughter, who was alive but away visiting her daughter in another village. Sudhakar informed me of her return to Rudravaram in December, so I revisited Rudravaram on 3 January 2017 and interviewed her at her residence. Additionally, I had telephone conversations with Moses and Kanakamma's daughter Sudarsanamma. On account of this I dis-

---

[53] Vansina, *Oral Tradition as History*, pp. xii, 12, 13, 28.

Fig. 1: With Aguta Kanakamma.

covered Nanchari's tomb as well. However, my efforts to get information on Nanchari in the Cuddapah prison were unsuccessful – as the
administration had no records from that far back.

I visited the Ahobilam temple on 5 November 2016. Ahobilam,
situated in the Nallamala Hills of the Kurnool District in Andhra Pradesh, is renowned as a major Vaishnava temple. It is in fact a complex
that comprises a lower Ahobilam temple in the foothills and an upper
Ahobilam temple approximately four miles uphill. Dedicated to the
worship of Narasimha, the man-lion incarnation of the god Vishnu, the
shrine is primarily overseen by Sri Vaishnava Brahmins. According to
Frykenberg, these Brahmins are known for their exclusivity, adherence
to pollution rules, and avoidance of interaction even with other Brahmins.[54]

The annual Brahmotsavalu (festival) is a significant event at the temple, typically held for ten days in the month of March or April.[55] Despite
my attempts, I could not meet the temple management or priests.
However, at the upper Ahobilam temple I engaged with some palan-
quin bearers who had worked there for years. They were unfamiliar with
the story of Nanchari's temple entry incident. I purchased some books

[54] Personal email correspondence, 26 April 2021.
[55] Nossam, *Nava Narasiimha*, p. 102; Vasantha, *Ahobilam*, p. 149.

from a bookstall within the temple premises which, though containing no information about Nanchari, offered insights into the temple's history and management.

Later that day I travelled from Ahobilam to Rudravaram, twenty-four kilometres distant. Rudravaram constitutes an important village in the SPG Telugu Mission because the mass conversion movement began in it. The founding of Rudravaram village is associated with Prataparudra, king of the Chalukya and Kakatiya dynasties in the early fourteenth century. In the colonial period this was a village of Sirvel Taluk in Kurnool District located at the border of Cuddapah and Kurnool districts. The first Collector of the Ceded Districts, Thomas Munro, arranged for an annual payment of 100 *varaha*s (gold coins) from this village to the Ahobilam temple. A weekly market is held in the village every Monday.[56]

In the late evening of Saturday, 5 November 2016, Sudhakar took me to the CSI (Church of South India). He introduced me to four elderly women who sat in the church premises after attending a prayer meeting. Jeevamma (85) and Leelamma (80) told me Nanchari went to Ahobilam and entered the temple, where the priests recognised him and said, "You are from the Mala caste, and you are not supposed to enter our temple."[57] Then they beat him and imprisoned him. Jeevamma said Malas were prohibited from visiting the temple; they worshipped gods and goddesses such as Sunkulamma, Maramma, Durgamma, Peddamma, Obulesu, and Lingamayya. She said she did not know where Nanchari had been imprisoned. Jameena intervened and said it was in the Madras jail. Jeevamma continued by saying that Thellollu (white missionaries) came to the jail to preach the gospel; Nanchari heard their words in the jail. Leelamma said Nanchari had come to Rudravaram from prison and, in his small hut, had started praying. The neighbours observed him at prayer and many Mala people soon became Christians. Subsequently, Nanchari established a church; during Nanchari's time this was a small hut; it was only in 1980 that a new church had been constructed. I asked

[56] Gopalakristnamah Chetty, *A Manual*, pp. 97, 214; Vasantha, *Ahobilam*, p. 73.

[57] All the translations of interviews and contents from the Telugu are mine.

whether Nanchari's name was inscribed anywhere on the church walls. Jameena said his name was inscribed over his tomb, and this was when I first learned about the tomb. I had never imagined finding Nanchari's tomb – it is in the graveyard next to the church. They took me to the graveyard and showed it to me.

When I asked about the descendants of Nanchari, Bhagyamma, Leelamma, and Jeevamma said "Aguta Kanakamma is alive" and lives in the village. They explained Kanakamma's relationship with Nanchari. Jeevamma said Nanchari's great-grandson Moses had two sons, Pedda (big) Nanchari and Chinna (small) Nanchari. Later, they were given the names Yesu Rathnam and Demesh, respectively. Kanakamma is married to Yesu Rathnam.[58] During my interview, Kanakamma, aged 85, said Nanchari's family name was Aguta; he was called Aguta Nanchari and his wife was called Nancharamma.

A Dalit Christian resident of Rudravaram, Moses (52), and Nanchari's great-granddaughter Kanakamma provided details on the Brahmin who identified Nanchari in the temple. Tapping into their collective community memory, Moses said that in the time before their conversion Malas had worshipped local gods such as Pothuluri Brahmam and Chennudu or Chenna Kesavulu; the village had a temple for their deity, Chennudu. It was on the day of Mukkoti Ekadasi – which Hindus

Fig. 2: Interaction with Jeevamma and others.

[58] Bhagyamma, personal interview, 5 Nov. 2016; Jameena, personal interview, 5 Nov. 2016; Leelamma, personal interview, 5 Nov. 2016.

consider important and auspicious for visits to their temples – that Nanchari, a community elder and devout man, made himself ready to go to the Ahobilam temple. On the same day a Brahmin named Venkateswarlu from Rudravaram also went off to the same temple. In the lower Ahobilam temple the Brahmin Venkateswarlu and the lower-caste Nanchari stood in the same queue. Since Nanchari was an elder of the community, he was known in the village. When the Brahmin recognised Nanchari, he alerted the priests by shouting, "*Apacharam, apacharam*, an untouchable person is in the line, drag him out."[59] Nanchari retorted, "I will not come out of the line. Is the god only for you, not for us?" At this the Brahmin priests and their associates thrashed Nanchari for polluting the temple and had him arrested. When Nanchari failed to return home, his family mounted a search and learnt of his arrest. But they did not know he had been imprisoned in Cuddapah jail. According to Moses, Thellollu from London visited the jail and preached to the convicts about sin and salvation. Nanchari, understanding the meaning of what they were teaching, went to the missionary and said: "I went to Ahobilam for the god, but the Brahmins beat me and put me in jail. They filed a case against me, but you brought the god to me. I accept Jesus. I don't want the god who doesn't want me, I want the god who wants me." Nanchari also told the missionaries that he was "from Rudravaram and an elder of the Mala community with seventy families. We worship the god of Chennudu." After listening to his story the Thellollu secured his release and helped dismiss the case against him. Nanchari brought the missionaries to Rudravaram and gathered seventy families. The missionaries preached to them about salvation and baptism and instructed them to abandon idolatry. Hearing them, thirty families responded and were baptised. These converts went to a nearby hill, cut the trees there, and brought the wood down to build a church hut. This happened in 1852, when Aguta Nanchari founded the Thalli Sangham (Mother Church) of the SPG Telugu Mission.[60]

As previously noted, the centenary celebrations of the first baptism occurred in Rudravaram on 27 July 1952. Leelamma, Premamma, Jee-

[59] *Apacharam* means non-conformity with the shastras.

[60] Moses, personal interview, 6 Nov. 2016; telephone conversation, 14 August 2021; Kanakamma, personal interview, 3 Jan. 2017.

vamma, and Kanakamma attested to their participation in these celebrations, reminiscing that they were approximately fifteen years old at
the time.[61] In those celebrations, they said, local people remembered and
celebrated Nanchari's memory in the form of a song. They said all Christians and invited guests went to the Pedda Cheruvu (Big Lake), where
the first baptisms occurred. From there they walked to the church
singing a song. In the church the "Laknoo Bisappu" (Lucknow bishop)
preached and said that it had been a hundred years since the church came
to their village.[62] Leelamma said various young people performed a play
and sang a song in memory of Nanchari. She and her three companions
recollected some lines of the Telugu song they had sung:

> Aguta Nanchari is a great lord, he was the founder of this church
> This is our joy and the joy of that establishment
> It has been a hundred years, for today the Church was established
> Hundred years that give happiness to the heart
> Great celebration, good celebration, centenary celebrations.

Rudravaram Church commemorated the 150th year celebrations of
the first baptism in 2002. The occasion was like a festival, and the Bishop
of the Nandyal Diocese was invited as chief guest. During those celebrations the Bishop and the church pastor, Benjamin, preached and
reminded their congregation about Nanchari.[63]

We don't have the year of Nanchari's death. As I indicated earlier, the
domestic chaplain Morley said Nanchari was very old when he and the
bishop met him in 1881.[64] However, Nanchari's tomb in the Christian
burial ground at Rudravaram shows a cross placed over the tomb with

---

[61] Leelamma, personal interview, 5 Nov. 2016; Premamma, personal interview, 6 Nov 2016; Jeevamma, personal interview, 5 Nov. 2016; Kanakamma,
personal interview, 3 Jan. 2017.

[62] When Leelamma uttered the words "Laknoo Bisappu", I did not understand and asked her to say them again. She uttered the same words. I thought it
was the name of a person. But later in 2017 when I read the SPG report of 1952,
I came across information that the Rev. C.J.G. Robinson, a bishop from Lucknow, had preached in Rudravaram as part of the centenary celebrations. I realised what Leelama had meant was the Lucknow bishop.

[63] Moses, telephone conversation, 14 August 2021.

[64] *The Mission Field*, 1882 p. 13.

an inscription which says (in Telugu) "Aguta Nanchari, established 1842".[65] Kanakamma and her daughter Nancharamma renovated the tomb in the 1980s with the money they earned selling wood from the nearby forest. They were invested in keeping alive the memory of their great-grandfather who had brought Christianity and Church to the village.

Fig. 3: Nanchari's tomb.

[65] These words were inscribed when the tomb was renovated. The year 1842 refers to the establishment of the SPG Telugu Mission in Cuddapah. Even the church nameplate has the same year. Moses said during my interview that by mistake they had inscribed 1842 instead of 1852, which indicates the year of establishment of the church in the village.

Defying Caste: Nanchari's Journey
to Christianity

Here I present my perspective on the motivations behind Nanchari's conversion. I emphasise the intricate factors influencing his decision to convert and its subsequent ramifications.

Missionary sources attribute agency to Howell and Davies in Nanchari's conversion. The SPG reports credit the Spirit of God, highlighting Nanchari's joy at receiving the Christian message, leading to his baptism and subsequent role as an evangelist.[66] Howell, who is said to have baptised Nanchari during a visit to Cuddapah prison, is celebrated for enabling Nanchari to lead his community to Christianity and initiating mass conversion movements. Nanchari is well positioned within the broader mission history of the region. The 1924 LMS annual report hails Howell as a hero for sparking a reformation through Nanchari's baptism.[67] Missionary narratives, in prioritising missionary agency, overlook the significance of caste discrimination in Nanchari's imprisonment.

Dalit oral traditions offer a contrasting perspective, attributing Nanchari with complete agency in his conversion. Oral accounts show the everyday ways in which caste domination prevailed, how Dalits were oppressed, and how Nanchari's defiance remains central in their collective memory. Dalits remember how Nanchari was caught, the Brahmin who recognised him, and how and why he was imprisoned. Their memories are all about defying caste oppression. His imprisonment makes him heroic, as does his violation of the caste sanctions which led to his imprisonment. He is more highly regarded than any missionary, remembered as a revolutionary figure in their lives and their history. In addition, as Kanakamma, Manikyamma, and Sudarsanamma told me during an interview, he is remembered as *Matham thechinodu, Sanghamunu thechinodu*, and *Mission thetchinodu* (he who brought religion, church, and mission) to Dalit communities, to their village, and to the surrounding villages.[68] In local social memory, it is not the missionary but Nanchari

---

[66] *To All Men*, p. 50.

[67] *ARLMS*, 1924, p. 47.

[68] Kanakamma, personal interview, 3 Jan. 2017; Manikyamma personal interview, 6 Nov. 2016; Sudarsanamma telephone conversation, 2 Dec. 2017.

who began a tremendous reform process. This inspires Dalits to view not just Nanchari's meeting with the missionary in prison but the entire process of caste domination and oppression which follows a Dalit from place to place. For them, this is the central issue; it is vital for their own sense of self and their collective identity to recall each and every detail of how he was caught, who caught him, and what he meant.

The aspects of Nanchari's character that are reconstructed in these recollections are also important. Unlike many others, it is said Nanchari did not rely on the dominant Reddy landlords for work; he sold thread in weekly markets across the Cuddapah and Kurnool districts. Beyond his livelihood, he harboured a spiritual bent of mind, evident from his visits to the Ahobilam temple. His realisation that caste should not hinder his access to temple prayers led him to the annual festival which drew participants from the surrounding villages. When his low-caste identity was exposed, he endured physical humiliation and imprisonment. The trauma justified his defiance of caste and ultimately his renunciation of Hinduism. Nanchari's activism represents a burgeoning form of Dalit resistance against entrenched caste norms. A century before Ambedkar, his experiences prefigure and highlight the evolving nature of the Dalit struggle against caste-based discrimination and oppression.

Oral accounts reveal the mechanisms of caste domination during Nanchari's time. It was a Brahmin from his own village who identified Nanchari as an untouchable to the community and temple priests. This sheds light on the intricate workings of caste relations within the village. The Brahmin's familiarity with Nanchari as headman of the Mala community and as a weaver-trader underscores the pervasive nature of caste norms beyond immediate interactions. Rather than merely admonishing Nanchari, the Brahmin priests used legal means to reinforce caste boundaries. Their reaction to Nanchari's attempt to enter the temple shows the extent of their determination to uphold caste order and associated restrictions. Their power is evident from the fact that they secured his imprisonment through the judicial system.

Nanchari's observations of the missionary's weekly interactions with his fellow prisoners seems to have been epiphanic, enabling him to internalise the teachings of Christianity and recognising it as a viable alternative to caste-driven Hinduism. It was clear too that the missionary was held in high regard by colonial officials, who treated him with a level of respect distinct from that of the dominant castes. Moreover, the concepts of God, sin, and salvation offered by Christianity resonated deeply in Nanchari's devout social context, where devotion to a deity was considered vital. Viewing Christianity as a potential catalyst for social change towards greater equality and inclusivity, he made his fateful decision to embrace it as a new way of life.

Upon his release Nanchari returned to his village a transformed individual. Shedding his former identity, he embraced a new one through baptism; he now came to be known as Abraham in the LMS accounts and as Moses in the SPG narratives. There is no doubt that his conversion was exemplary and marked a pivotal moment in the history of the Dalits in Rayalaseema, igniting community conversion movements.[69] The missionary Simmons recounts Nanchari's fervent sharing of his new-found faith with relatives and neighbours. His preachings extended outwards as he travelled to neighbouring villages, spreading the teachings of the new God he had found in jail.[70] In an interview, Yakobu, aged fifty-six, shared with me the oral tradition passed down from his grandparents, recalling Nanchari's memorable declaration: "I went to Ahobilam temple in search of God, but I was imprisoned. Yet, this new God, Jesus Christ, came to prison in search of me."[71]

References

ARLMS (Annual Reports of the London Missionary Society), 1824–1924.

Balasundaram, Franklyn J., Dalits and Christian Mission in the Tamil Country: The Dalit Movement and Protestant Christians in the Tamil Speaking Districts of Madras Presidency 1919–1939 with Special Reference to London Mission Society Area in Salem, Attur, Coimbatore, and Erode (Bangalore: Asian Trading Corp., 1997).

Benjamin, Busamella, Andhra Pradesh Christava Sangha Charitra (History of the Christian Church in Andhra Pradesh; n.p.: Telugu Theological Literature Board, 1976).

Bugge, Henriette, Mission and Tamil Society: Social and Religious Change in South India (1840–1900, (Richmond: Curzon Press, 1994).

[69] To know about mass conversion movements in Rayalaseema and their impact on Dalit community, see Chandra Sekhar, "In Search of a Touchable Body".

[70] Simmons, Hundred Years, p. 11.

[71] Yakobu, personal interview, 6 Nov. 2016.

Carman, John B., and Chilkuri Vasantha Rao, *Christians in South Indian Villages, 1959–2009: Decline and Revival in Telangana* (Cambridge: Wm. B. Eerdmans Publishing, 2014).

Cháirez-Garza, Jesús Francisco, "Touching Space: Ambedkar on the Spatial Features of Untouchability", *Contemporary South Asia*, vol. 22, no. 1, 2014, pp. 37–50.

Chandra Sekhar, C., "In Search of a Touchable Body: Christian Mission and Dalit Conversions", *Religions*, vol. 10, no. 12, 2019: 644, pp. 1–14.

Christhu Doss, M., "Repainting Religious Landscape: Economics of Conversion and Making of Rice Christians in Colonial South India (1781–1800)", *Studies in History*, vol. 30, no. 2, 2014, pp. 179–200.

Cole, Benaiah, *Indiana: The History of the Indians (Alias the Panchamas)*, vol. II, pt I (n.p.: Chandra Press, 1916).

Cornish, W.R., *Census Report of Madras Presidency, 1871, with Appendix*, vol. I (Madras, 1874).

Darling, T.Y., *A Telugu Convert: The Story of P. Venkayya* (London: CMS, 1893).

Devaraju, B.E., *Bharatadesa Christava Sangha Charitra* (History of Indian Christian Church; n.p.: A.S.R. Power Press, 1969).

Forrester, Duncan B., *Caste and Christianity: Attitudes and Policies on Caste of Anglo-Saxon Protestant Missions in India* (London, 1980).

Forrester, Duncan B., "The Depressed Classes and Conversion to Christianity, 1860–1960", in G.A. Oddie, ed., *Religion in South Asia: Religious Conversion and Revival Movements in South Asia in Medieval and Modern Times* (New Delhi: Manohar, 1977).

Frykenberg, Robert Eric, "The Impact of Conversion and Social Reform Upon Society in South India During the Late Company Period", in C.H. Phillips and M.D. Wainwright, eds, *Indian Society and the Beginning of Modernization c. 1830–1850* (London: University of London School of Oriental and African Studies, 1976).

Frykenberg, Robert Eric, "On the Study of Conversion Movements: A Review Article and a Theoretical Note", *The Indian Economic & Social History Review*, vol. 17, no. 1, 1980.

Frykenberg, Robert Eric, *Christianity in India: From the Beginnings to the Present* (Oxford, 2008).

Gladstone, J.W., *Protestant Christianity and People's Movements in Kerala: A Study of Christian Mass Movements in Relation to Neo-Hindu Socio-Religious Movements in Kerala, 1850–1936* (Trivandrum, 1984).

Gopalakristnamah Chetty, N., *A Manual of the Kurnool District in the Presidency of Madras* (Madras: Government Press, 1886).

Grewal, Inderpal, *Home and Harem: Nation, Gender, Empire and the Cultures of Travel* (London: Duke University Press, 1996).

Gribble, J.D.B., *A Manual of the District of Cuddapah in the Presidency of Madras* (Madras: Government Press, 1875).

Harper, S.B., *In the Shadow of the Mahatma: Bishop V.S. Azariah and the Travails of Christianity in British India* (Cambridge: Curzon Press, 2000).

Harvest Field, May 1893.

Hibbert-Ware, G., *Christian Missions in the Telugu Country* (Westminster: SPG, 1912).

Higgens, Alfred William Buckle, *Here and There in South India. Forty-six Illustrations and Three Maps* (Westminster: SPG, 1914).

Hosea, Bunyan, *Saga of the Humble Servants of God: Beginnings of SPG Telugu Mission in Rayalaseema* (Secunderabad: Junia Industries Pvt. Ltd, 2006).

Jangam, Chinnaiah, *Dalits and the Making of Modern India* (New Delhi: Oxford University Press, 2017).

Jenkins, Laura Dudley, *Religious Freedom and Mass Conversion in India* (Philadelphia: University of Pennsylvania Press, 2019).

Kawashima, K., *Missionaries and a Hindu State: Travancore, 1858–1936* (Oxford, 1998).

Kent, Eliza F., *Converting Women: Gender and Protestant Christianity in Colonial South India* (Oxford: Oxford University Press, 2004).

Kent, Eliza F., "'Mass Movements' in South India, 1877–1936", in Dennis Washburn and Kevin Reinhart, eds, *Converting Cultures: Religion, Ideology and Transformations of Modernity* (Boston: Brill, 2007).

Kooiman, Dick, *Conversion and Social Equality in India: The London Missionary Society in South Travancore in the 19th Century* (New Delhi, 1989).

Kooiman, Dick, "Mass Movement, Famine and Epidemic: A Study in Interrelationship", *Modern Asian Studies*, vol. 25, no. 2, 1991.

Lewis, Edwin, *History of the Telugu Mission of the London Missionary Society in the Ceded Districts* (Madras: Addison & Co., 1879).

Luke, P.Y., and J.B. Carman, *Village Christians and Hindu Culture* (New Delhi, 2009).

Mallampalli, Chandra, *South Asia's Christians: Between Hindu and Muslim* (New York: Oxford University Press, 2023).

Manickam, S., *The Social Setting of Christian Conversion in South India: The Impact of the Wesleyan Methodist Missionaries on the Trichy–Tanjore Diocese with Special Reference to the Harijan Communities of the Mass Movement Area 1820–1947* (Wiesbaden, 1977).

Marler, F.L., *A Century of Work in the Telugu Field, London Missionary Society, 1822–1922* (London: SOAS-CMWL MSS/116, 1928).

Millington, Constance, *An Ecumenical Venture: The History of Nandyal Diocese in Andhra Pradesh (1947–1990)* (Bangalore: Asian Trading Corporation, 1993).

Mission Field, The, 1859 and 1882.

MMCLMS (The Missionary Magazine and Chronicle of the London Missionary Society), 1845–91.

Mocherla, Ashok Kumar, *Dalit Christians in South India: Caste, Ideology and Lived Religion* (New York, 2021).

Mohan, Sanal, *Modernity of Slavery: Struggles Against Caste Inequality in Colonial Kerala* (New Delhi, 2015).

Mosse, David, *The Saint in the Banyan Tree: Christianity and Caste Society in India* (California, 2012).

Neelakantha Sasthri, Alladi, *Harijanudu (Harijan): A Play* (Cuddapah: Venkateswara Press, 1935).

Nicholson, Sydney, "Social Organization of the Malas – An Outcaste Indian People", *The Journal of the Royal Anthropological Institute of Great Britain and Ireland*, vol. 56, 1926.

Nossam, Narasimha Acharya, *Nava Narasiimha Kshetram-Ahobilam* (Tirupati: TTD Religious Publications, 2014).

Oddie, Geoffrey A., "Christian Conversion in the Telugu Country, 1860–1900: A Case Study of One Protestant Movement in the Godavery-Krishna Delta", *The Indian Economic & Social History Review*, vol. 12, no. 1, 1975.

Oddie, Geoffrey A., *Religious Conversion Movements in South Asia: Continuities and Change 1800–1900* (London: Routledge, 1997).

Paul, Vinil Baby, "Dalit Conversion Memories in Colonial Kerala and Decolonisation of Knowledge", *South Asia Research*, vol. 41, no. 2, 2021.

Pickett, Jarrell Waskom, *Christian Mass Movements in India: A Study with Recommendations* (New York: The Abingdon Press, 1933).

Phillips, G.E., *The Outcastes' Hope, or Work Among the Depressed Classes in India* (Edinburgh, 1912).

Proceedings of the South India Missionary Conference, Held at Ootacamund, 1858, 1879, etc.

QCTLMS (Quarterly Chronicle of Transactions of the London Missionary Society), 1824, 1831, etc.

Ranga Reddy, A., *The State of Rayalaseema* (Delhi: Mittal Publications, 2003).

Rawat, Ramnarayan S., "Occupation, Dignity, and Space: The Rise of Dalit Studies", *History Compass*, vol. 11, no. 12, 2013.

Satya Murthy, Z.E., *A Brief History of Zakkams and Woods* (Proddatur: Prasad Printers, 2007).

Simmons, A.T., *A Hundred Years in the Telugu Country, 1822–1922* (Mysore: Wesleyan Mission Press. 1923).

Sundara Rao, R.R., *Telugute Kristhava Sahityam* (Christian Literature in Telugu; Visakhapatnam: Rayi Publications, 2016).

Taneti, J.E., *Caste, Gender, and Christianity in Colonial India: Telugu Women in Mission* (New York, 2013).

Taneti, J.E., *Telugu Christians: A History* (Minneapolis, MN: Fortress Press, 2022).

Thurston, E., *Castes and Tribes of Southern India*, vol. 4 (Madras, 1904).

To All Men: S.P.G. Review of the Year's Work 1952–53 (London: SPG, 1953).

Vansina, Jan, *Oral Tradition as History* (Michigan: The University of Wisconsin Press, 1985).

Vasantha, R., *Ahobilam Sri Narasimha Swamy Temple* (Tirupati: Tirumala Tirupati Devasthanams, 2001).

Viswanath, Rupa, *The Pariah Problem: Caste, Religion and the Society in Modern India* (New York, 2015).

Viswanath, Rupa, "The Emergence of Authenticity Talk and the Giving of Accounts: Conversion as Movement of the Soul in South India, ca.1900", *Comparative Studies in Society and History*, vol. 55, no. 1, 2013.

Webster, J.C.B., *The Dalit Christians: A History* (New Delhi: ISPCK, 1994).

West, Shirley, "William Howell 1789–1867: Surveyor – Missionary – Priest", *The Journal of the Families in British Indian Society*, no. 11, Spring 2004.

Acknowledgements

I thank K. Satyanarayana, Rupa Viswanath, and Ramnarayan Rawat for their valuable comments on earlier drafts; all those who provided me with valuable information during my fieldwork; and the reviewers of this essay for their comments and suggestions.

3

An Ethical Community of Equals

A Dalit History of the Sant-Mat Religion in Twentieth-Century North India

RAMNARAYAN S. RAWAT

Yes! The proponents of Vedas have no doubt established their stamp on that fundamental doctrine [Brahma-gyan, the Atam-darshan philosophy], such as the Arya Samaj, which is now in the business of establishing a new Vedic way by pulling and pushing from the six shastras. Yet, that [philosophy of] Atam-gyan Anubhav's progress is separate from the Vedas, which is ever-present in the form of Sant-Mat, and still is.

– Speech by Swami Achutanand in 1926[1]

I FIRST READ about the Sant-mat in 1994, in Namvar Singh's 1982 study – a milestone Hindi literary-critical work – on the region's popular religious and cultural formations.[2] A major motivation,

---

[1] Achutanand, *Adi Hindu Sabha Mainpuri*, p. 3.

"देखो आदि बंश विज्ञान जो उपनिषद और शास्त्रों आदि में मूल रूप पाया जाता है वो ब्रह्मज्ञान आत्म दर्शन की फ़िलासफ़ी वेदों में पाई नहीं जाती क्योंकि ये बहुत प्राचीन थ्योरी है, हाँ। हां! वेद वादियों ने उस मूल सिदान्त [आतम देशन की फिलासफी] पर अपना रंग जमाया जरूर है जैसे अब की आर्य समाज षट् शास्त्रों को खींच तान कर एक वैदिक ढँग पर सिद्ध करने [के] उध्योग में है। पर वह आतमज्ञान, अनुभव विकास वेद से परे की बात है, जो सदा सन्त मत रूप में प्रचलित रहा ओर है।"

[2] Singh, *Dusari Parampara*.

as part of my earlier research on Dalit movements, was to understand the religious and literary history of medieval poet-saints such as Kabir and Raidas who belonged to the Nirgun bhakti tradition. Singh's pioneering study was built on an earlier landmark work in 1940 by Hazari Prasad Dwivedi. Dwivedi had highlighted Kabir's contribution not only to the formation of the Hindi language but also to the creation of an alternative religious worldview (especially in its third chapter, "Sant-mat").[3] In Dwivedi's view Kabir was important historically because his teachings used the people's spoken language, Hindi; because his devotionals songs (bhajans) praised an aniconic divinity, the Satguru (Supreme Lord); and because Kabir criticised caste.[4] Dwivedi argued that a popular religion (lok-dharma) had emerged in medieval India which represented a "glorious people's movement" (virat jana andolana) of those belonging to the lower classes.[5] Associated with the socialist wing of Hindi literary scholars in the twentieth century, Dwivedi and Namvar Singh argued that Kabir's collective teachings – in the shape of songs – represent an alternative radical tradition in North India.

By the 1980s the concept of "Sant-mat" occupied an important place in the discipline of Religious Studies, best represented by a collection of essays published in 1987, The Sants. According to its editor Karine Schomer, the "idea that there is a coherent body of Sant teachings (sant mat) and that individual Sants belong to a common spiritual line of descent (sant parampara) distinct from that of sectarian Vaishnavas did not become fully crystallised until the mid-nineteenth century."[6] Scholars have used the term Nirgun bhakti, i.e. devotion to God without attributes, and Sagun bhakti, i.e. devotion to God with attributes, to distinguish between two kinds of popular religious devotion.[7] Sagun bhakti

[3] Dwivedi, Hindi Sahitya, ch. 3, "Sant-mat", pp. 27–37.

[4] Sukla, Hindi Sahitya; Dasa, Hindi Sahitya; Dwivedi, Hindi Sahitya; Singh, Dusari Parampara; Agrawal, Azath Kahani. See also Barthwal, The Nirguna School.

[5] Dwivedi, Hindi Sahitya.

[6] Schomer, "Introduction", p. 3.

[7] See the essays by Frits Staal, Wendy O'Flaherty, Jack S. Hawley, Winand M. Callewaert, Charlotte Vaudeville, and David Lorenzen in Schomer and McLeod, The Sants.

is used to identify medieval sants (saints), such as Tulsidas and Surdas, who composed poems in praise of Lord Rama as a deity of mainstream Vaishnava Hinduism. However, in the disciplines of Hindi Literature and Religious Studies, the term Sant-mat refers to the teachings of poet-saints belonging to the Nirgun bhakti tradition.

During my research on the Adi-Hindu Mahasabha movement, which documents the Mahasabha's role in creating a language of liberal politics, especially its demand for separate and proportional representation in the legislative assemblies, I was equally surprised to discover its foundational intervention in promoting the Sant-mat religion in its publications as well as through its political activities (1920–40).[8] Dalit poet-activists – Swami Achutanand, Jagatram Jatiya, and Devidas Jatiya – founded the Adi-Hindu Mahasabha in 1923, after years of activism in Delhi and western Uttar Pradesh over 1916–23. Having founded the Adi-Hindu Mahasabha Press in 1925, Dalit poet-activists published song-booklets, speeches, dramas, and copies of the *Adi-Hindu* newspaper, all of which comprise the first body of work in which Dalit activists identify Sant-mat as a unique religion of untouchables in northern India. These poet-activists chose to use the term Sant-mat to describe the religious teachings associated with the poet-saints Kabir, Raidas, and Dadu: they rarely, if at all, used the term Nirgun bhakti. In line with them, I use the term Sant-mat to document the first sociological history of this distinctive devotional practice outlined by Dalit poet-activists in the Mahasabha's publications. I therefore use the term Nirgun bhakti only when discussing mainstream academic writing. The Mahasabha's publications offer a promising new Dalit perspective from which to unravel the sociological and literary histories of the Sant-mat religion.

Drawing from the Adi-Hindu Mahasabha's publications, I examine Dalit initiatives in appropriating and repurposing the Sant-mat religion to provide an ethical framework for social equality among all humans. It is clear that these poet-activists promoted the Sant-mat religion as an alternative to Vaishnavite Hinduism. In Section One of this essay I provide a brief history of the Sant-mat religion to illustrate the unique-

---

[8] Rawat, "Recovering the Dalit Public Sphere".

ly Dalit trajectory of its devotional paradigm, one which provides a unique comparative perspective to interpretations provided in the Hindi Literature and Religious Studies disciplines. Section Two recovers one of the most important principles of the Sant-mat religion emphasised in Mahasabha song-booklets, namely the notion of *atam-anubhav gyan* (sometimes *atam-anubhav*), referring to knowledge gained through personal experience. I first encountered extensive discussion of this notion in the 1926 *Vigyan Bhajan Mala*.[9] In Section Three I discuss the second-most important principle of the Sant-mat religion, the revelatory and liberatory role of Satguru – the aniconic divinity central to this religion. The first three song-booklets published by Swami Achutanand in 1916 and 1922 (11), and nearly all the Mahasabha publications (1924–40), begin with an invocation of Satguru, recognising him as the source of equality and dignity, and for promoting rational values. Section Four examines the critical role assigned to the poet-saint Raidas in the genealogy of the Sant-mat religion, and in the 1927 *Raidas Bhajan Mala* by the Mahasabha Press, projecting him as the chief ideologue of this new ethical framework. Section Five illustrates the relationship between the Sant-mat religion and the politics of liberty that was central to the agendas of the Mahasabha movement. For instance, the first six lines of the ten-page song "Adi-Hindu Vansh ka Prachin Gaurav", composed by Ramswarup Jaiswar, defined the core principles of the Sant-mat religion and reflected ideas associated with the politics of liberty:

> Through his knowledge, the Satguru has promised equal rights
>   (*sem-adhikar*),
> Erasing the evil distinctions of inequality, of high and low (*unch-niche*).
> Unfortunately, we were stuck in the web of darkness,
> Now, consciousness is waking us under the Raj.[10]

This essay, therefore, provides a history of Sant-mat devotion, including a new emphasis on Raidas, and shines a light on the significant role

---

[9] Achutanand, *Vigyan Bhajan Mala*. I have taken the term *atam-anubhav gyan*, from the song "Gyan Bhajan Mala" in *Vigyan Bhajan Mala* (1926), p. 7. Both *atam-anubhav* and *atam-anubhav gyan* appear in the text.

[10] Jaiswar, *Adi-Hindu Vansh*, p. 1. In the original, the Hindi words appear below the quoted lines, with a longer bhajan. All translations are mine unless otherwise specified.

of Adi-Hindu Mahasabha poet-activists led by Achutanand. It offers a historical perspective to contemporary studies which document the emergence of a powerful Raidas movement in the 1970s in the context of Punjab, but also in the United Kingdom and North America.[11]

The Sant-mat:
A Brief Conceptual History

In this short discussion of the Sant-mat religion I have two objectives: (i) to provide a much needed overview of the evolution of the term "Sant-mat", and (ii) to offer parallel histories of Sant-mat from the perspectives of the Literature and Religious Studies disciplines and Dalit vernacular sources. Through this discussion I hope to illustrate contrasting understandings of the Sant-mat religion and suggest that in Dalit writings this religion is claimed as belonging to the community as its unique inheritance, whereas in Hindi literary studies this religious tradition is considered part of the Nirgun bhakti tradition and projected as the "glorious people's movement".

The term Sant-mat, referring to the teachings of medieval poet-saints, appeared in the tracts of the Radhasoami sect in the late nineteenth century, and later in a popular tract series by the Belvedere Press from 1903 onwards. The Radhasoami sect, founded in Agra in the 1860s by Swami Shiv Dayal Singh, introduced the idea of Sant-mat into the literary public sphere.[12] The sect's members used the term to "designate the distinctive habit of mind that brought together more or less the same group of poet-saints" associated with bhakti devotional practices.[13] Juergensmeyer argues that the "phrase Sant-mat is occasionally used in the first tract published by the Radhasoami sect in 1884, *Sar Bachan Radhasoami: Poetry* (2 volumes)."[14] He emphasises catholicity in the use of the term when referring to the genealogy of medieval poet-saints.[15] However, the

[11] Ram, "Ravidass Deras and Social Protest", pp. 1347–8.

[12] Schomer, "Introduction", p. 3. For an excellent discussion on issues around Sant-mat, see ch. 6, "A Nation of Bhaktas", in Hawley, *A Storm of Songs*, pp. 231–84; Friedlander, "Ravidās / Raidās", pp. 14–15.

[13] Hawley, *A Storm of Songs*, p. 244.

[14] Juergensmeyer, *Radhasoami Reality*, p. 15.

[15] Ibid., pp. 21–2.

term Santbani (the voice of Sants) gained more currency in the public sphere when the Belvedere Press began to publish its cheap popular chapbook series. A leading member of the Radhasoami sect, Baleshwar P. Agrawal, founded the Belvedere Press in 1903 in Allahabad to publish the Santbani Pustakmala series ("The Voice of Sants" book series).[16] In his landmark 1936 study of the Nirgun school of Hindi poetry and its relationship to Indian mysticism, entitled *Nirguna School of Hindi Poetry*, Pitambar Datt Barthwal argued that the "Belvedere Press has played a prominent part in bringing the Sant literature to light," highlighting the role of the Santbani series in creating a new public in northern India.[17] Orsini argues that the Santbani Pustakmala series deployed a catholic meaning of "Sant" – as a saintly figure, a mahatma, or an ascetic who had created devotional religious songs that appealed to all social groups.[18] The Santbani series proved to be a major source in Barthwal's book, in which the terms "Sant-mat" and ' Nirguna-mat" describe the medieval poet-saints.[19] This genealogy may account for the circulation of the word Sant-mat in Hindi literary histories and textbooks such as Hazari Prasad Dwivedi's, in which Chapter 3 titled "Sant-mat", highlights an alternative rural vernacular religion to the Brahmanical religion.[20] The term Sant-mat emerged in the Hindi public sphere to describe medieval poet-saints who believed in divinity as aniconic and who used the Hindi language – as actually spoken by people at large – to compose their critical bhajans.

Thus, two parallel literary histories of Sant-mat emerged in the 1920s, first, the more established one led by mainstream caste-Hindu Hindi literary scholars, and second, the less known one led by Dalit poet-activists.[21] In the 1920s and 1930s the Hindi literary scholars Ramachander

[16] Orsini, "Booklets and Sants", p. 438.
[17] Barthwal, *The Nirguna School*, p. 284.
[18] Orsini, "Booklets and Sants", pp. 441–5.
[19] Barthwal, *The Nirguna School*, pp. ix, 284.
[20] Dwivedi, "Sant-mat", in *Hindi Sahitya*, pp. 27–37.
[21] Chapter 2, "The Nirgun Philosophy", in Barthwal, *The Nirguna School*. Hawley examines the relationship of Hindi literary scholars with the Bhakti tradition in Chapter 1, "The Bhakti Movement and Its Discontents", in Hawley, *A Storm of Songs*, pp. 13–58.

Sukla and Pitambar Datt Barthwal used the term Nirgun bhakti to describe devotion to the aniconic divinity associated with Kabir, Nanak, and Raidas in order to distinguish it from Sagun bhakti, which is associated with the devotion to Lord Rama in mainstream Vaishnava Hinduism and evident in the devotional songs of Tulsidas and Surdas. The works of socialist-leaning Hindi literary scholars – Hazari Prasad Dwivedi (1940), Namvar Singh (1982), and Purushottam Agrawal (2009) – characterise the Nirgun devotional tradition as *lok-dharma* (people's religion) and as "an ideology of ordinary people's rebellion" against the Brahmanical domination of Hinduism.[22] Recognising the medieval origins of Nirgun devotion, the three authors stress its longer Indic philosophical origins by showing its connections with the Upanishads, Buddhism, and the Tantric Nath sect (*sampradaya*).[23] By contrast, Mahasabha Dalit poet-activists in the early twentieth century and contemporary Dalit Hindi literary scholars in the late twentieth century, such as Dr Dharamveer and Kanwal Bharti, prefer to use the term Sant-mat rather than Nirgun bhakti. They argue that Kabir, Raidas, Dadu, and Nanak did not merely challenge Brahmanical hegemony, they rejected Hinduism. Dharamveer argues that the Sant-mat poet-saints embody a collective rejection of the Vaishnava Hindu religion and question the motives of Hindu scholars who represent them "within [the] Hindu and Vaishnava religious framework."[24] In his seminal book *Kabir ke Alochak* (1997; The Critics of Kabir), Dharamveer's objective is to document an alternative interpretation of Kabir and other Sant-mat poet-saints who, he says, created a new "hundred per cent Shudras and Antyajas religion."[25] Dalit Hindi writers in the twentieth century

[22] Dwivedi, *Hindi Sahitya*; Singh, *Dusari Parampara*, p. 79; Agrawal, *Akath Kahani*. They have stressed the role of poet-saints in using people's language to compose bhajans, giving them a voice, and actively creating and building the Hindi language.

[23] Chapter 3, "The Nirgun Panth", in Barthwal, *The Nirguna School*. Yet the dominant conservative stream within Hindi Literature Studies, located in the Nagari Pracharini Sabha in Allahabad, had dismissed Nirgun literature as lacking in literary and intellectual merit and later accepted it because of its connections with Vaishnavism: Sukla, *Hindi Sahitya*.

[24] Dharamveer, *Kabir ke Alochak*, p. 77.

[25] Ibid., p. 32. His objective in writing the book was to rescue Kabir and

emphasise a parallel literary and aural genealogy of Sant-mat religious practices.

This said, the Religious Studies historiography of Sant-mat has highlighted the rich hagiographical production of Sant-mat teachings between 1600 and 1800, and the emergence of leaders and movements that mobilised the poet-saints in late colonial India. Religious Studies scholars have recovered a large corpus of hagiographies of poet-saints containing collections of their bhajans. These were written by members of a number of religious sects belonging to the Sant-mat devotional genealogy.[26] These hagiographies – such as those by Dadu Dayal, Anantadas, and Nabhadas, for example – contain bhajans associated with various poet-saints who shared a philosophical and intellectual lineage with Sant-mat devotional practices, which also included the practice of citing the works of saints belonging to this genealogy. This distinctive history comprising Sant-mat hagiographies has laid bare the criticism of caste hierarchy, disagreements with Vaishnava scriptures, and the popularity of Satguru (the Supreme Lord) within a tradition that prioritises the aniconic.[27] Purushottam Agrawal has argued that Anantadas' hagiography of medieval poet-saints only looked at historical actors, or "ordinary humans", and stayed away from the Puranic gods.[28]

The Mahasabha song-booklets published in the 1920s suggest that Dalit movements in India had a strong social relationship with the Sant-mat religion. Historians of Dalit movements in northern India have documented the initiatives taken by Dalit groups to appropriate the Sant-mat tradition and Raidas because his teachings promoted egalitarian

---

other Sant-mat poets from a particular kind of interpretation which seeks to integrate him into a caste-Hindu view.

[26] In addition to the works of Karine Schomer, Mark Juergensmeyer, and Jack Hawley, cited above, I have benefitted immensely from David Lorenzen's two books, *Praises to a Formless God* and *Bhakti Religion*. I am grateful to Winand Callewaert's numerous works on the hagiographies of Sant-mat (Nirgun) poet-saints, and, for this article, Callewaert and Friedlander, *The Life and Works of Raidas*.

[27] Schomer, "Introduction", pp. 7–8; Hawley and Juergensmeyer, *Songs of the Saints of India*, esp. ch 1 on Ravidas, and ch. 2 on Kabir.

[28] Agrawal, *Akath Kahani*, p. 155. I found the general discussion on hagiography in ch. 3 very rewarding.

social values. The Ad-Dharm Dalit movement in 1920s' Punjab installed the statue of Raidas in newly created pilgrimage centres (*deras*) to further build on an already existing veneration for him among Dalits.[29] In the early twentieth century the "message of caste equality and the denial of ritual hierarchy in bhakti gave them [the poor untouchables in towns] means to question the discriminations, disabilities, and deprivation" in late colonial northern India.[30]

The Mahasabha poet-activists offered a contrasting definition of Sant-mat in the 1920s that encompassed an agenda for the social-cultural renewal of untouchable communities, and promoted this theme as a vital new feature of Dalit activism. First, at the heart of this concept was the notion of *atam-anubhav gyan* which recognised the agency of medieval poet-saints in challenging Vedic rote knowledge over human experience as a vehicle for acquiring new knowledge. Second, they emphasised the poet-saints' commitment to a Supreme Lord who is formless, nameless, and merciful. They distinguished devotion to Satguru, symbol of aniconic divinity, from devotional practices associated with "Hari-bhakti" – devotion to Lord Vishnu or Lord Rama. Third, these poet-activists promoted the divinity of Raidas to stress the principles of the Sant-mat religion which distinguished it from mainstream Vaishnavite Hinduism. Dalit poet-activists in the 1920s and contemporary Dalit writers insisted that Sant-mat is different from Hari-bhakti. The 1929 Hindi *Sabdasagar* dictionary defined "sant" as an ascetic or a Haribhakt, i.e. a devotee of Lord Vishnu. In contrast, Dalit writers and activists used the compound Sant-mat in the two distinctive senses mentioned above to register a unique devotional history. "Sant-mat" appeared for the first time in a 1993 Hindi dictionary, referring to "members of one of the sant communities of northern India (who believe in an unqualified and non-incarnated ultimate being)."[31] By the 1990s the study of Sant-mat had emerged as a distinct field in South Asian academia, even as a more visible and powerful Dalit political movement emerged in North India.

The Adi-Hindu Mahasabha poet-activists of the early twentieth century and the later Dalit writers used the term "Sant-mat" rather exclu-

[29] Juergensmeyer, *Religion as Social Vision*, p. 83.
[30] Gooptu, *The Politics of the Urban Poor*, p. 151.
[31] McGregor, *The Oxford Hindi-English Dictionary*, p. 964.

sively, rarely using "Nirgun bhakti". These contrasting interpretations of Sant-mat are evident in the shifting definition, especially in the 1993 Hindi dictionary which implicitly acknowledges the term's association with Dalit communities. The poet-activists clearly defined Sant-mat as an anti-caste religion which they associated with the teachings of Raidas and Kabir, locating its popularity and circulation in Dalit neighbourhoods. Further, they assigned to the Sant-mat religion a distinctive set of principles extant in Dalit neighbourhoods and highlighted their significance for Dalit social and political activism.

Atam-Anubhav Gyan: Social and Ethical in Sant-mat

The concept of *atam-anubhav gyan* first caught my attention when I read Swami Achutanand's May 1926 speech at Mainpuri and noted that the phrase appeared regularly in his oratory, most noticeably in May 1933 at Gwalior where he provided a detailed discussion of this idea.[32] So I decided to track the chronology of the appearance of this term in the Mahasabha's song-booklets. Swami Achutanand mentioned this term on several occasions in the song-booklets published by him in 1916 and 1922. A more systematic discussion of this concept appeared in the chapbooks and song-booklets published by the Adi-Hindu Mahasabha Press. The 1926 *Vigyan Bhajan Mala* offered the most extensive discussion of *atam-anubhav gyan*, portraying it as a vital category to highlight the role of a person's self-experience in evaluating, assessing, and building knowledge (*vigyan*).[33] In his 1930 Berar public speech (eight pages long) Achutanand added new insights to the concept, arguing that "among our ancestors [the Adi-Hindus] *atam-anubhav gyan* had achieved its highest scientific intellectual strength and development."[34] He insisted that Raidas and Kabir had played a singular role in developing this

[32] Achutanand, *Adi Hindu Sabha Mainpuri*, pp. 1–5. In his speech the words *atam-gyan* and *anubhav* appear together and separately. "Sabhapati ka Bhashana Sara", pp. 8–13 (President's Speech, Gist), in *Gwalior Rajya Adi-Hindu (Depressed Classes) Mahasabha Report* (1930).

[33] Achutanand, *Vigyan Bhajan Mala*.

[34] Achutanand's speech at the Adi-Hindu conference in Amrawati, Berar, on 20 April 1930: *Presidential All India Depressed*, p. 6.

notion to formulate their unique anti-caste agendas. The Mahasabha's song-booklets claimed that Raidas and Kabir also relied on this concept to engage in the religious and philosophical domains. The concept of *atam-anubhav* appears in Raidas and Kabir's teachings and is therefore interpretively deployed as the source of their actions and ideas in the Mahasabha's publications, where it becomes a valuable tool to explain agency in Dalit activism.

The association of *atam-anubhav* with the Sant-mat poet-saints as the source of this new philosophical principle emerged for the first time in the Dalit movement at the turn of the twentieth century, with the Adi-Hindu Mahasabha poet-activists led by Swami Achutanand and Jagatram Jatiya playing a critical role in promoting it. The notion gained popularity and strength in the Dalit Hindi literary public sphere to become a useful analytical tool for engaging with social and political inequities.

Systematic discussion of *atam-anubhav gyan* emerges after the formation of the Adi-Hindu Mahasabha (1923) and its press (1925), appearing in song-booklets as well as public speeches. Introducing the "philosophy" of Adi-Hindus (Dalits), as a distinct "ancient theory", Achutanand told his audience of 3000 Dalits in Mainpuri on 19 October 1926 that it is based on the notion of *"atam-gyan, anubhav vikas"*, a person's self-realisation through social experience.[35] He insisted in his speech that this philosophy had been present among Adi-Hindus in the form of the very Sant-mat that had informed the social and ethical objectives of the Mahasabha. Achutanand suggested that the Sant-mat religion had nurtured the principle of *atam-anubhav gyan* which built on the received knowledge extant in the Upanishads and it was recovered in the fifteenth century by the poet-saints Kabir, Nanak, and Raidas. He used this principle to highlight the agency of the learner in creating new knowledge by investigating the social at the heart of Sant-mat philosophy – as distinct from the Vedic literature and Brahman Sanskrit knowledge which orthodox caste-Hindus consider the final word on accumulated knowledge. At a public meeting in Kanpur on 13 January 1929 Achutanand argued that the teachings of the poet-saints rely on *atam-*

[35] Achutanand, *Adi Hindu Sabha Mainpuri*, p. 3.

anubhav gyan and are therefore vital to the Dalit political and ethical agendas.[36] He offered an original proposition about the history and role of the Sant-mat religion by emphasising its role in producing knowledge and the agency of personal experience.

The *Vigyan Bhajan Mala*, one of the first song-booklets published by the Mahasabha Press, offered a systematic treatment of *atam-anubhav gyan*. D.R. Jatiya, managing editor of the press, wrote on the cover page that their objective in publishing the tract was "to rescue and promote *atam-anubhav gyan* as the philosophy of Adi-Hindu's Sant-mat religion."[37] Disseminating the concept emerged as critical because the leaders of the movement recognised its vital role in empowering Dalits via new knowledge and a reshaping of activism. *Atam-anubhav* appeared in sixteen of the twenty-four songs. In the second song, "Prarthana Theater Dhvani", awareness of *atam-anubhav* is associated with a person's discovery and recognition of the divinity of Satguru, the Supreme Lord. It empowers a person's intellectual capacity, enabling them to learn from their experience and follow the example of Satguru, who reminds everyone to distinguish good from bad and equality from hierarchy.[38] Another bhajan credits the poet-saints for discovering *atam-anubhav* by emphasising the role of examiner (*paarakha*) and the value of examination (*parakha*) in directing individuals to the process of learning – and it is for this reason that the later poet-saints – Gorakh, Nanak, Dadu, and Sundar – claim that Kabir was a philosopher.[39] The song "Gyan Bhajan Nirvan" is in praise of learning based on the principle of *atam-anubhav gyan*, tested by Satguru to recognise the truth.[40] The song emphasises the search for truth through learning and lived experience over blind devotion to the Vedas, suggesting that the intelligent person will analyse social conditions to discover the facts. A number of bhajans in the *Vigyan Bhajan Mala* similarly highlight the philosophical

---

[36] Achutanand, "Sant Sangathan", in *Adi-Hindu*, p. 14. The *Adi-Hindu* was a monthly newspaper edited by Swami Achutanand.

[37] D.R. Jatiya's page-long note on the back cover page of Achutanand, *Vigyan Bhajan Mala*.

[38] "Prarthana Theater Dhvani", in Achutanand, *Vigyan Bhajan Mala*, p. 3.

[39] "Bhajan", in Achutanand, *Vigyan Bhajan Mala*, p. 3.

[40] "Gyan Bhajan Nirvan", in Achutanand, *Vigyan Bhajan Mala*, p. 7.

relationship between *atam-anubhav gyan* and the medieval poet-saints the Sant-mat religion.

The same reasoning lies behind all seven songs of the *Raidas Bhajan Mala* published by the Adi-Hindu Mahasabha Press in 1927. In the first bhajan of this tract, *atam-anubhav* is endowed an authority equal to that of the Vedas, especially in the second couplet which asserts that "one may read and study Vedas yet understand nothing if one does not use the knowledge of experience to interpret it."[41] The last two songs of the collection emphasise the notion of *atam* (individual self) to highlight the relationship between self and experience in producing knowledge.[42]

Dr Tej Singh, a writer and activist based in Delhi and founding editor of a quarterly Hindi magazine, *Apeksha* (Expectations), in a 2003 editorial essay entitled "Dalit Renaissance and Raidas", outlined the history of the *atam-anubhav* concept and its constructive role in helping poet-saints and present-day Dalit activists and writers to engage with the world.[43] He wrote an eight-page introduction to a special issue on Raidas which included contributions from leading Dalit writers. Associating the rise of a Dalit renaissance with Kabir and Raidas and asserting that it began around the same time as the "European renaissance", Dr Singh argued that despite the different contexts of these two movements they "had [the] same shared objectives", such as their basic voice being that of a "humanism centred on the individual human along with the desire for knowledge, rationalism, and wisdom."[44] At the time of the Dalit renaissance, he argued, Kabir and Raidas had relied on personal experience as the basis for investigation and acquisition of knowledge: "Dalit poet-saints' intellect moved forward with their experience and knowledge."[45] He distinguished *atam* from *atma*, the former referring to one's personal experience and the latter to matters of the soul; therefore, *atam-anubhav* refers to a person's knowledge gained from the real

---

[41] *Raidas Bhajan Mala*, p. 2.

[42] Ibid., p. 5.

[43] Singh, "Dalit Punarjagrana", pp. 2–8. He retired as professor from the Hindi Department, University of Delhi.

[44] Ibid., p. 4.

[45] Ibid., p. 6.

world.[46] Throughout his essay Dr Singh made two arguments, first that the Dalit poet-saints personally underlined the value of acquiring knowledge by engaging with the world, and second that for Dalit writers this principle defined their relationship with knowledge production.

As the example of Dr Tej Singh demonstrates, contemporary Dalit Hindi writers have recognised the critical role of *atam-anubhav gyan* in defining an alternative philosophical position of Dalit engagement. Dr Kanwal Bharati, a leading Hindi Dalit writer who has authored more than thirty books, argues that Achutanand's writings – primarily songbook collections and plays – represent a major intervention in the Hindi literary public sphere. Although Hindi literary historians have ignored Achutanand, he argues, Dalit writers and presses have continued to reproduce his writings because he radically reformulated Dalit political philosophy.[47] According to Bharati *atam-anubhav gyan* constituted the philosophical foundations of the Dalit movement and "the philosophy of Adi-Hindu religion was completely secular (*laukik*) because it was based on this principle."[48]

The Satguru and Aniconic Divinity: The Source of Human Dignity

In Dalit activism over the early twentieth century, devotion to Satguru, the Supreme Lord, and promotion of the Sant-mat religion emerged in this chronological order. The literary evidence in Achutanand's first three song-booklets (1916 and 1922) and the Adi-Hindu Mahasabha Press' song-booklets (1926 and 1940) indicate a broadening shift to include Sant-mat alongside Satguru in songs celebrating Dalit religiosity. Achutanand's three song-booklets highlighted Satguru centrally but did not comment on the Sant-mat religion, whereas the Mahasabha's publications

[46] Ibid., p. 5. On the difference between *atam* and *atma*, Tej Singh, writes here: "आतम का अर्थ आत्मा नहीं बल्कि खुद का अनुभव है, ... l इसलिए दलित संतों ने आत्मा की जगह आतम शब्द का इस्तेमाल किया है। आतम यानी खुद का अनुभव" (The meaning of *atam* is not *atma* [soul] but a person's self-experience . . . Therefore, Dalit Saints have used *atam* and not *atma*. *Atam*, meaning a person's self-experience).

[47] Bharati, *Swami Achutanand-ji*, p. 171.

[48] Ibid., p. 188.

after 1926 created a more robust discussion on the latter. Several British ethnographers in the late nineteenth century commented on the divinity of Satguru in Dalit neighbourhoods. The Mahasabha's publications played a leading role in promoting devotion to Satguru as the voice of dignity and freedom, identifying these two principles as central to the Sant-mat religion.

The notion of Satguru as fundamental to Dalit religiosity emerged as a substantive concept in Achutanand's earliest publications, *Hari-Bhajan Mala* (1916) and *Harihar Bhajan Mala Part II* (1922). Satguru was offered as a distinctive aniconic divinity to the Dalit community. From the very outset he occupied a vital place in *Hari-Bhajan Mala* and in *Harihar Bhajan Mala Part II* and appeared in the opening song composed in his praise.[49] The opening bhajan in *Harihar Bhajan Mala Part II* provides the most extensive discussion on Satguru. The eleven verses of the bhajan highlight unique features of the Satguru, the Supreme Lord, whose grace is boundless, whose essence is all around, whose light is present equally in every particle. The bhajan describes Satguru as the supreme convener (Sanyojaka) of every form of extant life, as the one who has nourished everyone in the world, from the meek (ant) to the powerful (elephant).[50] The latter part of the bhajan asserts the role of Satguru as an adjudicator and saviour who has appeared in different forms (avatars) to support the followers of the "sat-dharma" (Sant-mat) in their struggle against oppression. The last verse of the bhajan ends with the poet-activist composer praising the British government (the Raj) for having initiated policies that created new opportunities for freedom and dignity.

An appeal to the Satguru in the opening bhajan of the song-booklets became a novel practice. Compassion, knowledge, generosity, and human equality became the normative attributes associated with the divinity of Satguru in the songs and bhajans composed by Dalit poet-activists, which they contrasted with the ideals of caste inequality promoted by Brahman-centred Hinduism. The *Adi-Hindu Bhajanavali* (1924) opens with a bhajan praising universal values associated with Satguru (or Sirjanhar, meaning the Creator) who encourages his devotees to utilise their intellect and self-experience to acquire knowledge and contrasts this

---

[49] Achutanand, *Hari-Bhajan Mala, Part I*, p. 1.
[50] Achutanand, *Harihar Bhajan Mala, Part II*, pp. 1–2.

with the followers of Lord Rama/Vishnu (caste-Hindus) who consider the Vedas as the source of all learning.[51] An eleven-page poem published in the 1926 *Adi-Hindu Bansh ka Prachin Gaurav* starts with honouring the Supreme Lord who is considered the greatest source of knowledge because he promotes inquisitiveness.[52] These qualities of Satguru are eloquently captured in the second bhajan of the 1927 *Vigyan Bhajan Mala*:

> You are the lord, the Supreme Being, the knowledgeable,
> You are the extraordinary, primal harmoniser with good consciousness,
> You are the holy Incarnate the true lord [teacher],
> You are the compassionate deliverer of the fallen,
> You deny distinctions of us and them [among humans], between world and mind,
> You teach and propagate this wisdom,
> You remove the distinctions of I–You in the circles of life.[53]

Several bhajans in the *Raidas Bhajan Mala* published a year later, 1927, demonstrate Raidas' commitment to the Satguru, as do the two *Harihar Bhajan Mala*s published by Achutanand, and as do the Mahasabha song-booklets.

After the founding of the Mahasabha Press in 1925, Achutanand and other leading poet-activists began to promote Sant-mat as the unique religion of the Dalits. We see this emphasis in a number of Mahasabha publications, such as the 1926 *Vigyan Bhajan Mala* and the 1927 *Raidas Bhajan Mala*. A few years later Achutanand played a leading role in mobilising the bhagats (ascetics) connected with the Sant-mat religion, especially the followers of Raidas and Kabir, under the auspices of the Sant-Sangathan Mahasabha. Inaugurating the meeting of this organisation in Kanpur in January 1929, Achutanand urged members to promote the Sant-mat religion, demand equal rights guaranteed by the British government, and petition the government for *mulki-haq* (separate and proportional representation in legislative assemblies).[54]

The promotion of Sant-mat in print was a new development and yet

---

[51] "Doha", in *Adi-Hindu Brajanavali, Part IV*, p. 2.

[52] *Adi-Hindu Vansh*, pp. 1–2.

[53] "Prarthana Theatre Dhvani", in Achutanand, *Vigyan Bhajan Mala*.

[54] Achutanand, "Sant Sangathan Maha-Sabha Mahaotsav".

this devotional tradition already had a substantial presence in Dalit neighbourhoods. The teachings of Sant-mat poet-saints had occupied a significant place in the religious and philosophical domains of Dalit communities and were recited on various occasions. Dalit biographers have emphasised the influence of Raidas and Kabir's teachings on Achutanand during his childhood days in the 1880s. He grew up in the house of his paternal uncle, Mathura Prasad, in Ajmer; his uncle was an active member of a Kabirpanthi religious group and organised periodic Sant-mat *bhajan mandalis* (congregations) at home. This was what first made Achutanand aware of Kabir, Raidas, Nanak, and Dadu.[55] Over these early years he also learned about the social and religious elements within the teachings of these poet-saints. In his rich ethnography of Dalit political and religious activism in Punjab in the 1960s, Juergensmeyer argues that the veneration of Raidas, through temples and collective devotional practices, among untouchable communities in the state's rural areas had a longer history in late colonial India, and that this accounts for the appropriation of Raidas by the Ad-Dharm movement in the 1920s.[56]

The Mahasabha's promotion of Sant-mat and their integration of it with radical Dalit mobilisation added a new dimension to an already existing practice of adherence to alternative aniconic divinity. William Crooke's ethnography provides evidence of the prevalence of this religious practice among Dalit groups in northern India in the late nineteenth century. Crooke spent considerable time in the Rohilkhand region in central UP and commented on the popularity of "a deity [that Chamars] call Parmeshwar or 'the Supreme Being'." In most Dalit neighbourhoods, local deities known by colloquial names illustrated their relationship with a formless divinity.[57] In his book on the Chamars published in 1920, George W. Briggs emphasised the relationship between Chamars and several religious sects such as the Kabir Panthis, the Raidasis, the Dadu Panthis, and Maluk Dasis in northern India, and the Satnami sect

[55] This upbringing of Swami Achutanand is a major theme in his biographies: Bansal, *Jivan Parichay*, pp. 10–11; Singh "Raj", *Swami Achhutanand Harihar*, pp. 14–15; Jigyasu, *Swami Achutanand Harihar*, pp. 2–8.

[56] Chapter 8, "The Revival of Ravi Das", in Juergensmeyer, *Religion as Social Vision*, pp. 83–91.

[57] Crooke, *The Tribes and Castes, Vol. I*, pp. 184–6.

in the Chhattisgarh region of Madhya Pradesh.[58] The worship of Satguru occupied an important place in the Raidasi and Kabir Panth religious sects which were popular in the central and western regions of Uttar Pradesh (UP).[59]

Several Dalit religious sects, such as the Raidasis, the Kabir Panth, and the Shiv Narayani *sampradaya* (sect), became very visible in the urban centres of UP in the early twentieth century. The increased visibility of these religious sects within Dalit organisations may have had to do with their adoption of print media to circulate their objectives. These sects established places of worship to develop their identity and devotion to the Sant-mat religion. Nandini Gooptu has argued that new economic opportunities in urban centres provided Dalit groups the ability to acquire new resources.[60] Drawing from several years of thick ethnography in the erstwhile industrial city of Kanpur in the 1970s and 1980s, Maren Bellwinkel-Schempp shows convincingly that Dalit groups that migrated to Kanpur in the late nineteenth century built more visible markers of their relationship with the Sant-mat religion.[61] Bihari Lal, a prosperous building contractor belonging to the Khatik untouchable community, built a Shiv Narayani temple there in the 1870s. The Khatik untouchables took advantage of new professions in Kanpur – such as skilled masons, butchers in the pork and beef butcheries, workers in the bristles industry – and heavily patronised the Shiv Narayan devotional religion. Labourers from the Dhusiya and Jaiswara Chamar communities patronised Raidas. As they began to occupy new professions in the military, masonry, textiles, and leather enterprises, Chamars brought their devotion into urban areas from rural eastern UP.[62] Mahasabha activists led by Achutanand, along with other patrons and members of Sant-mat sects, built Raidas temples in both Kanpur and Lucknow in the 1920s.[63] Achutanand played a leading role in the task of forging a Sant-mat sensibility among Dalit groups in Delhi, Kanpur, and Lucknow.

[58] Chapter VIII, "Religion", in Briggs, *The Chamars*, pp. 205–14.
[59] Ibid., p. 210.
[60] Gooptu, *The Politics of the Urban Poor*, p. 144.
[61] Bellwinkel-Schempp, "Social Practice of Bhakti", pp. 15–32.
[62] Ibid., pp. 5–8.
[63] Ibid., p. 9.

One reason why Mahasabha leaders promoted devotion to Satguru in print was that this practice already existed in Dalit neighbourhoods where aniconic divinity was associated with human dignity. The Mahasabha publications extended this understanding of Satguru as a distinctive feature of the Sant-mat religion. The medium of print, along with temples and other visible markers, became important in sustaining more solid relationships among Dalits in the urban centres of North India, no doubt helped greatly by the new sources of secular income which funded such endeavours.

The Rise of Raidas: A Modern Saint

Cementing its association with the Sant-mat religious tradition, the Adi-Hindu Mahasabha used several of Kabir's teachings and couplets in its publications, especially those relating to the meaning of *achut* – the untouched and pure.[64] Achutanand actively promoted Raidas because he belonged to the Chamar community and specified his social identity in many of his bhajans. In January 1927 the Mahasabha Press published a collection of Raidas' bhajans entitled *Sant-Mat Sar Sangraha: Raidas Bhajan Mala*. This is an eight-page collection of five Raidas bhajans, with each containing a strong and sharp moral message for the Dalit public. This marks the beginning of a novel relationship between Dalit activism and the search by them for an alternative religious identity. The anthology addressed themes relating to the Sant-mat religion, the Satguru, the *atam-anubhav gyan*, and the Sant-mat's differences with Vaishnavite Hinduism.

As one of the earliest printed texts on Raidas by a Dalit organisation, this song-booklet marks an important intervention in establishing a historical relationship between untouchable social lives and medieval poet-saints. In the late nineteenth century British ethnographers commented extensively on the relationship between Dalits and Raidas. In his account of Benares District in 1872, M.A. Sherring described the pop-

---

[64] The cover page cites a couplet from Kabir's Bijak (compilation; anthology), defining *achut* as pure, free from the polluting touch, *chut*. Achutanand, *Vigyan Bhajan Mala*.

ularity of Raidas among the Chamars who, he says, regard the poet "as a great bhagat, or religious person, claim relationship to him, and speak of themselves as Raidasis, or disciples of Raidas."[65] Herbert Risley provided a more general description of Chamars and the Sant-mat poet-saints in his 1891 study of castes and tribes.[66] However, William Crooke provided the most comprehensive discussions on this subject in his 1894 castes and tribes survey of northern India. He was followed by George W. Briggs who in his 1920 study of the Chamars provided additional new information from the census, the gazetteers, and other government reports on Raidas. Achutanand, himself of the Chamar caste, recast the relationship between Raidas and Dalit society in print.

The language and composition of the songs in Achutanand's *Raidas Bhajan Mala* suggest a strong relationship with the Dadupanthi tradition of the Sant-mat religion dating back to the seventeenth century. Achutanand does not mention the sources from which the five bhajans of the tract are taken. Nevertheless, it is apparent that he drew from oral sources of the Dadupanthi sect, and from the Raidas and Kabir devotional traditions popular within Dalit neighbourhoods. The influence of the Dadupanthi devotional tradition on Achutanand's text is corroborated by Callewaert and Friedlander's 1992 edited volume, *The Life and Works of Raidas*. This comprehensive collection on Raidas contains his extant teachings in Gurumukhi (Punjab) and early modern Hindi (Rajasthan and UP) manuscript sources of the Sant-mat devotional traditions. The two substantive bodies of sources relevant for our purposes are (a) the *Adi-Granth* (1604) in the Punjabi language, written in Gurumukhi; and (b) the "Panch-Vani" manuscripts in the Rajasthani language source, written in Hindi between 1636 and 1698.[67]

Achutanand's 1927 collection was closer to the Dadupanthi tradition associated with the "Panch-Vani" manuscripts, especially in its metres and language forms. Peter Friedlander discovered the 1911 *Ravidas Ramayan* published by a Dalit activist, B. Jatav, from Ghaziabad and

---

[65] Sherring, *Hindu Tribes and Castes*, pp. 267–8.

[66] Risley, *The Tribes and Castes of Bengal, Vol. II*, pp. 241–3.

[67] On the use of Hindi and Gurumukhi in Raidas bhajans, Callewaert and Friedlander, *The Life and Works of Raidas*, pp. 13–15.

argued that its "structure of doha and caupia metres and language forms" was similar to those in seventeenth- and eighteenth-century sources.[68] Achutanand's text shares its verse structures and language styles with the *Ravidas Ramayan* as well as the "Panch-vani" manuscripts. It is for this reason strikingly different from the Belvedere Press' 1908 *Raidas-ji ki Bani*, which was the first printed collection on Raidas in the Hindi public sphere.[69] The difference is fundamental, though the Belvedere Press edition had also utilised the Dadupanthi sources. But the editors of the *Raidas-ji ki Bani* had substantially edited the early modern Hindi of the Rajasthani language and replaced it with standard spoken modern Hindustani in the new Devanagari script being increasingly used by the Hindu middle class. By contrast B. Jatav's 1911 *Ravidas Ramayan* and Achutanand's 1927 *Raidas Bhajan Mala* used a language closer to the Dadupanthi tradition because the Dalit public was familiar with this genre. Achutanand's upbringing in a Kabirpanthi family based in Ajmer seems to have equipped him with a unique aural archive of Sant-mat songs, including his knowledge of the Dadupanthi Sant-mat religious tradition.[70]

Achutanand's compilation of the song-booklet in 1927 offers a uniquely Dalit interpretation of Raidas' bhajans with implications for their movement. He reorganised the couplets in the bhajans and, on occasion, added a couplet to emphasise themes relevant in late British India. His motivation in publishing this tract was to highlight themes he considered vital for a definition of Dalit ethics and his advocacy of Sant-mat religious ideas as embodied in Raidas' teaching. This was a careful but necessary exercise in religio-literary taxonomy to categorise what was unique about Dalit religious practices and distinguish them from Vaishnavite Hinduism. It was a direct critique of Hindu religious texts, especially the Vedas. In this sense the *Raidas Bhajan Mala* also represented a response to the ongoing agendas raised by conservative Hindu reform organisations such as the Arya Samaj and the Hindu Maha-

[68] Peter Friedlander, "'Ravidās/Raidās", *Brill's Encyclopedia of Hinduism Online*, downloaded 11 May 2021, p. 5.

[69] *Raidass-ji ki Bani*.

[70] Bansal, *Jivan Parichay*, pp. 10–11; Singh "Raj", *Swami Achhutanand Harihar*, pp. 14–15; Jigyasu, *Swami Achutanand Harihar*, pp. 2–8.

sabha. This 1927 publication raised three key issues: (a) it emphasised *atam-anubhav gyan* over the Vedas; (b) it emphasised the ethical element in the divinity of Satguru; and (c) it emphasised the value of wisdom gained by engaging with the world.

This agenda is evident from the very outset: the first bhajan of the song-booklet outlines *atam-anubhav* as a cardinal principle of Raidas and contrasts it with the emphasis by Hindu reform organisations (such as the Arya Samaj) on the Vedas as the original foundation of all Hindu knowledge.[71] By offering an unorthodox interpretation of the Vedas, the Arya Samaj denied the mainstream Hindu view of caste as ordained by birth and instead offered up a model of caste as based on merit. Achutanand challenged what he saw as a deceitful reading of the Vedas because their novel interpretation of caste had not stopped members of the Arya Samaj from practising caste inequality. Having been a teacher at an Arya Samaj school in Sirsaganj, a town in western UP, Achutanand had personally experienced and witnessed the mistreatment of Dalit students at a function organised by the head teacher. In his 1916 song-booklet, the *Hari-Bhajan Mala*, Achutanand narrates this episode in a song in which he vows to fight against the duplicitous principles of the Arya Samaj.[72] Having worked for this Hindu reform organisation from 1905 to 1915, Achutanand had thereafter resigned from the school and from the Arya Samaj.

To deliver his sharp criticism of the Vedas, Achutanand completely reorganised the original structure of the first bhajan of six couplets: he retained the first couplet, moved the second couplet to the fifth position, reassigned the third couplet to the second position, inserted a new third couplet, and retained the existing position of the fourth couplet. This structural reorganisation of the first bhajan, which is bhajan no. 74 in *The Life and Works of Raidas*, was aimed at challenging the Arya Samaj's agenda to popularise the Vedas among the Dalits. In the first couplet, Raidas claims that reading the Vedas does not provide answers about the world, and therefore one should equally value learning gained through

---

[71] This paragraph is based on bhajan 1, *Raidas Bhajan Mala*, p. 2. See bhajan 74, in Callewaert and Friedlander, *The Life and Works of Raidas*, pp. 215–16.

[72] "Hari Geet-Chand", Achutanand, *Hari-Bhajan Mala Part I*, p. 14.

self-experience. Social experience is argued as equally important in the second couplet. The third couplet, a new one inserted by Achutanand, points to the Vedas' role in promoting segregation:

> the Vedas preach wicked ideas relating to Varna and discrimination claiming that Shudras cannot read the Sanskrit texts[73]

Achutanand chose the first bhajan of the song-booklet because it emphasised the philosophy of *atam-anubhav gyan* and promoted engagement with the world and not avoiding it. Instead of blindly following the Vedas, or instructions therein, claims Raidas, one is wiser discerning the true knowledge of what is ethical and socially desirable by following the principles of Sant-mat. According to Raidas, this is the only method to cure what ails the world – discrimination.

Bhajan Two clarifies the moral element in the devotion to the Satguru to mark differences from mainstream Hindu worship. It emphasises the need for moving beyond ego, pride, and delusion. Devotion to Satguru, recognising his universal presence, should help the devotee move beyond the domain of pride embodied in Brahmanical rituals and obsessions with the desire for heaven. Devotion to Satguru, claims Raidas, is accessible to all because the Satguru does not discriminate "between the master [*svami*] and the slave [*sevak*], the servant [*das*] and the priest [*bhagat*]." In the context of 1927 in British India – a time of discussion over separate representation for Dalits in legislative assemblies – Achutanand was using Raidas to create a community of equals.

The ethical divinity of Satguru represents an important theme in the *Raidas Bhajan Mala* and the third bhajan distinguishes the Satguru from the Vaishnavite Rama (or Hari).[74] Raidas asserts that the Satguru ("Naam") would not describe the world as illusion and unreal. Raidas says here that the material world holds no attraction for the Satguru because he is the compassionate lord. Greed (wealth or pride) holds no attraction

---

[73] Bhajan 1, *Raidas Bhajan Mala*, p. 2. The third couplet:
बरन भेद दुजन कहं वेदा (Varna Bhed Durjan Kahen Veda)
तिनहीं न शूद्र पढीजे (Tinha na Shudra Padi-je)

[74] This paragraph is based on bhajan 3, *Raidas Bhajan Mala*, pp. 4–5. See bhajan 9, in Callewaert and Friedlander, *The Life and Works of Raidas*, p. 185.

for the Satguru because his self, his body, and his mind are pure. Raidas insists that we should teach people about the Satguru, for he has no fixed place in the world, and the material world – its wealth – holds no attraction for him.

Bhajan Nos. Two and Three challenge the formulaic features of Hinduism associated with rites and rituals that privilege the role of Brahmans as well as promote solutions to all problems through the worship of Lord Rama.[75] The second bhajan distinguishes between devotion and pride, the former promoted by Raidas, in which Satguru recognises the dignity of all creatures in the world, and the latter advocated by Brahman, in which Lord Rama recognises rites and rituals that promote caste. According to Raidas, the practices of devotion promoted by the Vedas and Brahmans – such as shaving one's head, taking vows, performing pilgrimages, frivolously dancing and praying, washing one's feet, and practising insincere austerities – only advance a sense of false pride in the devotee. True devotion does not discriminate between the Lord and his servant, the slave and the devotee; it surpasses the pride created by such distinctions to recognise Satguru, who promotes dignity. Having witnessed the birth of the new piety initiated by the truly wiser person – Kabir – true devotion comes as the gift of self-realisation. Hence, the third bhajan distinguishes between Satguru and Rama, the former promoted by poet-saints to recognise the untouched Supreme Lord who promotes wisdom achieved by engaging with the world, and the latter promoted by Brahmans to promote worship of Rama untethered in reality.

The *Raidas Bhajan Mala*, one of the earliest Dalit publications on Raidas, was put together to promote the Sant-mat religion as a challenge to orthodox Hindu groups that promoted the Vedas. It represents a landmark intervention connecting untouchables within a longer history of Sant-Mat and Raidas religiosity. Evidence of this is provided by two sources: the shared language forms and structure with the "Panchvani" manuscripts of the Dadupanth devotional tradition dating to the seventeenth century; and British caste and tribe surveys in the late nineteenth century drew attention to the popularity of Raidas and Kabir

---

[75] This paragraph is based on bhajan 2, *Raidas Bhajan Mala*, p. 3. See bhajan 18, in Callewaert and Friedlander, *The Life and Works of Raidas*, p. 189.

in Dalit communities. As a leader of the Dalit movement and follower of the Sant-mat religion, yet committed to making it relevant to liberal politics, Achutanand published this song-booklet to promote dignity and equality but also emphasise a separate religious identity for Dalits.

The Sant-mat Ideology: Building a Relationship with Liberal Politics

The ethical and philosophical elements in the Sant-mat religion and the collective endeavour of Dalit activists to strive for a more just society contributed to an active engagement with liberal politics. The language of rights had entered the Dalit vernacular by the early decades of the twentieth century, and notions of equality, freedom, and human dignity, along with a political demand for separate and proportional representation in provincial legislative assemblies – in the context shaped by reforms introduced by the British government in 1919 – had substantially informed the Mahasabha-led Dalit movement.[76] The teachings of Raidas and Kabir, already popular among members of the Dalit community, had gained new meaning at this time. The Adi-Hindu Mahasabha poet-activists' promotion of Sant-mat as an ideological resource resonated with many of the core principles of liberal politics. The 1926 ten-page song-booklet *Adi-Vansh ka Prachin Gaurav* (quoted in the Introduction) had identified Satguru as the source of equal rights (*sem-adhikar*) and the struggle for equality against caste inequality (*unch-niche*). Yet it also recognised the social experience of liberal institutions in British India that had contributed to creating a Dalit consciousness. Dalit poet-activists saw Sant-mat as the charter for an egalitarian society, and their principles had a shared history in sections of Dalit society.[77]

The fourth bhajan in the *Raidas Bhajan Mala* addresses issues relating to the conditions of untouchables and the promise of new futures in early-twentieth-century British India.[78] The bhajan addresses the

[76] Zelliot, *Dr. Babasaheb Ambedkar*, pp. 111–18. Dr Ambedkar and G.A. Gawai had demanded separate electorates at their presentations to the Southborough Committee on Franchise during its tour of India between 1918 and 1919.

[77] Fuller, *The Camphor Flame*, p. 158.

[78] Bhajan 4, *Raidas Bhajan Mala*, pp. 5–6. See bhajan 4, in Callewaert and Friedlander, *The Life and Works of Raidas*, p. 183.

question of pride and arrogance, as well as religious and social divisions, and suggests that one can seek forms of devotion that emphasise a tolerant view of the Lord. To surpass religious and caste differences created by Hindu gods and texts, Achutanand uses Raidas' bhajan to assert the universal ethical promises of Satguru that nurture values of human dignity. In this bhajan Raidas claims that he is –

> Not known as a servant of [Lord] Rama, Nor I serve as a devotee (*das*)
> Know nothing of yoga, sacrifice [rituals], virtue, I live as an ascetic
>   (*udasa*)
> Nor do I [believe] in pride, delusion, charm, they shall all be destroyed
> [When I] became an ascetic my prestige grew, practised yoga and the
>   world revered
> Possessed virtue (*guna*) and became known as virtuous, I was called
>   worthy
> Heaven and hell are the same (*sem*), in both there is error, brother
> Seeing the world through I, You, and Me, I lost the self
> When mind and soul are one (*ek*), then self becomes one
> [The gods] Krishna, Karim, Ram, Hari, Self, until seen as One
> Vedas, the Book, Quran, Puranas, until seen simply as One
> Whatever you worship is unreal, only the Supreme Being (Sahaj) is real
> Says Raidas, I worship Him who has no village, no place, and
>   no name.[79]

Bhajan Four, but also the other bhajans in the text, raises issues that resonated with the contemporary concerns of the Adi-Hindu Mahasabha poet-activists in the 1920s and provided an ethical framework for their engagement with Liberal politics.

The terms *sem* and *ek* in the *Raidas Bhajan Mala* highlight claims for equality. Simultaneously, they reject differences built on one's pride in the Hindu religion, and reliance on the prestige and status of one's "place or name", all of which must be replaced by recognising the need for what is of benefit (*guna*) for all. These claims advanced the spirit of the new activism promoted by the Mahasabha poet-activists. Their moral agenda resonated with the institution of legislative assemblies in the provinces that were introduced by the British government through the constitu-

---

[79] Ibid. I have substantially revised the translation because the bhajan is slightly different from the one used in Callewaert and Friedlander, and also to stay closer to the original.

tional reform act of 1919, which allowed self-government to a small
section of Indians – 4 per cent.[80] The activists demanded separate and
proportional representation in provincial legislative assemblies, describing them as their *mulki-haq* rights. This term can be roughly translated as civil rights based on their territorial claims and as being coeval
with their assertion that untouchables were the original inhabitants of
Hindustan – hence Adi-Hindu.[81] Achutanand first raised the demand
for *mulki-haq* at a Mahasabha regional meeting on 19 October 1926 in
Mainpuri, a small town in UP.[82] In his speech he insisted that for the
proper representation of Dalits in legislatures "the objective of the Mahasabha is to demand the division of *mulki-haq* rights in line with the proportion of population."

Ideas of equality (*sem/ek*), goodness (*guna*), and civil rights (*mulki-
haq*) appear compellingly in the 1930 Mahasabha tract *Adi-Vansh (Mool
Nation) and Adi-Hindu Dharma Sant-Mat*.[83] This is a ten-page text that
includes a five-page title song and three additional songs on related topics. Stating the objectives of its production, the cover page says "the gist
of the Saints teachings, informed by their personal experience (*atam
anubhav*) is this: from their primeval origin, all humans have belonged
to one [equal] community of humans and this feature is their natural,
root trait."[84] It further states that "the Aryans have created all levels of
differences" (*bheda*). The Adi-Vansh song encapsulates several themes
relating to liberal rights, especially representative politics, and situates
notions of equality and freedom within the Adi-Hindu Dharma of Sant-
Mat. The opening couplet of the poem claims that "at the origin of the
universe, all [humans] were created as one." It asserts that they are made
of five elements (earth, water, fire, air, and space). The second bhajan
emphasises the *atam-anubhav* philosophy of the saints. The third bhajan draws attention to the leadership of the Mahasabha and describes

[80] Metcalf, *Ideologies of the Raj*, p. 230.

[81] The song "Raga hariana dhavani" in Achutanand, *Harihar Bhajan Mala,
Part II*, pp. 12–13, uses the term "*haq*", but subsequent editions of this song used
mulki-haq. Mulki-haq is used in "Bhajan", in *Adi-Hindu Bhajanavali, Part IV*,
pp. 9–14.

[82] *Adi-Hindu Mahasabha Mainpuri Report*.

[83] *Adi-Vansh (Mool Nation) and Adi-Hindu Dharma Sant-Mat*.

[84] Cover page, *Adi-Vansh (Mool Nation) and Adi-Hindu Dharma Sant-Mat*.

its role as an organisation established with the objective of demanding equal rights (*sem-adhikar*), human rights (*manav-hit*) for all. It asks readers to establish branches of the Mahasabha in their *mohalla*s (neighbourhoods) as these will benefit men, women, and Dalits. The bhajan describes the Adi-Hindu Mahasabha as an organisation committed to the Sant-mat notion of *samadarsi* ("viewing equally").[85]

Addressing the Sant-Sangathan Mahasabha meeting in Kanpur in January 1929, Achutanand reiterated these core points relating to the Sant-mat. He had founded the Sant-Sangathan Mahasabha on 3 April 1927 and addressed the meeting alongside two other leaders of the Mahasabha – Devi Din Verma and Swami Yuganand Bihari. He urged the religious heads of the Raidas and Kabirpanthi sects to work towards expanding the new ethical religion, demand *mulki-haq*, and organise campaigns to promote the rights of Dalits vis-à-vis representation in legislative assemblies, education, learning, and civil society. The meeting passed several resolutions: these pertained to the need for circulating the main principles of Sant-mat; their demand of *mulki-haq* which the Congress and Hindu Mahasabha had accepted for the Sikhs; and, by extension of this principle, employment for Dalits in the state apparatus and educational institutions.[86]

In these various ways the medieval poet-saints inspired an important ethical motivation among Dalit activists, resulting in enlarged efforts to promote democratic principles through a clear negation of the principles of the orthodox Hindu caste system.

~

The Mahasabha-led Dalit movement strongly promoted the Sant-mat religion as its unique ethical tradition in print and through activism in early-twentieth-century North India. This essay, therefore, has intervened in three specific areas of religious and social history. First, it has provided new sociological evidence demonstrating the incredible leadership of Mahasabha poet-activists as early as the 1920s in creating a political movement to support Sant-mat as the religion of Dalits. It has offered new insights to reconsider the study of the Bhakti religion in the

---

[85] Ibid., p. 7.

[86] Adi-Hindu Mahasabha ka Jalsa (Meeting), *The Adi-Hindu* monthly newspaper report, January 1929, Year 4, pp. 4–5 and 14–15.

disciplines of religious and literary studies, which have mainly looked at "radical bhakti" by exclusively focusing on the texts of Sant-mat poet-saints Raidas and Kabir.[87] Swami Achutanand and his associates recognised the role of these poet-saints in sustaining Dalit communities in the face of humiliation and exclusion. The circulation from the 1920s to the present of Hindi-language Dalit chapbooks of the Sant-mat religion has contributed to recovering this history: this study has greatly benefited from the research on hagiographies of Sant-mat poet-saints in the academic studies of Nirgun Bhakti in the religious and literary studies disciplines.

Second, this essay has revealed the foundational role of the concept of *atam-anubhav gyan*. The Mahasabha poet-activists introduced this concept to explain the relationship between the Sant-mat poet saints and the Dalit communities, especially the popularity of the teachings of Raidas and Kabir. They used this concept to explain Dalit participation in public discussions on the institutional politics of the early twentieth century.

Third, Sant-mat devotion, the Satguru, and the concept of *atam-anubhav gyan* emerged as vital mediums to intervene and create new democratic sensibilities to nurture the politics of social equality and human dignity.

References

Achutanand (Swami), "Sant Sangathan Maha-Sabha Mahaotsav", *Adi-Hindu* (monthly newspaper edited by Swami Achutanand), January 1929, vol. 4, no. 1.

Achutanand (Swami), *Adi Hindu Sabha Mainpuri Ka karya Saar Aur UP Conference ka Vivaran, 1926* (Mainpuri, UP: No publisher, no date).

Achutanand (Swami), Speech at the Adi-Hindu Conference in Amrawati, Berar, Central Provinces (Madhya Pradesh) on 28 April 1930, *Presidential All India Depressed (Adi-Hindu "Aborigines") Classes Social Conference Amrawati, Berar C.P.: Presidential Speech of Shri 108 H.H. Achhut-Swami* (Kanpur: Adi-Hindu Press, 1930).

Achutanand (Swami), *Vigyan Bhajan Mala: Satguru, Sant, Sharan* (Kanpur: Adi-Hindu Mahasabha Press, 1926).

[87] Omvedt, *Seeking Begumpura: The Social Vision of Anticaste Intellectuals*, p. 23.

Achutanand (Swami), *Hari-Bhajan Mala Part I* (Agra: Agra Akhbar Press, 1916).

Achutanand (Swami), *Harihar Bhajan Mala Part II* (Delhi: Mithanlal Chaudhari Haukumiram, Jatiya Committee, Delhi, 1922).

Achutanand (Swami), *Vigyan Bhajan Mala* (Kanpur: Adi-Hindu Mahasabha Press, Feb. 1926).

Adi-Hindu Bhajanavali, Part IV (Fatehgarh, UP: Achut [Pavitr] Adi-Hindu Sabha, 1924).

Adi-Vansh (Mool Nation) and Adi-Hindu Dharma Sant-Mat: Maha Kumbha, Prayag ka Prasad (Gift of Mahakumbh at Allahabad; Kanpur: Adi-Hindu Mahasabha Press, 25 January 1930).

Agrawal, Purushottam, *Akath Kahani Prem Ki: Kabir ki Kavita aur Unka Samaya* (Delhi: Rajkamal Prakashan, 2009).

Bansal, Mohan S., *Jivan Parichay: Shri 108 Swami Achutanand*, Third Edition (Gwalior: Saraswati Press, 1997).

Barthwal, Pitambar D., *The Nirguna School of Hindi Poetry: An Exposition of Medieval Indian Santa Mysticism* (Benares: Indian Book Shop, 1936).

Bellwinkel-Schempp, Maren, "Social Practice of Bhakti in the Śiv Nārāayan Sampradāya", in Monika Horstmann, *Bhakti in Current Research, 2001–2003* (New Delhi: Manohar Publishers, 2006).

Bharti, Kanwal, *Swami Achutanand-ji 'Harihar' and Hindi Navajagran* (New Delhi: Swaraj Prakashan, 2011).

Briggs, Geo. W., *The Chamars* (Calcutta: Association Press, Y.M.C.A., 1920).

Callewaert, Winand, and Peter Friedlander, *The Life and Works of Raidas* (Delhi: Manohar, 1992).

Crooke, William, *The Tribes and Castes of the North-Western Provinces and Oudh, Vol. I*, 4 vols (Calcutta: Office of the Superintendent of Government Printing, India, 1896).

Dasa, Syamasundar, *Hindi Sahitya ka Samskipta Itihasa* (Allahabad: Indian Press, 1931).

Dharamveer, Dr, *Kabir ke Alochak* (The Critics of Kabir; New Delhi: Vani Prakashan, 1997).

Dwivedi, Hazari Prasad, *Hindi Sahitya ki Bhumika* (1940; rpntd Bombay: Hindi Granth Ratnakar Pvt. Ltd, 1963).

Friedlander, Peter, "Ravidās / Raidās", in *Brill's Encyclopedia of Hinduism Online*, accessed 11 May 2021.

Fuller, C.J., *The Camphor Flame: Popular Hinduism and Society in India* (Princeton, NJ: Princeton University Press, 1992).

Gooptu, Nandini, *The Politics of the Urban Poor in Early Twentieth-Century India* (Cambridge: Cambridge University Press, 2001).

Gwalior Rajya Adi-Hindu (Depressed Classes) Mahasabha ke Pratham Mahaotsav, 8–9 February, 1933 ki Report (Gwalior: Kalyan Chandra Jatiya, Pradhan Mantri Adi-Hindu Sabha, 1933).

Harihar Bhajan Mala Part II (Delhi: Mithanlal Chaudhari Haukumiram, Jatiya Committee, Delhi, 1922).

Hawley, Jack S., and Mark Juergensmeyer, *Songs of the Saints of India* (New York: Oxford University Press, 1988).

Hawley, Jack S., *A Storm of Songs: India and the Idea of Bhakti* (Cambridge, MA: Harvard University Press, 2015).

Jaiswar, Doctor Ramswarup, *Adi-Hindu Vansh ka Prachin Gaurav* (Kanpur: Jaiswar Tract Samiti, 1926).

Jigyasu, Chandrika Prasad, *Swami Achutanand Harihar* (Lucknow: Bahujan Kalyan Prakashan, 1960).

Juergensmeyer, Mark, *Radhasoami Reality: The Logic of Modern Faith* (Princeton, NJ: Princeton University Press, 1991).

Juergensmeyer, Mark, *Religion as Social Vision: The Movement Against Untouchability in 20th Century Punjab* (Berkeley, CA: University of California Press, 1982).

Lorenzen, David, *Bhakti Religion in North India: Community Identity and Political Action* (Delhi: Manohar, 1996).

Lorenzen, David, *Praises to a Formless God: Nirguni Texts from North India* (Albany, NY: State University of New York Press, 1996.

McGregor, R.S., *The Oxford Hindi–English Dictionary* (Oxford: Oxford University Press, 1993).

Metcalf, Thomas R., *Ideologies of the Raj – The New Cambridge History of India III.4* (Cambridge: Cambridge University Press, 1995).

Omvedt, Gail, *Seeking Begumpura: The Social Vision of Anticaste Intellectuals* (New Delhi: Navayana, 2008).

Orsini, Francesca, "Booklets and Sants: Religious Publics and Literary History", *South Asia: Journal of South Asian Studies*, vol. 38, no. 3.

Raidas Bhajan Mala: Sant-Mat Sar Sangraha No. 1 (Kanpur: Adi-Hindu Mahasabha Press, 1927).

Raidass-ji ki Bani: Jivan-charitra Sahit, Ninth Edition (1908; rpntd Allahabad: Belvedere Printing Works, 1980).

Ram, Ronki, "Ravidass Deras and Social Protest: Making Sense of Dalit Consciousness in Punjab (India)", *The Journal of Asian Studies*, vol. 67, no. 4, 2008.

Rawat, Ramnarayan S., "Recovering the Dalit Public Sphere: Vernacular Liberalism in Late Colonial North India", *Comparative Studies in Society and History*, vol. 66, no. 3, July 2024.

Risley, Herbert H., *The Tribes and Castes of Bengal: Ethnographic Glossary, Vol. II*, 2 vols (Calcutta: Bengal Secretariat Press, 1891).

Schomer, Karine, "Introduction", in Karine Schomer and W.H. McLeod, eds, *The Sants: Studies in a Devotional Tradition of India* (Berkeley: University of California Press, 1987).

Schomer, Karine, and W.H. McLeod, eds, *The Sants: Studies in a Devotional Tradition of India* (Berkeley: University of California Press, 1987).

Sherring, M.A., *Hindu Tribes and Castes: As Represented in Benares* (Calcutta: Thacker, Spink & Co., 1872).

Singh, Dr Tej, "Dalit Punarjagrana and Raidas", *Apeksha*, vol. 3, April–June 2003, Special Issue on Raidas.

Singh, Namvar, *Dusari Parampara ki Khoj* (Search for an Alternative Tradition; New Delhi: Rajkamal Prakashan, 1982).

Singh, Rajpal "Raj", *Swami Achhutanand Harihar* (Delhi: Raj Laxmi Prakashan, 2003).

Sukla, Ramachander, *Hindi Sahitya ka Itihasa* (1929; Allahabad: Nagari Pracharini Sabha, rpntd 1965).

Zelliot, Eleanor, *Dr. Babasaheb Ambedkar and the Untouchable Movement* (New Delhi: Blumoon Books, 2004).

Acknowledgements

I am grateful to Anne Murphy, Davesh Soneji, Francesca Orsini, Jack Hawley, Margrit Pernau, Peter Friedlander, and the anonymous referees for their incredibly detailed reading and suggestions. A special thanks to Rohit Chopra for inviting me to present this paper at the virtual interdisciplinary conference, "Religion and Its Publics in South Asia", February 2022, Emory University. As always, special thanks to Lisa Mitchell for commenting on two drafts.

4

Dalit Futures and
Sexual Modernity in South India

LUCINDA RAMBERG

OW DO THOSE consigned to the waiting room of history work
to unsettle the time set for them by others? This is the central question I am working through in this essay. As many
scholars writing about the predicament of postcolonial modernity have
noted, this waiting room is an effect of colonial forms of knowledge and
the historicist fantasy that civilisation began in Western Europe and ra-
diated out from there across the world. In a prime and oft-cited example,
John Stuart Mill argued in the nineteenth century that the inhabitants
of the Indian subcontinent and African continent were *not yet* civilised
enough to be capable of self-rule.[1] Backwardness is also a sexual condition, a marker of gendered lack or womanhood. Sometimes these forms
of belatedness subtend each other, as pointed out by Mrinalini Sinha in
her introduction to the American reformer Katherine Mayo's 1927 tract
Mother India. In Mayo's characterisation, Indian inability to self-govern
was manifest in gendered embodiment: "[Men's] hands [are] too weak,
too fluttering, to seize or to hold the reins of Government."[2] As an ethnographer working on the everyday contemporary life of caste modernity, my interest here centres on the question of how belatedness is embodied and transformed by those who are made to embody it. This is

[1] Chakrabarty, *Provincializing Europe*, p. 8.
[2] Sinha, ed., *Mother India*, p. 93.

an ongoing dilemma for members of communities formerly designated as untouchable in the context of shifting regimes in bureaucratic state management and the political economy of caste. Focusing on these regimes, most scholars of caste and caste transformation have assumed or asserted a masculine subject of Dalit politics.[3] Focusing on sexual politics brings other instantiations of gender, power, and caste into view.

My thinking here emerges from research I have been conducting over the last fifteen years focusing on religious conversion in the context of the revival of Buddhism in Karnataka, South India. My own encounter with the phenomenon of Dalit conversion began twenty-five years ago in the course of the research for my first monograph, an ethnography of devadasi dedication and its reform.[4] Conversion to Buddhism is a common practice among the sons and brothers of the devadasi women I worked closely with in a village in Belgaum District of northern Karnataka, where twin offset posters of the Buddha and Ambedkar adorn many a household wall.[5] As many of the readers of this volume are aware, conversion to Buddhism among Dalits is inspired by Dr Bhimrao Ramji Ambedkar, the principal architect of the Indian Constitution and a founding father of independent India. An economist, philosopher, and political theorist whose collected works span eighteen volumes, Ambedkar took doctorates at Columbia University and the London School of Economics. Himself a member of a community formerly designated untouchable, he worked tirelessly against discrimination based on caste. His followers frequently note in particular that he wrote the abolition of untouchability and the provision of reservations into the constitution. A statue of him bespectacled, holding a book, and dressed in a three-piece suit, can be found in the Dalit quarter of virtually every town and city across

---

[3] For a diagnosis of this gendered dimension of caste politics, see in particular Rao, *The Caste Question*.

[4] Ramberg, *Given to the Goddess*.

[5] The secular literary and political anti-caste activism of the Dalit Sangharsha Samiti (DSS) has been more influential across the state of Karnataka than Ambedkarism, especially in the 1970s–1990s. However, in the northern districts of the state, formerly part of the Bombay Presidency, the influence of Bombay-based Jotiba Phule and Ambedkar has been more salient. For a brief overview of the DSS, see Yatanoor, "Dalit Movement in Karnataka".

India. Ambedkar became convinced that religion played a critical role in projects of social transformation, and, after conducting a systematic study of religion in relation to caste, he focused on Buddhism as an egalitarian religion indigenous to the subcontinent. In 1956, nearing the end of his life, he took *diksha* (initiation) into Buddhism from a Theravadan monk from Sri Lanka. On that occasion half a million Dalits followed him into Buddhism in what many have called the largest mass conversion documented in the history of the modern world.

It would be difficult to overstate the influence of Ambedkar or the ardent allegiance of his followers who refer to themselves as Ambedkarites. It would also be difficult to overstate the recalcitrance, not to say outright violence, that continues to meet those struggling against caste society. The forms of anti-caste activism and religious conversion Ambedkar inspired remain politically highly charged. To offer a comparatively mild but nonetheless egregious example from the archive of caste atrocity, in August 2018 a large platoon of police officers descended on the home of a notable Dalit scholar and professor of cultural studies and dean at the English and Foreign Languages University (EFLU) in Hyderabad, Dr K. Satyanarayana.[6] This was one of eight simultaneous raids on activists, lawyers, and academics across the country for their alleged involvement in an anti-caste uprising in Bhima Koregaon, Maharashtra. Professor Satyanarayana's laptops were confiscated, along with many books and papers, and he and his wife were questioned.[7] He was asked, "Why are you reading Mao, why are you reading Marx . . . why are you [displaying] photos of Ambedkar and Phule instead of gods and goddesses?" The slippage in between dissident politics and dissident religion in the police officer's question speaks to the force of Ambedkarism in the context of Hindu nationalism.

I want to underline the tenacity of caste and casteism not only as a feature of the Indian social but also as a structuring aspect of the field of South Asian Studies as well as the academy in the United States. My own

[6] See in particular Rawat and Satyanarayana, *Dalit Studies*, and Satyanarayana and Tharu, *The Exercise of Freedom*.

[7] For further information see https://scroll.in/latest/972412/bhima-koregaon-nia-summons-to-activist-k-satyanarayana-for-questioning, accessed 2 March 2021.

commitments to caste revolution are ethnographic, intellectual, and political, but as a white citizen of the United States teaching in the American academy I am, at best, an attentive witness to the unfolding life and death of caste. The stakes are not the same for me as they are for my colleagues, friends, and students whose life chances and possibilities of recognition have been organised through the virulent logics of caste supremacy and untouchability.

Inside/Outside

Most Dalit women in the central Deccan rural communities I work in become Buddhist at the time of marriage in response to the groom's desire for the marriage to be conducted "according to Buddha Dharma". Conversion and marriage ceremonies are typically conducted at once such that, for women, becoming a Buddhist and becoming a wife are wrapped up together in a single moment. In the words of one woman, "At the time of marriage I became Buddhist . . . [then], they made us clasp hands and they said: husband will follow wife till the end of her life and in all her sorrows and vice versa." In a typical ceremony the officiant – either a monk or ordained lay person – welcomes those gathered; leads them in reciting the five precepts; guides the bride and groom and their parents to light candles and offer incense and flowers to side-by-side portraits of Ambedkar and the Buddha, and then to recite the three refuges before them. After the bride and groom take the marriage vow, they exchange garlands of flowers. In 2015 at a wedding in Kalaburagi the vow was: "From today I marry in Buddha Dharma, so I will go for refuge in Buddhism and Ambedkar, and from today all your family members are as my family members, I welcome everyone who has come here and I say: Jai Bhim." The bride's *tali* (wedding necklace), if there is one, is placed over her neck with the garland.[8]

The egalitarian principle expressed in such vows is a familiar feature of caste-radical projects of marriage reform.[9] The question remains, how

---

[8] Some Buddhists eschew the practice of *tali* tying. As one woman put it to me: "I am not a slave as in the Hindu system, we are free, we are like friends, not like husband and wife."

[9] Such vows stand in a long tradition of caste radical marriage reform such as

might we think through the force of such egalitarianism in the context of the structural features of marriage as a social institution. Building on Lévi-Strauss' theory of marital exchange as the threshold of the social – the means by which bonds of solidarity were produced with "natural" enemies – Gayle Rubin argues that marriage vests in men "rights in women that women do not have in themselves."[10] In this structuralist formulation one of the effects of marriage is gender as a hierarchical relation of binary complementarity. Following Ambedkar, besides the sexual control of women, another effect of endogamous marriages is the reproduction of caste distinction as a territory of ranked belonging.[11] Given these critiques of marriage as a form that organises gendered hierarchies and caste distinction, how might we approach the question of the status of women in Dalit social reproduction?

In an early moment of the research for this project I interviewed a Buddhist family in their home in a village in Belgaum District of northern Karnataka. The mother and father described how they were inspired by their son to take up Dr Ambedkar's call to become Buddhist. "My son came home one day and tore the gods down from the wall. Being Buddhist is good, peaceful. In Buddhism there is no *jati* (caste, subcaste)," the father and head of the household explained. At the end of a long conversation over tea, I turned to their daughter who had not thus far participated in the conversation but who was sitting within earshot in an adjoining room on the edge of a metal bedframe. In her arms she held the child she had come back to her natal home to deliver.

"When did you become Buddhist?" I asked.

"When I was married. My husband wanted the marriage to be conducted according to Buddhist teaching (Buddha Dhamma), I took *diksha* and we were married."

Satyashodhak marriage rites conducted in the absence of any Brahmin acting in a priestly capacity organised by Jotiba and Savitri Phule in Maharashtra and Self Respect marriages promoted by Periyar in Tamil Nadu. See, in particular, Anandhi, "Women's Question"; Hodges, "Revolutionary Family Life"; and O'Hanlon, *Caste, Conflict and Ideology.*

[10] Rubin, "The Traffic in Women".

[11] Ambedkar, "Castes in India". For an important examination of history of the category of endogamy in the Indian social sciences, see Mitra, "Surplus Woman".

"How is it in your mother-in-law's house?"

"Inside [in the kitchen], we keep the gods, outside [in the sitting room] the men keep Buddha and Ambedkar," she responded, describing a gendered division of religious labour that I came to learn is found in many Buddhist households across India.

In these households, men and women adopt different religious orientations. Men turn toward world-historical Buddhism and its egalitarian promise. Women occupy themselves with the inner domain of the household where food is cooked and local gods and ancestral and fertility rites are kept. My interviews with Dalit intellectuals in Bangalore, Delhi, and Nagpur suggest that this spatial division of religious labour is widely recognised and discussed among Ambedkarite Buddhists across India as a *problem* for the community. In the words of one Ambedkarite and scholar of ancient Buddhism who reported that the women in his household in New Delhi continued to worship deities: "We know we must give up such backward practices, but it is difficult for our women to give up their gods."

What are the implications of the Delhi resident's formulation for Dalit futures in relation to gendered subjectivity? His statement is embedded within a number of assumptions about change and time. Even as he articulated the normative ideal of conversion as a radical break from the past, he acknowledged that this break is difficult, and not always possible. A convert should move forward, away from past practices and toward a present and future emancipation, but some remain "backward", caught in the past. Discourses of backwardness and conversion as decisive break from the past situate the woman I interviewed in northern Karnataka in the past as an obstacle to possible future emancipation. At the same time, she holds the future in her arms, literally – in the form of the child she brought into the world. Caught between her mother-in-law's allegiance to the household deities and her husband's commitment to Buddhism, she chooses both. She says, "I am Buddhist," and also, "I keep the gods," dissolving the dichotomy typically posed between them. In bearing the next generation as well as embracing both Buddhism and the gods her mother gave her, she is generating Dalit futurity, but not in modernist terms.

I encountered many such combinations of ancestral religion and Buddhism drawn together under one roof. Dravid works as a kind of barefoot social worker, travelling all over India and East Asia spreading Buddhist Dhamma and networking with other Buddhists. I spent an afternoon with him and his mother in 2015. Among other things we discussed the ways this gendered division of religious labour unfolded in their amicable household. He said: "I follow only Buddha, I tell her to throw the gods out, but I won't force her. Until I am on my own feet I cannot, I should not." For her part, as she showed me her *manedevara* (lit. house of the gods), his mother offered: "Whatever he is doing is good, but as long as I am here, I will continue to keep the gods, my mother gave them to me, I can't leave them." She had placed a Buddharupa alongside Durga, Ganesh, Vithoba, and a *purna kalasha* (metal pot filled with water and topped with a coconut representing the Devi) to make a polyvalent pantheon in her kitchen shrine.[12] Over his bed in the sitting room, Dravid had hung a single offset print of the seated Buddha offering the *abhaya mudra* (hand gesture) of fearlessness.

I hasten to add that I did not find this pattern to be *prevalent*; indeed I encountered many strictly Buddhist women and met men who regularly worship gods and goddesses.[13] Further, my arguments here are not generalisable to all Ambedkarites, nor certainly to all Dalits. That said, the gendered division of religious labour I have described is a common phenomenon, and as such it constitutes a rich site at which to examine the limits and possibilities of conversion in relation to caste transformation and gendered relations. I am interested in a set of interlinked questions raised by this kind of Dalit kin-making and religiosity in which Ambedkarite Buddhism and ancestral religion are combined and distributed according to gender, as well as how these practices are discussed and understood among Buddhists. In pursuing these questions,

[12] Vithoba exemplifies the difficulty of neatly dividing the embrace of Buddhism from the worship of deities. While his origins are not entirely clear, it is evident that he was associated with the Vakari sect that admitted women and untouchables and that he opposed the practice of untouchability. Ambedkar himself claimed in 1954 that the image of Vithoba at Pandharpur was in fact that of the Buddha. Keer, *Dr. Ambedkar*, p. 482.

[13] On Ambedkarite women, see in particular Kalyani, "Tathagata Buddha Songs"; Lynch, "Sujata's Army"; Moon and Pawar, *We Also Made History*; and Zelliot, "Religious Leadership".

I am working to render an account of how subjects of stigma produce possibilities of positive social recognition through everyday practices of kin-making and religiosity. This is an account of social transformation that takes into account *the normative and disciplinary* functions of kinship and religion as modern categories and institutions, but also turns towards kin-making and religiosity as *embodied practices with world-making effects.* Elsewhere I have framed kin-making as a technology, or a

> means of transforming persons that reiterates techniques of the body such as gender and caste as well as forms of knowledge about the nature of persons and their place in the world . . . Possibilities of human being and doing are made and unmade through everyday practices such as marriage, adoption, and domiciliation. Innovative kin-making practices open new pathways to forms of social and political recognition and inclusion.[14]

I am interested here in attending to how we reinvent ourselves and the world around us through our relations with each other and with Buddhas, gurus, gods, and spirits. Might the cultivation of such relations be one way Ambedkarite households corrupt the time set for them by others?

In 2015 an Ambedkarite activist and organiser in the Bahujan Samaj Party (BSP) gave me an invitation to his daughter's marriage.[15] At that point, we had been in conversation for over fifteen years and he was aware of my interest in marriages and weddings. Across the glossy white card stock in elegant Roman script the card read, "We are, because he was." This statement forwards a claim about the relationship between the material and existential presence of Dalits and the vision

---

[14] Ramberg, "Troubling Kinship", p. 671.

[15] Founded by Kanshi Ram in 1984 and inspired by the philosophy of Gautama Buddha, B.R. Ambedkar, Mahatma Jyotiba Phule, Narayana Guru, Periyar E.V. Ramasamy, and Chhatrapati Shahuji Maharaj, the Bahujan Samaj Party (BSP) is the third largest national political party in India. It represents *bahujans* – "people in majority" – from the Scheduled Castes, Scheduled Tribes, and Other Backward Castes (OBC), as well as religious minorities that together consist of 85 per cent of India's population. Mayawati, appointed by Kanshi Ram as his successor, was elected four times as the chief minister of Uttar Pradesh and is currently serving as the president of the party.

and work of Dr Ambedkar. His work is often cited by Buddhists as the very foundation of their possibility and survival. In fact, as I learned over the course of my research, this phrase reverberates across Ambedkarite worlds. How might we think about a political claim being wrapped up in an invitation to a wedding?

The activist, Pramukh, was marrying his daughter into another prominent Buddhist family active in the BSP, also from the Holeyar community – the same ex-untouchable jati. The invitation situated Dr Ambedkar as the ground of Dalit existence and placed this Buddhist marriage and the future of the community it promised on that ground. To put it slightly differently, becoming Buddhist and conducting life-cycle rituals according to Buddhist teachings are a means of enacting the caste revolution envisioned by Ambedkar: "Because of him, we are." And yet, at the same time the invitation announced an endogamous union between two families in the same jati would reproduce caste distinction as a central feature of social organisation. In a conversation with another activist who had married within his subcaste when he married his sister's daughter – enacting the kind of cross-cousin marriage that is ideal in the region – when I asked why he had not followed Dr Ambedkar's call to marry out of caste he replied, "Because of him, I got an education and a good job. If I don't help my family, who will?" Reservations had moved him out of outcaste marginality and precarity into salaried economic security and political citizenship, but, rather than taking a further step out of caste through exogamy, he felt ethically and affectively bound to pull his kin along with him.[16]

Tensions between Buddhist futures and marital and reproductive futures were not uncommon among Ambedkarites. Consider Sachin's dilemma: "I got married in 1995, I was eighteen. The marriage was conducted according to Hindu Dharma because at that time there was a gap. We had taken diksha, but we were not yet practising Buddhism and I was not able to catch hold of any Bhantajis (monks). I was not ready to get married without a Bhantaji. But there was no time. On Tuesday we went to see the girl and by Wednesday the marriage was fixed. I was

[16] On inter-caste marriages in the region, see Disha, "Practising Family"; Nemoto, "Becoming Dalit", and Tarikere, "Inter-caste Marriage".

not ready to get married. I kept asking them to call a *bhikkhu* (monk) to conduct the marriage."

"Who conducted the marriage?" I asked.

Sachin: "Some Brahmin [*pujari*] came. I was not ready to tie the *tali* in front of the house on the stage."

Sachin found himself in a gap between initiation into Buddhism and the practical realisation of Buddhist ritual conduct, and without the time to close the gap. Under the pressure of his family and in the face of his bride who followed him into Buddhism, he tied the *tali* on the wedding stage. I am interested in the contest between the endogamous conjugal future his family organised for him and his desire for a Buddhist ritual. He found himself in a gap. He lacked time. Three decades later we sat talking in the home he shared with his wife where strict adherence to Ambedkarite Buddhism or religious discontinuity and jati continuity had been brought together under one roof.

In his *Annihilation of Caste* Dr Ambedkar diagnosed caste as a social disease rooted in "belief in the sanctity of the Shastras" and the ritual authority of Brahmins. In his analysis, caste revolution called for the abandonment of Brahmanical religion. He also prescribed inter-caste marriage as the "remedy" for caste, that "solvent" which might disintegrate jati distinction and therefore the hierarchical ordering and downward distribution of stigma according to the Brahmanical logics of purity and impurity.[17] To risk a generality, the paradox my interlocutors' accounts present is this: In answer to Ambedkar's call, they work to embrace Buddhism and to renounce ancestral religion, but they turn away from inter-caste marriage: most choose endogamy over exogamy. In rendering these accounts of the stories Ambedkarites have told me I am working against the framing of this gendered division of religious labour as a *problem* and towards an account of it as a *solution*. This is a method that takes the critical consciousness and world-making capacities of Dalits for granted, as a necessary starting point and through line of analysis. What then are they solving? How might we think about why women continue to hold on to ancestral religion, and men persist in holding kin networks together by marrying within their jati? What does this

[17] Ambedkar, *Annihilation*.

paradox teach us about the gendered temporality and sexual politics of Ambedkarite Buddhism? What diagnosis of caste modernity does this pattern offer?

Religion and Kinship in Normative Time

Freedom from caste oppression has been conceived in relation to modern protocols for "proper" sexuality and "proper" religion. Within this framework, sexuality should be aimed at the extension of intimacy and reproduction within monogamous couplings of social equals. Religion ought to be a matter of chosen belief, devotion, and ethics clearly distinguishable from what is gathered under the stigmatising sign of superstition. This false religion is often referred to as "empty". In the words of one Ambedkarite: "Nothing is there, it's just a stone but they think it's god," pointing to the equation made between some kinds of aniconic worship and a lack of reason. Within the discourses and practices of both anti-caste struggle and feminist organising, modernist configurations of religiosity and sexuality have set the terms for who and what can be seen to move Dalit communities forward.

In the case of religion, anti-caste politics emerged on the ground of colonial missionary critiques of Hindu superstition in combination with Enlightenment principles of natural rights and freedoms.[18] The architects of Dalit emancipation in southern and western India agreed that superstition was a problem of Dalit false consciousness and Brahmin hegemony. There were differences among them, to be sure. Jotiba and Savitribai Phule concentrated on the ways Brahmanical religion reproduced Brahmanical supremacy and organised alternative egalitarian rituals. A champion of rationality, Ramasamy Periyar understood all gods and forms of religion to be obstacles to emancipation. Dr Ambedkar focused on what he termed the "hell of Hinduism" and called on his community to abandon the gods, throw them out of the house, and embrace the scientific reasoning and egalitarian ethics he found in Buddhism.

These architects of caste radicalism located the possibilities of critical consciousness, rationality, and Dalit progress in either the wholesale

[18] Rao, *The Caste Question*, pp. 31–2.

rejection of religion or conversion to a *modern* form of aniconic textual religion, such as Buddhism or Christianity. Others forged a pathway in the footsteps of guru renunciates in the anti-caste bhakti tradition of poets such as Ravidas and Kabir. In all these cases rituals that reproduce priestly authority, or conceptions of gods and goddesses as beings who might be directly petitioned by devotees or compelled by ritual enactments to act on their behalf, have been condemned as displays of irrationality that reproduce the stigmatised condition of Dalits. These turns to textual and devotional forms of religion as pathways out of caste abjection point to what can and cannot count as legitimate forms of Dalit religion, as well as how those who continue to keep, perform puja for, and petition their *manedevaru* (household ancestral deities) might be perceived.

In centring the value of rationality in the flight from Brahmanical religion, these programmes of caste revolution sidelined folk or popular religion.[19] One of the consequences of this marginalisation has been that Dalit religion has not been understood as meaningfully distinct from Brahmanical Hinduism, nor widely perceived to be a cultural and political resource for Dalits.[20] An emerging body of research, however, locates Dalit religiosity as a territory of caste critique, embodied belonging, and Dalit assertion across a range of world religions as well as autonomous regional traditions.[21] In *Why I Am Not a Hindu*, Kancha Ilaiah Shepherd writes: "Dalitbahujans never became part of Hinduism . . . the dalitbahujan castes have built a cultural tradition of their own, and Gods and Goddesses of their own."[22] Shepherd frames Hinduism as a fascist and colonising force and "Dalitbahujan" religion as a rich reservoir for the nourishment of critical and egalitarian consciousness. He contrasts Hindu gods and goddesses with Dalitbahujan gods and goddesses, identifying key distinguishing features: independent fierce goddesses; concern with material forms of human thriving; absence of mediating priests; egalitarian regard for all regardless of religion.[23]

How did Dalits come to be understood as Hindu? The common

---

[19] Ram, *Fertile Disorder*, p. 59.

[20] Elisha, "Liberative Motifs in the Dalit Religion".

[21] See Mohan and Lee, "Dalit Religion", for a useful summary.

[22] Ilaiah, *Why I Am Not a Hindu*, pp. 72–3.

[23] See also Elisha who offers a very similar characterisation of Dalit religion.

misconception that Dalits are primordially Hindu is rooted in British colonial and Brahmanical epistemologies and practices, including the category of religion, the genealogy of Hinduism, and taxonomies of caste. Religion was deployed as a mode of governance in 1772 when the British divided the population of the subcontinent into the categories "Gentoo" or "Mahometan". Later census protocols placed all non-Christian and non-Muslim Dalits as Hindu. In the context of "enumerative politics" and the felt need for an unassailable Hindu majority, Dalits were "purified" or nominated as Hindu. Joshua Samuel sums this history up: "[T]here was no one religion called Hinduism before the colonial era, and the Hinduism that we have today is a relatively newly constructed religious category in which Brahmic traditions were given primacy and into which the traditions of the lower castes and the Dalits were forcefully assimilated – only to be marginalized."[24] Indeed, it was in large part this history of assimilation and marginalisation which convinced Ambedkar that Hinduism must be renounced and displaced by Buddhism.

In my use of the term "ancestral religion" I mean to situate the gods and goddesses found in many Buddhist households as being of long durée but distinct from those in nationalised Hinduism or Brahmanical religion; meaningful materially and symbolically with regard to world-making orientations and practices; and as having belonged to and being passed along by elder kin. When people introduced me to the gods kept in their household shrines (*manedevaru*), more often than not they recounted receiving their *murtis* (icons) from mothers or grandmothers. Scholarly work on Dalit religion, alongside my archive of encounters with and instruction by Dalit women, leads me to situate "ancestral religion" as a non-modern cultural resource that might be drawn from and not necessarily a bond from which one must free oneself.

Modern antinomies between the past and the future, false and true, material and transcendental are upheld by the pedagogical and popular model of conversion as a break from inherited religion. Among Ambedkarites, this seems to be understood as a break men are able to make more easily. Gatherings of Ambedkarites on the public stages of life forward

[24] Samuel, *Untouchable Bodies*, p. 85.

men as those who are pulling the community into the future of conversion, rationality, and time discipline. The path of conversion laid out
by Dr Ambedkar prescribes a complete departure from the past. The
twenty-two vows he took and gave to his followers include: "I shall have
no faith in Gauri, Ganapati and other gods and goddesses of Hindus
nor shall I worship them." Conceptions of conversion as a radical break
from the past and of time as a forward march aptly characterise Ambedkar's vision of Dalit emancipation as well as contemporary ideological
accounts of community uplift and social mobility through the embrace
of Buddhism.

Sexuality too turns out to be a critical site for the enunciation of freedom from caste, as calls for inter-caste marriages suggest. Such calls ex-
plicitly or implicitly situate heterosexual forms of monogamous endogamy as the proper teleology of Dalit womanhood. The quest for decency
has taken shape within the predicament of sexuality within modernity.
Historians Chinnaiah Jangam and Sanal Mohan illustrate the dimensions
of this predicament. In the Telugu country, Jangam writes, "under the influence of caste Hindu reformist ideas . . . untouchable intellectuals tried
to 'purify' untouchable communities [in order] to create a respectable
social and political identity."[25] Writing from the missionary archives
of colonial Kerala, Mohan relates with great sensitivity the case of a
Pulaya man who was required to renounce one of his wives in order to
comply with the modern expectation of strict monogamy required to join
the mission.[26] Dalit men and women have understandably sought to
evade the ascription of indecency and humiliated condition. Upper-caste
men have claimed sexual access to outcaste women. Dalit women had
little grounds for refusal, Dalit men scant ability to protect, and upper-
caste women little recourse to either circumscribe their men or make similar claims on Dalit men. This uneven distribution of sexual rights pro-
duces two possible subject positions for Dalits, that of humiliation and
violation, and that of conjugality and respectability. Given this history, it cannot surprise us that the resolution to the caste question has
founded itself in jati endogamy, masculine authority, feminine decency,
and heterosexual reproduction.

[25] Jangam, *Dalits and the Making of Modern India*, pp. 112–13.
[26] Mohan, *Modernity of Slavery*, pp. 76–82.

It might seem self-evident that Dalit futures would unfurl on the grounds of conversion out of Hinduism and pursuit of endogamous conjugality. But ethnographic attention to everyday practices of kin-making and religiosity within the household as well as upon "the stage" brings a gap into view. This gap might be understood, as it was by Sachin when he was unable to catch hold of a monk, as an impediment to progress, a "waiting room of history". It might also be framed as an interval, a "mean time . . . not of revolutionary beginnings or historical completions . . . [but a time] to recognize [and make politically useful] the differences within and between various modalities of social transformation."[27] I am interested in the temporal dimension of the gap, and this question of temporality as a supplement to the mixing of religiosities that anthropologists working on projects of religious conversion have long taught us to expect. In Jean and John Comaroff's framing, "that curious mix of consent and contestation, desire and disgust, appropriation and accommodation, refusal and refiguration, ethnicization and hybridization" that characterises conversion in colonial and post-colonial contexts.[28] Speaking to the particular situation of Dalits seeking emancipation from caste, Milind Wakankar writes, "[The Dalit convert] is one who cannot assume a given religious, social or economic identity, and must remain temporally forever 'in-between' all ascription of place, location and identity."[29] Writing about the effect of Christian ideas on the consciousness of slave castes, Mohan notes: "This new mentality showed ambivalence, in the sense of values pulling in two directions . . . engaged in both the practices of their pre-Christian past and the new notions and practices that came through missionary Christianity."[30] One way to frame what projects of caste emancipation are aiming at is the question of *how not to get caught in the time set for you by others*. I have conceptualised the temporality of this gap as recombinant.[31] A recombinant organism contains a different combination of alleles than either of its parents. Recombinant proteins are artificially produced or un-

---

[27] Wiegman, "Feminism's Apocalyptic Futures", p. 86.
[28] Comaroff and Comaroff, *Of Revelation and Revolution*, vol. 2, p. 22.
[29] Wakankar, *Subalternity and Religion*, p. 51.
[30] Mohan, *Modernity of Slavery*, 84.
[31] Ramberg, "Backward Futures".

natural, fabricated through investments of human labour. In drawing on the language of recombination I seek to draw attention to this aspect of Dalit kin-making and religiosity – the ways they are producing futures in the gap between inheritance and break.

In my thinking about time and temporality I am drawing on conversations within feminist and queer theory about the forms of social life and death produced through heterosexual and patriarchal forms of sexual organisation. As feminist anthropologists have long argued, the reproductive time of patriarchy and patriliny spells forms of social abjection for women in the form of wifehood and motherhood. Queer theorists debate the possibilities of queer futurity and thriving in the face of the queer deathscapes incited by reproductive futurism which figures the innocent child as imperilled by, and in need of protection from, the narcissistic and anti-social homosexual.[32] Anthropological treatments of caste have long understood caste to be a product of endogamy; thus, jati endogamous marriages among Dalits might be said to produce forms of vibrant social continuity in lineage, community, and clan, and forms of social death in the perpetuation of caste distinction and hierarchy. To be clear, I am making a point about structural forms and their social effects, not a moral judgement about individual life choices that I see as always already unfolding in the territory between social life and death.

Within South Asian thought where the legacies of colonial representations of native others as stuck in the past stubbornly persist, the teleology of progress has also been subjected to critique. Here it has been less the straight time of sexual development and maturity and more the time of abstract labour, capital, and colonialism that have been deconstructed.[33] The concept of time as single and homogeneous, and of secular and modern politics as 'the unfolding of human sovereignty across that time" are inadequate to the task of accounting for political modernity in postcolonial India.[34] Adequate accounts of the social and political lives of those deemed non-modern, many scholars have argued, must eschew universalising categories and attend to alternative histories that

[32] Edelman, *No Future.*

[33] Notable exceptions include Arondekar, "In the Absence", and Cohen, "Song for Pushkin".

[34] Chakrabarty, *Provincializing Europe,* p. 15.

cannot be subsumed to the secular logic of political economy. Writing about Hindu nationalist invocations of the *kisaan* (farmer) as a figure situated in the present but also able to embody the rural past of "real India" and redemptive future of capitalism, Geeta Patel offers a model for such adequate attention. She writes: "The kisaan was a point at which different kinds of temporality were knotted together."[35] Her point has implications for who can be seen to bear the capacity to make history as well as for the subversive possibilities of knots in time. Might occupying the gap I am calling recombinant time be a means for stigmatised subjects to dislocate the time set for them by others? Might it be a means of embodying a different relation to the future, one that might be routed through the past?

The Reproductive Capacities of Promiscuous Religion

Many of the Buddhists I have spoken with worry about the impurity of their community's allegiance to Buddhism. In 2015 I had a long conversation with Suraj, an activist in Nandipur. I asked him about a wedding I had witnessed the previous week in the village in which Hindu and Buddhist ritual elements were mixed. How often, I wondered, did this happen. "About 30 per cent are like that," he responded, "Wherever I go I tell them clearly, choose one type, either Buddha Dharma or Hindu Dharma."

"Why is it important to choose?" I asked.

He replied: "It's important because they are different dharmas and if we conduct marriage in both dharmas people will get confused . . . In order to give a clear idea which dharma they are following it is important to conduct marriages under one dharma. On the stage we recite the *pancha shila* – don't kill animals, but in Hindu Dharma they start the marriage by killing animals. How can we say they are following Buddha Dharma? They have been following [Hindu Dharma] for thousands of years. It's not easy to tell people to come out of it and follow only one dharma, it is very difficult to make it happen."

[35] Patel, "Ghostly Appearances", p. 51.

"Why do you think it's difficult to leave the gods?", I asked. "It's a powerful belief (*nambikke*). People put *mowdya* (superstition) in the minds of people in so many ways. The number of people who think scientifically is very low. They are scared, they think that if they perform the marriage in another dharma, the *tali* may not be tied, so they go to temple, tie the *tali* and come [for the Buddhist ceremony]."

Suraj's account is sympathetic to the difficulty of breaking away from ancestral religion, but also demonstrates his clear commitment to the necessity of that break. He frames the obstacles in familiar terms: ignorance, superstition, fear. Strict adherence to Buddhist ethics and the cultivation of scientific rationality will usher in a better future for his people – in his vision. This is all consistent with the standard Ambedkarite narrative about the pernicious lure of the shastras as well as modernist understandings of proper religiosity and sexuality. Many of my conversations, however, brought other motivations and effects into view.

As I mentioned, sometimes ancestral rites and Buddhist ritual are combined in marriages. In November 2014 I interviewed two Buddhist social activists in Kalaburagi who often officiate at marriages. I asked them who calls on them to conduct the ceremony. Gautam said that in the most common scenario both families are Ambedkarites. His friend, Ashoka, disagreed.

"No. Hinduism, Buddhism, and Ambedkarism – each family is a combination of these things. Most mothers are following Hinduism, only a few are there who have much knowledge about Buddhism. After marriage, they again do the same things."

"What does doing the same things again mean?", I asked.

"Going to the temple, believing in Hindu gods and blind belief."

Ashoka explained the essential elements of a properly Buddhist marriage: "When we conduct marriages we keep a framed photo of Buddha, Ambedkar, a pot of water, four to five peepal leaves, a white thread, white clothes for both the bride and the groom, these are the basic requirements. Also candles. But sometimes they bring other things."

"Other things?" I asked.

"The women bring coconuts to break, but [breaking coconuts] is not part of Buddhism. They put camphor on the coconut, perform *aarthi* (waved offering of a flame) for the bride and groom, and break the coconut. When the time comes to exchange garlands I ask for the *tali*, which should go over the bride's neck along with the garland. But quietly they say, 'Carry on, it's already been done' and that is how I learn that the *tali* has already been tied in front of the *manedevaru*. Sometimes they even go to the temple!"

"How do you feel?" I wondered.

"I feel angry, because they have called me to do a Buddhist wedding, but they don't want a Buddhist wedding. They are doing it only for appearances (*showki*). But also I feel some sympathy. On the stage, once I see the *tali* has already been tied and if I insist the bride take off the *tali* so it can [be placed over her head and around her neck along with the garland], she starts to cry and all the women begin to crowd around saying, 'Let it be, let it be, let it be'."

The women step forward to prevent the marriage conferred by the tying of the *tali* from being broken. The Buddhist activist is conflicted. He is irritated to encounter a Hindu practice in the middle of his Buddhist ceremony. These converts, he feels, have failed to make the break from Hinduism and therefore their attachment to Buddhism is superficial. But he is also moved by the press of women and their gentle but insistent claim that the bride be allowed to have both – her *tali*, tied in the Hindu manner before the ancestral gods, and her Buddhist rite of marriage. With a chorus "Let it be, let it be, let it be" (*irili bidi:* more literally, "leave it there") the women press forward, making a new ritual in which the blessings of the household gods are combined with the promise of egalitarian religion and political modernity.

For some Buddhists, such mixing is unproblematic, even mundane. In 2015 I attended a double Buddhist wedding where two brothers were getting married at the same time. As the two brides faced their future husbands, waiting to receive their wedding garlands, I saw that one already wore her *tali*. This did not seem to concern either of the two monks leading the ritual. Confused, I turned to the women behind me, members of the grooms' family, to seek clarification. "Yes," one explained, "today marks the auspicious time for only one of the couples. That *tali* was tied at the auspicious time for that couple."

"Where?" I asked.

"In front of the gods."

"Is Buddha in that household shrine?" I asked.

"Yes, of course, we are Buddhists," she said, with the air of one stating the obvious. In the *tali* a knot is tied between the backward future of superstitious attachment to astrological tellings of time and the forward past of rational and egalitarian Buddhism.

Ironically, Ambedkar himself tied such a time knot in 1954 on the occasion of the inauguration of a Buddhist temple. He had been invited to dedicate a temple to the fourteenth-century Mahar poet Cokhamela, but requested a Buddhist temple be constructed instead. In his speech he pulled the revival of Buddhism and remembrance of Cokhamela together by saying that the image of the god Vithoba – associated with Cokhamela – was a form of the Buddha.[36] Recall that Vithoba was among the pantheon arrayed in Dravid's mother's shrine.

In conclusion, I want to turn to the question of how we might think about these accounts of the mixture or combination of aspects of Hindu and Buddhist dharma within the Dalit domestic, as well as how we might think about the gendered division of religious labour within Buddhist households and the gendered discourse circulating this phenomenon. What are the women doing when they press forward with their gods? Within the categories and logic of modernity, these combinations constitute failures – of masculine ethics, reason, and science. They demonstrate the stubborn hold of past degradation, its drag on the present, the difficulty of moving into an emancipated future, and the backwardness of women.

Why then do Buddhist women continue to keep the ancestors, bringing them inside the house after death and doing puja for them, offering incense, the flame of oil lamps, and flowers? Why do they do this even as their sons, husbands, and brothers scold and berate them for failing to follow Ambedkar's injunction against keeping the gods and making offering to ancestors? Their keeping of the ancestral and familial gods is a way to secure the future – the fertility and prosperity of the family and its lineage. Even as they call for a radical break from old religion, many men reproduce such ties by pursuing endogamous marriages

[36] Zelliot, *Ambedkar's World*, p. 169.

within caste. Through this gendered division of religious labour, men and women are securing different kinds of futures for the household. Where this gendered division of religious labour is found, Dalit everyday life practices are enacting recombinant time. They draw the backward future of the ancestral gods and the forward past of a recuperated Buddhism together within a household. This recombinant time unsettles the domestic time kept by obedient wives, the Christian secular time of true converts, and the Hindu time of national hegemony and coherence.

Women make a bridge in the gap between the aspirations of their husbands and the commitments of their mothers and mothers-in-law for the reproduction of the lineage into a future in which the promises of political modernity and rational religion might be combined with the protection of the ancestors. When their sons scold them, they defer, "Whatever you are doing, following Ambedkar, it is good. But as long as I am here, I will continue the worship. These gods came from my parents, I have to keep them." They accept the stigma of backwardness – "What are we to do, our women find it difficult to let go of their gods" – as the cost of carrying the lamp of the ancestors forward: "Let it be, let it be, let it be."

Through the lens of queer theory, another set of effects comes into view. In a conversation with a colleague, another anthropologist working in Karnataka, about the gendered division of religious labour I have been describing here and the ways it works to produce both the reproductive future of health and lineage and the political future of rational progress and national inclusion, he offered an evocative idiom: "They are riding two horses." To ride two horses at once is to risk the terrible and dangerous possibility that they veer apart and tear your life in two. It is also to harness and gather the force and power of two trajectories, to pull together and multiply the possibilities of your life course and the future you can pass forward. The backwardness of deity propitiation and the forwardness of conversion to Buddhism might seem obvious. However, what I attempt to show here through ethnographic attention to everyday practice is that Dalit converts are out of joint with the straight time of progressive emancipation. They queer time by multiple enactments of it, perverting modernist protocols for religion while multiplying Dalit futures. At the same time, they are reproducing gender as a respectable relation of binary opposition, women and men as persons naturally tending to different spheres, standing in complementary relation to each other and together comprising a whole. In other words, they are producing themselves as sexual moderns.

I began this essay by outlining an empirically observable pattern occurring within many Ambedkarite households. I situated the stigmatising narratives that typically accompany this pattern as undergirded by modernist assumptions about religious conversion, history, and sexual personhood, including the idea that women's reproductive labour (the gestation and rearing of children, care of home and hearth, tending the ancestors) is less valuable than productive labour. Setting the modernist assumptions aside (without forgetting their disciplinary force) I suggest we consider this pattern as a solution to a problem rather than a problem to be solved. That is, that we ask: what are the effects of this gendered and spatial division of religious labour rather than what it tells us about the character of those performing it. I have suggested two key effects: the multiplication of possible Dalit futures and the consolidation of gender as a binary and complementary relation naturally contained within endogamous, heterosexual, and reproductive couples. Reading these practices through the lens of repair, I situate them as reproducing Dalit futures otherwise, neither modern (pure/break) nor traditional (continuous) but both, producing futures in the gap between inheritance and break. Rather than standing as evidence of failed conversion, I argue that this gendered division of religious labour is a solution for the precarity of outcaste existence that multiplies possibilities for the next generation.

To the extent that we want to remove the history-making capacities of Dalit women from the mark of erasure they have been set under, we need to document transformations in household and family as Dalit history in the making too. As many critical caste feminist scholars have noted, where women appear in Dalit historiography it is almost always as victims and survivors of unrelenting exploitation and violence. Where this trope has been exceeded and Dalit women's agency has been foregrounded, it has typically emerged in readily recognisable public forms of self-assertion and collective action such as the pursuit of higher education, participation in party politics, or autobiographical writing.[37] What ethnographic attention can bring to light are ways that seemingly backward everyday small acts of devotion and ritual constitute forms of transformative reproductive labour and history in the making.

References

Ambedkar, Bhimrao Ramji, "Castes in India: Their Mechanism, Genesis and Development", *Readings in Indian Government and Politics Class, Caste, Gender* (2004).

Ambedkar, Bhimrao Ramji, *Annihilation of Caste* (London: Verso Books, 2014).

Anandhi, S., "Women's Question in the Dravidian Movement c. 1925–1948", *Social Scientist*, vol. 19, nos 5–6, 1991.

Chakrabarty, Dipesh, *Provincializing Europe* (Princeton: Princeton University Press, 2009).

Ciotti, Manuela, "The Conditions of Politics: Low-caste Women's Political Agency in Contemporary North Indian Society", *Feminist Review*, vol. 91, no. 1, 2009.

Cohen, Lawrence, "Song for Pushkin", *Daedalus*, vol. 136, no. 2, 2007.

Comaroff, Jean, and J.L. Comaroff, *Of Revelation and Revolution: The Dialectics of Modernity on a South African Frontier* (Chicago: The University of Chicago Press, 1997).

Disha, K.R., "Practising Family, Intimacy and Caste: Narratives of Dalit Women in Non-endogamous Marriages", *Caste in Everyday Life: Experience and Affect in Indian Society* (Cham: Springer Nature Switzerland, 2023).

Edelman, Lee, *No Future* (Durham: Duke University Press, 2004).

Elisha, James, "Liberative Motifs in the Dalit Religion", in *Bangalore Theological Forum*, vol. 34, no. 2, 2002.

Hodges, Sarah, "Revolutionary Family Life and the Self Respect Movement in Tamil South India, 1926–49", *Contributions to Indian Sociology*, vol. 39, no. 2, 2005.

Jangam, Chinnaiah, *Dalits and the Making of Modern India* (New Delhi: Oxford University Press, 2017).

Kalyani, Kalyani, "Tathagata Buddha Songs", *Caste: A Global Journal on Social Exclusion*, vol. 1, no. 2, 2020.

---

[37] See in particular Ciotti, "The Conditions of Politics"; Paik "The Rise of New Dalit Women"; and Rege, *Writing Caste/Writing Gender*.

Keer, Dhananjay, *Dr. Ambedkar: Life and Mission* (1954; rpntd Bombay: Popular Prakashan, 1971).

Lynch, O.M., "Sujata's Army: Dalit Buddhist Women and Self-emancipation", *Women's Buddhism, Buddhism's Women: Tradition, Revision, Renewal* (Boston: Wisdom Publications, 2000).

Mitra, Durba, "'Surplus Woman': Female Sexuality and the Concept of Endogamy", *The Journal of Asian Studies*, vol. 80, no. 1, 2021.

Mohan, P.S., and J. Lee, "Dalit Religion", *Religion Compass*, vol. 16, no. 4, 2022.

Mohan, P. Sanal, *Modernity of Slavery: Struggles Against Caste Inequality in Colonial Kerala* (Delhi: Oxford University Press, 2015).

Moon, Meenakshi, and Urmila Pawar, *We Also Made History: Women in the Ambedkarite Movement* (New Delhi: Zubaan, 2004).

Nemoto, Tatsushi, "Becoming Dalit: Ambedkarite Movements and Inter-caste Marriages in and Around Nagpur", *Inclusive Development in South Asia* (London: Routledge, 2022).

O'Hanlon, Rosalind, *Caste, Conflict and Ideology: Mahatma Jotirao Phule and Low Caste Protest in Nineteenth-century Western India* (Cambridge: Cambridge University Press, 2002).

Paik, Shailaja, "Mangala Bansode and the Social Life of Tamasha: Caste, Sexuality, and Discrimination in Modern Maharashtra", *Biography*, vol. 40, no. 1, 2017.

Paik, Shailaja, "The Rise of New Dalit Women in Indian Historiography", *History Compass*, vol. 16, no. 10, 2018.

Patel, Geeta, "Ghostly Appearances: Time Tales Tallied Up", *Social Text*, vol. 18, no. 3, 2000.

Ram, Kalpana, *Fertile Disorder* (Honolulu: University of Hawaii Press, 2013).

Ramberg, Lucinda, "Backward Futures and Pasts Forward: Queer Time, Sexual Politics, and Dalit Religiosity in South India", *GLQ: A Journal of Lesbian and Gay Studies*, vol. 22, no. 2, 2016.

Ramberg, Lucinda, *Given to the Goddess: South Indian Devadasis and the Sexuality of Religion* (Durham: Duke University Press, 2014).

Ramberg, Lucinda, "Troubling Kinship: Sacred Marriage and Gender Configuration in South India", *American Ethnologist*, vol. 40, no. 4, 2013.

Rao, Anupama, *The Caste Question: Dalits and the Politics of Modern India* (Berkeley: University of California Press, 2009).

Rawat, Ramnarayan S., and Kusuma Satyanarayana, *Dalit Studies* (Durham: Duke University Press, 2016).

Rege, Sharmila, *Writing Caste/Writing Gender: Narrating Dalit Women's Testimonies* (Delhi: Zubaan, 2014).

Rubin, Gayle S., "The Traffic in Women", in idem, *Deviations* (1975; rpntd Durham: Duke University Press, 2011).

Samuel, Joshua, *Untouchable Bodies, Resistance, and Liberation* (London: Brill, 2020).

Satyanarayana, K., and Susie J. Tharu, eds, *The Exercise of Freedom: An Introduction to Dalit Writing* (Delhi: Navayana Publishing, 2013).

Shepherd, Kancha Ilaiah, *Why I Am Not a Hindu: A Sudra Critique of Hindutva Philosophy, Culture and Political Economy* (Delhi: Sage Publications India, 2019).

Sinha, Mrinalini, ed., *Katherine Mayo: Selections from 'Mother India'* (Ann Arbor: University of Michigan Press, 2000).

Sturman, Rachel, *The Government of Social Life in Colonial India: Liberalism, Religious Law, and Women's Rights* (Cambridge: Cambridge University Press, 2012).

Tarikere, Rahamath, "Inter-caste Marriage and Shakta Myths of Karnataka", *Economic and Political Weekly*, vol. 52, nos 42–3, 2017.

Wakankar, Milind, *Subalternity and Religion: The Prehistory of Dalit Empowerment in South Asia* (London: Routledge, 2010).

Wiegman, Robyn, "Feminism's Apocalyptic Futures", *New Literary History*, vol. 31, no. 4, 2000.

Yatanoor, Chandrakant, "Dalit Movement in Karnataka and the Role of the Dalita Sangharsha Samiti (DSS) in the Emancipation of Dalits", *Voice of Dalit*, vol. 3, no. 1, 2010.

Zelliot, Eleanor, *Ambedkar's World: The Making of Babasaheb and the Dalit Movement* (New Delhi: Navayana Publishing, 2020).

Zelliot, Eleanor, "Religious Leadership among Maharashtrian Women", *Women's Buddhism, Buddhism's Women: Tradition, Revision, Renewal* (Boston: Wisdom Publications, 2000).

5

Between Blasphemy and Martyrdom

The Formation of the Ravidassia Religion in Punjab

KOONAL DUGGAL

We will gladly mount the gallows for the community
We will bravely bare our chests to face bullets
We have learnt to combat the blows of swords
Think before you challenge Chamars.

– Roop Lal Dhir, "Panga", 2010[1]

THE LINES ABOVE are from a song entitled "Panga" (Fight) written and sung passionately by Roop Lal Dhir, a Punjabi singer from the Chamar caste. Appearing in his 2010 album *Mundé Chamaran De* (Sons of Chamars), it begins with sounds and beats typical of Punjabi pop music. A combination of traditional folk and modern instruments – synthesiser, tumbi, dholak, alghoza – generates

---

[1] Dhir, "Panga". All translations in this essay are mine, unless otherwise specified.

Asi qaum di khatir hass ke suli chhad jaiye
Asi goliyan agge hikk taan ke chad jaiye
Asi muh modne sikkh laye talwaaran de
Panga soch samajh ke payo naal Chamaraan de

119

Fig. 1: Still from Roop Lal Dhir's "Panga".
Source: YouTube.

the music, with shouts from a chorus adding a revolutionary dynamism.
The configuration of aural, lyrical, and visual elements presents the
song as a call for revolution, throwing out an open challenge to enemies.
In the music video of the song, directed by P.K. Kaler, we see the lead
singer in the foreground, with co-singers in the background, all carrying
mashaal (torches) symbolising revolution. This combination of visual
signs is emphasised through sartorial elements borrowed from various
iconographies visible in both the lead and co-singers/actors. The lead
singer Roop Lal Dhir appears wearing a suit and a tie – but not the blue
suit of Dr B.R. Ambedkar usually worn by Dalits – and a *basanti* (yellow)
turban identified with the revolutionary and *shaheed* (martyr) Bhagat
Singh who, though an atheist but also claimed as a Sikh, is seen as being
specific to Punjab's context.[2] The background actors in their yellow turbans are shown wrapped in a shawl similar, to Ravidassia religious representations of Guru Ravidass.[3] In the Dalit community the wearing

[2] For more detailed discussions on various contestations around the legacy
of Bhagat Singh, see Moffat, *India's Revolutionary Inheritance*.
[3] The term Ravidassia refers to followers from the Chamar caste, normatively
linked with leather tanning and the shoemaking profession, who worship the
medieval bhakti poet Guru Ravidass. The Ravidassia religion is dedicated to the
Bhakti poet Sant Ravidass not only because he is one of the major historical and

Fig. 2: B.R. Ambedkar.   Fig. 3: Representation of Guru Ravidass (left);
and Shaheed Bhagat Singh (right).
Author's collection.

of a tie and suit has always been symbolically associated with modernity.[4] This is also connected with the upward mobility of the Chamar/
Ravidassia community of Punjab, gained from entrepreneurial ad-
vances in their caste trade (in the leather industry), well-paying government jobs because of affirmative action, and, most importantly,
from deep links with the prosperous diasporic community in the West.[5]

---

religious figures who come from the Chamar caste – like his contemporary Sant
Kabirdass, who also belonged to the untouchable caste of Julaha (weavers) – but
because his poetry asserts his caste identity and protests against all kinds of discriminations and inequalities. Therefore, for the Ravidassia community the figure
of Ravidass embodies "A Symbol of Liberty": see Suman, *Miracles of Jagat-guru*,
p. 91. In my doctoral thesis I have looked at transformations in the iconography of
the Ravidass from saint to god (Sant/Bhagat to Guru/Satguru) which is also interlinked with the rise in Ravidassia religiosity.

[4] Tartakov emphasises that the strikingly modern sartorial elements embedded in the iconography of Ambedkar make three key points: "this is a city man,
a man of learning, and *only* a man – not a god." Tartakov, "Art and Identity",
p. 411.

[5] According to Singh, Simon, and Tatla this contribution of Chamars from the
diaspora to their caste and religious community should be seen as "transnationalism from below", and it can be characterised in four ways. First, the subaltern
groups among migrants "remained as marginal actors within both their home-
lands and their host societies because of their low levels of income and social
status. Second, driven by religion as a 'social vision' – in which the assertion of a

These developments have played a significant role in the assertion and territorialisation of the Chamar caste and Ravidassia religious identity. It is important to note that Chamars are the second largest in proportion among Dalits in the state of Punjab, and that Punjab has the largest Dalit population of any Indian state.[6] Therefore, one should read this juxtaposition of sartorial references as a combination of *bhakti* (Guru Ravidass) and *inqalabi* (Shaheed Bhagat Singh), a simultaneously devotional and revolutionary identity that arrives as a unified *shakti* (power).[7] The use of the term Chamar not only foregrounds caste identity but also the violence, stigma, and humiliation attached to the caste name, as it operates through humiliation via caste slurs to other forms of violence against Dalits. However, Roop Lal Dhir's song is not about victimisation; rather, it is entirely about asserting a new dignity and the will to power by Chamars. In this sense, the song attempts to reverse the

---

distinctive religious-caste identity is used as a basis for assisting the material and social development of the members of the group in the homeland; third, this contribution is not engaged primarily in conventional forms of religious philanthropy. Rather, their use of religious-caste identity for the mobilisation of resources in the North (their host countries) is undertaken mainly for economic development aimed at enhancing the group's social prestige, thereby enabling it to realise its quest for equality. Fourth, committed to using religious-caste identity to redefine the public sphere, pursue inclusionary governance, and combat religious-caste discrimination in both host and homeland countries". See Singh, Simon, and Tatla, "New Forms", p. 12.

[6] According to the 2001 census, Punjab has a much larger proportion of seats reserved for the SCs – around 29 per cent as against 15 per cent at the national level. According to the 2011 census, this reached 36.74 per cent. The Dalits of Punjab are divided into different communities, such as the Churha caste (also called Mazhabi Sikhs) and the Balmikis/Bhangis. The Chamar caste is made up of the Ad Dharmi Chamars/Ravidassis/Ramdasi Sikhs. The remaining comprise thirty-three caste groups. See Jodhka and Kumar, "Internal Classification of Scheduled Castes".

[7] During my first field visit to Dera Sachkhand Ballan (DSB) in 2012 I noted that there was a music shop inside the Dera complex selling music and video VCDs and DVDs produced by the Dera as well as an overall collection of Ravidassia and Chamar music. I was told by the singers Kulwant Kajla and Raj Dadral that they have songs varying from *bhakti* to *shakti*, where *bhakti* meant reference to a Ravidassia genre and *shakti* to a Chamar genre of music.

normative meanings and representations attached to Chamar caste identity.

The assertion of a masculine Chamar identity, which is intimately associated with Guru Ravidass, represents a new development in the evolution of the Ravidassia religion in Punjab and in the diasporic community. It is associated with the emergence of Chamar singers within Punjabi music who have openly asserted a religious and caste identity to lay claim to a new dignity. Moreover, these two developments are good examples of a fundamental transformation in Ravidassia religious identity that had occurred after what is now known as the "Vienna attack", referring to the assassination in May 2009 of a saint, Sant Ramanand, who had belonged to one of the most prominent Ravidassia Deras, namely Dera Sachkhand Ballan (henceforth DSB).[8] The Ad Dharm movement in Punjab first appropriated Guru Ravidass in the

---

[8] The word Dera, also spelt Dehra, means "encampment", or the dwelling place of a *sant* (saint). See McLeod, *The A to Z of Sikhism*, p. 55. Jodhka argues that "Babas, sants, gurus, peers and their deras have been an important part of the religious landscape of Punjab for a long time. As institutions of popular or folk religion outside the more organized structures such as mosques and temples, they represent the enchanted universe of pre-modern religiosity." See Jodhka, "Of Babas and Deras". According to Surinder Singh, "The Deras in Punjab that existed prior to the Sikh Panth belonged to the Muslim Peer and Yog Nath's Dera." Therefore, "a study conducted in 2008–9 by *Desh Sewak*, a Punjabi newspaper published from Chandigarh, provides figures showing more than 9000 Sikh as well as non-Sikh Deras in the 12,000 villages of Punjab. See Singh, "Deras, Caste Conflicts". However, now Deras as institutions of "popular" religion function almost in the manner of new religious movements. At present, Deras attract a large number of followers from different castes and religions precisely because of the "charismatic" presence of living gurus and sants. Their popularity is not only limited to the religious sphere but rather plays an important role in the political sphere too, with political parties seeking their support during elections. See Duggal, "The 'Vexed' Status of Guru Images". DSB is a Ravidassia Dera located in Ballan, a village in Jalandhar District (the Doaba region). It was founded by Sant Pipal Dass in the beginning of the twentieth century, then the second and best-known *sant*, Sarwan Dass (DSB is also referred to as Dera Sant Sarwan Dass), followed by other *sants*. In brief, the contribution of each *sant* is narrated as hagiography within DSB literature. For instance, the founder guru Sant Pipal Dass is said to have ended his search for truth in Ballan by performing a miracle which confirmed his sacredness. After donations of land from nearby villagers, the Dera occupied

1920s as the embodiment of an alternative religious identity for the Chamars, and over the past hundred years this movement has gained in depth and solidarity.[9] While I will not here be able to examine all aspects of their religion and music, I will focus on the impact on the politics and aesthetics of this music created by the "martyrdom of Sant Ramanand". The rise of the Ravidassia religion alongside that of Chamar singers represents a new moment of performative intervention, or a rupture in the form of sub-cultural practices in the field of religion and Punjabi devotional pop music. Furthermore, it represents a qualitatively new form of countervisuality vis-à-vis normative ideas of representational aesthetics and religiosity, as well as the overall conditioning of one's being (individual/community) by asserting, as Nicholas Mirzoeff puts it, one's "right to look".[10]

In the contested terrain of sight the right to look is entwined with the right to be seen. On the one hand visuality is dominated by the policing of hegemonic forces that not only control the grammar of representation and seeing but also claim visuality as their divine/natural right. On the other hand, countervisuality makes a claim for visual subjectivity against naturalised "invisibilisation" from the ruling regimes of representation. In short, there is a claim for subjectivity through the politics of recognition initiated not by the state or a political party but by a religious movement: in this case by the historically marginalised Dalits who have been systematically invisibilised and dispossessed of their rights. They assert their claim to show the dominant Other that they too have the right to be visible, to sing songs and practise their religion. Therefore, this counter-normative self-image of Dalit individuals/community can be presented as "the claim to a right to the real,"[11] where "the realism of the right to the real highlights the 'struggle for existence', meaning a genealogy of the claim of the right to existence."[12]

---

its present place in Ballan and soon became a place of pilgrimage for its lower-caste followers because of the veneration associated with Ravidass since its inception. For more details, see Suman, *Miracles* pp. 8–9.

[9] Chs 8 to 11 and 21 and 22 in Juergensmeyer, *Religious Rebels*.

[10] See Mirzoeff, *Right to Look*.

[11] Ibid., 26.

[12] Ibid.

I argue here that cultural forms narrate and represent the genealogy of the Ravidassia religion starting with Guru Ravidass, and thereafter with the DSB and its consolidation after the martyrdom of Sant Ramanand. Yet I do not seek to argue that the struggle for representation as a caste-religious identity is settled with religious formation. Rather, I hold that the opposite is true: the fight for recognition in terms of religious identity is asserted since the right to be seen as equal – as a fully formed (citizen) subject as promised by democracy and Dr B.R. Ambedkar's Constitution of India – is yet to be realised. Moreover, this essay demonstrates that it is through the deployment of the cultural tropes of martyrdom that an alternative religious identity is carved out to counter the policing by dominant religious forces. I show the clash between two religious views: first, that of the dominant Sikh, which uses acts of violence to punish the Other's view of religion through charges of blasphemy; and, second, that of the Other, i.e. Chamars/Ravidassias, who counter the dominant claims of blasphemy through their own articulation of martyrdom. It is the orthodox and mainstream groups in Sikhism that lead the charge of blasphemy against Chamars and the Ravidassia religion. The clash between these views of blasphemy on the one hand and martyrdom on the other represent a clash between dominant Sikh visuality and Chamar/Ravidassia countervisuality. This is not to refute the idea that Chamar/Ravidassia religious and cultural forms borrow elements from dominant traditions of religion and visuality. In fact, countervisuality emerges only because of visuality, when the push and pull from each side not only sustains but reconfigures the other. But during this process countervisuality reveals the inherent contradictions and narrow construction of reality in the dominant visuality. This countering "right to the real" is a move towards imagination and an assertion of the marginalised Other.

Ravidassia Countervisuality: Song and Sant Dignity

The emphasis on Ravidassia countervisuality highlights the points of departure from the established norms of visuality, and such a formulation avoids adopting a simplistic appropriation and reversal framework. An emphasis on a more nuanced understanding and recognition of the contexts and its politics establishes a firm ground of countervisuality and gives the latter a meaning and a context for intervention. For instance, in Roop Lal Dhir's song we could connect formal and generic linkages with a number of songs about Bhagat Singh and around the theme of *panga*. The most popular one that comes to mind is Diljit Dosanjh and Honey Singh's song of the same title ("Panga") from the album *The Next Level* (2009) that touches upon a range of issues, such as the Jat Sikh (colloquial: Jatt) brotherhood's caste-based male bonding/friendship (*yaarian*) which not only celebrates Jat masculinity through "gun culture" but represents caste hegemony overall.[13] This hegemony is maintained through domination over all structures of power – the complex of land, politics, and religion – which becomes a precondition for the normalisation of routine violence and the humiliation of Dalits and lower-caste communities. This hegemony of the Jat Sikh is the universal representation of being a Sikh in a dominant visuality that gets manifested in popular Punjabi music (folk, Bhangra, and pop music) and films, and which serves to mainstream electoral and religious politics. In contrast to this, in Dhir's song anger merges with the overall response to an act of religious violence, a tragic event in the Chamar/Ravidassia community's history and memory that would change the course of religion and politics. As we hear in the song:

> Through attacks on our saints what do you want to prove?
> We are not cowardly people, your forceful attempts are futile.

These lyrics are aligned with a montage of images and video footage which indeed appears throughout the music video, zooming into Sant Ramanand's body in the coffin, zooming out to show believers mourning and paying homage to their departed saint in Vienna. This is followed

---

[13] In rural Punjab's agricultural set-up, Jats occupy different structures of power, be it social, ethnological, economic, political, religious, or numerical. Jats are 60–65 per cent of the Sikh population and the largest caste group in Punjab, consolidating the notion of "Jatt Power". They became a formidable force from the time of Maharaja Ranjit Singh. Their domination and power grew during British rule, be it through the grant of the status of "martial" race, or their construal of them as "farmers" via the Land Alienation Act in 1902 (which made them farmers and landlords at the same time). Even in the post-colonial context it was the Jats who reaped the success of the Green Revolution, adding to their dominance.

by a sequence of still images of protests in the Doaba region across Jalandhar District against Sant Ramanand's assassination (Figs 4 and 5).[14] These stills show protesters, irrespective of gender, registering their anger by occupying publics spaces like roads and highways. They hold sticks in the air and clash with the police, whilst trains, buses, and cars are shown in flames.

This is the historic moment that we see in Dhir's song, a moment that further shaped the politics and aesthetics of the Chamar/Ravidassia community. Let me provide a brief background of the 2009 incident.

The Ad Prakash: The Book of the Ravidassia Religion

On 25 May 2009 five gunmen from the Sikh brotherhood attacked the DSB chief Sant Niranjan Dass, and his second-in-command Sant Ramanand Maharaj, in front of worshippers at a Ravidassia temple in Vienna. This resulted in the death of Sant Ramanand. The attack was rationalised via the claim that a portrait of Guru Ravidass cannot be placed next to the Sikh holy book, the *Guru Granth Sahib*, on the same platform – neither in the DSB nor in other affiliated Deras in India and abroad. It was condemned as blasphemous to have an idol or image of Ravidass and a living Dera guru/sant sitting at the same level as the *Guru Granth Sahib* since, according to Sikh religious rituals, one is not allowed to bow down to anyone else in the presence of the *Granth Sahib*. This is because the holy book is considered an embodiment of the Guru. Prior to the formation of a separate Granth, the *Guru Granth Sahib* used to be placed there.

As we can see in the image (Fig. 6), and possibly imagine, there is a "distributed guruship" in which the Guru Ravidass idol is displayed next to the holy book along with a living Dera guru, so that all share the same platform before Ravidassia congregations. This practice of distributed guruship became the subject of ire for Sikh radicals. Their objection to Ravidassia practice was justified by them on the grounds that

[14] Punjab is divided into three regions: Malwa, Majha, and Doaba. Doaba is predominantly dominated by the Chamar caste and historically, since the Ad Dharm movement, has been the centre of Dalit resistance.

Fig. 4.

Fig. 5.

it contradicted the tenets of a document called *Khalsa Sikh Rahit Mar-yada*.[15] According to the political scientist Ronki Ram, "most of the attacks on [non-Sikh Deras] happen when the mainstream religion thinks that the Deras are not adhering to Sikh *maryada*. But if the Dera follow-

[15] The *Sikh Rahit Maryada* is a booklet containing codes of conduct and conventions that a Sikh should follow. It argues for maintaining "uniformity" and "cohesion" among the Sikh community and its followers in everyday religious

Fig. 6: The idol of Guru Ravidass placed next to the
Holy Granth, the Guru Ravidass Amritbani, inside the
Shri Guru Ravidass Mand__, Hadiabad, District Phagwara (Punjab),
September 2012.

(bodily) conduct and observances. It was first published in 1950, after long deliberations among Singh Sabha reformers. The work is divided into two parts: personal discipline and panthic discipline. The first part covers such topics as behaviour in a gurdwara and reading the *Guru Granth Sahib*. It also details the order to be followed in rituals for birth and naming, marriage, and death. The second section largely comprises the order for Khalsa initiation. See McLeod, *The A to Z of Sikhism*. It insists on "recitation or repetition", or the singing of religious hymns, *Naam* (word) and scriptural compositions, thus emphasising the importance of text and words in the form of writing and speech over anthropomorphic images of gurus. The main concentration of all reverential ceremonies and bodily conduct revolves around the *Guru Granth Sahib* as eternal guru in its present avatar. It states: "No book should be installed like and at par with the Guru Granth. Worship of any idol or any ritual or activity should not be allowed to be conducted inside the gurdwara . . . installing statues, or idols inside the gurdwaras, bowing before the picture of the Sikh Gurus or elders – all these are irreligious self-willed egotism, contrary to *Gurmat* (the Guru's way)." See Kulraj, trans., *The Code of Conduct*, p. 13.

ers do not identify themselves as Sikhs, where is the question of *mar-yada*?"[16] In short, the ritual was seen from the normative Sikh Khalsa (pure) perspective that refuses to acknowledge a Ravidassia ritual. As the sociologist Surinder Singh Jodhka also notes, "Their reverence for the *Guru Granth* is primarily because it also contains the writings of Guru Ravi Das."[17] This not only foregrounds the Ravidassia way of reverence for the *Granth*, but has value for them as one of the most important and earliest compilations of Ravidass *bani* (hymns) recorded in the Gurumukhi script. Therefore, from this perspective the spiritual preference for Ravidass' *bani* takes precedence over every other *bani*. This indicates the awareness and presence of Ravidass in the religious landscape of Punjab much before the inception of Ad Dharm (Original Religion) in 1925, evident from religious practices in the Sikh tradition as well as through a loose network of Ravidassia *panth*s (paths) and Deras headed by *sant*s from the Chamar caste. Note that Ad Dharmi leaders collaborated with Ravidassia saints in the formation of their holy book, the *Ad Prakash* (Original Light). Historically, this shows the overlaps in religiosity between the Sikh and Ravidassia *panth*s, which is contrary to the contemporary claim of Sikh ownership over the *Guru Granth*.

Hence, it is important to underline that the Sikh religion as we understand it today is a formation that started in the early twentieth century. This genealogy would bring both the Lahore Singh Sabha (1870s) and Ad Dharm movement (1920) into a comparative perspective, since these two movements, which argued for an independent religious identity, were contemporaries. Even the leaders from both movements – figures from the first generation of educated new-elite Dalit and Sikh intellectuals – came from educational institutions and affiliations of the Arya Samaj.[18] And both movements initially followed the Arya Samaj model to articulate their independent religious identity. To break away

---

[16] See Mahaprashasta, "Inflamed Passions".

[17] See Jodhka, "The Ravi Dasis of Punjab", p. 79.

[18] The first generation of radical Dalit leaders in northern India were also educated in schools run by the reformist Hindu Arya Samaj. A number of these leaders, such as Swami Achutanand, would eventually distance themselves from the Arya Samaj. See ch. 4, "Struggle for Identities", in Rawat, *Reconsidering Untouchability*. Similarly, in the context of Punjab, the Ad Dharm movement's founder Mangoo Ram Mugowalia, the Singh Sabha movement reformer Dalit Sikh,

from this given model, both movements undertook several measures to carve out an autonomous identity, but one thing that connected both movements was the *Guru Granth Sahib*. Both movements approached this sacred object/text – a compilation of verses and hymns from Sikh Gurus, Sufis, pirs, and bhakti saints – with a Judaeo-Christian understanding of religion, i.e. a religion wherein a sacred book, such as the Bible, serves as the foundation of the whole religious edifice. In this sense the formation of Sikhism, as a well-defined religion with codes of conduct, is a twentieth-century formation. On the other hand, in order to encourage participation in the Ad Dharm movement, which was modernist in its vision of equality and had a new religious identity, a history or connection with tradition remained important. Therefore, the process of making the *Ad Prakash* the holy book of Ad Dharmis involved giving a traditional and spiritual background to a modern faith. This was accomplished through the revival and reclamation of Ravidass as an icon and main Guru, and through the promotion of his poetry as the core teachings of the Ad Dharm religion.[19] However, even after the Ad Dharm transitioned into a movement for Ravidass and the leaders of the movement took the name Ravi Dass Mandal in 1946, the urgency of possessing their own holy book had not been felt within the Ravidassia community. During this period, the Ravidassia community had, however, developed its own identity markers, with an active role being played by DSB *sant*s in all the Ravidassia Deras; and this had continued alongside worship of the *Granth Sahib* – until the Vienna attack.[20]

The Luminous Deras: Building a Community

The most important contribution by the DSB *sant*s was their "missionary" role, mainly among the diaspora communities. This had resulted in

---

and the intellectual Giani Ditt Singh were associated with the Arya Samaj and grew distant from it.

[19] To understand Sikh and Ad Dharm religious movements historically, see Oberoi, *The Construction of Religious Boundaries*, and Juergensmeyer, *Religious Rebels in the Punjab*.

[20] For more details, see Jodhka, "From *Zaat* to *Qaum*".

spreading Ravidassia religiosity and the commencement of what became known as "Mission Begumpura" – the ambition to connect the entire religious community through a centre and a site of pilgrimage. The significance of the DSB *sant*s is noted in several songs in Ravidassia music mourning Sant Ramanand's death. For instance, in the song "Sant Ramanand Ji", which is sung by the female singer Amrita Virk and the child singer Master Ragav Mahi, in an album entitled *Prabhat Pheri Mata Kalsa De Lal Di* (2011; Morning Procession of Mother Kalsa's Son), we see performers, with the DSB in the background, evoking the relationship between a mother and her child who are mourning the loss of their community's father figure. In their contrasting voices they sing the following lines:

> Who will take the train [the Begumpura Express] to Kashi (Benaras),
> Who will sing the verses of Guru Ravidass for us? [Master Ragav Mahi]
> The gardener [signifying Sant Ramanand] of Sachkhand Ballan, who broadened the fragrance of *Har naam* [name] in the entire world . . .
> *Guru Ravidassji Sant Ramanand ik janam layi bhejo hor* (Guru Ravidass-ji, send Sant Ramanand for one more lifetime) [Amrita Virk].[21]

Unlike Dhir's "Panga", this song is mellow and emotional; it exemplifies the idea of loss in the Ravidassia community by showing followers crying and mourning the loss of their departed saint. Towards the end of the song Virk herself breaks down. Her tears show her performing vulnerability, not to mention femininity (in a normative gendered understanding), on account of the loss.

In all Ravidassia Chamar songs the singer performs not only as an individual but to index representation of the larger community, the individual as part of the whole. Altogether, the song urges the Sant's rebirth for the community to achieve the emancipation that is the fulfilment of Mission Begumpura. Both lyrically and visually, the song narrates the role played by Dera *sant*s, with the main focus being on Sant Ramanand spreading the Ravidassia religious "mission" – as marked by these various indicators of identity formation. Again, through a montage of diverse video footage and still images, the music video focuses on the missionary task of *sant*s in travelling and addressing congregations in Ravi-

[21] Virk and Mahi, "Sant Ramanand Ji".

dassia temples all over Europe. This shows the expansion of the Chamar caste and religious identity through the DSB, which not only facilitated community-building but also provided spiritual certitude to a community that was alienated from its homeland. This language of montage – clippings showing the *sant*'s travels, with planes flying and being welcomed by followers at an airport in Birmingham, etc. – can also be seen in souvenir objects.

In this photo-montaged image (Fig. 7) we see DSB *sant*s in an airport setting with a Virgin Atlantic airliner in the background, symbolising the close ties between Dera *sant*s and England's Ravidassia *sangat* (community). The showering of flowers on their chief personage, Sant Niranjan Dass, from the airplane flying above has replaced the flying angels usually seen in traditional religious representations. This transition from angels to airplanes highlights the modernity of

Fig. 7: A souvenir object showing the foreign visit of Dera Sachkhand Ballan *sant*s, the present head Sant Niranjan Dass (standing left) and Sant Ramanand. At the top of the image, we see written "Sant Niranjan Dass' foreign visit". Collected from Seer Goverdharpur, Varanasi, February 2013.

migration via the technique of image-making, and in the conception of Ravidassia religiosity. The flying plane thus symbolically serves the imagery of the transnational Ravidassia community welcoming their auspicious visitor's arrival.

It is important to recognise the importance of video montage as a technique that accompanies a certain kind of politics and aesthetics in almost all Chamar/Ravidassia music videos. The videos and still images are brought in and put together from various archival sources – such as documentation footage and materials from DVDs to online videos and stills from various Ravidassia congregations in Punjab – at the pilgrimage site of Seer Goverdhanpur and across the globe. These are then reconfigured to suit the thematic of each song. In this way, the song not only becomes a reconfigured archive but also a testimony, a *shaheed* (witness) account of the *shaheed* (martyr), justifying its claims.[22] All such claims and assertions to community by Ravidassia members, foregrounded through a range of sources, are presented to the viewer/listener as archival testimony. These include claims of upward mobility that can facilitate the community's presence in the diaspora through temples and congregations, the DSB *sants'* travels, the community's religious presence in Punjab, in Varanasi (Uttar Pradesh), and in parts of Europe and North America. All these varied sources together signify the upward mobility of the community. They also assert, in both material and spiritual realms, the identity and sense of being a Chamar who is simultaneously a Ravidassia Dalit.

This development, incorporating the montage technique of sourcing and putting together visual forms, also shows the development of Ravidassia religiosity from provincial Deras to a fully formed religion and global community. This form of montage is realised through a well-networked collaboration between various actor-networks and organisations, underlining the "community-run" aspect of Ravidassia countervisuality. These include the Dera's charismatic *sants* whose following is located in the diaspora and within India, the flow of transnational/local capital, cultural forms and practices such as the formation of religious identity markers, and mythologisations of Guru Ravidass and of the

---

[22] The term *shaheed* conveys both these meanings.

Chamar/Ravidassia community. These mythologisations in literature and song take the form of linguistic (texual/aural), visual (still/moving), and media (printed, digital, and social media) phenomena; within their respective contexts they interweave and overlap to contribute to an over-all formation of Ravidassia cultural identity and religiosity. This "community-run" network is not centralised, but what binds it to a larger network is a caste-religious communitarian consciousness working through new media cultures to create an overarching montage. One finds instances of such fusion on community-run television broadcasts, online channels such as Kanshi TV, and channels on YouTube, as well as on production and distribution networks run by the DSB and others (Fig. 8). Both DSB and some established Ravidassia individuals (mainly from the diaspora) sponsor and promote singers who come mostly from their caste-religious community – such as Roop Lal Dhir, Amrita Virk, S.S. Azad, S.H. Tajpuri, Sudesh Kumari, Rajni Thakkarwal, Ginni Mahi, and many more.[23] Others also contribute in different ways, such as those who provide the lyrics of the songs. For example, on the flex hoardings, banners, posters, and VCD covers, we can see along with pictures of singers studio portraits of producers, music directors and lyricists. In most of these instances the emphasis on "location" in addition to the name and picture – such as when "Kapil Canada presents . . ." is written on top of the poster of Bibey Putt Chamaran De's song – shows the producer in the centre of the composition like a hierarchical, guardian figure.[24] Other posters and VCD covers would have locations like the USA, Italy, and the UK, highlighting not only the transnational capital invested in the production, circulation, and consumption of Chamar/Ravidassia cultural forms, but also showcasing individuals performing various roles in different capacities as a form of *seva* (selfless

[23] The self-identification of these singers from Chamar and Ravidassia background as "mission singers . . . who sing for the community and its gurus, rather than for money", and who don't want to be seen simply as folk singers, adds another layer to the term mission in the post-Vienna context. See Singh, "The Caste Question and Songs of Protest in Punjab".

[24] This aesthetics of juxtaposition of words and images hierarchically arranged is not only borrowed from religious but also from political hoardings and advertisements.

Fig. 8: A shot from an evening show featuring a panel discussion
around the meaning and relevance of Guru Ravidass *amritbani*.
This webcast comes live from London on 10th August 2015 and it is
produced by Kanshi TV and Venus TV, run by the Shri Guru Ravidass
Mission International. Beneath the frame, the trending account details
an individual contributor's name and the amount of each contribution
foregrounds the community-run aspect of the channel.

service) towards the *krantikaari* (revolutionary) mission of the community.[25] This relationship of part with whole is wrought through the
mutual desire of *seva*, of "giving back" to the community and with a
desire to be visible. The community's increased consolidation and assertion constitutes the politics of this aesthetic.

The Temple of Ravidassia Religiosity

Yet another layer of meaning can be gathered from Virk's song, namely the important role that transnational capital has played in the development of the Ravidassia religious mission for a desired Begampura –

---

[25] The terms *seva* and *krantikaari* were often used in the interviews on Kanshi
TV. This also connects with the previously discussed point about *bhakti* and
shakti.

meaning a city without sorrows – through a temple built on the site of Guru Ravidass' birthplace as the centre of pilgrimage. Virk's song highlights this:

> So far our Begumpura mission has not reached its peak. So far we have not converted Guru Ravidass' temple into gold.

In any process of religious institutionalisation, symbols and markers of identity hold great importance, and a pilgrimage centre is one such significant marker. The DSB *sants* initiated this by founding the pilgrimage site as a centre that would contain the entire Ravidassia community as a united whole. The second Dera guru, Sant Sarwan Dass, assigned this task to a select group of people who went to Varanasi and traced the place at Seer Goverdhanpur. On 14 June 1965 construction began at the traced site and, after several phases of building, the temple came into being. Therefore, the desire of discovering Begumpura, symbolising the worldly egalitarian utopia which figured in Ravidass' poetry, was unearthed, reclaimed, and reiterated through cultural forms, and most specifically in the form of a temple.

This was furthered from the year 2000 with a ritual – that of conducting an annual pilgrimage to the site on a special train, the Begumpura Express, which ran from Jalandhar Cantonment to Benaras on Ravidass' birth anniversary. All this further consolidated the image of Begumpura as the community's centre for pilgrimage – resembling Mecca in Saudi Arabia and the Golden Temple in Amritsar – as "a symbol of Dalit identity and Dalit awakening" in the Ravidassia religious imagination.[26]

The idea of a temple had haunted Dalits as an impossible dream because of their age-old systemic exclusion from the sacred spaces of temples. Access to Hindu temples and Sikh gurdwaras under upper- and dominant-casteist factions has always been an area of contestation. This oppression, which has been confronted with temple-entry movements by Dalits at various historical junctures right down to recent times, has now been overthrown via the coming into being of their own temple reachable by pilgrimage. This possession of their own symbol and location of worship that Dalits had long been denied represents

[26] See Suman, *Miracles*, p. 54. Also, on the development of these religious identity markers, see Ram, "Ravidass Deras and Social Protest".

Fig. 9: The image of the Ravidass Temple printed on the cover
of a brochure. Collected from Dera Sachkhand Ballan,
September 2012.

the actualisation of their hitherto impossible dream, the arrival of utopia into their real inhabited world. Begumpura is a universal idea realised as a temple where all are welcome. This conception is absorbed by Ravidassias as an aspect of their liberation, taking them a step nearer the idea of equality and democracy: in short, to their right to partake of religion and their own desired representation. This need for a temple plated with gold was the call for a community that had issued from the martyred Sant Ramanand (Fig. 10): in the form of a *bhajan* (devotional song):

> Let us go to Benaras saints and followers, we have to create history by having the temple of Guru Ravidass plated in gold.

The first phase of having the temple plated in gold started in 2008, a year before the Vienna attack, which we can see also in the unveiling of gold plating within Virk's music video. Speeches in several Ravidassia congregations suggest that Sant Ramanand's vision offered the community its own Golden Temple (*unhone humein humara swarn mandir diya*).[27] This desire amongst materially dispossessed Dalits to plate the Ravidass temple in gold shows their upward mobility, or, at the very least, their great aspiration for it. This question of materiality and how it is tied with aspirations and will to power, dignity, and pride can be seen in the use of stone and bronze materials for statues and reliefs of Ambedkar and other subaltern figures and leaders in Mayawati's monuments.[28] Similarly, not far from Jalandhar, in Amritsar (in the Majha region) we see the Valmiki community's successful appropriation and reclamation of a popular Hindu pilgrimage centre. Previously named Ram Tirath, this was renamed Valmiki Tirath in 2016 and an 8-foot-tall, 800-kg gold-plated idol of Valmiki was installed.[29] This not only completed the

[27] This in reference to speeches made at the congregations held during Guru Ravidass Birth Anniversary celebrations at Seer Goverdhanpur, Varanasi (Uttar Pradesh), in February 2013.

[28] For a detailed analysis of Mayawati's monuments, see Jain, "The Handbag that Exploded".

[29] A popular Hindu pilgrimage site in Amritsar named Ram Tirath. "A site believed to be the abode of Rishi/Bhagwan Valmiki where Sita, the wife of Rama took refuge [and] apparently gave birth to Rama's two sons, Lav and Kush." See Snehi, "From Ram Tirath", p. 23.

Fig. 10: A representation of Sant Ramanand with quoted lines
in one of the printed posters at Seer Goverdhanpur,
February 2013.

Valmiki community's successful reclamation of a contested pilgrimage
site, it demonstrated how the celebrated Hindu god "Rama, therefore,
becomes peripheral" in Valmiki religiosity.[30] It shows the Valmiki community's "right to look" as a "right to the real" and "right to religion", as

[30] Ibid., p. 25.

we have seen with Ravidassia religiosity. In this way we see the missionary role played by the DSB *sant*s in making possible a Ravidassia religious identity, with the DSB itself emerging as a powerful entity within and outside Punjab.

The Martyrdom and Public Protests

The funeral of Sant Ramanand in June 2009 was attended by leading political figures from Punjab and Uttar Pradesh. They included the chief minister of Punjab, Parkash Singh Badal, who belonged to the mainstream Sikh political party the Shiromani Akali Dal; the deputy chief minister Sukhbir Badal; the chief minister of Uttar Pradesh Ms Mayawati who was the Dalit leader of the Bahujan Samaj Party; and Captain Amarinder Singh, leader of the Indian National Congress. Sant Ramanand's funeral was carried out with full state honours. The status accorded to Sant Ramanand's funderal demonstrates the power that the DSB holds within the larger politics in Punjab and beyond.[31]

As mentioned earlier, the Vienna attack on the Dera Guru Sant Ramanand resulted in several protests from the Chamar/Ravidassia community in Punjab and the diaspora regions. In both contexts, the protests registered the community's sense of injury in the face of violence unleashed on them through an attack on their *sant*s and gurus who, as icons, embody the idea of their community.[32] As part of the protests, the affected community asserted itself through an occupation of public spaces. As a result, the emergence of two contrasting images or languages of protest became apparent. The first was the mode adopted by the diaspora in London, where people carried out peaceful rallies indicative of the language of protests by civil society groups (Fig. 11).

And second, contrary to this, the protests in and around Jalandhar and other parts of Punjab took shape as the "vandalism" of public property –

[31] The Dera's connection with figures from the political class – such as the Bahujan Samaj Party founder Kanshi Ram, who was himself a Ramdassia Sikh from Punjab – and leaders from other political parties can be seen in the form of photographs displayed within the DSB.

[32] This can also be seen in the context of desecration of Ambedkar statues in Dalit localities, which are clearly instances of violence against the Dalit community. See Jain, "Taking and Making Offence".

Fig. 11: Protesters in 2009 in the UK holding placards that read "A Great Saint Ramanandji Killed by Control Freak Sikhs", with banners showing the attack on Dera gurus as "terrorism" and the death of Sant Ramanand as a "sacrifice". Source: https://ravidassia.wordpress. com/wallpapers/#jp-carousel-479.

as defined in the language of the state. However, acts of violence – such as the burning of the train coaches of the Himsagar Express at the Jalandhar Cantonment railway station, the burning of buses and other vehicles, and clashes with police forces (as we saw in Dhir's song) also represent a stigmatised response against the dominant groups' control over resources. What needs to be noted is that the violence was not carried out against any specific community or caste group. This kind of violent protest follows the language of what has been called "political society" and was largely misrepresented by the mainstream media as a riot between Dalits and Jat Sikh followers. These events, as performative and affective expressions, were enacted to convey feelings of injury, anger, and frustration to the larger public in Punjab and elsewhere.

Their violence, I suggest, also needs to be contextualised against the backdrop of the persistent suppression of Dalits by dominant castes over a long period of time. For instance, in 2003 caste violence was per-petrated against Ad Dharmi Dalits by Jats in Talhan village.[33] This hap-pened when Ad Dharmis demanded an equal share in the structures of power. Such instances show that despite instances of economic upward mobility by Dalits, the social discrimination against them persists. It is against such conditions within the Doaba region of Punjab that the forms of protest in Jalandhar should be understood – as symbolic out-bursts against a historical suppression of Dalits. By occupying the public domain, these Ravidassia followers resisted their vulnerability and the precarious position of humiliation they were put in by the assassination of their saint. As Judith Butler notes, "So, despite being aware that we are vulnerable . . . We come in a public platform to resist that precarity and in doing that we know while enacting that we are vulnerable. Also, we are exposing ourselves for attack, assault, of being killed, of teargas shells, and, still, we do enact that resistance."[34]

In these conditions that connect vulnerability and resistance, pro-testers participate despite knowing that their enactments of protest make them susceptible to state violence – evident, within the case dis-cussed, from the death of four protesters by police action. The images of four martyred Ravidassia protesters (Fig. 12) appeared in the mon-tage of protest images in Dhir's song, juxtaposed with the line "We will bravely bare our chests to face bullets."

The death of four Ravidassia Dalits in the protests against the as-sassination of Sant Ramanand, and the violent death of the Sant, were

[33] Talhan village has only 20 to 25 per cent Jats, while nearly 65 to 70 per cent of Chamar-caste Dalits are Ad Dharmis. Caste violence in 2003 between Ad Dharmis and Jats took place over the management of a jointly revered shrine – of Baba Nihal Singh – which was a heterodox shrine but which in the course of time turned into a Sikh gurdwara with mostly Jat Sikhs holding positions of power. Therefore, the Ad Dharmis of the village, despite having less share in landholding while being upwardly mobile, remained excluded from the processes of decision-making and the administrative body of the shrine. This demand for representa-tion by Dalits (since 1998) led to tensions between them and the Jats within the village, resulting in violence and the social boycott of Dalits, and leading thence to protests by Dalits in Jalandhar. For details see Jodhka, *Sikhism and the Caste Question*; and Ram, "Untouchability in India".

[34] See Butler, *Rethinking Vulnerability*.

Fig. 12: Photographs of martyred protesters – from left to right
Telu Ram, Vijay Kumar Dugal, Rajinder Kumar, and Balkar Singh.
Entitled "Ravidassia Qaum de Shaheed" (Martyrs of the
Ravidassia Community), this panel is displayed inside the
Dera Sachkhand Ballan, September 2012.

collectively articulated as *shahadat* (martyrdom). This occurred on
13 June 2009, during the Shraddhanjali Samagam (congregation to
pay tributes to the departed) at the DSB. Here, it was pronounced:
"For the *qaum brahmleen* (absorbed in god's love) Shri Sant Ramanand Maharaj was martyred, and to remember his martyrdom our
qaum's true selfless servants (*sachhe-suchhesevak*) could not bear the
sadness [of losing Sant Ramanand], and for their community they too
become martyrs."

This is not the first time that the Dera's followers were protesting
publicly against attacks on their respective Deras, fuelled by charges of
blasphemy from mainstream and radical Sikh organisations and individuals. The Vienna attack on DSB *sant*s indicates a general unease at
the ritual practices in Deras by mainstream and radical Sikh organisations that propound the ideology of a single and unified community of
Khalsa (pure) Sikhs. Therefore, the Vienna attack on the DSB needs to
be seen in conjunction with a series of prior controversies concerning the
Deras, such as Dera Sacha Sauda and Dera Bhaniarawala (henceforth
DSS and DB). It is noteworthy that most of the orthodox Sikh charges
of blasphemy against these Deras were centred on the nature of iconography, text, and ritual. For instance, in the DB controversy of 2001, the

Dera chief Piara Singh Bhaniarawala was accused of copying the image/ iconography of Guru Gobind Singh in his performative act of riding a horse. He was also accused of appropriating the *Granth Sahib* in his *Bhavsagar Samundar Granth*. In 2007 the DSS chief Gurmeet Ram Rahim Singh Insan was charged with copying and subverting the tenth Guru's iconography in terms of his attire and the baptism ritual performance of Jaam-e-Insan.[35] Both controversies led to protests and violent clashes between the respective Deras and the followers of radical Sikh groups.[36] In the 2007 controversy of DSS, protesters who were killed in clashes from both sides were declared martyrs by their respective religious communities.[37]

The Discourse of Martyrdom: Building a New Religion

The trope of martyrdom is often deployed in the politics of religious assertion and commemoration in Punjab. The act of policing the Dera's ritual and cultural practices by dominant Sikh groups stems from the viewpoint that these practices are "displacing" the "particularity" of meaning attached to Sikh religious practices and images. However, irrespective of each controversy's context, what this dominant viewpoint obliterates is the question of difference – the reconfiguration of given meanings, and the different ways of seeing within each Dera. This different perception represents a point of departure from the idea of "borrowings" out of the dominant traditions and their visual apparatus – as we have seen, for instance, in the Ravidassia understanding of the *Guru Granth Sahib*. The dominant view has attempted to define these persistently popular religious practices and religiosities as deviant precisely

[35] The etymological meaning of Jaam-e-Insan can be interpreted as a "drink that is this-worldly" and linked to humanity. On the other hand, the Sikh ritual of Amrit Sanchar, where Amrit literally means "deathless", is the eternal holy nectar, which can be considered as otherworldly. McLeod defines *amrit* as the nectar of "immortality". See McLeod, *The A to Z of Sikhism*, p. 12.

[36] For more detailed discussion around the DSS controversy, see Duggal, "The 'Vexed' Status", and Copeman, "The Mimetic Guru".

[37] To understand Sikh and DSS martyrs, see Baixas and Simon, "From Protestors to Martyrs", and Duggal, "Crossing Religious Boundaries".

because they have continued in the public domain despite the formal institutionalisation of Sikhism in the twentieth century. Before the coming of modern ideas of religion, the religious practices of Sikh *panth*s and Ravidassia *panth*s showed many shared features.

The charge of blasphemy by radical Sikhs resulting in Sant Ramanand's assassination has raised several questions: Who has legitimate hold over the *Guru Granth Sahib*? Do only Sikhs have the right to revere the *Granth*? Can the holy book be read and revered only by following the rituals of the *Sikh Rahit Maryada*? The alleged blasphemy is a clash of two views – the puritan Sikh view of the Khalsa which stresses the need to follow a code of conduct; and opposing this the Dalit Ravidassia view which identifies the *Granth* with the *bani* (voice) of Guru Ravidass. The need for their own *granth* emerged in the Ravidassia community subsequent to the implicit violence in the charge of blasphemy by Sikh radicals. For the same reason, the violence that led to Sant Ramanand's death was countered by the Ravidassia community with their definition of it as martyrdom. One can argue that blasphemy countered by martyrdom was responsible for the founding of the Ravidassia religion: the obvious analogue is Christianity where Christ, who claimed divine powers, was accused of blasphemy, leading to his crucifixion.

In the context of larger debates around the formation of religions, Talal Asad says that "[E]very new tradition, whether it is called religious or not, is founded in a discursive rupture – which means through a kind of violence."[38] However, Asad problematises this reason – which comes from an outside perspective (mostly that of historians) – by bringing in the view of a believer:

> In the foundation of Christianity, the blasphemy was not perceived as such by believers. From a Christian point of view, the charge of blasphemy was merely an expression of disbelief. And although that disbelief eventually led to Christ's death, Christians have historically held that the violence done to him was part of a divine plan . . . Strictly speaking, of course, what founded Christianity was not blasphemy itself but a new narrative of sacrifice and redemption – a story of martyrdom (witnessing) that would be, for believers, the door to eternal life.[39]

[38] See Asad, "Free Speech", p. 33.
[39] Ibid., p. 34.

The rhetoric of martyrs and martyrdom was deployed in the formation of the Ravidassia religion, post-Vienna, in the ceremonial congregations and practices involving the ritual of the Antim Darshan (last divine viewing) of Sant Ramanand, which foregrounded the community's sentiments that were voiced through their *sants* and leaders. In the present essay I have relied on one digital source, a DVD produced and distributed by the DSB, entitled *Antim Darshan, Asthi Kalash Yatra, Shraddhanjali Samagam* (Last Seeing, Procession of Last Remains and Homage Gathering).[40] At one level, the DVD functions as a "document", a well-arranged documentation of the event that is widely circulated and disseminated through several channels (from markets to the new media). However, at another level the DVD functions as a way of keeping this event alive in the community's history and memory through the precarious materiality of the medium. Here, the ritual of Antim Darshan gets transformed through the mediation where

> photographs and film footage as artefacts enable forms of mourning and remembrance that move away from the principles of disintegration and disappearance of the corpse and extend *muh dekhna* well beyond its encapsulation in a ritual moment. By its very nature the still and moving image captures and preserves the present of a moment, but also breaks with

[40] Darshan is a mode of interaction which means "'seeing and being seen' by the deity, but which also connotes a whole range of ideas relating to 'insight', 'knowledge', and 'philosophy'." See Pinney, *Photos of the Gods*, p. 9. The iconography of gods and spiritual figures in the form of statues, calendars, framed pictures, etc. is mainly "frontal, directly facing the worshipper, in accordance with the ritual imperative of darshan: both seeing and being in the presence of the iconic figure; a reciprocal encounter of gazes where being seen or blessed by the deity is as important as having votive access to it." See Jain, *Gods in the Bazaar*, p. 90. However, darshan in the context of seeing a dead guru and sant negates the possibility of the frontality and interaction of gazes between viewer and viewed. Here, in various South Asian religions, the ritual practice of *muh dekhna* (viewing the face of the dead) during the funeral and before cremation is part of the tradition. This is irrespective of whether there is a televised public viewing of the corpse of a famous historical, religious, or political figure, such as Indira Gandhi or Mother Teresa, or an intimate gathering of kinsmen who are viewing the dead body of their kin. *Muh dekhna* is an act of retaining the memory of the corpse in the minds of the viewers – whether they be devotees, followers, or kinsmen – in various South Asian religions. See Chopra, "Seeing Off the Dead".

the immediacy of a single moment of viewing, transforming the whole process of how we remember.[41]

And it is through the production, circulation and consumption of Antim Darshan in DVDs, with affective songs and music videos like Dir's "Panga", Virk's Sant Ramanand ji and many others foregrounding the martyrdom of Sant Ramanand, that the archive is not only reconfigured but the viewing is turned, as Radhika Chopra would say in the context of post-mortem photographs of Sikh militants, into a "political act".[42]

The video as document not only offers the viewer the experience of partaking in the last glimpse of Sant Ramanand through the camera's eye, it also gives a glimpse of the discourse, rhetoric, and deliberations that were undertaken before the formal declaration of the Ravidassia religion.

Fig. 13: Live projection of the dead body of Sant Ramanand to female followers who reached the Dera to attend the Antim Darshan and funeral on 4 June 2009. Here the viewer joins the rest of the mourners for a video-projected darshan of Sant Ramanand's body.

[41] Chopra, *Seeing Off the Dead*, p. 209.
[42] Ibid.

The last part of the video, titled "Shraddhanjali Samagam" (Homage Gathering), by the DSB sheds light on the nature of the Sant's martyrdom. Among the claims for martyrdom, the one made by Sant Surinder Dass Bawa insists: "Sant Ramanand throughout his life produced awakening, and in the end, on 25 May for society, for the nation. For the Shri Ravidass society, he partook of the drink of martyrdom (*shahadat da jam pinde*) and was absorbed in god's love (*brahmleen ho gaye*)."

Equating Sant Ramanand's martyrdom with the nation, society, and Ravidassia society, this speech made a connection between the specific and the universal, suggesting that the act of killing the saint was an act of terrorism because it was not just against the Dera but against the nation. Sant Surinder Dass Bawa urged the Ravidassia community to be united on a single platform so as to fulfil the *sant*'s mission for equality, brotherhood, and love among humans. Yet another *sant* stressed the need to remember Sant Ramanand as one who sacrificed himself for the backward (*pichhde*) and oppressed. However, the most radical voice that gave a call for unity to preserve the community's identity came undoubtedly from a UK diaspora representative, Harbans Lal Shonki, who was also a regular presenter on Kanshi TV. He articulated the need to follow religious ideals and principles in practice and questioned followers by emphasising the deprived state of the community:

> We hear *bani, kirtan, katha* and *parchar*. We listen, we read in some way or the other, but we don't follow them. If we had followed these, Ramanand wouldn't have been martyred . . . there is an urge to forge community. They [Sants like Ramanand] have done their work. Today it's your duty; it would be a failure if Sant Ramanand's martyrdom goes unnoticed. For Sant Ramanand's martyrdom's sake, we need to connect with the roots.

This idea of staying connected to roots demonstrates the significant role of the Dera's *sant*s in reconstructing Ravidass as an icon and forming a religious tradition through his poetry. Through the construction of a pilgrimage site, moreover, the Ravidassia community is now connected with Kashi, the birthplace of Ravidass (*kanshi de darbaar naal jodeya*). Hence, it can be posited that those who remain connected to roots flourish while others perish. In the end, Shonki urged his audience to understand the urgency of the moment, of the May 2009 Vienna martyrdom of the Dera Sant as a moment of grief, anger, and of crisis which required an urgent response: "If we want to pay tribute to Sant Ramanand from a true heart I request all babas, *sants*, the Ravidassia *qaum*, and the Ad Dharmis who are sitting here: if even today we don't unite under one flag, our name will vanish." His speech highlighted the need for a united religious movement, or, in short, a proper religion.

One can assert that, aside from the development of Ravidassia religiosity, the identity of being a Ravidassia is fluid.[43] For instance, despite having Guru Ravidass as their main guru, the followers remain within the folds of Sikhism, Hinduism, and Ad Dharm. And this fluidity is evident within religious practices inside the DSB temple complex where they continue to revere the *Guru Granth Sahib* as their core text and use it in their rituals. At the same time the DSB felt it necessary to develop independent religious identity markers for the Ravidassia religion. It had the example of the Ad Dharm movement in the 1920s which had distanced itself from the Sikh religious text through its religious devotion to Ravidass. Therefore, the imperative of creating their own *Granth* emerged after their saint was attacked and they were accused of blasphemy.

External threats such as possible attacks on Dera *sants* and their following were brought into focus by the Vienna incident. Defence preparations entailed ensuring internal unity by visibly bringing together all the dispersed religiosities within the Chamar caste under one flag – an overarching identity for Ravidassias. It was through these deliberations within the Guru Ravidass religiosities that the Ravidassia religion, in the formal sense of the term, came into being. In less than a year's time, on 30 January 2010, during the occasion of Guru Ravidass' birth anniversary, the formation and declaration of the Ravidassia religion (*Ravidassia Dharm ka elaannama*, Fig. 14) happened with the release of the holy *Granth Guru Ravidass Amritbani*, which contains the Ravidass *bani* (teachings) extracted from the *Guru Granth Sahib*.

[43] This can be historically contextualised after the Poona Pact, when the Ad Dharm religion had to give up its status as an independent religion – because to get the benefits of reservation they had to identify themselves with Hinduism. At a later juncture, though, the Sikh religion (being the first non-Hindu religion) ensured reservation for Dalit converts such as the Ravidassias and Mazhabi Sikhs.

श्री गुरु रविदास जन्म स्थान मंदिर सीर गोवर्धनपुर, वाराणसी (यू.पी.) में जगतगुरु रविदास महाराज जी के 633वें प्रकाश पर्व पर श्री 103 संत निरंजन दास महाराज जी हज़ारों की संख्या में संत समाज एवं विश्व के कोने-कोने से पधारे लाखों की संख्या में श्रद्धालु संगतों की हाज़री में रविदासिया धर्म की पावन पुस्तक ''अमृतवाणी सतगुरु रविदास महाराज जी'' रिलीज़ करते हुए।

Fig. 14: Release of the *Guru Ravidass Amritbani* on the occasion of
Guru Ravidass' birth anniversary on 30 January 2010 at Seer
Goverdhanpur (the centre of pilgrimage for the Ravidassia religion),
Varanasi.

The lines on the displayed picture (Fig. 15) on the right of Sant
Ramanand say:

> When the earth and the skies tremble, when the page of history opens,
> that world worships where the blood of martyrs falls.

This highlights the historic moment of the foundation of the Ravidassia religion while the image displayed next to Sant Ramanand charts
out the principles of the newly founded religion as pedagogic rules.
The quoted lines establish a genealogy with several religious figures
who have had their blood spilled for the sake of their religion. Interestingly, a similar link can be drawn with the Sikh rhetoric of martyrs and
martyrdom. As Louis Fenech explains it:

> What is indeed fundamental to the idea, as the word "shahid" or witness de-
> notes, is resistance [to oppression] and defiance [of tyranny] . . . "as a wit-
> ness he [the martyr] is, as it were, on the offensive against the persecuting

Fig. 15: Displayed pictures showing the principles of the newly formed Ravidassia religion with a photo of *Qaum ke Mahaan shaheed* (Community's Great Martyr) Sant Ramanand. Ravidass Janam Asthan Mandir, Seer Goverdhanpur, Varanasi, February 2013.

power." Implicit in the present-day idea of shahid, in other words, is that which is testified against, namely oppression. The shahid is one who dies heroically, testifying to his or her faith on the path of God. It is this emphasis which is undeniably at the very core of the contemporary Sikh understanding of the Shahid.[44]

∽

[44] See Fenech, *Martyrdom in the Sikh Tradition*, pp. 6–7.

A rhetoric of martyrs and martyrdom began taking specific shape at the end of the nineteenth century and became what we understand today as the dominant version of Sikhism via the work of the Singh Sabha movement, which played an important role in the formation of an independent Sikh identity and community. Ironically, the important aspect in the formation of the Ravidassia religion is that their oppressors have been Sikh radicals from the orthodoxy. The trope of martyrdom with its invocation through several cultural forms has played an important role in mobilising the Sikh community throughout its modern history. And so it continues, even into contemporary times.[45] Such tropes have been reconfigured by the Ravidassias as a weapon to formally counter and dissociate themselves from all related religious identities and ambiguities.

Ravidassia, the subsequent new religion is, as we have seen, in a continuous process of remaking. It has, I believe, potentially reached a climax through its reliance on the trope of martyrdom. However, this undoing of normative religious understandings in Ravidassia religiosity forms the crux of Sikh objections that enfold and unfold a larger problem which is reflective of the crisis within the Sikh community and identity, namely that, as a consequence of the caste practices of Sikhs, many non-Sikh Deras have a large following of Dalits and lower-caste communities. This has been popularised through various academic and media discourses. In fact, all the aforementioned "controversial" Deras have a large Dalit and lower-caste following; the Guru of Dera Bhaniarawala is Dalit while the Guru of Dera Sacha Sauda is a Jat with a majority following of Dalits and lower castes. These controversies, I have argued, through their charges of blasphemy not only made the visibilisation of caste and casteism possible in the state of Punjab, but also further demystified the idyllic image of Punjab and the Sikh religion as egalitarian. Caste discrimination within Sikhism has been long known but widely unacknowledged, and the participation of Dalits and other Sikhs in non-Sikh Deras has pushed this contradiction into

---

[45] The attribution of martyrdom via the term *shaheed* is common to several contemporary figures from the community, dead or alive, such as (Sant) Jarnail Singh Bhindranwale and Zinda Shaheed Balwant Singh Rajoana.

the open.[46] From the dominant Sikh view, Deras are the Other, they represent divisive forces against Sikhism. And the continuous violence against Dera gurus and their followers can be seen as desperate acts from (Jat-dominated) Sikhs to enforce their dominant ideas of religion and bring "deviant" Dera Sikh followers back into the Sikh fold. This has only resulted in a further consolidation of these Deras – as we have seen with the formation of the Ravidassia religion.

It is useful to invoke the work of Kajri Jain who, drawing from Anupama Rao, notes in her work on Mayawati's monuments that "anti-Dalit violence becomes 'a locus for further politicizing Dalit identity'. This politics reoccupies corporeal grounds, such that new forms of embodied violence continue to define Dalit personhood."[47] I see this in the consolidation of Ravidassia religious identity, which is an outcome of caste-religious antagonism performed through blasphemy. Therefore, the countervisuality in Chamar/Ravidassia religion and (visual) cultural practices foregrounded through the articulation of martyrdom challenges not only the hegemony of dominant caste-religious forces but also exposes their contradictions. This "right to look", manifested through Chamar/Ravidassia songs, rituals, and temples, performs the role of fulfilling and reclaiming denied rights and desires as part of the process of religious formation; this is, in short, the right to possess and practise one's own religion.

References

Asad, Talal, "Free Speech, Blasphemy and Secular Criticism", in T. Asad, W. Brown, J. Butler, and S. Mahmood, *Is Critique Secular? Blasphemy, Injury, and Free Speech* (Berkeley: University of California Press, 2009).

Baixas, Lionel, and Charlene Simon, "From Protestors to Martyrs: How to Become a 'True' Sikh", *South Asia Multidisciplinary Academic Journal*, no. 2. 2008, accessed 16 January 2021, https://journals.openedition.org/samaj/1532.

Butler, Judith, "Rethinking Vulnerability and Resistance", June 2014, accessed 27 February 2015, http://www.institutofranklin.net/sites/default/

---

[46] See Duggal, "The 'Vexed' Status of Guru Images", pp. 108–9.
[47] See Jain, "The Handbag that Exploded", p. 159.

files/files/Rethinking%20Vulnerability%20and%20Resistance%20 Judith%20Butler.pdf.

Chopra, Radhika, "Seeing Off the Dead: Post-mortem Photographs in the Darbar Sahib", *Sikh Formations*, vol. 12, no. 2–3, 2016.

Copeman, Jacob, "The Mimetic Guru: Tracing the Real in Sikh-Dera Sacha Sauda Relations", in Jacob Copeman and Aya Ikegame, eds, *The Guru in South Asia* (New York: Routledge, 2012).

Dhir, Roop Lal, "Panga", *Hummer-Charhat Chamaran Di*, Smi Audio Video, 2010, YouTube, accessed 15 September 2015, https://www.youtube. com/watch?v=tbVcptVp5Qs.

Duggal, Koonal, "Crossing Religious Boundaries: Representation, Caste and Identity in Contemporary Punjab", unpublished dissertation, Hyderabad, The English and Foreign Languages University, 2015.

Duggal, Koonal, "The 'Vexed' Status of Guru Images: Visuality, Circulation and Iconographic Conflicts", *South Asian Popular Culture*, vol. 20, no. 1, 2022.

Fenech, Louis E., *Martyrdom in the Sikh Tradition: Playing the Game of Love* (New Delhi: Oxford University Press, 2000).

Jain, Kajri, *Gods in the Bazaar: The Economies of Indian Calendar Art* (Durham: Duke University Press, 2007).

Jain, Kajri, "Taking and Making Offence: Husain and the Politics of Desecration", in Sumathi Ramaswamy, ed., *Barefoot Across the Nation* (New York: Routledge, 2011).

Jain, Kajri, "The Handbag that Exploded: Mayawati's Monuments and the Aesthetics of Democracy in Post-Reform India", in Partha Chatterjee, Tapati Guha-Thakurta, and Bodhisattva Kar, eds, *New Cultural Histories of India: Materiality and Practices* (New Delhi: Oxford University Press, 2014).

Jodhka, Surinder S., "Sikhism and the Caste Question: Dalits and Their Politics in Contemporary Punjab", *Contributions to Indian Sociology*, vol. 38, no. 1–2, 2004.

Jodhka, Surinder S., "From Zaat to Qaum: Fluid Contours of the Ravi Dasi Identity in Punjab", in Ramnarayan S. Rawat and K. Satyanarayana, eds, *Dalit Studies* (Durham and London: Duke University Press, 2016).

Jodhka, Surinder S., and Avinash Kumar, "Internal Classification of Scheduled Castes: The Punjab Story", *Economic and Political Weekly*, vol. 42, no. 43, 2007.

Jodhka, Surinder S., "Of Babas and Deras", *Seminar*, vol. 581, 2008.

Jodhka, Surinder S., "The Ravi Dasis of Punjab: Global Contours of Caste and Religious Strife", *Economic and Political Weekly*, vol. 44, no. 24, 2009.

Juergensmeyer, Mark, *Religious Rebels in the Punjab* (New Delhi: Navayana, 2009).

Mahaprashasta, Ajoy Ashirwad, "Inflamed Passions", *Frontline*, 26 December 2006–9 June 2009, accessed 30 April 2010, http://www.frontline.in/static/html/fl2612/stories/20090619261203300.htm.

McLeod, Hew, *The A to Z of Sikhism* (Lanham, Maryland: Scarecrow Press, 2009).

Moffat, Chris, *India's Revolutionary Inheritance: Politics and Promise of Bhagat Singh* (Cambridge: Cambridge University Press, 2019).

Mirzoeff, Nicholas, *The Right to Look: A Counterhistory of Visuality* (London and Durham: Duke University Press, 2011).

Oberoi, Harjot, *The Construction of Religious Boundaries: Culture, Identity and Diversity in the Sikh Tradition* (Delhi: Oxford University Press, 1994).

Pinney, Christopher, *Photos of the Gods: The Printed Image and Political Struggle in India* (London: Reaktion Books, 2004).

Ram, Ronki, "Untouchability in India with a Difference: Ad Dharm, Dalit Assertion, and Caste Conflicts in Punjab", *Asian Survey*, vol. 44, no. 6, 2004.

Ram, Ronki, "Ravidass Deras and Social Protest: Making Sense of Dalit Consciousness in Punjab (India)", *The Journal of Asian Studies*, vol. 67, no. 4, 2008.

Rawat, Ramnarayan S., *Reconsidering Untouchability: Chamars and Dalit History in North India* (Bloomington: Indiana University Press, 2011).

Singh, Kulraj, trans., *The Code of Conduct and Conventions* (Amritsar: Dharam Parchar Committee, n.d.).

Singh, Surinder, "Deras, Caste Conflicts and Recent Violence in Punjab", *Mainstream*, vol. 26, 13 June 2009, accessed 15 September 2015, http://www.mainstreamweekly.net/article1425.html.

Singh, Gurharpal, Charlene Simon, and Darshan Sigh Tatla, "New Forms of Religious Transnationalism and Development Initiatives: A Case Study of Dera Sant Sarwan Dass, Ballan, Punjab, India", Religions and Development Working Paper 52, 2010, accessed 3 September 2011, http://www.rad.bham.ac.uk.

Singh, Santosh K, "The Caste Question and Songs of Protest in Punjab", *Economic and Political Weekly*, vol. 52, no. 34, 2017.

Snehi, Yogesh, "From Ram Tirath to Valmiki Tirath: The Making of Valmiki Religious Identity in Amritsar", *Nidān: International Journal for Indian Studies*, vol. 8, no. 1, 2023.

Suman, Chain Ram, *Miracles of Jagatguru Ravidass Ji* (Banaras: Shri Guru Ravidass Janam Sthan Mandir, n.d.).

Tartakov, Gary, "Art and Identity: The Rise of a New Buddhist Imagery", *Art Journal*, vol. 49, no. 4, 1990.
Virk, Amrita, and Shehzada Ragav Mahi, "Sant Ramanand Ji", *Prabhat Pheri Mata Kalsa De Lal Di* (Goyal Music, 2011).

Acknowledgements

This essay was presented at the International Dalit Studies Conference at CSDS (Delhi) in 2018. I thank its discussant, Shail Mayaram, and others there for their helpful comments. I am grateful to Ramnarayan Rawat, K. Satyanarayana, Santhosh Sadanandan, Hugo Gorringe, Lotte Hoek, and Lotte Segal for their many invaluable and perceptive comments and suggestions. I would also like to acknowledge Ria De, Sneha Ragavan, Kavita Bhanot, and James Mooney for their helpful feedback.

6

Oppression, Resistance, and the Formation of a Faith Community among the Dalit Christians of Kerala

JESTIN T. VARGHESE

Introduction

I N THE WAKE OF reason and science, it was widely believed that in daily life religion had become more concerned with moral values than God, and that religious faith would be undermined in a secularising society.[1] But contemporary scholars have argued that the twentieth-century experience has disproved this belief,[2] and that the intellectual justification of religious faith has become very central to contemporary concerns.[3] It is in this larger context that I analyse Dalit Christianity in contemporary Kerala.

I am grateful to Professor P. Sanal Mohan, my PhD supervisor, for his exceptional guidance and support throughout my research and the development of this paper. I am grateful to Peter Mathew for his support during the fieldwork and to Anish R. for his encouragement and support of my research. I am also grateful to Professors K. Satyanarayana, Ramnarayan S. Rawat, and Joy Pachuau; to the participants of the Dalit Studies Conference 2018; and to Professor Corrine Dempsey for critical comments on my essay. My wife Anupama and daughter Norah deserve my thanks for their care and love.

[1] Mair, *An Introduction*, p. 200.
[2] Asad, *Genealogies of Religion*.
[3] Joas, *Faith as an Option*, p. 2.

Dalit Christianity in the context of Kerala offers an intellectual justification for embracing Christianity as their religion by Dalits. In Dalit
Christianity God is conceived as the Saviour who rescues Dalits from
worldly sufferings caused by structural oppression. However, several
studies on Dalit "conversion" in India have failed to engage with the question of the faith and the agency of Dalit Christians in accepting Christianity. Academic knowledge and popular understanding represent
Dalit Christians as "inauthentic" and attribute conversion to material
advantages, duress, and patronage.[4] More importantly, the same argument is reproduced in official documents, legislative acts, and state policies. The dominant views on Dalit Christians show no change despite
the passage of time.[5] This essay attempts a critical analysis of the social
world of Dalit Christians from a bottom-up perspective and uncovers
the formation of a faith community in the context of oppression. It also
questions dominant knowledge and the insulting perceptions that have
been constructed by "higher-caste" Christians about Dalit Christians.

As descendants of the untouchable "slave castes" – such as the Pulaya,
Paraya, Kurava, and Cherumar – Dalits converted to Christianity in
the early nineteenth century.[6] The Protestant missions, including the
Church Mission Society (CMS), the London Missionary Society, and the

[4] The discussion on "authenticity" of conversion was a part of Hindu nationalist politics in India. For a detailed analysis, see Viswanath, "The Emergence
of Authenticity". Also see ch. 4 in Roberts, *To Be Cared For*; Alexander, "Caste
and Christianity", pp. 551–60; and Kooiman, *Conversion and Social Equality*.

[5] For example, in 2017 a Syrian Christian MLA (Member of the Legislative Assembly) made derogatory comments on Dalit Christians in front of the media.
"PC George Abusing Pulayas", YouTube Video, anonymous, 1:31, 14 August
2020, https://www.youtube.com/watch?v=pF3ELYmUvnU, accessed 14 January
2021. In 2018 a Dalit Christian boy was murdered by a Syrian Christian family
for marrying a girl from that family; "Kevin Murder a Case of Honour Killing",
The Hindu, accessed 20 August 2020, https://www.thehindu. com/news/
national/kerala/ kevin-murder-a-case-of-honour-killing/article29223133.ece.

[6] The term "slave caste" denotes the differences between modern slavery of the
Blacks and the system of caste slavery in Kerala. Caste slavery had social, religious,
and philosophical consent for its combination of caste and slavery. For a detailed
analysis of caste slavery and slavery in the Atlantic world, see ch. 2 in Mohan,
Modernity of Slavery; also see Saradamoni, *Emergence of a Slave Caste*.

Basel Mission, provided a religious space for Dalits. Others joined en masse during the work of Catholic missions such as the Chirackal Pulaya Mission in northern Malabar, which was part of the British Malabar presidency. The slaves had made several attempts to join the CMS Mission even before it started accepting the slave castes.[7] It has been noted that the slave-owning communities either tortured Dalit groups for choosing emancipation through Christianity or treated them as "Christian slaves" who worked "sincerely" and earned for their masters.[8] Traditional Syrian Christians, as a slave-owning community, refused to treat slave-Christians differently and continued to oppress them. They used a derogatory term, "Puthukristhyanikal" (Neo-Christians), for Dalit Christians to emphasise their "lack" of a base in Christian tradition. Thus, the "conversion" of the slave castes was accompanied by caste-based discrimination by "traditional" Christians.

In fact, "the Syrians have a history of power and privilege which dates from many centuries before the coming of European rule."[9] But the hagiographical construction of St Thomas in Syrian Christian tradition claims that Syrian Christians are descendants of Brahmins christened by St Thomas, one of the apostles of Christ who came to Kerala in AD 52. Another group of Syrian Christians identify themselves as the descendants of Thomas of Cana and consider themselves the most pure-blooded race among Christians today: they are known as Knanaya Christians.[10] Historians have disproved the story of St Thomas and Brahmin conversions, but Syrian Christians continue to believe in this story to legitimise their Brahmin origin and caste supremacy in the Church. Elite families among the Syrian Christians of Kerala trace their origins to one of the five families supposedly christened by St Thomas. T.M. Yesudasan, criticising the Syrian Christian supremacy in the Church of South India, satirically terms this tendency the "Pakalomattam Complex".[11] Pakalomattam is the name of one of the five families.

By asserting a Brahmin origin story to their conversion to Christianity, Syrian Christians show a remarkable similarity with caste-Hindus

---

[7] Yesudasan, *Baliyadukalude Vamshavali*, p. 35.

[8] Kawashima, *Missionaries and a Hindu State*, pp. 157–8.

[9] Bayly, *Saints, Goddesses and Kings*, p. 243.

[10] Ibid., p. 246.

[11] Yesudasan, *Chettitheruvile Dwishadabdhikal.*

on the question of caste. Currently, there are several church denominations in Kerala. In their organisational structure, most of these churches show separate dioceses, separate churches, and even separate cemeteries for Dalits and Syrian Christians, substantiating and reinforcing the fact of hierarchy and caste divisions among them. It is in this context that the present essay is situated.

Karikkottakkari: An Overview of the Village

My fieldwork was conducted in January 2015, September–October 2016, and May–September 2018 in two Dalit Christian Catholic congregations in Kottukappara and Parakkappara of Karikkottakkari, a village in the Kannur District of Kerala. Peter Mathew, a Dalit Christian activist and member of the community, helped by conducting additional interviews with elder members of the community who had migrated in the 1950s. My arguments here are supplemented with data available in the Audio Visual Archives of the SSRC-NDSP project 2012–14 at the Inter University Centre for Social Science Research and Extension (IUCSSRE).[12] My central focus is the caste conflict between "higher-caste" Syrian Christians and Dalit Christians in the 1950s that resulted in forming the Kottukappara and Parakkappara congregations. Karikkottakkari is a village located in the eastern part of Kannur, the northern district which under colonial rule was part of British Malabar. The village consists of 500 Dalit Christian households in two exclusive Dalit Catholic parishes, one being the Our Lady of Lourdes Church Kottukappara established in 1962, and the other being the Karunyamatha Church Parakkappara founded in 1977. The village of Karikkottakkari was itself established by Syrian Christian farmers in the late 1930s, when they migrated to it from Kottayam District in southern Kerala.

For nearly a decade these migrants walked six kilometres to attend church at a nearby village. In 1954 the Syrian Christians and the Dalit

---

[12] This archive comprises ethnographic interviews of elderly Dalits, collected as part of a project supported by SSRC New York called "New Directions in the Study of Prayer" (NDSP) at the IUCSSRE, Mahatma Gandhi University, Kottayam, Kerala.

Christians founded the St Thomas Syrian Church, with the two groups parting company in 1959. In 1962 the Dalit congregation set up its own church. Almost simultaneously, Dalit Christians migrated from Kottayam to Karikkottakkari in search of land and livelihood – most were Catholic Christians at the time they migrated. One can view the migration of Dalit Christians of this region as a collective movement, a willed escape from caste slavery and oppression by landlords, and as a search for a better, dignified life in the period following the abolition of slavery.[13]

Dalit Christians protested the exclusionary practices of Syrian Christians in the newly formed St Thomas Church. Although subordinated as former slave labourers to upper-caste Syrian Christians, Dalit Christians had begun to exhibit a new assertive identity as marginal peasants with landownership in Karikkottakkari. This led to tensions in the parish and the spaces of the church came to be contested along caste lines. The ensuing contestation spread to all aspects of social and religious life. The conflict came to an explosive head in the wake of the infamous "liberation struggle" (Vimochana Samaram) of 1958–9 led by propertied and elite groups in Kerala, including Syrian Christians and upper-caste Hindus, against the first elected government in Kerala led at the time by the Communist Party. The Syrian Christian-led Church in Kerala had issued pastoral letters to propagate and struggle against the government, arguing that the policies of the government in the spheres of education and land reforms were against the Church.[14] The Dalit Christians, though, were convinced of the transformative potential of the new government policies and refused to join the elite struggle. Nor did the Dalit Christians lend support to the government's policies through a movement: given the precariousness of their conditions, they continued as daily-wage labourers. Despite this, Syrian Christians, with the blessing of the Church authorities, unleashed a reign of terror on Dalit Christians, abusing them as communists with no faith in God.

[13] Even though slavery in Travancore was abolished by law in 1855, the practice continued until at least the 1930s. The related practices of slavery and untouchability continued until the early decades of India's independence.

[14] See for details, Salim, "The First Popular Government in Kerala".

According to local informants from the Kottukappara and Parakkappara congregations, during this "liberation struggle" Syrian Christian violence over Dalit Christians was boundless and exceeded all limits. Syrian Christian gangs patrolled the public roads day and night and assaulted every black person, identifying them as Dalit. Such violence occurred even within the church premises. The priest at St Thomas Church blessed wooden sticks that he distributed among his Syrian Christian congregation – to beat up Dalit Christians with.[15] Dalit Christian households suffered even higher levels of poverty and hunger on account of the prolonged absence of men who were forced by marauding Syrian Christian gangs into hiding at places distant from their homes. Dalit Christian women and children, already destitute, were further traumatised by illnesses and crop failure, there being no one to harvest the crops.[16] At this stage Dalit Christian women showed exceptional leadership because, in spite of the threat of violence from Syrian Christian men, they decided to find where their own men were hiding and rescue them from exile. These women were abused and humiliated by upper-caste "volunteers" when they appeared in public in search of their men.

During the peak of this Syrian Christian oppression in 1959, Dalit Christians left the St Thomas parish en masse and separated themselves from the Christian community in the village. After about six months they approached an Italian Jesuit missionary at the Chirackal Catholic Mission, Fr. Joseph Tafferel, S.J., famous for his interventions in saving the oppressed Pulaya Christians of Malabar. Fr. Taffarel was a missionary of the Society of Jesus who had worked for Fr. Peter Caironi, also of the same missionary organisation: the latter had established the Chirackal Catholic Mission in Malabar in the late 1930s.[17] Taffarel gladly accepted the invitation and established a mission station at Kottukappara, offering a safe zone to Dalit Christians. This mission station was

[15] Interviews with Chacko Mekkuttiyil (aged 70) Peter Mathew (aged 71), Michael (aged 62), and Savior Palakudiyil (Aged 80) between 29 September and 26 October 2016.

[16] Mathew, "Interview with Kuriakkose Tharoth".

[17] This mission had made credible transformations in Pulaya lives in Chirackal and other coastal areas of Malabar. See for details Taffarel, *Jottings of a Poor Missionary*.

not far from St Thomas Church, Karikkottakkari. A Dalit Christian community soon flourished there under the leadership of Fr. Taffarel, apparently with a fullness of life in which faith was central. Sanal Mohan has argued that the schools for the schools for slave castes in the CMS Mission centres of Travancore were social and cultural spaces of freedom for these groups.[18] It became clear that, in the context of their historical and structural oppression, the establishment of an alternative social sphere and religious space by Dalit Christians was foundational to the flourishing of their own community and spirituality.

The Formation of a Faith Community

Anthropological studies of Christianity have shown its transformative power via creating ruptures in the indigenous and dominant cultural pasts of "converts".[19] Analysing the history of Dalit Christianity in Kerala we find various dimensions to these ruptures, the most obvious of which is their crucial role in creating a new community among the Dalits who joined one of the various Christian missions. A rupture is necessary to the formulation of a new spiritual world which is the promise of some of the desired life changes. The arrival of this new spirituality has played a key role in resistance to oppression and in the formation of community life. M. Merrill highlights the centrality of spirituality: "In many ways, spirituality is the application of beliefs and propositions, not just the theoretical formulation. To be spiritual is to put into daily, lived practice the values and doctrines one has. It is to take the teachings of an institution and live out those teachings in praxis."[20]

Elderly Dalit Christians noted that Dalit Christian leaders like V.D. John referred repeatedly to a Biblical verse which goes: "Here are my mother and my brothers. For whoever does the will of my Father in heaven is my brother and sister and mother." Peter Mathew recollects V.D. John having planned meticulously for the social movement he led. In Mathew's view the virtues that John wished for were attainable only if the followers of the movement executed his plans.[21] Discussing the history of cultural resistance, Stephen Duncombe situates the relationship

[18] Mohan, "Creation of Social Space".
[19] Robbins, "Transcendence and the Anthropology of Christianity".
[20] Merrill, "Personal Spirituality", vol. 3, p. 46.
[21] V.D. John founded the Backward Class Christian Federation (BCCF)

between cultural resistance and community development by pointing out that cultural forms of resistance, "unless translated into political action, become 'imaginary' solutions to real-world problems and create 'magical' communities in the place of real ones."[22]

The formation of a faith community based on the modern Christian worldview has been the most important form of resistance that Dalit Christians have mounted against caste discrimination, injustice in the Church, and in society at large. As Richard Sennet has argued, Christian faith and values have been the major resources of the community in this resistance: Dalit Christian faith and spirituality are formed and renewed in the context of the dominant oppressive structures. According to Sennet, "[R]esistance only exists in relation to the dominant power and without that dominant power, resistance has no coherence or purpose."[23]

The social memory of Dalit Christians in Kottukappara and Parakkappara congregations highlights the structural barriers against their new spiritual community formation, which began with their conversion in the late nineteenth century in Travancore and following their migration to Malabar. Later too, in the second half of the twentieth century, there was severe opposition to the formation of a faith community of Dalit Christians in the Catholic parishes. Reading or interpreting the Bible was strictly forbidden, with a high penalty on violators. Peter Mathew remembers the experience of his grandfather's brother who was beaten on his knees by a Syrian Christian priest for reading the Bible.[24] This scene was repeated in many places in Catholic congregations in twentieth-century Travancore.[25] The denial to Dalits of the knowedge of Christian doctrines was a precautionary measure by "higher-caste" Christians against Dalits forming their own critical worldview and

---

and became instrumental, along with Fr. N. Stephan, for the legitimate claim of reservations for Dalit Christians in government jobs and education in Kerala. For details see John, *Ente Jeevithavum Kalavum*.

[22] Duncombe, "(From) Cultural Resistance to Community Development".

[23] Ibid., p. 497.

[24] Interview with Peter Mathew, 29 September 2016.

[25] NDSP interviews reveal that this practice was common in Catholic parishes. Audio Visual Archives of NDSP Project at Inter University Centre for Social Science Research and Extension, Mahatma Gandhi University.

generating a community rooted in that new perspective. Learning the scriptures is the basis of achieving "revelation" by the oppressed – as noted by many scholars who have studied the uses of religion among the oppressed. According to R.A. Bennett, the "Bible as revealed word . . . tries to communicate something about the purposeful ordering of society as a sign of God's intentions for his creation. The literature of the old and new Israel is religious literature because it witnesses to God as the one not only creating but also maintaining and forcefully working out freedom for the oppressed in a community for the alien or alienated."[26]

By disregarding the history of discrimination in the Travancore churches, Dalit Christians continued their attempts to form a common congregational life in St Thomas Church, Karikkottakkari, by engaging in church activities, including the conducting of an annual feast and observance of the sacraments. They also provided the church their labour for the construction of a new church building. As one informant put it, Dalits "worked with pride" to show that they were no less than anyone else when it came to affairs of the Church.[27] Despite this, in the recollection of Dalit Christian informants the priests of the Syrian church were much too emphatic on the need for sacramental discipline by Dalit children – an expression of their biased perception that Dalit Christians were not committed to the faith. The real problem in the early phase of Dalit migration was their extreme poverty, not to mention illness and other obstacles such as the lack of ready cash for contingencies. In this context, the observation of sacramental requirements by church-going children was far from easy: preparing them for the sacrament of confirmation with its ritual paraphernalia and white clothing was beyond the means of nearly all Dalit families. Chacko recollects this difficulty and says his parents managed to somehow get him a white shirt for his confirmation day.[28] Moreover, there were notable personalities within the community who were well versed in all the Catholic prayers. By this time, in the 1950s, such people had managed leading

---

[26] Bennett, "Black Experience and the Bible", quoted in Loue, *Understanding Theology*, p. 16.

[27] Mathew, "Interview with Kuriakkose Tharoth".

[28] Ethnographic interview with Chacko Mekkuttiyil, aged 70, at his residence in Ayyankunnu, Karikkottakkari on 4 October 2016.

positions for themselves in the spiritual affairs of the community. They were also in the forefront of other community activities, providing leadership to the resistance movement against the caste oppression unleashed by Syrian Christians in the wake of the "liberation struggle".

In all these ways Dalits were extending their new Christian community spirit, acquired in the first instance as their inheritance – the values and doctrines that they had learned over many generations. Their new activities and engagements showed that their resolve against caste rules communicated to the larger society their desire for all that symbolised a good Christian life. They were careful to observe rituals and sacraments properly, and in order to transform their identity and image they demonstrated their devotion through more than merely habitual acts.

In the history of Dalit Christianity religion comprises not just moral codes but also takes the form of political codes rooted in the history of resistance. The engagement of Dalit Christians in political struggle provided the congregation an opportunity to change themselves into a Christian brotherhood. This also demonstrated that Dalits had no hesitation living out an autonomous Christian spirituality while following Christian values in their daily life and lived practice. This argument is contrary to the observations of the sociologist K.C. Alexander, who suggests that Dalits "lack deep conviction in Christianity" and "do not like a joint congregational or denominational life."[29] Affirmations of faith in the context of discrimination and oppression by fellow Christians can in fact be the most valid form of Christianity.

Faith versus Caste: Foundational Factors for a Dalit Christian Faith Community

According to Louis Dumont, the separations among various castes and the idea of the impurity of the lower castes have survived conversion.[30] He views the impurity associated with untouchables as "permanent", and the idea of pollution for the higher castes as "a matter of eventual fall of social status or risk of such a fall."[31] Analysing the Dalit Christian

---

[29] Alexander, "Caste and Christianity in Kerala".
[30] Dumont, *Homo Hierarchicus*, p. 205.
[31] Ibid., pp. 47–53.

experience in the Kottukappara and Parakkappara congregations, and elsewhere in Kerala, it is obvious that the "higher-caste" Syrian Christians have replicated Hindu fears of pollution by keeping Dalits away from sacred spaces in churches. They resisted the very presence of Dalit Christians inside the church – opposing them listening to sermons and receiving sacraments, including Eucharist and confession. Chacko recalls that during Eucharist Dalit Christian children, including he himself, were forcibly removed from the front row as it was close to the altar.[32] He claimed that Syrian Christians "would not allow us to kneel down in front of their God! So, during those times we could only stand outside the church."[33] There were incidents of Dalit Christian corpses being removed from their graves and disposed of elsewhere because "presumably [they] threatened to defile" the Syrian Christian cemetery.[34] Such incidents were noted in the 1930s, 1990s, and most recently in 2019 when the burial of a Dalit was delayed for a month because the Dalit family resisted burying the body near the ablutions area of the cemetery.[35] The notion of the Dalit Christian as untouchable continues and is rearticulated in relation to those who should enjoy equal status under the shelter of the Church.

Most Syrian Christians in Karikkottakkari, as elsewhere in Kerala, view the impurity of the untouchable castes as permanent, an irredeemable feature of their very being. As strong supporters of a tradition in which they have an imagined connection with Brahmins, they validate their view of Dalit Christians also via tradition – the untouchables are seen by them to belong to the tradition of slavery. This caste consciousness persists despite the concepts of secular education, constitutional democracy, and Christian interpretations of equality. In the larger ideological context, however, liberation theology and Dalit

---

[32] According to Chacko, high-caste children in the same row pushed them back with their elbows and those who were behind them pinched them until they moved out of the church. Interview with Chacko Mekkuttiyil on 4 October 2016.

[33] Ibid.

[34] Yesudasan, "The Upper Caste Tip of a Dalit Pyramid", postscript in Koshy, *Caste in the Kerala Churches*.

[35] "Discrimination and Victimisation".

theology have posed serious challenges to the institutionalisation of caste discrimination in the Church. The penetration of these theologies in Syrian Christian consciousness have forced them to modify and re-formulate the fundamental idea of caste, which instead of stressing the "impurity of untouchables" shifts to viewing them as less cultured or as naturally and inherently uncivilised. Stereotyping contributes to the distancing and separation of Dalit Christians from higher-caste Syrian Christians.

Racist slurs are another dimension of this ring-fencing of one church-going community from another. Addressing Dalits as "Poocha" (cat) and "Poochakristhyani" (Cat Christian) was common and resulted in many violent brawls in Karikkottakkari as well as in the villages of Travancore. The term "poocha" is a reminder to Dalits of an enslaved past during which the behavioural characteristics of a slave and a cat were made a proximate relationship in order to revile the untouchable.[36] It was in such a context that Syrian Christians produced a cat for auction in St Thomas Church during the "liberation struggle".[37] This was a varia-tion on the template of ethnic slurs that exist across the globe, includ-ing the association of subordinated identities with beasts.[38] A.M. Croom has noted that "slurring terms offered the racist speakers a linguistic resource with which to dehumanize their targets and identify them in 'subhuman' rather than fully human, terms."[39] He points out

[36] Cats walk silently without making their presence felt, particularly to their ad-versaries – just as the slave castes do not approach the "high born". The slur "poo-cha" also incorporates the negative qualities of cats. From an analysis of proverbs and idioms in Malayalam and omens related to cats, it is clear that cats are hated and feared (termed "silly and trivial", "cheats and frauds", "bad and mischievous", etc.) by the traditionally "civilised" and "upper-caste" communities. For proverbs and phrases related to cats, see Pillai, *Dictionary of Malayalam Phrases*.

[37] The Dalit Christian trustee was forced to auction off the cat and Syrian Christians laughed raucously at Dalits during the auction. Mathew, "Interview with Kuriakkose Tharoth".

[38] Some of the most offensive ethnic slurs are "coon", "ape", "monkey", and "crow", pejoratively used to address Blacks and other ethnic people. See for details Hund and Mills, "Comparing Black People"; and Hughes, *An Encyclopedia of Swearing*.

[39] Croom, "How to Do Things with Slurs", p. 8.

the derogatory language of British and other colonialists to "maximize the idea of difference between themselves and their African captives."[40] The same maximising of difference is clear from the caste slurs deployed by upper-caste Christians to position themselves above Dalit Christians.

The experience of Dalit Christians in the Kottukappara and Parakkappara congregations is similar to those in other comparable congregations across Kerala. It has made Dalit Christians believe that Syrian Christians challenged the basic Christian affirmation in the Bible requiring equality of prayer: to "pray also for those who will believe in me that they all may be one."[41]

Faith, Belovedness, and Resistance

"The threat from Syrian Christians was the major reason why we all got more united than ever before. It was as if the odd man out among us would fall victim to their machinations. A casual passing of information was enough to bring all men, women, and children to our meeting place, no matter where it was located."[42] So said one interviewee during my fieldwork, outlining the reasons for community cohesion and solidarity among Dalit Christians. Physical violence and social suffering have created a "spirit of belovedness"; the urgent meeting up in togetherness of Dalit Christians became necessary in Karikkottakkari during the violent days of the "liberation struggle", which lasted several months in the fall of 1959. Gatherings in household spaces and over shared dining were used by Dalit Christians to discuss resistance strategies and the future of the community. In the context of their oppression, the sharing of joy, sorrow, hopes, fear, thirst, hunger, and knowledge became the beacons to an improved future. The little space of Dalit huts was the efflorescence of a "beloved community" necessary to their survival.

Has this situation created a sense of shared victimhood and self-pity among Dalit Christians? In this context, "Many scholars have argued that social protest serves more of an ego function to build up the self-

[40] Ibid.
[41] See John, 17:20, 21, in the Bible, New International Version.
[42] Interview with Kunjoutha Chittakkattu on 10 October 2016.

esteem of individuals and that many people primarily engage in activism because of their self-pity and sense of victimhood."[43] In the case of the Dalit Christians I interviewed, their prayer gatherings became the principal and enduring practice that symbolically healed the wounds of their bodies and minds and strengthened the resolve of the community to move forward. In their congregations the sharing of pain and experiences of oppression were often accompanied with prayers and tears. The community could collect contributions that would help meet the travel expenses to go to Thalassery to meet Fr. Taffarel and invite him to their village – to these emotional events, during which several people cried out of joy and hope.[44] Oppressed labouring communities are known to pray for blessings for their hard work and in the hope that their prayers will be heard. This is part of the context of faith that is created for God to become a force for liberation, to bring people closer and engender feelings of self-respect.

To protect the lives and holdings of Dalit Christians from higher-caste assault, a new leadership within the community showing physical and intellectual strength was also deemed necessary. Kunjoutha recollects: "If P.M. Peter – their leader – held one end of the rope tightly, we all together held the other end. If he had shaken the rope, we would all have been shaken to the core."[45] Martial art practitioners with expertise in the famous martial art of Kalaripayattu were brought to the village to train those interested in learning forms of self-defence. Those fearing assault tended to gather in groups, preferring to stay together and adopting an appearance as well as behavioural patterns that betokened resistance. Sharp objects began to be carried as weapons. Dalits ascribed their success in "this war" to their use of physical strength because "no other dealings with them [the Syrian Christians] were possible."[46]

A form of resistance commonly adopted by Dalits – mainly by the Pulaya caste – is to circulate a counternarrative of humiliation against the higher-caste practice of humiliating Dalits by calling them "poocha". This counternarrative is circulated secretly and in it the sexual

[43] Atkinson, *Journey into Social Activism*, p. 5.
[44] Mathew, "Interview with Kuriakkose Tharoth".
[45] Interview with Kunjoutha Chittakkattu on 10 October 2016.
[46] Ibid.

exploitation of Dalit women is described as common under caste slavery; so also are episodes of sexual liaison between Dalit men and upper-caste women. In one narrative, an upper-caste husband arrives home unexpectedly and the wife hides her Dalit man in the attic. But the Dalit man's hand hits certain vessels that fall with a clatter. On enquiring who is upstairs, the husband is told it is a cat ("poocha").[47] This counternarrative is the attempt of Dalit men to construct an idea of their masculinity as capable of attracting upper-caste women, which goes against upper-caste definitions of Dalit men as inferior. Sociologists have shown the importance of looking at "underlives" in studies of resistance to see how a a sense of identity develops among the oppressed. James Scott uses the term "hidden transcript" to explain the discourses of subordinated social groups that take shape "offstage", beyond the direct observation of power holders. Hidden transcripts of indignation are produced by the subordinated to bolster the self-esteem by which they insulate themselves against insults to their dignity.[48]

It could be argued that this counternarrative by Dalit men to assert the power of their masculinity demonstrates a lack of gender sensitivity. The larger picture to be kept in mind is that the counternarrative resists humiliation in a society where the power wielders are patriarchs with a history of violence against women. If there is violence and a lack of ethics in the representation of women in Dalit counternarratives, the justification could lie in their need for discursive forms of vengeance against the dominant practices of oppression and humiliation.

The Purification of Learned Christianity and the Scope of a Beloved Community

In the context of caste conflict, the question of "integration" between Dalit Christians and Syrian Christians becomes important. The dominant view in this regard is that it is "the inability" of Dalits to "change their social image" that prevents "their integration with the traditional

[47] This counternarrative is in circulation among Dalit men mainly in the northern Travancore region. When I asked some of the Dalit Christian respondents in Karikkottakkari village about such a counternarrative, they were aware of it.

[48] Scott, *Domination and the Arts*, p. 7.

Christians."[49] The idea of a "beloved community" assumes significance here. This "beloved community" of people of various races and ethnicities was envisioned by African-American philosophers and activists, including Josiah Royce, Howard Thurman, and Martin Luther King Jr. It was modified and put into practice by King throughout his life. His vision was to develop a community of "genuine intergroup and interpersonal living" among diverse humans, based in non-violence, love, brotherhood, forgiveness, reconciliation, respect for personhood, caring, and sharing. It was to be a "non-sectarian and cosmopolitan siblinghood of persons."[50] Howard Thurman points out the importance of taking "personal responsibility" in social change and the meaning of "commitment" in the formation of a "beloved community" of people of various ethnicities. For him "there can never be a substitute for taking personal responsibility for social change. The word 'personal' applies both to the individual and the organization – in this instance, the church."[51] He is of the opinion that "individuation consisted in expressions of sincere loyalty to some communal cause . . . [c]ommitment means that it is possible for a [person] to yield the nerve centre of [his or her] consent to a purpose or a cause, a movement or an ideal, which may be more important to him [or her] than whether he [or she] lives or dies."[52]

How far is it possible to create such a beloved community in a caste society? What are the basic requirements for its formation? To realise a beloved community of Dalits and Syrian Christians, both these groups would have to work towards ensuring certain basic conditions in their own respective communities. We can find examples of significant incidents that contributed to the formation of this basic requirement initiated in the Syrian Christian community before, during, and after the "liberation struggle" in Karikkottakkari. One such incident was the nomination of a Dalit Christian member of the St Thomas Syrian Catholic Church, Mathai Pazhayakalayil, as one of the trustees before the "liberation struggle". A Syrian Christian priest, Fr. Paul Vazhuthalakkattu, took the initiative for this inclusion of Dalits in the church

[49] Alexander, "Caste and Christianity", p. 559.
[50] Jensen and King, "Beloved Community".
[51] Ibid., p. 23.
[52] Ibid., 22–3.

administration despite opposition from members of the dominant community.[53] Furthermore, during the "liberation struggle" some Syrian Christians were sympathetic to Dalit Christians and opposed the caste violence that their brethren "volunteers" unleashed upon Dalit Christians. In yet another notable incident, which occurred in 2010, a leading personality from the Syrian Christian community – a retired schoolteacher – urged in a public meeting the need for Syrian Christians to apologise for the caste violence against Dalits in 1959. By all accounts, he personally expressed regret for the "wrong things committed to the poor people of the village."[54] From these episodes we see the occasional manifestation of "inclusion", "nonviolence", and "reconciliation" in the oppressor community.

Before the 1959 liberation struggle, Dalits had shown their commitment to the formation of a beloved community in the joint congregation of St Thomas Syrian Church at Karikkottakkari by their active involvement in church affairs. They had shown their willingness for "brotherhood", "forgiveness", and "reconciliation" with their caste oppressors. But it was the Syrian Christians who had denied this attempt at brotherhood and unleashed the caste violence of which the consequence was violent resistance. It was Fr. Taffarel who prepared Dalits for "reconciliation", developing the values necessary for the formation of a larger beloved community through purification, resulting in a learned form of Christianity among Dalits. The missionary Christianity of Fr. Taffarel introduced purification among the Dalit Christians of the Kottukappara and Parakkappara congregations, leading to their separation of society's modern values from spirituality's non-modern or pre-modern values. This also meant separating out the human tendency to follow natural instincts from the cultural frame of an ideal Christianity based on faith. In sum, purification here meant developing Dalit members of the congregation as individual subjects impervious to insulting objectification by others.

Fr. Taffarel and his team wanted Dalits to be good Christians in their

[53] Mathew, "Interview with Kuriakkose Tharoth".

[54] This meeting was organised by the Council for Dalit Christians (CDC) in remembrance of V.D. John, the late Dalit Christian leader and founder of the BCCF. Interview with Peter Mathew on 18 May 2018.

souls. He spoke to them about how to behave and what to avoid in life. He had a clear definition of bad and good people. His sermon in the church was a call for the spiritual as well as material transformation of individuals. Some of his regularly used phrases included *kuppaya kristhyanikal venda* (no Christian pretenders), *meeshakkar venda* (no one sporting twirling moustaches), *kommeesakkar venda* (no to communism). He also taught his audience to forgive others; he himself forgave them for many of their mistakes and asked them to behave mercifully. Where individual and family quarrels occurred, Fr. Taffarel made the warring parties reconcile. The lives of both Fr. Taffarel and his assistant Fr. Valerian D'Souza represented the Christian ideal as lived experience among Dalit Christians. Unlike higher-caste priests, they brought about changes among Dalits by invoking the finer aspects of their learned variety of Christianity. Their presence mitigated the Dalit interest in both violent resistance and communism as a possible resource of resistance. What these priests successfully imparted was the need for individual dignity and peace in community life through a reconciliation with caste opponents.

The emergence of activity based on Christian values among both oppressor and oppressed communities is an important requirement in the formation of a beloved community. But the more important question is whether such values can continue to be nurtured and furthered within the communities and larger common spaces. This expansion of values can only happen with more organised attempts. Here, the problem is the absence of shared joint initiatives towards a common platform of opposed caste groups based on forgiveness, reconciliation, and brotherhood in church and society. Without such joint initiatives, the integration of Dalits and Syrian Christians remains a pipe dream.

Social Experience and Faith

The transcendent and immanent nature of God has been one of the major themes in the anthropology of Christianity.[55] Experiencing the

[55] See, for example, Cannell, ed., *The Anthropology of Christianity*; Robbins, "Transcendence and the Anthropology of Christianity"; Webster, "The Immanence of Transcendence", pp. 380–402; Saler, *Conceptualizing Religion*.

liberatory face of God in everyday life in the context of oppression is
a fundamental aspect of Dalit Christian faith and spirituality. This experiencing of God has been possible in the relationship between Dalits
and Western Christian missionaries because of its basis in Christian
love and brotherhood. The mutuality of Dalit and missionary imagin-
ings regarding human dignity, emancipation, and a possible good life
were conducive to the development of the faith of Dalit Christians in
Jesus as Saviour. Discriminated and oppressed, the Dalits in Karikkottakkari welcomed an Italian priest, Fr. Taffarel, with his modern
worldview interpreted through Christian theology. Missionaries of this
variety were not part of the caste system, nor in need of perpetuating
it. Their modern outlook and Christian values formed an ideological
frame in support of the oppressed. Fr. Taffarel's very first activity was
the settling of violence and caste conflict in Karikkottakkari. The visit
of a "Mooppachan" – a colloquial way of addressing Western missionaries – alerted the Syrian Christian community. They feared that
they would perish if the Mooppachan's curse fell upon them.[56] But by
his words and assurance Fr. Taffarel resolved the issue of lost spaces of
worship among Dalit Christians even over his very first visit. During this
visit, women, children, and mothers wept, and seeing them Fr. Taffarel
himself "could not stop his tears rolling down his cheeks."[57] According to Dalit Christian respondents, Fr. Taffarel's arrival among them
was like God himself coming down to slaves and subordinated people.
Many felt that Dalits started to experience *sarva swathanthryam* (complete freedom) from the time of Fr. Taffarel's interventions.[58] Even
several years after his demise, Dalits identified him as a godly figure
blessed with abilities for spiritual transactions in the mundane.[59]

After Dalits quit the St Thomas Syrian Church, questions were
raised about future options for the community. The community's very
survival was at stake since they were mostly dependent on Syrian Christian landlords for daily-wage work. As they searched for survival strate-

[56] Interview with Peter Mathew on 9 May 2018.
[57] Mathew, "Interview with Kuriakkose Tharoth".
[58] Interview with Kunjoutha Chittakkattu on 10 October 2016.
[59] During my fieldwork I observed that many people had set Fr. Taffarel's
photos as their homescreen picture on their mobile phones. Some people keep
big portraits of him in their homes.

gies as well as a place for worship, someone suggested conversion to Hinduism as the way forward, since conversion to Hinduism came with offers of support by the state.[50] But the community rejected this idea and followed the advice of its elders, who decided it would be best to choose any one of the other Christian churches. This decision not to quit Christianity and not to join Hinduism despite feeling they had reached a dead end in their quest for survival was the most important evidence of undisputed faith in the Christianity of Dalit Christians. Similar examples exist all over Kerala, showing the resolution of Dalits to remain Christians despite the efforts of Hindu missions to bring Dalits into the Hindu fold, specially during the first half of the twentieth century.[61] Webster has described a similar situation in Punjab – of Punjabi Dalit Christians choosing the "inner peace that Christ gives" as against the "worldly advantages gained from scheduled caste status."[62]

Commitment to their Christian faith and the revelation of caste divisions as sinful and satanic are two important aspects of Dalit Christianity. They show the importance of sacred–profane binaries that Dalits have learned from Christianity in the democratisation of the Church and their struggles for liberation from caste. In Dalit Christianity the casteist spaces of the church signify a sinful setting, and their belief that only a casteless church can be sacred. These binaries can be made evident only through the theological framework of Dalit Christianity. One cannot conclude that Dalit Christianity is an "impossible religion" in the Hegelian sense. The idea of God does not simply reside in the notion of "transcendence"; Dalit Christianity is in fact rather a worldly religion. In other words, it includes both elements of "transcendence" as well as the visibility of God.

≈

[60] They would have acquired Scheduled Caste status if they joined Hinduism as that would make them eligible for reservations in government jobs and other legal protections.

[61] The NDSP fieldwork shows the strong convictions of elderly Dalit Christians, demonstrated as well in many parts of Kerala in matters of their Christian faith, the politics of "conversion", and the strategies of Hindu nationalist forces. Also see Gladstone, *Protestant Christianity*.

[62] Webster, *Verities of Dalit Christianity*, pp. 97–118.

This essay has argued that Dalit Christian spirituality and a faith community emerged in response to oppressive social structures, including those in the Syrian Church, and by challenging dominant knowledge and the perception of Dalit Christians by the upper castes. It tries to demonstrate that the dominant knowledge and "high-caste" perceptions of Dalit Christians is built on shaky foundations, casteist stereotyping, and ethnocentrism. This dubious structure has ignored the complex and productive social world of Dalit Christians who have attained deep religious faith and a critical consciousness by making use of the liberatory aspects of modernity and Christian values. Their values and faith in Christianity have for Dalits been instrumental in the formation of faith communities resistant to caste oppression. Dalit Christians have, moreover, acquired a social and political identity on account of their history of resistance to social oppression. The material and spiritual resources for their ethical resistance are drawn from Christianity, which was purified by accepting God imagined as Saviour, and rejecting other lures of patronage.

Dalit Christianity is a religion alive in the mundane world while consisting of both material and spiritual elements. On the material side it involves historical knowledge and the rejection of objectification and patronage from political opponents. On the spiritual side it involves an engagement with Christianity and acceptance of its objectification of God as Saviour. In this lived Christianity, Dalits challenge the "high-caste" Christian claim to the status of "real" and "authentic" Christianity.

The Israeli philosopher Avishai Margalit is of view that "A decent society is one whose institutions do not humiliate people. I distinguish between a decent society and a civilized one. A civilized society is one whose members do not humiliate one another, while a decent society is one in which the institutions do not humiliate people."[63] Relying on Margalit, as well as the analysis offered in this essay, we could say that the Christian community in Kerala has proved neither decent nor civilised despite its attempts to appear so. It is in this context that Dalit Christianity shows a capacity to democratise society and truly christianise the Church. By engaging with Christian values, sacraments, and other

---

[63] Margalit, *The Decent Society*, p. 1.

church activities amidst the humiliation and indignities heaped on them, Dalits present to the world the authenticity of their conversion and disprove dominant ethnocentric constructions of Dalit Christianity. Critical and nuanced understandings of Dalit Christian life-worlds and their faith community can, indeed, provide new resources for the democratisation of hegemonic societies in general.

References

Alexander, K.C., "Caste and Christianity in Kerala", *Social Compass*, vol. xviii, no. 4, 1971.

Asad, Talal, *Genealogies of Religion: Discipline and Reasons of Power in Christianity and Islam* (Baltimore: The Johns Hopkins University Press, 1993).

Atkinson, Joshua D., "The Study of Social Activism", in idem, *Journey into Social Activism: Qualitative Approaches* (New York: Fordham University Press, 2017), https://www.jstor.org/stable/j.ctt1hfr0rk.4.

Audio Visual Archive SSRC-NDSP Project-Collection of Interviews with Elderly Dalits in Kerala, 2012, Inter University Centre for Social Science Research and Extension, Mahatma Gandhi University, Kottayam, Kerala.

Bayly, Susan, *Saints, Goddesses and Kings: Muslims and Christians in South Indian History, 1700–1900* (Cambridge: Cambridge University Press, 2003).

Bennett, R.A., "Black Experience and the Bible", in G.S. Wilmore, ed., *African American Religious Studies: An Interdisciplinary Anthology* (Durham, NC: Duke University Press, 1989).

Cannell, Fenella, ed., *The Anthropology of Christianity* (Durham, NC: Duke University Press, 2006).

Croom, A.M., "How to do Things with Slurs: Study in the Way of Derogatory Words", *Language and Communication*, vol. 33, 2013, http://dx.doi.org/10.1016/j.langcom.2013.03.008.

"Discrimination and Victimisation Based on 'Caste' Against Dalit Christians in Thuruthikkara Parish in Adoor Diocese of Marthoma Syrian Church, Kollam District in Kerala", Fact Finding-Preliminary Report, National Dalit Christian Watch (NDCW), 20 June 2019.

Dumont, Louis, *Homo Hierarchicus: The Caste System and Its Implications* (New Delhi: Oxford University Press, 1999).

Duncombe, Stephen, "(From) Cultural Resistance to Community Development", *Oxford University Press and Community Development Journal*, vol. 42, no. 4, 2007, DOI: 10.1093/cdj/bsm039.

Gladstone, J.W., *Protestant Christianity and People's Movements in Kerala:*

A Study of Christian Mass Movements in Relation to Neo-Hindu Socio-Religious Movements in Kerala, 1850–1936 (Thiruvananthapuram: The Seminary Publications, 1984).

Hughes, Geoffrey, *An Encyclopedia of Swearing: The Social History of Oaths, Profanity, Foul Language, and Ethnic Slurs in the English-Speaking World* (London: Routledge, 2006).

Hund, Wulf D., and Charles W. Mills, "Comparing Black People to Monkeys has a Long, Dark Simian History", *The Conversation Africa*, updated 28 Feb. 2017, https://theconversation.com/_comparing-black-people-to-monkeys-has-a-long-dark-simian-history-55102.

Jensen, Kipton, and Preston King, "Beloved Community: Martin Luther King, Howard Thurman, and Josiah Royce", *The Journal of Friendship Studies*, vol. 4, no. 1, 2017, DOI: https://doi.org/10.5518/AMITY/20.

Joas, Hans, *Faith as an Option: Possible Futures for Christianity* (Stanford: Stanford University Press, 2014).

John, V.D., *Ente Jeevithavum Kalavum* (Thodupuzha: V.D. John Darshana Kendram, 2014).

Kawashima, Koji, *Missionaries and a Hindu State: Travancore 1858–1936* (New Delhi: Oxford India Paperbacks, 2000).

Kooiman, Dick, *Conversion and Social Equality in India: The London Missionary Society in South Travancore in the 19th Century* (New Delhi: Manohar Publications, 1989).

Koshy, Ninan, *Caste in the Kerala Churches* (Delhi: CISRS, 2014).

Latour, Bruno, *We Have Never Been Modern*, trans. Catherine Porter (Cambridge: Harvard University Press, 1993).

Loue, S., "Understanding Theology and Homosexuality in African American Communities", Springer Briefs in Social Work, DOI: 10.1007/978-1-4614-9002-9_2, © The Author(s) 2014.

Mair, Lucy, *An Introduction to Social Anthropology* (New Delhi: Oxford University Press, 1965).

Margalit, Avishai, *The Decent Society*, trans. Naomi Goldblum (Cambridge: Harvard University Press, 1996).

Mathew, Peter, "Interview with Kuriakkose Tharoth", in idem, "Interviews with Dalit Christian Elders of Kottukappara, Karikkottakkari and Parakkappara", unpublished manuscript, 2018.

Merrill, M. Hawkins, Jr., "Personal Spirituality", in Charles H. Lippy, ed., *Faith in America: Changes, Challenges, New Directions*, vol. 3 (London: Praeger, 2016).

Mohan, P. Sanal, "Creation of Social Space through Prayers among Dalits in Kerala", *Journal of Religious and Political Practice*, Routledge: published online, 19 Oct. 2015, DOI:10.1080/ 20566093.2016.1085735.

Mohan, P. Sanal, *Modernity of Slavery: Struggles Against Caste Inequality in Colonial Kerala* (New Delhi: Oxford University Press, 2015).

Pillai, T. Ramalingam, *Dictionary of Malayalam Phrases and Idioms* (Kottayam: DC Books, 1975).

Robbins, Joel, "Transcendence and the Anthropology of Christianity: Language, Change, and Individualism", Edward Westermarck Memorial Lecture, October 2001, accessed online 10 December 2017, https://www.asnc.cam.ac.uk/_conversion/Westermarck.pdf.

Robbins, Joel, "Transcendence and the Anthropology of Christianity", *Suomen Antropologi: Journal of the Finnish Anthropological Society*, vol. 37, no. 2, 2012.

Roberts, Nathaniel, *To Be Cared For: The Power of Conversion and Foreignness of Belonging in an Indian Slum* (Berkeley: University of California Press, 2016).

Saler, Benson, *Conceptualizing Religion: Immanent Anthropologists, Transcendent Natives, and Unbounded Categories* (New York: Berghahn Books, 2000).

Salim, P.M., "The First Popular Government in Kerala and Liberation Struggle 1957–59: A Historical Study", PhD diss., University of Calicut, 2013.

Scott, James, C., *Domination and the Arts of Resistance: Hidden Transcripts* (London: Yale University Press, 1990).

Taffarel, Rev. Joseph, S.J., *Jottings of a Poor Missionary* (Calicut: Feast of the Sacred Heart, 1950).

Viswanath, Rupa, "The Emergence of Authenticity Talk and the Giving of Accounts: Conversion as Movement of the Soul in South India, *ca.* 1900", *Comparative Studies in Society and History*, vol. 55, no. 1, 2013.

Webster, John C.B., "Verities of Dalit Christianity in North India", in Rowena Robinson and Joseph Marianus Kujur, *Margins of Faith: Dalit and Tribal Christianity in India* (New Delhi: Sage Publications, 2010).

Webster, Joseph, "The Immanence of Transcendence: God and the Devil on the Aberdeenshire Coast", *Ethnos*, vol. 78, no. 3, 2013.

Yesudasan, T.M., *Baliyadukalude Vamshavali* (Thrissur: Prabhath Books, 2010).

Yesudasan, T.M., *Chettitheruvile Dwishadabdhikal* (Kottayam: Thaipparambil Books, 2016).

7

Presenting the Dalit Body
Caste and Sartorial Dignity in North India

ANUPAMA

Under British rule, you can no longer be forced. All those things that mark you as an untouchable – you must drop them. The way you drape your saris marks you untouchable. You must begin the practice of wearing your saris in the same fashion that upper-caste women do, it will not cost you anything. Similarly, your habit of wearing heavy necklaces around your necks and bracelets and bangles of *Kathil* on your arms up to the elbow, mark you out as being untouchable. There is no need for more than one necklace. Clothes bring more grace than jewellery. Rather than spending money on artificial ornaments, you should spend it on good clothes. If you must wear ornaments, get gold ornaments and wear them or else you need not wear any. Also you must take care to be clean in your person . . .[1]

THE TRANSFORMATION wrought by the British in Indian society was felt most by the "Untouchables". Their leader, Dr B.R. Ambedkar, highlighted the new liberalism of British India that offered them opportunities to transition towards a dignified personhood. In this transition, clothes were to play an important role and Ambedkar highlighted the distinctiveness of this sartorial aspect of Dalit life.

This essay is derived from my PhD thesis, "Caste, Class and Clothing: North India in the first half of the Twentieth Century". I would like to thank Professor Janaki Nair for editing a previous draft, and Professor Neeladri Bhattacharya for his comments on earlier drafts.
[1] Speech by B.R. Ambedkar, 25–26 December 1927, at the Mahad Satyagraha, in Pawar and Moon, *We Also Made History*, pp. 120–3.

182

The objective of wearing good clothes, as he saw it, was to acquire grace and dignity.

Caste in India had long been visualised through forms and styles of dress, as well as bodily markings and comportment, all these indicating the position of people in the caste hierarchy. In British India the visible markers of caste discrimination included ornaments (copper, metal, leather),[2] sartorial styles (unclean clothes; bare-breasted women), and forms of apparel that had long been informally prescribed or imposed on Dalits.

Here, a clarification on the term "Dalit" would be in order. In colonial India the categorisation of oppressed castes with the term "Depressed Classes" was an administrative innovation of 1911. In various different parts of India, the prefix "Adi" was used, particularly from the start of the first decade of the twentieth century, to indicate a new self-awareness of the indigeneity of the Depressed Classes. Examples of this were terms such as Adi Dravida and Adi Karnataka. Following Mahatma Gandhi, the Congress Party coined the term Harijan (Children of God) to refer to the lower castes/Depressed Classes, which, as Ramnarayan Rawat has pointed out, was part of a salvationist rhetoric.[3] More recently, Dalit has become the standard term for those formerly known as the Untouchables. During the 1970s, with the activities of the Dalit Panther Movement, the term acquired a radical nomenclaturing method of self-identification. The word Dalit has found large acceptance across India among "Untouchable" communities to express their political and social identity. Although the term meant "downtrodden" or "broken down", it was accepted as a community's self-chosen name to emphasise their oppression and humiliation rather than the idea of pollution; potentially it could include all who identified themselves as oppressed by the caste system. I have therefore used the term Dalit to signify the radical alterity of "Untouchables" in colonial India, even if it is an anachronism in the context of the time before the 1970s.

At times, when members of the ruling castes felt a Dalit sartorial style signified an affront to them, they enforced their upper-caste notions of

[2] Hutton, *Census of India,* 1933, vol. I, pp. 485–6.
[3] Rawat, *Reconsidering Untouchability*, p. 168.

a "proper" dress code through violence. It was necessary from this caste-Hindu perspective for Dalits to look inferior. These forms of discriminatory practice came under increasing challenge by Dalit groups thanks to the coming into being of a new liberal order that entitled them to the same rights as caste-Hindus.[4]

Several violent incidents occurred on account of the clothes worn by Dalits, and these help us understand the nature of sartorial regulation and resistance. In May 1927 caste-Hindu groups in fifteen villages of Indore District in the Central Provinces imposed a complete social boycott against the Dalit groups known as Balais for their "daringness to wear clean clothes and gold ornaments."[5] In 1928 two Mahar "Untouchable" brothers in Ahmedabad (Gujarat) were treated savagely for wearing clean clothes that had apparently concealed their identity.[6] The 1931 census documents instances of attacks on Chamars by Rajput groups in Agra District for wearing gold ornaments and Western clothes.[7] In 1933, in a village near Agra, caste-Hindu groups forced a Dalit woman to remove her nose-ring and crushed her toes with a stone for wearing silver toe-rings.[8] In Sevra, a village in Agra District, the Golas (Purva Thakurs) mercilessly beat several unarmed Jatavs because a Jatav bridegroom among them wore a glittering crown (*pukka mohar*): he was what in the American South, in relation to Black slaves, was called "being uppity" by white slave owners. In the Agra District marital context, a Dalit seen as proclaiming high social station had offended the Thakurs.[9] Across the country, Dalits who took the initiative to wear clean Western clothes or who decided to wear a local outfit associated with sta-

---

[4] Moon, *Dr Babasaheb Ambedkar*, vol. 5, pp. 21–2. The wearing of a clean dress, shoes, a watch, and gold ornaments was considered an offence by Dalit communities in the late nineteenth century. Some of these prohibitions continued through much of the twentieth century. These were a part of various codes of dress, behaviour, and conduct which lower-caste communities were supposed to follow, primarily in Indian villages.

[5] Ibid., pp. 48–51.

[6] "Orthodoxy Run Mad, Alleged Barbarous Treatment of 'Untouchables': Crime of Being Mahars", *Bombay Chronicle*, 25 February 1928, in Moon, *Dr Babasaheb Ambedkar*, vol. 2, p. 453.

[7] Hutton, *Census of India*, vol. I, pp. 485–6.

[8] *Harijan*, 13 June 1933.

[9] Moon, *Dr Babasaheb Ambedkar*, vol. 5, p. 77.

tus and dignity met swift and violent retaliation. In such cases caste-Hindus made it ferociously clear that the act of wearing supposedly prohibited items of clothing was an attempt to transgress caste boundaries.

Ambedkar had advised Dalit women during the December 1927 Mahad satyagraha to forsake those items of ornamentation and dress which marked them out as "Untouchable". These women, mainly Mahar and Chambhar, of the Konkan region in Maharashtra, particularly from the Thane and Colaba districts, were used to wearing nine-yard saris exposing their knees and even their thighs.[10] Their style of draping the sari was different from that of upper-caste Hindu women. Dalits were not supposed to wear new clothes and precious jewellery: only tin, brass, and iron ornaments were permitted. Dalits in Pune District wore saris in the traditional way as there were rules even for how the sari pleats were to be tucked.[11] Mahar women had to tuck saris to ensure their borders remained hidden, else it was considered an offence against the high castes.[12] Dalit women's draping styles were thus meant to distinguish them from caste-Hindu women, making their identification as inferiors easier. Dalit women recalled the huge impact of their leader's speech. Many who had attended the conference cast off their jewellery and from the next day began to drape their sari down to their ankles, as Brahmin women did.[13] Ambedkar's argument that the new legal institutions established by the British government had presented Dalits an opportunity to break away from the traditional markers of their subordination made absolute sense to his followers. Their adoption of new styles of dressing, which also entailed shedding earlier forms of ornamentation, represented powerful new ways of presenting a transformed Dalit selfhood.

Caste prohibitions were also densely prescribed in the spatial organisation of villages, with segregated Dalit villages kept safely distant from caste-Hindu villages, and this principle of distance had been taken in the direction of sartorial practices as well as bodily movements.[14] Most

---

[10] Pawar and Moon, *We Also Made History*, p. 120.
[11] Kamble, *The Prisons We Broke*, p. 54.
[12] Ibid.
[13] Rege, *Writing Caste*, pp. 55–9.
[14] Hardgrave, "The Breast Cloth Controversy", pp. 171–87.

of the regulations forbidding specific clothes and ornaments had been outlined in the *Manusmriti*.[15] Manu, author of the *Manusmriti*, had recommended that Dalits wear only the garments of the dead, or old and torn clothes discarded by caste-Hindus, and ornaments made of iron.[16] In British India these restrictions were extended to shoes, watches, umbrellas, and cheap new factory-made clothes.[17] Dalits aspired to change these oppressive caste rules, having been enabled by the new liberal institutions that entitled them the freedom to present themselves in "casteless" clean clothes and gold ornaments. A Dalit bridegroom now had the right to ride on a horse during his marriage procession.[18]

A reaction against reform was to be expected from caste-Hindus alarmed by the challenge to their supremacy in the caste hierarchy. Several kinds of offence and punishment were recorded by the British official E.A.H. Blunt with respect to the transgression of social codes set by caste rules.[19] What makes the history of caste and dress regulation in India so necessary to any study of clothing is that although such regulation was never imposed as legislation, it was in fact far more rigid and onerous because of the caste power of the dominant groups, and because dress codes were an expression of both social and economic hierarchy. In twentieth-century India too, despite the winds of modernity and capitalism, free choice in the matter of clothing and dress has tended to be restricted to the caste-Hindu sections of society while Dalit groups have continued to confront oppressive social-sartorial codes and informally enforced dress rules. Wearing Western clothes and being seen in conspicuously clean clothes have thus come to represent social aspiration as well as an important site of the Dalit struggle to alter or eliminate imposed caste markers. Their sartorial rebellion also shows how caste identity, personhood, power, and domination are linked and closely interconnected in processes of social ordering and control.[20]

[15] Moon, *Dr Babasaheb Ambedkar*, vol. 5, p. 277.

[16] Ibid.

[17] Hutton, *Caste in India*, p. 74; Blunt, *The Caste System of Northern India*, pp. 117–24.

[18] Moon, *Dr Babasaheb Ambedkar*, vol. 2, p. 135.

[19] Hutton, *Census of India, 1931*, vol. I, pt I, p. 485.

[20] Moon, *Dr Babasaheb Ambedkar*, vols 1 and 5. These volumes cite various examples of caste prohibitions on the clothing of the "Depressed Classes".

Sartorial Historiography

South Asian historiography has not paid adequate attention to the decisive role of caste on Dalit sartorial practices. Ambedkar first raised the clothing question and a small body of scholarship developed around his recognition. This has begun to show clothing as vital to social classifications that mark out the wealthy from the poor, the high caste from the low caste, men from women, East from West, colonial masters from colonised subjects. The choice by Dalits of Western forms of dress and behaviour as an aspect of dissent, though under-represented in South Asian historiography, has fortunately occupied a central place in Dalit autobiographies – which I will discuss later.

Robert Hardgrave's 1969 study was probably the earliest to address the relationship between caste and clothes. In the southern Travancore region of Kerala, lower-caste women of the Nadar community were not allowed to cover their breasts and the upper parts of their body, this having traditionally been part of a larger regime to manage their spatial space and bodily movements.[21] Missionary activities in the region changed Nadar attitudes. Many who converted to Christianity now saw sense in women covering the upper body and donning themselves in clean new clothes. Consequently, caste-Hindu groups of the Namboothiri and other upper-caste communities attacked missionary schools and Nadar women. Hardgrave, who narrated this history, considered the breast-cloth controversy critical to the constitution of community dignity and identity. His focus was not so much on understanding clothing and dress, but studying how transformations occur in caste positioning and practice. Emma Tarlo, who was interested in similar ideas and measures, documented the differing responses by Indians to sartorial cultural norms introduced by the British in the nineteenth century.[22] She showed the disturbance in and recasting of elite customary clothing practices, with upper-caste Hindus from elite backgrounds readily adopting British dress styles alongside language.[23] Another contributor to this terrain of analysis was Narayana Guru who, alongside other social reformers in Kerala, led a campaign against prescribed caste attributes pertaining to

[21] Hardgrave, "The Breast Cloth Controversy", p. 172.
[22] Tarlo, *Clothing Matters*, pp. 12–39.
[23] Ibid., pp. 39–41.

the human body and urged people to free themselves of physical caste markers.[24] Following this broad line of thought, I focus here on the sartorial experiences of Dalits in late British India.

Sartorial considerations played an important role in Dalit conversions to Christianity in South India. Eliza Kent argues that Christianity offered various opportunities to Dalits, allowing them the possibility of changing their status through self-presentation.[25] While focusing on cultural change and social habits, she analyses the emergence of new ideals of Dalit Christian femininity.[26] New dress habits became a vital means for Dalits to assert their new identity and claim social respectability.[27] Kent's work documents social conflicts that emerged between on the one hand Dalit Christian converts who adopted new sartorial styles, and on the other the dominant caste-Hindu groups wishing to preserve the status quo.

Another historian, Charu Gupta, studies caste in colonial North India from the perspective of gender, focusing on practices of distinction and hierarchy among Dalit castes.[28] She analyses a wide range of colonial archives and focuses on visual representations popular in the print media of the northern region, examining also religious conversion by Dalit women to Christianity and Islam. Gupta points out that converted Dalit women saw changes in their social status by, in part, their adoption of new dress styles which challenged traditional notions of caste- and class-appropriate clothing. The reformist voices of caste-Hindus found in the visual archives of cartoons and photos that she displays illustrate the sartorial change that was instrumental in social change. In the wake of her work, I look more closely at questions of dress from the perspective of Dalit subjectivity.

Histories of clothing suggest that sartorial conventions not only represent identities, they also express notions of correct behaviour in communities by shaping individual and group notions of modesty, shame, and humiliation. We have seen how, through new processes of conversion and education that came with colonial rule, many marginalised

[24] Kumar, "Self Body and Inner Sense", pp. 247–50.
[25] Kent, *Converting Women*.
[26] Ibid., p. 221.
[27] Ibid., pp. 199–233.
[28] Gupta, *The Gender of Caste*.

castes were able to fashion a new collective self. Although the opportunities generated by colonial modernity were uneven and distorted, new institutional spaces such as schools, factories, and the army provided unprecedented opportunities for fresh varieties of self-definition.[29] My interest here is in the various strategies adopted by "Untouchable" groups to recast their self via clothing, deportment, and ornamentation in the early twentieth century.

The earnings of many of the Doms of eastern Uttar Pradesh came through contracts for construction-related work. They began to adopt Western and Indian dress styles to claim dignity and equity with caste-Hindus.[30] Dalit men, more than women, took to these Western sartorial styles, wearing suits, trousers, shoes, ties, gowns, jackets, and carrying an umbrella.[31] But both sexes embraced ornaments made with the forbidden metals silver and gold. They even took to wearing clothes that signified entry into hitherto non-ascribed forms of labour, such as the army, police, and bureaucracy.

Within the "Untouchable" cultural universe clothing was also seen as the instrument of patriarchal and upper-caste constraints on "Untouchable" bodies, which even included notions of when it was imperative for Dalits to cast off their clothes. The most grotesquely insulting instance of this demand was when the body of a deceased Dalit was placed on the funeral pyre, at which point the white shroud covering the corpse had to be removed and thrown away. Dalits from Mahar-wada ("Untouchable" villages) were then required to arrive and collect castoff shrouds to make clothes.[32] In Uttar Pradesh too, Dalits, apart from having to provide funeral supplies, were expected to collect the clothing items of the dead, including the shroud.[33] The Dom "Untouchables" of eastern Uttar Pradesh were required to wear the clothes of the dead, and one among them was when required assigned the duty of being the village executioner.[34]

British policies and activism by missionary organisations introduced

[29] Moon, *Growing up Untouchable*, p. xii.
[30] Crooke, *The Tribes and Castes*, vol. IV, p. 338.
[31] Nair, *Miners and Millhands*, p. 95.
[32] Kamble, *The Prisons We Broke*, p. 79.
[33] Briggs, *The Chamars*, p. 100.
[34] Crooke, *The Tribes and Castes*, vol. IV, p. 338.

a new sense of shame over the unclothed or naked body. The under-standing of nakedness, as Philippa Levine argues, varies from culture to culture and through different eras. However, the British emphasis on clothing has to begin with Christianity and their idea of civilisation. New notions of shame and decent clothing were introduced into India from the late nineteenth century, in particular to lower-caste groups.[35] Con-ditions of nakedness and wearing torn clothes now began to be experi-enced as signs of humiliation, against which lower-caste protests were in-creasingly organised.

In the section that follows I trace the role of various codes of conduct and restrictions on dress that were set up to stigmatise the Dalit body. I examine Dalit memories of their experiences of altering and adapting to new styles of clothing over the first part of the twentieth century. In Dalit autobiographies, as mentioned, memories of poor clothing are a central theme, especially memories of torn clothes or the impoverishment indicated by the lack of a school uniform. Such memories were often overcome or compensated in autobiographical celebrations of a transi-tion to Western clothes, clean clothes, fashionable clothes, and work clothes which cast the Dalit writer anew. I also look at the responses of caste-Hindus to the assertive sartorial choices being exercised by Dalits. Decoding taste in clothing is an important dimension of my analysis since it constituted one aspect of positioning the individual's identity in the social hierarchy. The choice of one kind or colour of cloth over others acquires significance here. Through texts, pamphlets, short stories, cartoons, autobiographies, and journals I look at both personal styles of dressing, dress choices, and community responses to changes in dress codes over much of the twentieth century. My argument is that over this period sartorial choices and styles introduced new affective elements into society – new notions of modesty and shame, pride and self-esteem, and national as well as community identity. As R.S. Khare puts it, the "Untouchable" woman or man reconstituted her or his own body and self through both organised and individuated struggles.[36] These struggles were strongly signified in sartorial choice.

---

[35] See Levine, "States of Undress", pp. 189–219.
[36] Khare, "The Body, Sensoria, and Self", pp. 147–68.

Sartorial Questions and Codes
of Caste

According to this code [of behaviour], an untouchable . . . should not dress in style superior to that of his status, nor should the untouchable woman adorn herself with ornaments after the fashion of the higher class Hindu women. An Untouchable must not wear clean clothes, must not use brass or copper pots and must not wear gold or silver ornaments . . .[37]

The extract from Ambedkar's *Speeches and Writings* quoted above emphasises the role of Hindu social codes defining the kinds of clothes and ornaments "Untouchable" groups were expected to follow. As noted, Ambedkar was keenly aware of rules and codes prohibiting his community from wearing clean or new clothes and "fancy gowns".[38] Knee-length saris were enforced among Dalit women and they were prohibited from wearing gold-bordered saris.[39] This exposé of the role of clothes in the construction of caste boundaries was among the many facets of Hindu caste oppression pioneered by Ambedkar.

Among caste-Hindus the commonest clothing item, typically worn by men, was the dhoti. The word is usually defined as the loincloth covering the lower part of the body. The dhoti was generally a cotton garment five yards in length, a single piece of cloth wound around the waist, its width hanging downwards till below the man's knees, its ends tucked in.[40] In the twentieth century middle-class Hindus had taken to wearing shirts, coats, and even suits. However, the dhoti was the commonest garment of choice among rural areas and the poorer Hindu men of Central India.[41] Caste-Hindu women continued to wear traditional saris and their class background determined the quality of the cloth. In general, therefore, while men in the towns and cities took to Western clothes, the

---

[37] Moon, *Dr Babasaheb Ambedkar*, vol. 5, ch. 15, p. 133. Ch. 15 of the volume analyses the various ways India's population was classified – into (a) Primitive Tribes, (b) Criminal Tribes, (c) Untouchables – and the effect of Hindu communities on these classes.

[38] Ibid.

[39] Ambedkar, *Jati Bhed ka Uchhed*, pp. 7–8.

[40] Burn, *Imperial Gazetteer of India*, vol. I.

[41] Ibid., ch. entitled "Caste, Tribes and Race", p. 40.

women continued with saris. Given the sartorial transformations taking place in the cities and towns, several British officers perceived that Western clothes had the effect of mitigating or even removing caste distinctions.[42]

Yet in relation to Dalits the sartorial codes ensured the virtual impossibility of change: Dalits continued to wear caste-specific clothes. Among the Bhangis of Lucknow, women could not wear the bodice (*angiya*), chemisette (*kurti*), or gold ornaments; they could not even pierce their nose to wear a nose ring.[43] Muslim Bhangi women could not wear gold ornaments, nor sky-blue clothes, nor lac bangles (*churi*).[44] The use of brass ornaments was considered unlucky, but alloys were allowed. Chamar women of eastern Uttar Pradesh were only allowed to wear metal bangles (*mathiya*), arm ornaments, and heavy bell-metal anklets; they could not wear nose rings.[45] Dom "Untouchable" men in the Garhwal region, in the foothills of the Himalayas, were barred from wearing shoes and using an umbrella in front of caste-Hindus; the women were barred from using silver and gold ornaments.[46] William Crooke, that sharp colonial observer of North Indian society, noted that until recent times a sweeper, when walking through the streets of a town, was expected to carry a broom under his armpit to convey he was a menial scavenger by caste.[47] For working Dalits the broom was akin to a caste ornament required by Hindu social codes.

Among large Dalit groups in Uttar Pradesh, such as the Chamars, the use of caste marks and tattooing was popular, being connected to a belief in protection from evil forces.[48] Mushar women in the eastern districts of the province tattooed their wrists, cheeks, and nose.[49] They believed that God (Parmeshwar) would bar heaven to women who sought

---

[42] Eyde, *Census of India 1921*.

[43] Crooke, *The Tribes and Castes*, vol. II, p. 290.

[44] Ibid.

[45] Ibid., p. 190.

[46] Turner, *Census of India, 1931*, p. 559.

[47] Unknown, "Chapter XI: Caste", Civil and Military Gazette Press, 1912, p. 413, *South Asian Archive*, accessed 25 January 2016.

[48] Briggs, *The Chamars*, p. 145.

[49] Crooke, *The Tribes and Castes*, vol. IV, p. 36.

to enter the divine domain without these protective marks. The men of this community typically wore earrings (*pagara*), bracelets (*dharkana*), and arm ornaments made of base metal.[50] The women wore two kinds of nose rings – the *nathiya*, in the inside of the nose, and the *bulaq*, in the septum. They also wore ear ornaments (*karnphul*), bead necklaces, and glass bangles (*churi*). The ethnographer Briggs noted the popularity of caste marks and tattooing among the Chamars of the United Provinces.[51] Some Chamar women wore a distinguishing caste mark on their feet – a specially shaped anklet called *dhundhni*. Tattooing was more common among Chamar women than among other lower castes. Briggs also recorded the custom among Chamar men who worked with other caste men, and who did not wish to conceal their caste, of tying a small leather thong around their pipes (*chillam*) or tongues.

Several comportment restrictions were discerned as applicable to Dalit groups at the start of the twentieth century. A prohibition on specific colours of clothing was noted among the Manjhi in the Mirzapur region.[52] Manjhi women were not allowed to wear yellow clothes and glass bangles, and they could not apply red decorative markings on their foreheads. They were required to keep their heads bare and disallowed covering them to make clear their contrast with upper-caste women. Manjhwar women were prescribed an especially warm heavily woven cotton cloth known as the *darab*, which had an ornamented border.[53] The *darab* made their caste visible, being seen as a typically "Untouchable" garment.[54] Gond women had customarily to dress in a short petticoat which was tucked between the legs to leave their thighs and legs bare – they wore jewellery on both arms and legs. Among wealthy Gond women silver ornaments were permissible, suggesting the perennial argument about affluence being at least a partial gateway out of caste immobility. The poorer class of Gonds were, naturally, restricted to wearing brass, iron, and coloured glass jewellery.[55]

[50] Ibid.
[51] Briggs, *The Chamars*, p. 145.
[52] Crooke, *The Tribes and Castes*, vol. III, p. 449.
[53] Ibid., p. 114.
[54] Ibid.
[55] Crooke, *The Natives of the British Empire*, p. 22.

Chad Bauman notes the prevalence of similar exclusionary practices among the Satnami (Chamars) community in the Chhattisgarh region of Central India.[56] He provides a number of instances when Satnami men were not allowed to wear full-length dhotis, turbans, and shoes in the proximity of upper-caste people.[57] He notes that Satnami women were forbidden saris with brightly coloured borders and ornaments of silver and gold. His ethnography underscores the power of such distinctions in rural India.

The codes and rules in this domain of life were so rigid that even those who could afford new Western clothes feared violent reactions from orthodox Hindus. Nonetheless, by the turn of the second decade of the twentieth century certain changes had appeared in dressing styles, and once again British colonial ethnographic writers provide the first written accounts of them. These also provide an important background to newspaper reports and Dalit accounts of the 1920s, when Ambedkar raised the question of sartorial codes.

Dignity, Desire, and Respect: The Freedom to Choose Clothing

Several commentators noted that travel by train in the early twentieth century was an inescapably jostling experience which brought all castes together, creating the conditions of a previously unexperienced equality.[58] Social change also took shape with the entry of Dalit men and women in the public sphere, a result of changes in education, increased conversion, domestic service in European and British families, army or military recruitment, and employment in the government services. These collectively represented a large threat to the caste order.[59] The initial impetus towards a visibly transformed sense of Dalit selfhood was seen as escaping caste-prescribed styles of clothing (or undress) through a comprehensive abandoning of what was sartorially Indian and, by con-

[56] Bauman, *Christian Identity*, p. 92.

[57] Ibid., p. 41. The Chamar caste in Chhattisgarh, Central India, changed its name to Satnami during the colonial period.

[58] Crooke, *The Natives of the British Empire*, p. 413.

[59] Moon, *Dr Babasaheb Ambedkar*, vol. 2, pp. 451–84.

trast, a wholesale adoption of what was Western. At stake was the need to bring into being a Dalit dignity visible to all that the upper castes would be forced to acknowledge. Conversion to Christianity and Islam, as well as the acquisition of some level of education, enabled this new impetus. Colonial ethnographers recorded the new opportunities available to sections of Dalits to a new life and some dignity via conversion. In this, economic change played a significant part. Crooke showed that in Cawnpore the extension of the leather trade had made it a great Chamar centre, so that many in this community had become wealthy and aimed at a standard of social respectability much higher than their ascribed position in the Hindu hierarchy.[60]

The appearance in 1936 of *Untouchable*, an autobiography by a Dalit using a pseudonym, Hazari, offers a window on the quest for a new identity between the 1920s and 1950s.[61] Hazari's narrative demonstrates a complicated but strong relationship between religious identity and sartorial change.[62] His conversion to Islam allowed Hazari to adopt new styles of clothing appropriate to his new identity. He says, however, that he could not escape his "Untouchable" status even by changing his religion and clothing. During his time in Bombay, a friend of Hazari's, Yusuf, had asked him to remove his turban and alter clothing which identified him as an "Untouchable". It was at this point that Hazari realised what wearing Western clothes and parting his hair like Europeans really signified: they were necessary to the forging of a new identity which would allow him to mix more easily with other people. Much the same is made clear in Mulk Raj Anand's 1935 novel *Untouchable*, in which the protagonist Bhaka, a Bhangi by caste, expresses his desire to wear trousers and a jacket like those worn by soldiers in the military cantonment in order to change his sense of self.[63] However, the adoption of Western clothes was in emotional or affective terms not a simple process: Hazari says as much: "When I put on my new shirt for

---

[60] Crooke, *The Tribes and Castes*, vol. II, p. 191.

[61] Hazari, *Untouchable*, p. 66.

[62] The exact year of Hazari's birth is not known since his illiterate parents had maintained no record of it. However, an analysis of the events Hazari mentions in his autobiography suggests he was born before Indian independence in 1947.

[63] Anand, *Untouchable*, pp. 8–10.

the first time, I felt very self-conscious and uncomfortable. I did not like the idea of dressing in European fashion; I felt it was not the dress for India and I am still of that opinion. I came to like it only because it made me look different from what I was and gave me a social status I could not have otherwise acquired, except changing my religion."[64] Yet the discomfort had to be borne: he continued to wear coat, trouser, and tie. The internal conflict had to be an aspect of lived life: "everything about [me] was wrong, [my] clothes were wrong, I was born in the wrong family and could not see how I could overcome the difficulties inherent in my parenthood, the community and the karma . . ."[65] Western clothes gave him much needed solace, though not much else. All the same, even the solace was something.

Sometimes these early attempts at the acquisition of a new sense of being were brought about by a response to Christian notions of a modest" and "respectable" body.[66] Bauman argues that among the Satnami Christians the Victorian values of missionaries and indigenous notions of respectable womanhood influenced the sartorial choices of Dalit converts.[67] The colonial ethnographer J.H. Hutton, however, repeats a point made in Hazari's autobiography – which was that though social barriers impelled Dalit conversions to Islam or Christianity, the social stigma attached to them did not vanish at once.[68] Gait was astute in pointing out that the low-caste individual had little left to lose, making conversion a preferred option as it meant at least some alleviation of his oppressed condition. The converted had less to lose and gained something material and concrete via access to education, assistance in employment, and the dropping of a caste designation.

> The great majority of the converts from Hinduism belong to the low castes
> such as the Churas of the Punjab, the Mahars of the Central Provinces and
> Berar, and the Shanars of Madras for whom conversion means an accession
> of respectability as well as cleaner and purer life. The missionaries have raised

[64] Hazari, *Untouchable*, p. 86.
[65] Ibid.
[66] Kent, *Converting Women*, p. 205.
[67] Bauman, *Christian Identity*, p. 136.
[68] Hutton, *Census of India 1931*, vol. I, pp. 485–6.

their converts' standard of cleanliness in dress and habits and their position in general estimation has improved accordingly.[69]

Hindu nationalist reformers in colonial North India also noted that social mobility was enabled by conversion. Cartoons and articles published in journals around the 1930s depicted upper-caste anxieties about conversion. These cartoons caricatured outcaste men and women, even if in the process they had the unintended effect of showing "Untouchables" attaining dignity and status. One of the cartoons which appeared in 1932 in the journal *Hamare Harijan* helps us understand the politics of representation. It caricatured two Harijan women together, one who had converted and the other who had not.[70] The unconverted woman was reduced to the status of a servant whereas the converted woman was wearing European clothes and behaving like a memsahib. The relationship between the two is that of mistress and servant. Western clothing accessories – shoes, hat, gown – and modern furniture appear in this as distinguishing markers of modernity.

Similar caricatures of Dalit men and women in other journals used similar items, such as the umbrella and high-heeled shoes.[71] An image from the journal *Chand* in its special issue *Achoot Ank* in May 1927 represented conversion to Christianity as the path to a decent and civilised body in accordance with notions of decent apparel as propagated by missionaries. The young converts are photographed in their new clothes after their conversion.[72] Madhava Prasad argues that while images reflect a particular type of clothing they are also the conscious productions of a self-image.[73] By claiming the right to footwear, adornments such as hats and umbrellas, and in Kerala wearing the breast cloth in the proximity of upper-caste Hindus showed Dalits taking collective action and asserting what they could wear into a politically

[69] Gait, *Census of India, 1911*, vol. 1, pt 1, p. 137.

[70] *Hamare Harijan,* May 1932, p. 34. The quote in the cartoon of Fig. 1 translates as "Both are from the Harijan caste, one becomes a Christian. While one pets the dog, the other becomes the superior."

[71] Gupta, "Feminine, Criminal or Manly", pp. 309–48.

[72] Tiwari, *Chand, Achoot Ank*, p. 48.

[73] Prasad, "The Struggle to Represent", pp. 527–88.

दोनो हरिजन रक्त-जाति में, किन्तु हृदे इंसाहन एक ।
नीचे एक मेहमानी कुलिया, बैठी करे हुकूमत एक ॥

Fig. 1: The Christian Harijan and the "Untouchable"
Harijan woman.

अछूत बालक ईसाई होने के बाद अपने इस नए बस्त्र पर अभिमान कर रहे हैं !

Fig. 2: Untouchable boys after converting to Christianity,
feeling proud in their new clothes.
Source: Achoot Ank, May 1927, p. 48.

radical issue.[74] Cartoons and images may have exaggerated the difference between converted and unconverted, but they were nevertheless representations of the public perception of the difference.

Sujatha Gidla, a Dalit woman from Andra Pradesh, narrates an incident in her autobiography concerning one of her relatives during the 1930s.[75] Maryamma, her relative, and Maryamma's husband Prasanna Rao, had been raised in the Christian faith and educated from early childhood. On one Christmas day Maryamma went into the village (where no "Untouchable" was allowed to live) to buy spices for the holiday feast. She was wearing a new sari that the missionaries had given her as a Christmas present, and a flower-print blouse she had stitched for herself out of a cast-off dress. Her clothes were seen in the village as a challenge: upper-caste men standing outside a store were infuriated by her apparel and insulted her crudely. The incident was then escalated, resulting in the entire Dalit community of the village being penalised.

For Hazari, his new clothes meant discomfort – even if short-lived. For Bhaka, the adoption of a Western style produced neither the same discomfort nor the same dramatic effect. For Maryamma in South India the sartorial change on account of conversion to Christianity is reminiscent of the experiences of Dalits in North India.

Ambedkar's own sartorial and other life-style choices were meant to be exemplary, intended as one of the pathways to Dalit emancipation from humiliation. They were completely rooted in his strife for the social respect and egalitarian perspective required by the Dalit community. In his autobiography he narrates the first time he travelled out – to Koregaon in the year 1901, to meet his father – as a nightmare.[76] He was a child at the time and his innocent mind was puzzled by the sense of hostility he and his siblings faced despite being well-dressed and looking like they were from a well-to-do family. Ambedkar's father was employed in the army, which had provided them financial security. "Great preparations were made. New shirts of English make, bright bejewelled caps, new shoes, new silk – bordered dhotis, were ordered for the journey . . . We were well-dressed children. From our dress or talk no

[74] Gupta, *The Gender of Caste*, p. 197.
[75] Gidla, *Ants among Elephants*.
[76] Ambedkar, *Autobiography of Dr Ambedkar*.

one could make out that we were children of untouchables. Indeed, the stationmaster was sure we were Brahmin children . . ."[77] However, when Ambedkar revealed his caste identity, the stationmaster was stunned – indeed, he now seemed overcome by repulsion. The vividness of this recollection, when Ambedkar and his brothers faced discrimination all through their journey despite their Western attire, is paradigmatic. Dalit memories in autobiographies and other forms of recorded recollection echo the power of their leader's experience of humiliation.

It is hardly surprising, then, that unlike most Indian nationalist leaders, who could be said to have worn their nationalism on their sleeve by clothing themselves in Indian-style elite apparel, Ambedkar decided to forsake Indian clothing and took pains to project his image as that of a cultured and superior westernised person.[78] His sartorial style worked as a metaphor for the ambitions of his community; it was a deliberate personal choice to assert a political message. In fact, Ambedkar rarely abandoned the suit that he wore as a sign of personal achievement, as his proclamation of the dignity and self-respect every Dalit needed to obtain.[79]

Sartorial choices for Dalits constituted in Ambedkar's mind a more important avenue of his community's struggle than has perhaps been acknowledged and properly studied. He challenged nationalists and Hindu reformers when raising this important question: "[A]re you fit for political power even though you do not allow them to wear what apparel or ornaments they like?'[80] He constantly argued that the "Untouchable" community's clothing prohibitions were part of a semiotic network of hegemonic restrictions. Congress could not claim to be any kind of true representative for Dalits so long as even the clothing of the leaders of that party flaunted their caste-Hindu credentials.[81]

[77] Ibid., pp. 2 and 3.

[78] Deliege, *The Untouchables of India*, pp. 178–9. Personal accounts describe Dalits as filthy, dirty, and foolish. Baby Kamble clearly recalls women of her caste seeming disgusting to her, their hair crawling with lice, their clothes filthy. Kamble, *The Prisons We Broke*, p. 66.

[79] Prasad, "The Struggle to Represent", p. 592.

[80] Moon, *Dr Babasaheb Ambedkar*, vol. 1, p. 41.

[81] Ibid., vol. 2, p. 358.

Baby Kamble records how Ambedkar's advice to change their clothing habits had a deep impact on the Mahar community in the Maharashtra region during the 1930s.[82] She recalls his arrival to give a speech in her region – his sturdy physique, fair complexion, European attire, suit and boots. Everything about him impressed the audience, and Ambedkar's advice, "we must reform ourselves", had a big impact.[83] Soon after his Mahad speech of 1927, Dalit women felt inspired enough to drape their saris like upper-caste women, and cover their legs down to their ankles. In this they were helped by upper-caste women such as Lakshmibai Tipnis and Indirabai Chitre from the Chandraseniya Kayastha Prabhu community.[84] To help, the women were given eight annas for *choli baangadi* (blouse bangles). Ambedkar's speech also influenced the men: they gave up wearing jewellery on their hands and ears.

Dalit autobiographies in post-colonial India illustrate the continuing relationship of clothing and caste privilege; they recall the wearing by Dalits of apparel that seemed uppity and objectionable to the upper castes, resulting in the usual mockery and violence. Omprakash Valmiki's autobiography, *Joothan* (meaning the leftover food in Hindu houses), offers a poignant tale of the pain arising from inhuman caste practices which forced the Dalit community to eat the leavings of elites for sheer survival.[85] Valmiki's book is set in Uttar Pradesh and, beyond its narration of the author's life, tells us of lives more broadly in an "Untouchable" (Bhangi) community. It narrates an incident of 1955 when Valmiki was a child in Class IV at his local school: "If we ever went to school in neat and clean clothes, then our class fellows said, 'hey you untouchable, he has come dressed in new clothes.' If one went wearing old and shabby clothes, then they said, 'hey, you untouchable, get away from me, you stink'."[86]

---

[82] Kamble, *The Prisons We Broke*, p. 65.

[83] Ibid. p. 66.

[84] Paik, *Dalit Women's Education*, p. 171.

[85] Valmiki, *Joothan*, p. 13.

[86] Ibid. "*saaf suthre kapde pehenkar kasha mein jao toh ladke kehte, 'abe chuhre ka, naye kapde pehen kar ayah ain.' Maile purane kapde pehan kar jao toh kehte, 'abe chuhre ke, dur hat badbu aa rahi hain'* . . .", p. 13. For the English translation, see Valmiki, *Joothan: A Dalit's Life*, p. 3.

In rural India too, Dalit groups saw the danger of wearing new clothes. Caste-Hindu antagonism to even minimal finery shown on the body of a Dalit was something Dr Tulsi Ram, who later taught at New Delhi's Jawaharlal Nehru University, discovered in the 1960s. In his autobiography, *Murdahiya* (the cremation ground), he recounts his childhood experiences in a Dalit village, Dharampur in eastern Uttar Pradesh.[87] Primarily, the recollections are of mundane life among Dalits of the Chamar community facing unending barriers and caste stigma. In 1962, when Tulsi Ram wore a "pajama" for the first time, he became the butt of mockery by caste-Hindus.[88] This was because, being embarrassed about wearing it, he tied the pajama as high up his waist as a dhoti. The Brahmins in his village used regional idioms to satirise his appearance: "When the father doesn't even know how to fart, the son tries to show off by playing a conch!"[89] His father being a field labourer, the son had to suffer these taunts in silence. "During these days," he says, "I accidentally touched a cycle's handle which was there in the veranda of the school premises. This cycle belonged to Ranvir Singh. Suddenly somebody slapped me on the back and I heard . . . 'after wearing the Pajama you have lost your mind, You swine!' This incident was the extent of my pajama. After all, because of this I got beaten. This pajama had become a problem for me."[90]

Sheoraj Singh Bechain's autobiograpbhy, *Mera Bachpan Mere Kandho Par* (My Childhood on My Shoulders), set in independent India, narrates his life story as a Chamar in Uttar Pradesh. His community people were summoned for unpaid work during ceremonial feasts around Hindu religious rituals and were expected to pick up the leftovers. Against the usual norm, he dressed in his best clothes for the feast. For this

[87] Ram, *Murdahiya*.

[88] Ibid., p. 140.

[89] Ibid. *"Pyjama pahne dekh kar gaon ke brahman kahte: baap ke paad na aawe – poot shankh bajawe."*

[90] Ibid., p. 141. *"Issi beech ek din meine school ke baramde mei khali ek cycle ke handle ko chu dia jo cycle ranvir singh ki thi. Achanak piche se mere sir par jor ka tamacha laga aur mujhe sunna pada: 'Charjama pahir ke tohar dimagwa kharab hoi gayil hai, sarau kahin ke yah ghatna mere pajame ki parkastha thi. Akhir isne mujhe pitwa hi diya. Yah pyjama mere liye ek musibat ban gaya tha."*

he was ridiculed by the Hindu Yadav of the village who was hosting a traditional ceremonial feast at the death of an elder.

> In order to partake of the feast, it was expected that one should appear piti-able. Once at Master Mokkam Singh Yadav's feast I went all dressed up. I had washed my shirt with *reh* (a salty, snow-white weed used as a natural de-tergent), oiled my hair and polished my shoes to a brilliant shine. On seeing me, the master commented, "You hardly look like a chamar! All dressed up like a Nawab, did you hope to gain entry into our courtyard? Out you go!" I left immediately. It was then that I felt the first stirrings of my sense of self-respect . . .[91]

In most cases, encounters such as these generated a new politics of dignity critical to the sense of Dalit selfhood. The works of Hazari and Bechain, Sujatha Gidla and Vasant Moon, Om Prakash Valmiki and Tulsi Ram corroborate and amplify Ambedkar's first exhortation to shed imprisoning cloth and don a new garb for Dalit self-confidence, self-identification, and self-assertion. Each of these writers, in his or her own way, illustrates the coming into being of new perspectives on the processes of sartorial and personality change believed necessary among Dalit communities.

There have been other voices. In a recent Dalit memoir, Yashica Dutt writes of her dilemma in forging her Dalit identity by dressing differently from upper-caste Hindus.[92] The Dalit activist and entrepre-neur Chandra Bhan Prasad says that "the pressure to look good, to be clean, is so much on Dalits because everyone assumes we are filthy un-touchables. Even if a Brahmin is wearing torn clothes, he is still babu saheb."[93]

Then there are the representations of the Dalit body in the main-stream Indian cinema. Broadly, these have echoed traditional caste codes when putting costumes on Dalit characters in films. In early films

---

[91] Bechain, *My Childhood*, p. 61.

[92] Dutt, *Coming Out as Dalit*, p. 24. She says: "I didn't understand why we needed to dress in good clothes when we couldn't afford them, but for mum, her jewellery and personal vanity mattered a lot less than social (upper-caste) acceptance of her children."

[93] https://www.livemint.com/Leisure/ avsrwntNuBHG3THdAb5aMP/ The-changing-fabric-of-Dalit-life.html.

such as *Achoot Kanya* (Hindi, 1936; Gujarati, 1940), and *Sujata* (Hindi, 1969), various characters – such as Kasturi, Dukhiya, and Sujata – were often the Dalit receivers of upper-caste reform. In some of these films costume as caste marker was blurred, which could lead to a conflict of identity for the Dalit individual – as in the case of Sujata (played by the actress Nutan). In recent regional cinema we have *Sairat* (2016), *Fandry* (2013), *Kabali* (2016), and *Karnan* (2021), in which we see a more active voice for Dalit subjectivity. Caste is more visible, and the politics of protest now has a different language. For the young boy Jabya in *Fandry* (2013), buying blue jeans remains an unfulfilled aspiration throughout the film. In *Kabali* (2016), Rajinikanth's character constantly makes references to Ambedkar's politics and wears a suit as a symbol of defiance against the upper castes. Over a climactic moment he says: "If it's a problem for you that I progress, then I will definitely progress more than you, I will get educated, I will wear a coat and suit, I will sit with my legs before you, stylishly."[94] Films now offer us different approaches to Dalit identity and subjectivity via what is worn and spoken.

Finally, the media. Despite recent changes in India, stories of caste-led conflict over sartorial choices are frequently reported. Caste markers have been enforced in schools by educated caste-Hindu teachers, as for example in 2015 in a school in Tirunelveli near Chennai, where students were required to wear differently coloured wrist bands to indicate their caste.[95] In 2018 in Gujarat a 13-year-old Dalit boy from the Valmiki community was allegedly attacked for wearing a pair of Mojris – leather shoes traditionally seen as royal footwear and worn by upper-caste people in certain parts of India.[96] In 2020 the *Indian Express* reported a 20-year-old Dalit man in Cuddalore being attacked by a group of caste-Hindus for wearing sunglasses and riding a bike.[97]

∾

[94] Suresh Ravichandran, "Kabali: A Film to Celebrate", https://www.round-tableindia.co.in/kabali-a-film-to-celebrate/.

[95] https://indianexpress.com/article/india/india-news-india/wearing-caste-on-my-wrist-green-for-dalits-red-for-thevars/.

[96] https://www.bbc.com/news/world-asia-india-44517922.

[97] https://www.newindianexpress.com/states/tamil-nadu/2019/aug/07/dalit-man-in-cuddalore-village-attacked-for-wearing-sunglasses-2015366.html.

Drawing inspiration from Ambedkar's comments, I have here tried to show and argue for a Dalit perspective on the necessity of a modified sartorial perspective as a form of identity transformation, selfhood, and social defiance – especially in rural contexts, where Dalits were most victimised by sartorial exclusion. Dalit responses were naturally far more varied across different Dalit caste groups, genders, and regions than may be evident in the present essay. But there is no doubt that the "clothing question", if it can be called that, attained a special meaning in the Dalit language of protest and aspiration.

References

Ambedkar, B.R., *Autobiography of Dr. Ambedkar: Waiting for a Visa* (Chennai: Xpress Publishing, 2019).

Ambedkar, B.R., *Jati Bhed ka Uchhed*, in Vasant Moon, ed., *Dr Babasaheb Ambedkar: Writings and Speeches*, vol. 5, pp. 7–8.

Anand, Mulk Raj, *Untouchable* (1935; rpntd New Delhi: Penguin Books, 2001).

Bauman, Chad M., *Christian Identity and Dalit Religion in Hindu India, 1868–1947* (London: William B. Eerdmans Publishing Company, 2008).

Bechain, Sheoraj Singh, *My Childhood on My Shoulders*, from Hindi trans. by Deeba Zafir and Tapan Basu (New Delhi: Oxford University Press, 2018).

Blunt, E.A., *The Caste System of Northern India: With Special Reference to the United Provinces of Agra and Oudh* (Allahabad: Superintendent of Government Press, 1931).

Briggs, Geo, *The Chamars* (Calcutta: Association Press / Oxford University Press, 1920).

Burn, R., *Imperial Gazetteer of India, Provincial Series: United Provinces of Agra and Oudh*, vol. I (Calcutta: Superintendent of Government Printing, 1908).

Crooke, W., *The Natives of the British Empire: Natives of Northern India* (London: Archibald Constable and Company, 1907).

Crooke, W., *The Tribes and Castes of the North Western Provinces and Oudh* (Calcutta: Superintendent of Government Printing, 1896).

Deliege, Robert, *The Untouchables of India* (Oxford: Berg Publishers, 1999).

Dutt, Yashica, *Coming Out as Dalit: A Memoir* (New Delhi: Aleph Book Company, 2019).

Eyde, E.H.H., *Census of India 1921: United Provinces of Agra and Oudh* (1901), vol. XVI, pt I (Allahabad: United Provinces' Government Press, 1923).

Gait, E.A., *Census of India, 1911, Volume 1, Part 1, Report by E.A. Gait* (Calcutta: Superintendent, Government Printing, 1913).

Gidla, Sujatha, *Ants Among Elephants: An Untouchable Family and the Making of Modern India* (Delhi: Harper Collins, 2017).

Gupta, Charu, "Feminine, Criminal or Manly: Imagining Dalit Masculinities in Colonial North India", *The Indian Economic and Social History Review*, vol. 47, 2010.

Gupta, Charu, *The Gender of Caste: Representing Dalits in Print* (Ranikhet: Permanent Black and Ashoka University, 2017).

Hardgrave, Robert, "The Breast Cloth Controversy: Caste Consciousness and Social Change in Southern Travancore", *Indian Economic and Social History Review*, vol. 5, no. 2, June 1968.

Hazari, *Untouchable: The Autobiography of an Indian Outcaste* (New York: Praeger Publishers, 1969).

Hutton, J.H., *Caste in India: Its Nature, Functions and Origin* (Cambridge: Cambridge University Press, 1946).

Hutton, J.H., *Census of India 1931, Volume I: India, Part 1: Report; Corresponding Member of the Anthropologische Gesellschaft of Vienna; To Which is Annexed an Actuarial Report by L.S. Vaidyanathan* (Delhi: Manager of Publications, 1933).

Hutton, J.H., *Census of India, 1933, vol. I: India – A Report* (Delhi: Manager of Publications, 1933).

Kamble, Baby, *The Prisons We Broke*, trans. from the Marathi *Jina Amucha* by Maya Pandit (New Delhi: Orient Longman, 2008).

Kent, Eliza F., *Converting Women: Gender and Protestant Christianity in Colonial South India* (New York: Oxford University Press, 2004).

Khare, R.S., "The Body, Sensoria, and Self of the Powerless: Remembering/ Re-Membering, Indian Untouchable Women", *New Literary History*, vol. 26, no. 1, 1995.

Kumar, Udaya, "Self Body and Inner Sense: Some Reflections on Sree Narayana Guru and Kumaran Asan", *Studies in History*, vol. 13, no. 2, 1997.

Levine, Philippa, "States of Undress: Nakedness and the Colonial Imagination", *Victorian Studies*, vol. 50, no. 2, February 2008.

Moon, Vasant, *Growing up Untouchable in India: A Dalit Autobiography* (New York: Rowman and Littlefield Publishers, Inc., 2001).

Moon, Vasant, ed., *Dr Babasaheb Ambedkar: Writings and Speeches*, 5 vols (New Delhi: Dr Ambedkar Foundation, 1979).

Moon, Vasant, ed., *Dr Babasaheb Ambedkar: Writings and Speeches*, vol. 2 (Bombay: Education Department, Government of Maharashtra, 1982).

Nair, Janaki, *Miners and Millhands: Work, Culture and Politics in Princely Mysore* (New Delhi: Sage Publications, 1998).

Paik, Shailaja, *Dalit Women's Education in Modern India: Double Discrimination* (Delhi: Routledge, 2014).

Pawar, Urmila, and Meenakshi Moon, *We Also Made History: Women in the Ambedkarite Movement*, trans. from the Marathi *Aamhihi Itihas Ghadawla Ambedkari Chalwait Streeyancha Sahabhag* by Wandana Sonalkar (New Delhi: Zubaan, 2016; English translation 2008).

Prasad, Anupama, "Caste, Class, and Clothing: North India in the First Half of the Twentieth Century", PhD Dissertation, New Delhi: Jawaharlal Nehru University, 2016.

Prasad, M. Madhava, "The Struggle to Represent and Sartorial Modernity: On a Visual Dimension of Indian Nationalist Politics", *Inter-Asia Cultural Studies*, vol. 15, no. 4, 2014.

Ram, Dr Tulsi, *Murdahiya: Atamkatha ka Pahla Khand* (New Delhi: Raj Kamal Publishers, 2012).

Rege, Sharmila, *Writing Caste / Writing Gender: Reading Dalit Women's Testimonies* (New Delhi: Zubaan, 2006).

Tarlo, Emma, *Clothing Matters: Dress and Identity in India* (Chicago: University of Chicago Press, 1996).

Tiwari, P. Nandkishore, *Chand, Achoot Ank,* year 5, no. 2, May 1927.

Turner, A.C., *Census of India, 1931, vol. 18, pt 1: United Provinces of Agra and Oudh* (Allahabad: The Superintendent, Printing and Stationery, 1933).

Valmiki, Omprakash, *Joothan: A Dalit's Life*, English trans. Arun Prabha Mukherjee (Kolkata: Samya, 2003).

Valmiki, Omprakash, *Joothan: Autobiography* (Delhi: Radhakrishna Prakashan, 1997).

8

Inheritance and Caste
Formations in Kerala

SHARIKA THIRANAGAMA

Introduction

IN MAY 2016, Vinu Palissery and I made a trip to KIRTADS (Kerala Institute for Research Training & Development Studies of Scheduled Castes and Scheduled Tribes).[1] It was a hectic time for the staff there: they were handling large workloads relating to the entrance of applicants to the university, which involved investigating and verifying caste certificates. One employee, Renuka, an upper-caste woman, described the "vigilance work" involved in investigating cases.[2] One of

[1] This research was funded by the National Science Foundation (Award No. 1460012) and the Wenner Gren Foundation. I would like to thank the editors of the volume, especially Sanal Mohan, K. Satyanarayana, and Ramnarayan Rawat, for their excellent feedback and support. Ram in particular has seen multiple drafts of this essay and I am deeply grateful. I would like to thank all the participants in the original workshop at the CSDS whose comments helped this essay grow. Vinu Palissery was my research assistant and companion, none of this research would have been possible without her. Finally, I would like to thank Thomas Blom Hansen, who offered his characteristically thoughtful advice on earlier drafts of this essay. Of course, my primary thanks are to those who kindly talked to me throughout 2016–17 and whom I always hope to honour in this work.

[2] All names in this article have been anonymised to protect confidentiality.

the many methods was to verify an applicant's caste through knowledge of hereditary occupations. I asked her how this method could be trusted if there had been significant changes in traditional occupations. Bemused, she asserted firmly that "people should know their *culture and practices.*" Hereditary occupations, in this case, referred to historical forms of landless agricultural labour, which were considered part of the traditional occupation of formerly enslaved Dalit communities in Kerala, alongside basket weaving and other such work. In contrast to Renuka, Krishnan – another officer we met – was impassioned on the subject of traditional occupations and change: "In my opinion, all SCs [Scheduled Castes] and STs [Scheduled Tribes] should abandon their traditional occupations," he told us, adding, "It is their stigma and form of subjugation." Krishnan himself was from a Dalit community. He believed "all agricultural labour should vacate and diversify and enter new jobs." While for people of his generation it is still possible to link people to agricultural labour and their traditional occupations, he said he hoped it would be a different story in fifty years.

I had asked both Krishnan and Renuka about occupational changes because months of sustained research in the Palakkad District with agricultural labourers, from both Dalit and OBC (Other Backward Class) Ezhava communities, had shown me that very few young people wish to continue their parents' occupation as agricultural labourers. Many viewed it – as one of my older Dalit friends explained to me – as *nainakidu* (shameful) work, as caste-based forms of labour. Krishnan and Renuka's opposed views on the issue knot together caste as a deeply consequential inheritance. Their differing responses to my query also show us that people from different castes tend to differ on whether people should be tethered to their pasts.

Another story now, about Balan Chettan, a man in his sixties from the Dalit Cherumar Pulaya community.[3] Balan Chettan's family had worked for a landlord who employed around thirty families. Chettan no longer laboured in agricultural work, he was a nightwatchman for a bank. He told us his life had been entirely dependent on the "landlord". In most cases, this is the lease-holding tenant farmer rather than the distant

---

[3] *Chettan* means elder brother, and, along with *ettan*, is a respectful term for an older man.

jenmi (outright) landlord. As they were paid in kind via *edangazhi* (measures of unhusked rice), expenses for weddings or emergencies had to be borrowed from the landlord. One was tied down by work and debt. There were, he said, "friendly relations because there was no choice. You have to go to them for everything. You have to please the landlord." As with the upper castes, relationships with the OBC Ezhavas, both landlords and labourers, could never be absent of caste difference: "You can't go to their house . . . if the *cherumakkal* get in the house, the Ezhava and others will say that their pots will break."[4]

Balan Chettan described the house he had grown up in as a *chala/chalam* (a small thatched hut). The landlord provided a small space, and that was where people like him lived. By contrast, our interviews were in Balan Chettan's house, sitting on his sofa in his front visiting room, the sofa a marker of the family's pride and respectability. This house was in a sparsely inhabited area, a new road winding from the main road, the houses facing open spaces. It was a new residential colony still in the early phase of being established, not historically a Dalit colony. Balan and Kalyani came to this formerly panchayat land in 1982 when offered 4 cents (c. 1750 sq. ft) through the state's new housing assistance schemes. Balan Chettan saw this as part of the journey for dignity and respectability that he and his family were embarking on. This was the third house he had built on the land. When they first came, he had put up a small thatched hut. Then he tore that down and built a tiled house. Now, finally, with the help of the panchayat's Rs 200,000 building scheme, he had built this concrete home that we were sitting in.

Chettan's three houses, and the future stretching in front of him that he had worked so hard to create, is true of every Dalit agricultural labourer I met, man and woman alike. Every labourer I met had acquired the right to his or her homestead in the 1970s and built their third house in this sequence of thatch, tile, concrete. Each of their stories reflected this steady commitment to a future.

These two stories illustrate the main theme of this essay, i.e. both undesired and desired inheritance, as well as histories and futures enabled.

---

[4] *Cherumakkal:* An umbrella term for Cherumar communities. *Makkal* means "people".

This allows us to discuss the durability of inequality as well as aspirations for new futures. First to the *undesired* inheritance: in Kerala, the various different communities, especially Dalits and Adivasis, continue to be understood through their "traditional" occupations. For the Dalit Cherumar and Paraya communities in Palakkad this is a history of agricultural labour and enslavement. I examine below the legacy of this agrarian history of servitude. Throughout I discuss how, despite recent transformations, the forms of work, the interactions, the disparities, and the aspirations are tethered to the longer histories of stratification through which they are inhabited. Second, as regards the *desired* inheritance: the acquisition of land for a homestead is a significant symbolic and material asset for labouring families that have been able to establish themselves as self-enclosed families. Houses are central to how people imagine and invest in durable futures. For most people I spoke to, such as Balan Chettan, the idea of expenditure was centred on children's marriages, education, home improvement, and house construction. These avenues were seen as intertwined in the pursuit of well-being. However, homesteads as aspirations also could not be disentangled from caste disparities.

Depictions of Kerala's post-colonial developmental state have stressed the unique nature of the state's reduction of poverty through extensive public provisions, emphasis on social entitlements, rises in literacy and public health, and regard for political mobilisation and protest.[5] The transformations in Kerala are impressive, but with significant disparities for Dalit and Adivasi communities. My writings address contemporary caste formation in two modes. In a state where welfare-oriented measures have comprehensively transformed everyday life, I try to examine caste as structuring socio-politico-economic formations that differentially apportion life chances, assets, and mobility, and that profoundly shape Dalit struggles to raise themselves towards shared visions of well-being. Second, I examine how caste relations are experienced in everyday life, particularly by Dalit communities. This, I suggest in my wider work, resides not only in the better explored new public spaces and contests but is actively entrenched in and makes up the fabric of

[5] See Heller, *The Labor of Development*; and Ramakumar, "Public Action, Agrarian Change".

new kinds of private spaces, such as the home/house, and the neighbour-hood.[6] Here, I focus on my first concern – disparity and caste as a struc-turing force – critically examining how agrarian labour as "traditional occupation" shapes contemporary life chances and desires while ex-amining Dalit aspirations for transformation, particularly around the family. Following Patricia Hill Collins, I suggest this also allows us to place Dalit women at the centre of our discussion on mobility, aspira-tion, work, caste discrimination, and new futures.[7]

Here I draw on my fieldwork from June 2015 to June 2016. My work was predominantly with female agricultural labourers in Palakkad Dis-trict, which continues to be the district in Kerala with the highest pro-portion of (Hindu) Dalits – 16.5 per cent.[8] This is the percentage for them given in the 2011 Census.[9] I worked with three Dalit communi-ties: Cherumar Kanakan, Pulaya, and Paraya. The Kanakan and Pulaya communities were referred to by the colonial authorities as subcastes of the Cherumar caste, who, alongside the Parayas, were considered by com-mentators such as Francis Buchanan (in 1807) to live and work in some of the most wretched conditions he had seen.[10] My friend and research assistant Vinu Palissery and I worked largely in three colonies in one large rural eastern panchayat.[11] These were K Colony, composed of both OBC Ezhava and Dalit Kanakan Cherumar communities, and O Colony and P Colony, two adjacent and predominantly single-caste colonies comprising the Dalit Paraya and Pulaya Cherumar commu-nities. This was supplemented with fieldwork in a western panchayat with Namboodiri, Nair, and Gupta "landlords", and Dalit Cherumar labourers. We conducted ethnographic interviews and participant ob-servation as well as broad genealogical surveys with thirty-three house-holds.

Relations between the OBC Ezhava and Dalit communities are

[6] See, for example, Thiranagama "Respect Your Neighbor".

[7] Collins, "Gender, Black Feminism".

[8] https://censusindia.gov.in/ Tables_Published/SCST/dh_sc_kerala.pdf.

[9] The SC population of Palakkad is around 403,833, 14.4 per cent of the whole population of Palakkad, https://www.censusindia.co.in/district/palakkad-district-kerala-593.

[10] Buchanan, *A Journey from Madras*, pp. 370–1.

[11] There were twenty-four Dalit colonies in the panchayat.

complex. The Ezhavas are around 23 per cent of the population, the largest Hindu community in Kerala. Historically associated with toddy-tapping, in fact they are to be found in multiple occupations across the class scale.[12] Despite my focus on relations between Ezhavas and Dalits, these economies, histories, and interactions were still structures shaped by upper castes such as Nairs and Namboodiris, who, while not always physically present in these rural areas, are the undoubted beneficiaries then and now of economic, social, and political caste privilege.

I have used initials for these colonies to preserve their anonymity and negate derogatory naming. Many Dalit residential areas have names denoting them as malodorous, haunted, or plainly bad, or they are known by a caste name. Many are located near waste dumps, cemeteries, and other "polluted" lands. In areas attached to large Namboodiri or Nair "estates", they are known as owned by those big houses. However, I note it here because it is significant: that people were positioned within land-scapes that designated them by their caste name, their association, or their environment.

Rural areas like Palakkad are often presumed to be casteist because they are "stuck in the past", rather than have their caste relations ana-lysed as part of the contemporary *"rural modern"* – as I term it here. Not least, the 2011 census reported that though 47.5 million Dalits are now listed as living in urban areas, around 153.9 million are still un-derstood to be living in rural areas.[13] Thus, rural areas in the process of transformation represent the conditions of life for most Dalit commu-nities. While what I sketch here is specific to the lives of the people I have come to know, I hope nonetheless to provide insights into the histories, struggles, and dilemmas that many like them grapple with.

Caste Inheritance and
Racial Formations

In Kerala some scholars and many upper-caste Malayalis understand caste as a symbolic, residual, and customary form persisting only as a fragmented remainder of the past in the face of large-scale social trans-formation. For example, Patrick Heller sees caste as symbolic and as the

[12] Osella and Osella, *Social Mobility in Kerala*.
[13] *Census of India, 2011*.

source of "non-economic" forms of domination, which he contrasts with "economic" transformation.[14] This is a disturbing distinction that both misrecognises the fact that Kerala's wealth and economic forms of domination entailed and were enabled by caste, and that for Dalits inequality compounds social humiliation and economic domination.[15] However, as Jodhka and Manor argue, we fail to understand caste if we see it as residual, or if we analyse it only as identification and symbolic form implemented materially.[16] Rather, like race, caste persists within substantialised forms that both determine individual identification and interactions, and is continually materially secured institutionally and historically.[17] Caste ideologies, structures, and relations are embedded within a whole range of institutions ranging from associations, political parties, and occupations to everyday social and material practices. These render caste's significance to be its promise of being more *durable* than anything else. To Manor and Jodhka's suggestion that we need to examine caste empirically by focusing on its "articulations" with "the patterns and processes of social and economic change",[18] I highlight caste formations and aspirations as realised *durationally*, both intergenerationally in families and through being historically situated and enacted.

The family is a central site for examining caste across Kerala's various communities. In colonial and post-colonial Kerala, debates about marriage, kin, and sexual relations have been *the* critical sites through which ideas about modernity, tradition, backwardness, "tenancy", and land rights were debated in colonial and post-colonial Kerala.[19] This scholarship has extensively discussed upper-caste Nairs and Namboodiris, and

[14] Heller, "Degrees of Democracy", and idem, "Kerala: Deepening a Radical Social Democracy".

[15] See Devika, "Egalitarian Developmentalism", for a critique of Heller, "Kerala: Deepening a Radical Social Democracy".

[16] Jodhka and Manor, *Contested Hierarchies*.

[17] Ibid., pp. 14–17; also see Rafanell and Gorringe, "Consenting to Domination?"; on race, cf. Omi and Winant, *Racial Formation in the United States*.

[18] Jodhka and Manor, *Contested Hierarchies*.

[19] Jeffrey, "Matriliny, Marxism"; Jeffrey, "Legacies of Matriliny"; Kodoth "Shifting the Ground"; Kodoth, "Courting Legitimacy"; Saradamoni, *Matriliny Transformed*.

OBC Ezhavas.[20] Families are always members of caste communities, their marriages and organisation reflecting upon the community as well as enacted within caste networks of relations.

The axiomatic good of all families is *inheritance*, the possibility of generating and transmitting reputation, children, houses, property, jewellery, and other goods through birth and marriage.[21] Feminist work on gender and inheritance has particularly focused on blocked forms of female inheritance.[22] I wish to retool this discussion into focusing on concrete familial and household models, ideologies, practices, and aspirations among Dalit communities. This means examining caste-segmented inheritance as it appears within Dalit communities and for the purpose of Dalit Studies.

Broader sociological discussions of inheritance are now heavily influenced by the economist Thomas Piketty's argument that contemporary inequality rests on examining intergenerational transfers of *familial* wealth rather than simply income: inheritance accumulated from "fortunes accumulated in the past" has more weight than savings accumulated from "work in the present".[23] Oliver and Shapiro argue that "wealth signifies the command over financial resources that a family has accumulated over its lifetime along with those resources that have been inherited over generations . . . most often it is used to create opportunities, secure a desired stature and standard of living, or pass class status along to one's children . . . *wealth taps not only contemporary resources but material assets that have historic origins.*"[24] While Piketty's analysis concentrates on wealthy families and largely ignores race, Oliver and Shapiro describe the cost for those who have struggled to accumulate and transmit because of racialised structures.

In examining blockages to inheritance in the US, scholars have

[20] Nineteenth-century marriage-reform movements were at the forefront of modernisation campaigns by upper-caste associations seeking new political and social roles. See Kodoth, "Gender, Caste and Matchmaking"; Devika, "Egalitarian Developmentalism".

[21] E.g. Kapadia, *Siva and Her Sisters*.

[22] E.g. Roy, "Empowering Women"; Basu, *Dowry and Inheritance*.

[23] Piketty, *Capital*; see also Oliver and Shapiro, *Black Wealth, White Wealth*.

[24] Oliver and Shapiro, *Black Wealth, White Wealth*, pp. 2–3 (my italics).

emphasised particular foci in explaining how histories of racial formations have shaped contemporary disparities in wealth, the major focus
being home ownership.[25] Home ownership emerged in the US as one
of the most critical aspects of a safety net for working families, as well
as a differentiating source of wealth accumulation for upper-middle-
class families, resources that grew over time. Herring and Henderson
argue that the denial of the opportunity – through active federal legal
discrimination and everyday racism – for African Americans "to acquire and pass down accumulated wealth until the 1960s" has "created
generational consequences that continue to impact African Americans
today."[26] There are obvious parallels I wish to draw upon in my discussion of histories of agrarian enslavement, disparities in land accumulation, and the emergence of a real-estate market in post-land reform
that continues to impact and shape Dalit life in Kerala. This is the profound effect of *cumulative* historical inequality as a specific form of
inequality for particular communities which is intrinsically tied to the
privilege of other communities.

Foregrounding the family while examining inheritance also allows
us to reposition Dalit women and their work at the centre of understanding durable inequality and caste. Patricia Hill Collins describes the
family as an intersectional paradigm.[27] She locates the household and
family as both an ideological form and principle of social organisation
at the centre of intersecting hierarchies.[28] In the US, Collins argues,
the family both organises racial and social hierarchies and attachments,
as well as differentially distributes access to property, security, and debt.

[25] E.g. Rothstein, *Colour of Law;* Herring and Henderson, "Wealth Inequality". However, Darity, Jr, *et al.*, "What We Get Wrong", argue that home ownership is *one* and not *the* component of racialised wealth gaps.

[26] Herring and Henderson, "Wealth Inequality", p. 6; see also Coates, "The
Case for Reparations".

[27] Collins, "Gender, Black Feminism"; see also Collins, "It's All in the Family".

[28] An intersectional paradigm is when "certain ideas/or practices [here the fam-
ily] surface repeatedly across multiple systems of oppression" and serve as "focal
points for intersecting systems of oppression", making them "central to how
gender, sexuality, race, class and nation mutually construct one another." Collins,
"Gender, Black Feminism", p. 48.

Differentiations within and between families are produced by and re-produce hierarchical structures.[29] Collins proposes that accounting for "the family" (the "institutionalised group access to wealth") would reinvigorate social class analysis often focused on measuring individuals and their mobility. Gender and family would thus not be secondary or part of a putative "private", only to be studied in relation to women (and vice versa where women would not only be studied in relation to family) but the family itself would be understood as central to ra-cial formations, thus also reconceptualising black women's lives and struggles as central to black political economy.[30]

For the Dalit communities I work with, household structure and family organisation (upper caste and Dalit) historically structured work, transforming only latterly into the possibility of a self-enclosed Dalit family as the primary mode of transmitting forms of property, distinc-tion, mobility, and aspiration. This family was located now in a neigh-bourhood and transmitted land onwards to their children as saleable. Home ownership, new ideas of work, and new ideas of education were critical. This argument, I propose, gives us a distinct perspective on the articulations of caste which centrally locates Dalit women and the everyday aspirations towards well-being which inform people's narra-tives and practices.

Agrarian Histories of Caste: Inheriting the Traditional Occupation

In academic writing on upper and middle castes, "traditional occupa-tions" recede into a distant past, celebrated as "culture", as upper castes embarked on "modernisation".[31] In contrast, "traditional occupation" for lower and Dalit castes is a form of stained inheritance, one that be-comes biologised and difficult to efface. As Ramnarayan Rawat remarks, "the factor that has contributed most to the continued subordination of Dalits has been the ghettoization of their communities into so-called

[29] Ibid., pp. 48–50.
[30] Ibid., pp. 51–2.
[31] E.g. Singer, *When a Great Tradition Modernizes*; and Natarajan, *Cultural-ization of Caste*, for a thorough critique.

'traditional' and 'ritually impure' occupations."[32] In fact, as Mendelsohn and Vicziany emphasise, "the majority of Untouchables never perform the 'traditional' work that is the presumptive basis of their Untouchability."[33] Instead, Rawat suggests we pay real attention to the "actual social experiences – both past and present – of those defined as 'untouchables'."[34]

Despite the list of occupations that are supposed to define the traditional work of Dalit castes, Dalits in South India are predominantly agricultural labour.[35] Thus, arguments about pollution and purity have to be connected to the political economy of agrarian life.[36] Across India, in the 1991 census almost exactly half (49.06 per cent) of "main" Scheduled Caste workers are agricultural labourers.[37] The next highest classification is "cultivators" at 25.4 per cent. While the percentage of agricultural labour as main work has declined in the 2001 census to 39.16 per cent (from 49.06), this does not take into consideration women workers who predominate in agricultural labour but are categorised as marginal workers (working for less that 183 days a year). In 2001, every third Dalit in Kerala was still an agricultural labourer,[38] and overwhelmingly rural.[39]

In British Malabar (Palakkad District was in southern Malabar) every inch of land was owned, right down to the riverbed, by large corporate family houses, upper-caste Namboodiri Brahmin and Nair; some private individuals, most often from dominant castes; and corporate

---

[32] Rawat, *Reconsidering Untouchability*, p. 3.

[33] Mendelsohn and Vicziany, *The Untouchables*, p. 31.

[34] For example, Rawat shows that Chamars were most likely primarily a peasant caste, comprising multiple levels of the agrarian economy. This does not square with the colonial characterisation of them as "landless labourers" who were "alienated" from their traditional "polluting" occupation as "leatherworkers". See Rawat, *Reconsidering Untouchability*, pp. 54–84.

[35] Harriss, Jeyaranjan, and Nagaraj, "Land, Labour and Caste Politics".

[36] Mosse, "A Relational Approach"; idem, "The Modernity of Caste".

[37] *Census of India, 1991*, "Chapter 3", https://ncsc.nic.in/files/Chapter%20 3_2.pdf.

[38] "Kerala Data Highlights, the Scheduled Castes", *Census of India, 1991*.

[39] It should be noted that, as per the 2011 census, 81.8 per cent of Dalits reside in rural areas in Kerala.

temple bodies (*dewaswoms*), predominantly Tamil Brahmin residential groups.[40] All labour relations were structured through caste. Namboodiri and Tamil Brahmins were forbidden from engaging in any form of labour as all the upper castes deemed labour demeaning. Those from the upper castes, Namboodiri, and Nair known as Jenmis, would have large housing complexes – *illoms* by Namboodiris and *tarawads* by Nairs – inclusive of large joint families, livestock, growing areas, ritual shrines – and would also possess agricultural land in nearby as well as far-flung places. Agricultural land would then be leased to tenants, most often from dominant castes such as Chettiars, poorer Nairs, Guptas, and sometimes wealthy (OBC) Ezhavas. They might then have labourers to work the land, or they might lease the land further on, to other tenants, often Ezhava and Mappila Muslim, who would then have labourers themselves. The bulk of the actual labour was done by landless labourers from, predominantly, the Dalit, Kanakan, Pulaya, and Paraya castes.

This caste economy was built on deep servitude. Kumar argues that landless agricultural labour was predominantly from the Dalit castes, people who were held in some variety of "servile" status, supplemented with hired "free" labour from other castes who were often paid slightly better or had shorter working hours.[41] Kumar points to three zones of agrestic servitude across the Madras Presidency in South India: an eastern, middle, and western zone including Malabar, where Malabar represented the most rigid agrestic servitude.[42] In Malabar, agrestic slaves were mortgaged, leased, and sold, and could be sold independently of the land.[43] Slave status was inherited. Slaves were always understood to be from particular "untouchable" castes and not from the castes that are now OBC – i.e. Ezhava, Thiyas, or "forward castes"

[40] See Menon, *Caste Nationalism and Communism*. Following William Logan's (1887) *Manual of the Malabar District*, scholars argue that British regulation transformed rights in land and share of produce into fixed forms of outright landownership.

[41] Kumar, *Land and Caste*; idem, "Caste and Landlessness".

[42] Ibid., cf. Hjejle, "Slavery and Agricultural Bondage", and Saradamoni, *Emergence of a Slave Caste*. Also see Mohan, *Modernity of Slavery*, for an extensive discussion of enslavement and caste, and Christian Dalit movements.

[43] See also Paul, "Dalit Conversion", for accounts of slave auctions.

such as Nairs, though Ezhavas had also worked as labourers in some areas.[44] This is clear in "Graeme's Report on the Revenue Administration of Malabar, 1822",[45] a work which describes in detail prescriptions of spatial distance that "slave castes" must keep from Brahmins, Nairs, and Teeans (Thiya) as well as other castes (para 42, p. 72), prices for leasing, mortgaging, and selling agrestic slaves under each (Dalit) caste (para 34, pp. 65–70), and the differences in daily allowances of paddy between *slaves* and *free labourers* (para 55, p. 77).[46] "Graeme's Report" became central to how the colonial authorities saw and enforced agricultural norms; it was circulated and cited widely, and reproduced as a history of the region in other documents such as William Logan's equally influential 1887 *Manual of the Malabar District*.

While the nineteenth century shows heavy dependence on low wages and the constant presence and employment of attached Dalit labour, there have been surges in agricultural labour from the 1920s to the 1950s, and then between the 1960s and the 1980s.[47] These surges have meant a contemporary rather heterogeneous caste labouring population and marks the feminisation of agricultural labour.[48] For example, economists have shown that, in most states in India between 1961 and 1981, "the percentage of agricultural labour in the total rural workforce has nearly doubled" and "agriculture remains the mainstay of female employment."[49] Duvvury suggests that not only have significant populations of those previously classifiable as cultivators and engaged in household industry become a part of agricultural labour, but that "caste-wise analysis . . . indicates [that] with the exception of four states (i.e. Madhya Pradesh,

[44] Dharma Kumar cites as illustrative examples comments made by the Collector of Tanjore and the Magistrate of Madras in the Slavery Papers of 1828 and the Report of Slavery 1841, respectively: see Kumar, *Land and Caste*, pp. 1, 55, and also the short discussion on pp. 3, 61.

[45] "Graeme's Report on the Revenue Administration of Malabar, 1822" was reprinted in Logan, *Manual of the Malabar District*.

[46] See also other works such as Paul, "Dalit Conversion", for documentation in Travancore of the sale of the enslaved within church histories.

[47] Jose, "Origin of Trade Unionism"; Kumar, *Land and Caste*; Patnaik, "On the Evolution"; Roy, *Rethinking Economic Livelihood*.

[48] Bardhan, "Women's Work".

[49] Duvvury, "Women in Agriculture", p. 98.

Orissa, Rajasthan and West Bengal), *more than 50 per cent of the growth in female agricultural labourers is due to the increase in the number of non-scheduled caste and tribal agricultural labourers.*[50] In Kerala, the historical expectation that agricultural labour was the lot of enslaved Dalit communities meant that, even as agricultural labour was also performed by other castes, the shaping of agricultural labour's history, its working conditions, and the expectations and kinds of dependencies and bonds that characterised agrarian labouring in Malabar came from the agrarian slavery of Dalit castes. Dalit women's historic labour in Palakkad determined the depressed conditions, low wages, and expectations of availability to which women from other castes then became subject.

While some labourers I met were OBC Ezhava, agricultural labour in contemporary Palakkad was nonetheless mainly thought of as a Cherumar occupation. It became clear over a year of fieldwork that, for Ezhava women, agricultural labour is seen as degrading because it is also seen as Dalit work and working with Dalits, the two being mingled as "polluting". Some middle-aged Ezhava labourers told us that when they had first married and begun working in the fields in the 1970s, their mothers-in-law still washed outside the house and purified themselves there after work before entering in order to "cleanse" themselves of the pollution of working with Scheduled Castes. While such practices had lapsed, caste distinctions continued to determine relationships between female labourers in contemporary Palakkad, including forms of humiliation and restricted commensality. Manual agrarian labour is seen as degrading by all communities engaged within it. However, does the tying together of caste and enslavement in Kerala account for this deep association between Dalits and agrarian labour as a caste formation beyond the associations with manual labour? Is agricultural labour polluting work in itself or because for other castes it means working with Dalits? I have no clear answers, but only these questions which actually animate struggles within interactions. These are questions that discussions on the traditional occupations – centring on predetermined "polluting" professions – don't quite answer, as Rawat shows us.[51]

---

[50] Ibid., my italics.
[51] Rawat, *Reconsidering Untouchability*.

Transformations

Kerala's land reforms are often hailed as more comprehensive than other contemporaneous land reforms in India.[52] The Communist Party enacted the Kerala Land Reforms Act of 1963 in the Assembly in 1969, its implementation being from 1 January 1970.[53] The 1963 Act and its amendments had three major aspects: (1) the transfer of property above newly instituted land ceilings from upper-caste Jenmi landlords to their tenants; (2) the right and subsidisation of the purchase of homestead land for the landless; and (3) the confiscation and reallocation of surplus land. The first two provisions are acknowledged to be more successful than the third – which continues to be an incomplete project.[54]

Scholarly evaluations of Kerala's land reforms thus see little benefit for the predominantly Dalit landless labourers.[55] As Rammohan points out, Dalits, who were the backbone of wetland rice agriculture in Kerala along with tribal communities, remain overwhelmingly landless.[56] The large transfer of land to tenant farmers, whether upper caste or OBC Ezhavas or Muslims, meant very little in everyday terms for labourers. Their distant landlords, most of whom they never met, had vanished. The tenant landlords who oversaw their work and with whom they had deeply iniquitous relationships became their landlords. Not least, Dalit leaseholders were few and unable to capitalise on the reforms. Ponni Veliyamma, a Kanakan Cherumar woman, recalled that her parents held a small lease on land prior to the 1963/69 land reform.[57] The tenant leaseholder from whom they subleased had taken back their lease immediately prior to land reform. In the few stories we heard of Dalits who had held small leases, most had relinquished their leases either because of a straightforward demand from the holders of their lease or because they had been harassed into giving up leases by scare stories of supposedly impending land tax that would have to be paid on the land. Veliyamma told us her father never recovered from the anger of this loss.

[52] Raj and Tharakan, "Agricultural Reforms"; Herring Land to the Tiller.
[53] Radhakrishnan, "Land Reforms"; Herring Land to the Tiller.
[54] Radhakrishnan, "Land Reforms"; Yadu, "The Land Question".
[55] Krishnaji, "Agrarian Relations"; Sivanandan, "Economic Backwardness".
[56] Rammohan, "Caste and Landlessness", p. 15.
[57] "Veliyamma" is a respectful term for an older woman.

For the Communist Party, as well as for many scholars and commentators, the end of upper-caste landlord *jenmism* as a structure and the transfer of land to other castes become the hallmark of Kerala's new class-based society and class bargaining.[58] Within this schema, Dalits emerge not in relation to their caste, which was so visible under the upper-caste landlording economy, but through a class-based language of workers, wages, and voters which only partly allowed their caste-based predicament to be imagined, even though on the ground Dalits continued to be understood mainly in relation to caste-based economies. For newly endowed class-based workers (not as caste-bonded communities) wage improvements superseded land. The CPM sponsored strikes throughout the 1970s to improve wages and labouring conditions: shorter working hours and severance from one's permanent landlord with a lump-sum pension so one could work for different landlords.

Balan Chettan was a CPM member who had been prominent in organising labourers and strikes; he was the mainstay of one three-year strike locally in the late 1970s against eleven landlords. The strikes were against tenants who had just become the major beneficiaries of land reforms, not the Jenmis of old but those newly consecrated as landlords, predominantly OBCs. There was some new class solidarity across Ezhava and Dalit labourers, as organising had to be done across castes. However, this wasn't easy. Balan Chettan noted that the strikers had received encouragement from CPM-affiliated Ezhava landlords; nonetheless, there were caste issues within their strike. Ezhava landlords would try to rally Ezhava labourers to stand with them in caste solidarity. Ezhava labourers and landlords met not only as employer and employee (as with Dalits) but as a community in meetings of the local Ezhava caste assembly. Class solidarity did not equate to caste transformation. In contemporary Palakkad older female Ezhava labourers, who were fellow strikers, still observe commensal restrictions.[59]

Strikes and resulting wage increases mirrored the rise in real wages within agricultural wages across India in the 1970s.[60] However, wage increases were soon followed by deep stagnation.[61] Palakkad had already

[58] For example, Heller, "Degrees of Democracy".
[59] Thiranagama, "Respect Your Neighbor".
[60] Jose, "Agricultural Wages".
[61] Ibid.

started with the lowest wages in Kerala. When Balan Chettan was younger and still working within agricultural labour, he had been one of the delegates from Palakkad to the state-wide meetings of agricultural unions in the 1970s. It was then, he told us, that he realised that the three taluks Alathur, Chittoor, and Palakkad in Palakkad District were the most "backward" in relation to the rest of the state – wages in these districts were still paid in rice, not cash. Balan Chettan dated the change-over to money to 1975; however, we could not find any precise date for the switch. Most labourers as well as the local panchayat agricultural officer thought it happened in the 1980s. This meant, as Balan Chettan explained, that even though they did manage to get somewhat better wages, the new wages were still so low that the real effect on their lives was not manifest until the late 1980s and 1990s.

Over the long term, wages in kind gave way to monetisation as labourers preferred money, and, landlord families told us, as rice became an increasingly expensive method of paying wages. Many of the women I worked with saw monetisation as an overwhelmingly positive moment, allowing them some measure of control over their circumstances. The two other most consequential changes within the agrarian economy were the increasing mechanisation of agriculture and a decrease in days of work. Women who had depended on multiple days within a month of employment were no longer being called for work. Men began to leave agriculture in large numbers. In the 1990s, amongst the families that I worked with, school-going rose. Young men and women now saw education as a possibility. The colony was no longer a workplace but a residential area where older women without work spent their days.[62] This was all made possible by the acquisition of homestead land.

New Foundations

Leaving Agricultural Labour and Building New Houses

When we carried out genealogical surveys, the major pattern we noted for Dalit families was that only in and after the 1990s could we see significant shifts in profession out of agricultural labour for *men*. Dalit

[62] On the neighbourhood, see Thiranagama, "Respect Your Neighbor".

men who were labourers as children and adolescents helping their families were able to shift to construction and other industries in the 1990s. Young men born in the 1990s skipped the stage of participation in agricultural labour. By contrast, through interviews and the limited sample of Ezhava families we surveyed, one could see already in the 1980s Ezhava male labourers moving into the construction industry – painting, point work, etc. Most younger Ezhava men who were not employed in workshops or professional activity were, if they did manual labour, in construction. Tractorisation replaced some of the men's work in agriculture, but other work such as "bordering" remained. However, agricultural labour not being considered desirable for men, in Palakkad, as elsewhere in India, agricultural labour and NREGA work was carried out by women. The NREGA salary at around Rs 250 a day was considered decent wages for women in Palakkad and unthinkable for men. Construction was understood as the respectable pathway and a good money-earning method away from agricultural work.

Conversely, while construction offered a structure for mobility and aspiration for men, it represented a structure of degradation for women. Velumany Chettan, who had become a construction worker, explained that while it was a good job for him, it would not be a good job for his wife: "If a woman goes to work in the construction field, she will be watched with *randam kannu'* [lit. second eye, meaning "seen in a different way"] by her community." Women who work on construction sites have to work with men all the time, and others would remark that these women would be changed in their demeanour and speech as a result. Women who work, in short, have to continually weigh the necessity of wages with reputational risk. Devaki Chechi, his wife, had remained an agricultural labourer and was now a NREGA worker. Similarly, Ezhava women remained agricultural labourers when their husbands moved into other forms of labour. Gender is inextricable from a consideration of work and aspiration.

To return to Collins and her suggestion of examining shifting the "family/work nexus",[63] we gain a different perspective on the transmission of well-being and mobility when we examine Dalit women's lives. Agricultural labour was shaped by labouring and landholding

---

[63] Collins, "Gender, Black Feminism".

household structures. Landholding/leasing households extended from landowning living space to their fields, their livestock, their family shrines (all of which were regulated by caste) to the households of their attached workers which were owned and transmitted through the family structures of upper-caste families.[64] Agricultural work was commonly done through a work group. A standard work group in K Colony would consist of around 7–8 women and 2–3 men. The men were the husbands of some of the women. The women were predominantly Dalit but also included at least two or three Ezhavas. The women in the work group would be related to each other or were often neighbours. For the now-middle-aged women I interviewed, it was understood that as a young woman you inherited a work slot from your mother-in-law and that you would work with her and your sisters-in-law. Work groups were organised around the household of the landlord and its needs. In K Colony, for example, when the main landholder partitioned his land across his five sons, he also partitioned his workers across his sons, which resulted in the make-up of the small work groups that I encountered when I met women in K Colony.

Women in their fifties and above had mostly married very young – in their early to mid teens. They came from families that had also been agricultural workers, and all the Dalit women I talked with had been shown how to do fieldwork by their families from a young age, around eight onwards. Older and middle-aged Dalit women had been born into agricultural labour and expected that to be the substance of their working life. Vasantha Chechi, Thanga, and all the other women that I interviewed struggled with the fact that their wages were always lower than a man's. When I interviewed women in eastern Palakkad, I discovered they earned a daily wage of Rs 250, whereas men earned Rs 450/500. In western Palakkad, where wages were higher, women might earn up to Rs 300/350 and men Rs 550/600. While many have written about the integral role that Dalit women play within Dalit families as bread-winners,[65] Dalit women's labour and wages, especially when they support whole families, have always been valued at much lower levels than

---

[64] Gough, "Kinship and Marriage"; Arunima, *There Comes Papa;* Saradamoni, *Matriliny Transformed.*

[65] E.g. Kapadia, *Siva and Her Sisters*; Still, *Dalit Women.*

men's. This is hardly only a symbolic matter – it is deeply material in many ways.

Women's income and work is central to agricultural labouring households, as pointed out in relation to South Indian rural Dalit women who inherit this as their history. In a study conducted by Mencher and Saradamoni of agricultural labourers in rice production in six villages within Bengal, Tamil Nadu, and Kerala in the 1970s, they found that "among the landless agricultural labourers, income given to the household by females accounts for more than half the total amount of household income."[66] They add that "without the female income these households might not be able to survive at all."[67] Any account of the agrarian economy, especially because of the centrality of agrarian economies to Dalit life, has to acknowledge or give a careful account of Dalit women's work. Balan Chettan and other men who were active in the local party acknowledged that without women joining in their strikes, they would have gone nowhere. Women had to withdraw their labour for the strikes to be successful. Moreover, as has been demonstrated, gendered ideologies shape the allocation of men's and women's income. Major financial schemes of the state and NGOs thus target women as their ideal recipients to improve the general welfare of the family.[68] For Tamil Nadu Vera-Sanso argues that "men are understood to be autonomous and able to withhold their income" while "women are understood as 'family-centred'", meaning that their whole income is understood as the family's income.[69] Karin Kapadia describes such assumptions also in relation to work done by Dalit Pallar women in Tamil Nadu.[70]

"Marriage is difficult," Vasantha Chechi told me; she, not her husband, was responsible in her family for their welfare, still working in NREGA in her sixties, in debt for her children's marriages and home improvements. This was true of others. Which is not to say husbands were

[66] Mencher and Saradamoni, "Muddy Feet", p. A149.

[67] Ibid.

[68] A different body of work on poverty and gender in India (e.g. work on micro finance, etc.) has emphasised how central women's income is to the well-being of the household.

[69] Vera-Sanso, "Community, Seclusion".

[70] Kapadia, Siva and Her Sisters.

not concerned with the welfare of the household, but it was their wives who went into debt for their children's marriages and managed household transfers: it was their money that was seen as entirely for the household. In the past, this gendered equation was much more a senior/ junior relation. Many of the older women had lived in larger households where all the sons and their wives would give over their income – in the case of Palakkad the daily measures of rice – to their parents. The father-in-law would manage purchases and allocate money even for the clothes of daughters-in-law and their children. The mother-in-law would manage the household, food purchases, and allocation of the daily work in the household. Married couples sought to move into new houses when they had children, but that was not always possible given that landownership was dependent on the landlord. Post-1970s, land became purchasable and thus families could live across different houses, and the monetisation of wages allowed for greater freedom with one's own wages. However, for women unlike for men, such freedom meant more money committed to the household, not less.

Not least, in our genealogical surveys we could see that previously male mortality was high, and especially pronounced in Paraya family genealogies. The effect for women left as widows and sole earners was dramatic. In most cases – as with Ponni Veliyamma, who was widowed at the age of thirty-two while pregnant and with three children under ten years of age – her oldest son began work at fourteen and already commands a wage equivalent to his mother's. Many men in the older generations had no choice but to begin agricultural labour as their wages were critical to their mother's household. In one household, which was a series of single women and children born out of marriage, the absence of continuous male wages rendered the family (in K Colony) among the absolutely poor, and with marriageability for their young women dramatically reduced. Despite a history of strikes and wage action, there has never been a campaign for raising female wages within manual labour, and this has a crushing effect on households that depend on female manual labour. The intergenerational transmission of mobility in Dalit households has to be understood through this gendered inequality.

What did it mean to inherit agricultural manual labour? Older women who had been agricultural labourers and learned to do such work as small children would laugh and tell me that younger women were too soft to do the kind of work they had done. This teasing was ubiquitous in every family situation. Nonetheless, they also made it clear that they did not want their daughters and daughters-in-law to do agricultural labour. It was an inheritance they refused to transmit. Prema Chechi, a woman in her seventies, told me that had she been educated she would have liked a good job in a "company". Another, Vasantha Chechi, would have liked to travel. Ponni Veliyamma asked what the point was in us asking them what they would have liked to do given money and opportunity – her view was that this was their life, and that was it. Women transposed such hypothetical desires instead to their children. They wanted them to be educated, get good jobs or be housewives, have soft hands, and not do agrarian labour. Young people don't want to get muddy, I was told all the time – with pride, not reproach.

Aspirations for their children centred on good jobs and education. Older women could write their names because of having attended adult education programmes. Women in their forties were fully literate and most had studied at least to the eighth or the tenth class. Younger women had often studied to Plus 1, Plus 2 (Grades 11 and 12); a few had a university degree. Educating their daughters was as important to them as educating their sons. This may seem out of sync with larger Indian patterns, which show that many of the children of agricultural labourers do not have ready access to an advanced secondary education. In the context of widespread literacy in Kerala, which has very high rates of secondary and college education, Dalits fit the Malayali pattern; however, and this is significant, they enter these structures at a much later time than many other castes who came to be educated in larger numbers prior to the 1990s and 2000s – large populations of Ezhava college students, for example. They enter various Malayalam education streams at a time when English education affords access to higher paid and more mobile professional employment. English-language familiarity, use, and education were all part of intangible class inheritances that the upper castes brought to the table as part of the intergenerational transmission of wealth. The most highly desired jobs were working for the government, i.e. the "Sarkar", though difficult to acquire. Desirable jobs in companies and factories needed money and connections for all, not only Dalits.

Those who were farmers were able to mobilise money and caste connections, as were some Ezhava labourers. Without there being many prominent Dalit business people and professionals sympathetic to poorer Dalits, Dalits were shut out of these networks. Moreover, in the absence of a politically unified Dalit movement in Palakkad, the Kanakan, Pulaya, and Paraya communities did not consider themselves a pan-Dalit community network to help others – their common inheritance lay in similar histories of untouchability.

Let me contrast this briefly to our encounters with upper-caste rural families. In the Valluvanad region west of Palakkad, we became acquainted with the hilly landscape and caught sight of Nair *tarawads* and Namboodiri *illom*. Narayanan, an elderly Namboodiri Brahmin and former landowner who was in his eighties, told us that he was the first Namboodiri Brahmin boy in his family to be allowed to go to school instead of being made to study the Vedas. His uncles had opposed such a move but his father, who was "forward thinking", had had him educated along with his sisters. This meant that in the 1940s when Narayanan was in his twenties he found employment in the government, lodging with his father's sisters' households and Tamil Brahmin *agraharams* so that he could manage employment and simultaneously maintain his caste identity. His brothers were also educated; one became a teacher, another a steel engineer. This was a big move for his landed family, whose primary income was previously through land. Through the caste-reform movement, by the 1930s it had already become clear to many upper castes that agricultural land had to be supplemented by professional employment. Lowering his voice, Narayanan and his wife explained to us the humiliation that they as a family in the 1970s, after land reform, had had to suffer by depending upon rice rations from the state. Post-reforms, without a regular income from the land, many Namboodiri families that had never done any form of labour were completely unable to support themselves. We were quite "useless", he explained. His family managed because of his professional employment.

While we heard these stories containing feelings of deep loss by elderly Brahmins, Nairs, and Guptas, their loss was primarily expressed as the deprivation of agricultural land and the attendant income derived from it. They had retained their houses. We realised from our brief genealogical surveys of Narayanan's family as well as some Nair and Gupta families that while the 1970s represented a loss of land and income for this generation now in their seventies and eighties, their children and their children's children came to be highly educated and professionally employed. It was rare for their children to be around when we spoke to them, most being abroad or elsewhere. This is significant in Kerala, because from the 1980s wealth creation and status has rested primarily in non-agricultural professional employment often combined with migration across India or abroad. As Narayanan explained to us, because both Namboodiri women and men are educated and now have higher degrees (i.e. better qualifications), they go and work in "Bombay, UK, Australia". Currently, "having a career" is a must. Even poorer upper-caste families that had never possessed large tracts of land had obtained an education and entered the professions early. Thus there was an intergenerational "bounce back" among the upper-caste families we encountered after land reform. This is what longer patterns of inheritance look like when there is accumulated status: early entrance into education and professional work, physical and social mobility, marriageability, and extensive networks – all because of caste status. These inheritances are what count when there are sudden dips or a fall in income. This generational bounce-back pattern was of a very different type from that seen among Dalit or Ezhava labourers. This was also true of the houses that became central to new Dalit aspirations.

What I have described in relation to caste has often been discussed in relation to class in Kerala.[71] Dalits and Ezhavas are both agricultural labourers. Ezhava landless agricultural labourers also found themselves impoverished and struggling to transmit goods. My argument here is not that being a poor Ezhava landless agricultural labouring family is not a difficult life (it *is*, as I saw in Palakkad). It is more that, first, despite organised forms of class solidarity through CPM mobilisation, on the ground deep caste-residential segregation and differentiated hospitality and sociality continued to mark relations between Ezhava and Dalit labourers. Second, Ezhavas as a caste community were internally very

[71] There is of course a complex discussion around the relationship between caste and class that is also well discussed – e.g. Beteille, *Caste, Class, and Power*, and Fuller and Narasimhan, *Tamil Brahmans*.

class differentiated; Ezhavas were landlords, educated professionals, government workers, high-ranking CPM members, and activists as well as labourers. Ezhava labourers compared themselves to other Ezhavas where being a labourer was both embarrassing in class terms as well as seen as degrading oneself and becoming Dalit-like. Becoming upwardly mobile for Ezhava labourers was to move in class terms. Moreover, unlike Dalits, they were also able to somewhat mobilise caste networks and party networks given the preponderance of Ezhavas within the CPM, and in all kinds of professions and positions. Given the general impoverishment of Dalit communities, there were few networks of patronage or wealth outside the party, and even these were limited to a few Dalit members and some associated families.[72]

For Dalits, with very recent and limited socio-economic mobility in Palakkad, leaving agricultural labour is always seen as a *caste-based* endeavour of upliftment. Agricultural labour, which was a low-class position among Ezhavas, was a Dalit-*caste* position among the Kanakan, Pulaya, and Paraya communities, and an inheritance of deep forms of subordination, inequality, and humiliation that spanned pre-colonial, colonial, and post-colonial Dalit life in Palakkad. Individuals could not lose this history through upward mobility either. Given the concentration of Dalit communities that had agricultural landless labour as their primary historical *traditional* occupation, this concentrated these difficulties of inheritance and lack of access to accumulating and transmitting even limited forms of wealth and a safety net. In turn, this meant that these are both the outcome of and central in maintaining and reproducing caste inequality. This is why I find class overdetermined by caste for Dalits.

Thatch, Tile, Concrete

Undoubtedly, the most important reformative impact of the 1963 Land Reform Act (though it was the 1969 amendment that expanded the definitions[73]), for Dalit communities, were the rights of landless labourers as *kudikidappukar* to purchase at nominal rates their home-

---

[72] Pramod, "Subordinated Inclusion".
[73] http://www.bareactslive.com/KER/ker062.htm.

stead or the land on which they already lived.[74] A *kudikidappukar* was a person who was "allowed' by the landholder, tenant, or landlord to put up a residence in order to provide work for that landholder, and who owned or leased "a homestead or any land exceeding 3 cents in any city or municipality or ten cents of land in any panchayat area or township on which he could erect a homestead."[75] Subsequently, the state also launched schemes, including the Lakshanweedu scheme, to provide housing for labourers and others with low incomes and no right to land.[76] For the first time, homes were now ownable and alienable for landless labourers. This represented the possibility of independent inheritance as well as the beginning of localities as residential areas as opposed to only workplaces. This gave Dalits an important new stake in the inheritance society: they owned land which they could pass on to or parcel out amongst their children.

After the reforms, activists such as Balan Chettan collected information about which Dalit colonies existed within the panchayat and took a list of twenty-eight colonies to the panchayat. In registering these as colonies, not workplaces, they made it possible for the colonies to be recognised as residential areas in need of services. While individual houses were made possible by hutment rights, the possibility of realising these as homes came only with the extension of panchayat schemes to provide some minimal services, roads, water, and electricity, including the extension of schemes to help Dalits build permanent structures. This transformation of workplaces into colonies was absolutely central in creating new forms of Dalit possibility even as such areas also served to re-entrench Dalit communities in land that was considered low value.[77]

Homestead land established new familial forms of aspiration and micro-level mobility. Houses are absolutely critical across the class and caste structure in Kerala to forms of respectability and marriageability. Having a good house became a real possibility for Dalit communities after the 1980s. It was imagined as critical to both horizontal expansion – houses from the same families began fanning out; and vertical –

---

[74] Krishnaji, "Agrarian Relations".
[75] Section 25, Malabar Land Reform Act 1963.
[76] Pramod, "Subordinated Inclusion".
[77] Ibid.

houses could be inherited as property not tied to one's labour for a land-lord. This created new visions of possibility for marriage and family. When I asked local families what they needed and were looking out for in order to contract a decent marriage, they said two things were essential: some dowry and a "good" house for both the bride and the groom. As everyone told me, neither of these were historically given in their community: dowry-giving had been minimal and houses had never counted when everyone lived in large joint families working for landlords. Dowry-giving had risen steadily after the 1980s. The women I interviewed in their forties had often been given around 1–2 sovereigns of gold as dowry. Now the expectation was around 10 sovereigns of gold as dowry. In addition, the expectation of household goods and assets that the woman's family were expected to send to the groom's family after the new mother and first child returned to the marital home had risen. I was told that when visiting prospective grooms or brides to judge whether this was a good family to marry into, their possession of a decent house was considered critical. The groom's house was an indication of where the bride would later live. The bride's house was a measure of occasional inhabitation for confinements, the setting for many wedding events, and fundamentally a measure of the "quality" of the family. Prior to his son's marriage, Velumany Chettan stayed home from work to finish up and fully cement his house to make it a "good house". Only when the house was finished could the wedding take place. Many of these expenses – dowry, weddings, house building and goods – were financed by deep debt, i.e. debt to the local co-operative banks, the CPM bank, and to a variety of moneylenders who came to the colony regularly and were known in K Colony as the "Saturday man" and the "Sunday man".

However, while Dalit communities have acquired rights and continuously improved houses through building them, investing in them, and acquiring assets, comparatively speaking they are still at a considerable disadvantage in relation to others. Land reforms created a new class of the land rich, both in terms of agricultural land and through the new valuation of housing land. Older landlords retained their housing land as most were not officially tenanted.[78] Secondly, in relation to those

[78] Franke, "Land Reform", p. 89.

who benefited from land reform, while some tenants were small holders, those who leased large tracts joined a new land-rich category that
could use these assets in multiple ways.[79] This was consequential when
land prices and the real-estate economy rose dramatically in Kerala
from the 1980s onwards.[80]

In his analysis of the 2011 NSS Employment and Unemployment
Survey, Yadu provides data examining land distribution for Kerala.[81]
He also shows that the differential holdings of land post-land reform
had very different outcomes for Dalit and Adivasi communities in
this highly monetised land economy: "Inter-group differential in land
ownership post-land reform has created a wedge between the mobility
options of communities which gained from land reform and those which
did not gain much."[82] In short, gains were undercut by the differences
between different groups' absolute holdings. Yadu's calculation from
the NSS data puts SCs as "clustered in the lowest land class".[83] Almost
85 per cent of Dalits/Scheduled Castes are in the lowest 60 per cent land
class (in terms of quantity of land owned). This contrasts with almost
61 per cent of Adivasis/Scheduled Tribes (ST), and 64 per cent of
Other Backward Classes (OBC) who are distributed in the lowest 60 per
cent land class.[84] In turn, this shows not only that SCs, STs, and OBCs
still remain overwhelmingly in the lowest land class, but also Dalits/
SCs disproportionately so.[35] In short, Yadu concludes that the current
pattern of land transactions in the state, driven by the real-estate boom,

[39] See the discussion in Tharakan, *When the Kerala Model*.

[80] Yadu, "The Land Question".

[81] Ibid., pp. 334–8.

[82] Ibid., p. 329.

[83] Ibid., p. 336.

[84] Ibid.

[85] While OBCs do not constitute large numbers of those in the highest land
class, Yadu shows them to be 28.16 in the middle category. Those in "forward"
castes constitute 29.76 of the lower land class, 43.95 of the middle class, and
26.29 of the top class. To put these figures into proportion, the lowest land class
comprises around 60 per cent of those surveyed, the middle 25 per cent, and the
top only 15 per cent. For the forward castes to constitute 26.29 per cent of the
smallest category of high quantity of land ownership, as well as the nearly half
of those in the small middle category of ownership, gives some insight into land
inequity. See Table 4 in Yadu, "The Land Question".

is resulting in "disproportionate benefits for the rich";[86] and moreover that the patterns of land accumulation, land poor, and land rich can be understood through caste and community categories.[87]

Homes, both rented and owned – as real estate one of the major wealth accumulators across India – have to be thought of in relation to caste and community. In spatial terms, residential houses consolidate segregated caste patterns, with ideas about whom one sells to and rents to shaped by the approval and disapproval of other members of one's caste and neighbourhood community. This contemporary spatial pattern is shaped by the historical caste economy of neighbourhoods. Further, as new assets accrue within inheritance societies, their monetary valuation rests on caste status. This is why Pramod, for example, argues that Dalit colonies are socially enclosed spaces which may further stigmatise those living within them.[88]

To return to the question of names, Dalit neighbourhoods are marked by their location and emplacement in a long history of caste segregation. Not least, differentiated duration, time lags, and delayed entry into particular status and land economies leave Dalits at a consequential disadvantage even if their situation seems to show equality of opportunity. Dalit communities' late entrance into real estate came at a point where, in order to realise the symbolic and economic potential of being homeowners, they were both utterly dependent on limited municipal schemes and party loyalties, and in debt to multiple lenders. Duration and intergenerational inheritance matter. Deep intergenerational inheritance provides forms of mobility in the present and a safety net in times of trouble.

However, despite this disparity, in my fieldwork people's three houses, "thatch, tile, concrete", were really important. Dalit families know they live in highly unequal economies and have to contend with humiliation and disparity. So they strive to make their families and houses into structures and symbols that celebrate their own aspirations – as well as complex community spaces in which their full humanity can be allowed to abide.[89]

[86] Ibid., p. 338.
[87] See also Yadu and Vijayasuryan, "Triple Exclusion".
[88] Pramod, "As a Dalit Woman".
[89] Rawat, "Occupation, Dignity and Space".

Jegathesan provides a parallel example when writing about Malaiyaha Tamil plantation workers in Sri Lanka.[90] For all Tamil-speaking communities in Sri Lanka, the notion of an "ur", a home, is vital for personhood, but often Malaiyaha Tamil line-rooms are described – especially by NGOs, activists, government officials, and plantation officials – as debilitating and degraded spaces indicative of the poverty of Malaiyaha Tamils.[91] Jegathesan instead describes all the home improvements through sacrificing and saving that families build within their line rooms, even though they do not formally own them. She remarks that "this process of terraforming is a pragmatic task taken on by Tamil plantation residents who recognize that the allotted line room spaces are uninhabitable and unaccommodating to the fullness of the lives workers wish to lead. Realizing this, they terraform lands that they do not own and find alternatives to transform these spaces into places more commensurate with their aspirations."[92] For me, the carefully maintained and decorated houses and neighbourhoods that I was welcomed into were marked, as for Jegathesan, by "generative signs of life, investment, and desire."[93] They were spaces of sociality, hospitality, and new life. People were building their futures and the futures of their families. Women endeavoured to make these spaces and families their new foundations.

~

This essay has suggested that we think about caste in relation to inheritance, both the inheritance of "traditional occupations" and blockages as well as struggles to transmit durable intergenerational futures. Agricultural labour in Palakkad has been imagined as a form of degrading work associated with Dalit labour. The middle-aged Dalit female labourers I worked with have inherited this form of work over multiple generations – agricultural labour has been intergenerationally transmitted and written on their bodies. When young women choose not to work in agricultural labour but stay at home, or work in NREGA or other forms of casual and

---

[90] Jegathesan, *Tea and Solidarity*.
[91] Ibid., p. 101.
[92] Ibid., p. 115.
[93] Ibid., p. 101.

professional labour, they are making conscious choices based on this intergenerational transmission. I have suggested that focusing on households as a means of resisting, inhabiting, and differentially transmitting aspiration and inequality is one key way to understand ordinary Dalit worlds in Kerala by looking at housing.

Thus, this essay has also suggested that we think about inheritance in relation to new forms of aspiration and desire to transmit new futures through the inheritance of houses. I have proposed we examine temporal structures in relation to aspirations and possibilities. The entrance of different caste communities at different times in Kerala's twentieth-century transformation has been critical for contemporary possibilities of upliftment. The significant lag in the effects of transformation and the late beginning of accumulation of inheritance and new forms of contacts and work mean that Dalits continue to feel the effects of long histories of servitude. They come to the table late and at a time when the possibilities for their accumulation are still disadvantaged vis-à-vis other castes. At the same time, I have told stories throughout of how people sought to transform their lives, always imagining themselves moving towards a better future.

Beena in K Colony, a middle-aged woman with enormous determination and drive, epitomised this fierce drive. She came from a labouring family and had contracted an early marriage. When we met her, she was in NREGA work and participating in the state "Kudumbashree" programme, Kerala's flagship poverty eradication and women's empowerment programme.[94] While she had thought about CPM work, she and others told us that it would be hard for her to advance, given how dynamic and outspoken she was. Other women's representatives preferred by the local party were much more willing to be guided. By the time we left, Beena had begun a women's co-operative canteen with some of the other Dalit women we knew. She poured all her ambition and love into her two children – her son who was still at school and her very clever daughter entering university. Beena had two things she was saving for: her daughter's dowry and renovating her house. When we were there, Beena

---

[94] https://www.kudumbashree.org/pages/171. For a detailed analysis of the programme, see Devika and Thampi, " Between Empowerment and Liberation".

was engaged in supervising renovation, and we visited her to help with the construction crew. The house was surrounded by her husband's kin; however, it was Beena who was the driving force within the street. She had a dry and biting wit with a taste for caustic commentary. She was always open about the caste humiliation that others showed Dalit women, even while offering her judgment on the inhumanity of those who inflicted such caste discrimination.

It was with Beena in mind that I began sketching out issues around work, houses, and education, all strategies and pathways to which Beena introduced Vinu and myself. She looked always to the future as something that she could claim, that might be more hospitable than the past, and that would eventually unfold if one claimed it in the present. I write of her here in the hope that we can also understand what the women I work with dream of, and how they want to carry their histories without being bound by them.

References

Arunima, Gopinath, *There Comes Papa: Colonialism and the Transformation of Matriliny in Kerala, Malabar, c. 1850–1940* (New Delhi: Orient Black Swan, 2003).

Bardhan, K., "Women's Work, Welfare and Status: Forces of Tradition and Change in India", *Economic and Political Weekly*, vol. 20, no. 50, 14 December 1985.

Basu, S., *Dowry and Inheritance*, vol. 3 (London: Zed Books, 2005).

Beteille, André, *Caste, Class, and Power* (Berkeley: University of California Press, 1971).

Buchanan, F., *A Journey from Madras Through the Countries of Mysore, Canara, and Malabar*, vol. 2 (1807; rpntd Cambridge: Cambridge University Press, 2011).

Census of India, 1991, "Chapter 3: Economic Development of the Scheduled Castes", https://ncsc.nic.in/files/Chapter%203_2.pdf.

Census of India, 2001, "Kerala Data Highlights: The Scheduled Castes", https://censusindia.gov.in/nada/index.php/catalog/27906/download/31075/PC01_PCA_IND_SC_DH_32.pdf.

Census of India, 2011, https://www.censusindia.gov.in/2011census/PCA/PCA_Highlights/pca_highlights_file/India/4Executive_Summary.pdf.

Coates, Ta-Nehesi, "The Case for Reparations", *The Atlantic*, June 2014.

Collins, Patricia Hill, "Gender, Black Feminism, and Black Political Economy", *The Annals of the American Academy of Political and Social Science*,
vol. 568, no. 1, 2000.

Darity, Jr, W., *et al.*, "What We Get Wrong About Closing the Racial Wealth
Gap", *Samuel DuBois Cook Center on Social Equity and Insight Center for
Community Economic Development*, 2018.

Devika J., "Egalitarian Developmentalism, Communist Mobilization, and the
Question of Caste in Kerala State, India", *The Journal of Asian Studies*,
vol. 69, no. 3, 2010.

Devika, J., and B.V. Thampi, "Between 'Empowerment'and 'Liberation': The
Kudumbashree Initiative in Kerala", *Indian Journal of Gender Studies*,
vol. 14, no. 1, 2007.

Duvvury, N., "Women in Agriculture: A Review of the Indian Literature",
Economic and Political Weekly, vol. 24, no. 43, 28 October 1989.

Franke, R.W., "Land Reform versus Inequality in Nadur Village, Kerala",
Journal of Anthropological Research, vol. 48, no. 2 , 1992.

Fuller, C.J., and Haripriya Narasimhan, *Tamil Brahmans: The Making of a
Middle-Class Caste* (Chicago: University of Chicago Press, 2014).

Gough, K., "Kinship and Marriage in Southwest India", *Contributions to
Indian Sociology*, vol. 7, no. 1, 1973, https://doi.org/10.1177/00 69
96677300700107.

Harriss, J., J. Jeyaranjan, and K. Nagaraj, "Land, Labour and Caste Politics in
Rural Tamil Nadu in the 20th Century: Iruvelpattu (1916–2008), *Economic and Political Weekly*, vol. 45, no. 31, 2010, http://www.jstor.org/
stable/20764363.

Heller, P., "Degrees of Democracy: Some Comparative Lessons from India",
World Politics, vol. 52, no. 4, 2000.

Heller, P., "Kerala: Deepening a Radical Social Democracy", in Richard Sand-
brook, Marc Edelmann, Patrick Heller, and Judith Teichman, eds, *Social
Democracy in the Global Periphery: Origins, Challenges, and Prospects*
(Cambridge: Cambridge University Press, 2006).

Heller, P., *The Labor of Development: Workers and the Transformation of Capitalism in Kerala, India* (Ithaca: Cornell University Press, 1999).

Herring, C., and L. Henderson, "Wealth Inequality in Black and White: Cultural
and Structural Sources of the Racial Wealth Gap", *Race and Social Problems*, vol. 8, no. 1, 2016.

Herring, R.J., *Land to the Tiller: The Political Economy of Agrarian Reform in
India* (New Haven: Yale University Press, 1983).

Hjejle, B., "Slavery and Agricultural Bondage in South India in the Nineteenth Century", *Scandinavian Economic History Review*, vol. 15, nos 1–
2, 1967.

Jeffrey, R., "Legacies of Matriliny: The Place of Women and the 'Kerala Model'", *Pacific Affairs*, vol. 77, no. 4, 2004.

Jeffrey, R., "Matriliny, Marxism, and the Birth of the Communist Party in Kerala, 1930–1940", *The Journal of Asian Studies*, vol. 38, no. 1, 1978.

Jegathesan, M., *Tea and Solidarity: Tamil Women and Work in Postwar Sri Lanka* (Seattle: University of Washington Press, 2019).

Jodhka, S.S., and J. Manor, eds, *Contested Hierarchies, Persisting Influence: Caste and Power in 21st Century India* (Hyderabad: Orient Blackswan, 2018).

Jose, A.V., "Agricultural Wages in India", *Economic and Political Weekly*, vol. 23, no. 26, 25 June 1988.

Jose, A.V., "The Origin of Trade Unionism Among the Agricultural Labourers in Kerala", *Social Scientist*, vol. 5, 1977.

Kapadia, K., *Siva and Her Sisters: Gender, Caste, and Class in Rural South India* (Boulder: Westview Press, 1995).

Kodoth, P., *Shifting the Ground of Fatherhood: Matriliny, Men, and Marriage in Early Twentieth Century Malabar* (Trivandrum: Centre for Development Studies, 2004), http://localhost:8080/xmlui/handle/123456789/257.

Kodoth, Praveena, "Courting Legitimacy or Delegitimizing Custom? Sexuality, Sambandham, and Marriage Reform in Late Nineteenth-century Malabar", *Modern Asian Studies*, vol. 35, no. 2, 2001.

Krishnaji, N., "Agrarian Relations and the Left Movement in Kerala, a Note on Recent Trends", *Economic and Political Weekly*, vol. 14, no. 9, 1979.

Kumar, D., "Caste and Landlessness in South India", *Comparative Studies in Society and History*, vol. 4, no. 3, 1962.

Kumar, D., *Land and Caste in South India* (Cambridge: Cambridge University Press, 1965).

Logan, W., *Manual of the Malabar District* (Madras: Madras Government, 1887).

Mencher, J.P., and K. Saradamoni, "Muddy Feet, Dirty Hands: Rice Production and Female Agricultural Labour", *Economic and Political Weekly*, vol. 17, no. 52, 25 December 1982.

Mendelsohn, O., and M. Vicziany, *The Untouchables: Subordination, Poverty and the State in Modern India*, vol. 4 (Cambridge: Cambridge University Press, 1998).

Menon, D., *Caste, Nationalism and Communism in South India* (New York: Cambridge University Press, 1994).

Mosse, David, "A Relational Approach to Durable Poverty, Inequality and Power", *The Journal of Development Studies*, vol. 46, no. 7, 2010, DOI: 10.1080/00220388.2010.487095.

Mosse, David, "The Modernity of Caste and the Market Economy", *Modern Asian Studies*, vol. 54, no. 4, 2020.

Natrajan, Balmurli, *The Culturalization of Caste in India: Identity and Inequality in a Multicultural Age* (London: Routledge, 2011).

Oliver, M.L., and T.M. Shapiro, *Black Wealth, White Wealth: A New Perspective on Racial Inequality* (London: Taylor & Francis, 2006).

Omi, M., and H. Winant, *Racial Formation in the United States* (New York: Routledge, 2014).

Osella, Filippo, and Caroline Osella, *Social Mobility in Kerala: Modernity and Identity in Conflict* (London: Pluto Press, 2000).

Patnaik, Utsa, "On the Evolution of the Class of Agricultural Labourers in India", *Social Scientist*, vol. 11, no. 7, 1983.

Paul, Vinil Baby, "Dalit Conversion Memories in Colonial Kerala and Decolonisation of Knowledge", *South Asia Research*, vol. 41, no. 2, 2021.

Piketty, T., *Capital in the Twenty-first Century* (Boston: Harvard University Press, 2017).

Pramod, K.M., "Subordinated Inclusion: The Developmental State and the Dalit Colonies of Southern Kerala", *Development and the Politics of Human Rights*, vol. 198, 2015.

Pramod, M., "As a Dalit Woman", *CASTE: A Global Journal on Social Exclusion*, vol. 1, no. 1, 2020.

Radhakrishnan, P., "Land Reforms in Theory and Practice: The Kerala Experience", *Economic and Political Weekly*, vol. 16, no. 53, 26 December 1981.

Rafanell, I., and H. Gorringe, "Consenting to Domination? Theorising Power, Agency and Embodiment with Reference to Caste", *The Sociological Review*, vol. 58, no. 4, 2010.

Raj, K.N., and P.K.M. Tharakan, "Agricultural Reforms in Kerala and Its Impact on the Rural Economy: A Preliminary Assessment", in A.K. Ghosh, ed., *Agrarian Reforms in Contemporary Developing Countries* (London: Croom Helm, 1983).

Ramakumar, R., "Public Action, Agrarian Change and the Standard of Living of Agricultural Workers: A Study of a Village in Kerala", *Journal of Agrarian Change*, vol. 6, no. 3, 2006.

Rammohan K.T., "Caste and Landlessness in Kerala: Signals from Chengara", *Economic and Political Weekly*, vol. 43, no. 37, 13 September 2008.

Rawat, Ramnarayan S., "Occupation, Dignity, and Space: The Rise of Dalit Studies", *History Compass*, vol. 11, no. 12, 2013.

Rawat, R.S., *Reconsidering Untouchability: Chamars and Dalit History in North India* (Bloomington: Indiana University Press, 2011).

Rothstein, R., *The Color of Law: A Forgotten History of How Our Government Segregated America* (New York: Liveright, 2017).

Roy, S., "Empowering Women? Inheritance Rights, Female Education and Dowry Payments in India", *Journal of Development Economics*, vol. 114, 2015.

Roy, T., *Rethinking Economic Livelihood in India: Labour and Livelihood* (London/New York: Routledge, 2006).

Sanal Mohan, P., *Modernity of Slavery: Struggles Against Caste Inequality in Colonial Kerala* (New Delhi: Oxford University Press, 2015).

Saradamoni, Kunjulekshmi, *Emergence of a Slave Caste: Pulayas of Kerala* (New Delhi: People's Publishing House, 1980).

Saradamoni, Kunjulekshmi, *Matriliny Transformed: Family, Law and Ideology in Twentieth Century Travancore* (New Delhi: Sage Publications, 1999).

Shapiro, T.M., *The Hidden Cost of Being African American: How Wealth Perpetuates Inequality* (New York: Oxford University Press, 2004).

Singer, M.B., *When a Great Tradition Modernizes: An Anthropological Approach to Indian Civilization* (Westport, CT: Praeger, 1972).

Sivanandan, P., "Economic Backwardness of Harijans in Kerala", *Social Scientist*, vol. 4, no. 12, 1976.

Still, Clarinda, *Dalit Women: Honour and Patriarchy in South India* (London: Routledge, 2017).

Tharakan, P.K.M., *When the Kerala Model of Development is Historicised: A Chronological Perspective* (Trivandrum: Centre for Socio-Economic & Environmental Studies, 2008).

Thiranagama, S., "Respect Your Neighbor as Yourself: Neighborliness, Caste, and Community in South India", *Comparative Studies in Society and History*, vol. 61, no. 2, 2019.

Vera-Sanso, P., "Community, Seclusion and Female Labour Force Participation in Madras, India", *Third World Planning Review*, vol. 17, no. 2, 1995.

Yadu, C.R., "The Land Question and the Mobility of the Marginalized: A Study of Land Inequality in Kerala", *Agrarian South: Journal of Political Economy*, vol. 4, no. 3, December 2015.

Yadu, C.R., and C.K. Vijayasuryan, "Triple Exclusion of Dalits in Land Ownership in Kerala", *Social Change*, vol. 46, no. 3, 2016.

9

Caste, Occupations, and (Im)mobility in Modern Indian Industry, 1870–2006

SUMEET MHASKAR

Introduction

THE PERSISTENCE OF caste in Indian urban settings has historically been viewed as an aberration. Especially in relation to occupational choices, the initial scholarship influenced by the
"modernisation" framework attributed the weakening of caste in cities
to large-scale manufacturing industries and the rapid urbanisation process. These twin processes, scholars expected, would make caste irrelevant as employers prioritised individual skills rather than social background, which included caste, religion, and gender. The American
sociologist Davis Kingsley took this line of thought to an extreme by arguing that "If industrialisation proceeds rapidly [in India] . . . the caste
system will have essentially disappeared by the end of this century."[1]
Later scholarship advanced similar claims when the Indian state adopted economic liberalisation policies in the 1990s.[2] However, such claims
were rarely tested with detailed empirical evidence. It was probably for
this reason that the sociologist M.N. Srinivas noted in the late 1950s
that "[n]ext to nothing is known about the social background of indus-

[1] Davis, *The Population of India and Pakistan*, p. 176.
[2] Panini, "The Political Economy of Caste", p. 60.

trial workers in different parts of the country."[3] Srinivas' observation was not entirely correct, as the Bombay Mill Owners Association (BMOA) Survey of 1940 provided detailed insights into the role of caste, religion, region, and gender in segmenting occupations inside the textile mills.[4] In fact, before Indian independence in 1947, the British colonial state's census and labour commission reports, as well as academic scholars, had gathered information on the caste, race, gender, and religious background of individual workers and demonstrated their influence when making occupational choices.[5]

Post-1947, however, the Indian state made a significant decision with far-reaching consequences. It consciously discontinued the documentation of information on caste and subcaste to prohibit "caste consciousness", which the members of the Constituent Assembly argued was at the root of "caste patriotism" and "caste hatred". As a result, the state sought to prohibit the gathering of caste and subcaste data in "any forms supplied by Government or in any records or registers kept by the Government." However, the Indian state did not impose *official restrictions* on academics gathering data on caste. Scholars dominated by the upper castes voluntarily followed the upper-caste nationalist diktat and avoided data collection on castes. They took refuge in the discourse on modernity – that caste would eventually be irrelevant, so there was no need to count it. These decisions by the Indian state and academic scholarship profoundly impacted our understanding of caste dynamics in rural and urban settings.

In some cases, scholars gathered data on caste but did not examine its impact on an individual's livelihood choices. Ironically, however, the Indian state and academic scholarship did examine urban occupations, skills, wages, and migratory patterns with respect to the language, regional, religious affiliation, or gender background of workers.[6] Neither

---

[3] Srinivas, "Social Anthropology", p. 137.

[4] Gokhale, *The Bombay Cotton Mill Worker*, p. 116.

[5] Burnett-Hurst, *Labour and Housing in Bombay*; Rutnagur, *Bombay Industries*; Pradhan, *Untouchable Workers*; Cholia, *Dock Labourers*; Gokhale, *The Bombay Cotton Mill Worker*.

[6] Patel, *Rural Labour*; Joshi and Joshi, *Surplus Labour*; Papola, "Small Establishments"; Deshpande, "The Bombay Labour Market"; Dandekar, *Men to*

of these varieties of information and analysis were seen as divisive forces promoting "patriotism" of a certain kind. Furthermore, even today, without using large-scale scientific data on caste, there are arguments about the disappearance or weakening of caste in urban settings that remain part of the intellectual and political discourse. The conclusion can only be that by their approach the state and academic scholarship have contributed to the invisibility of caste. More crucially, this has created a gap in how traditional institutions such as caste function in modern economic settings. While a large body of scholarly literature on urban large-scale industries has focused on strikes and lay-offs in modern industries, hardly any longitudinal study exists that examines the role of gender, caste, religion, and region in shaping occupational choices in modern Indian industries.

The present essay fills a significant empirical and analytical gap by examining the role of caste in shaping occupational choices in large-scale modern factories from the late-nineteenth to the early-twenty-first century. To put it briefly, five varnas (caste groups) exist that are ranked hierarchically. The Brahmins (priests) are at the top, and below them are Kshatriya (warriors), Vaishya (traders), Shudras (labouring people), and Ati-Shudras (untouchables). Occupational flexibility and mobility decreased as one moved down the caste ladder. The untouchables had practically no economic rights, and severe restrictions were imposed on their occupational choices as physical contact with them resulted in "pollution" for the other four groups. From the late nineteenth century onwards, numerically dominant jati (sub-castes) among the Shudras, such as the Marathas, successfully claimed a socially superior position. Although in the textile industry the top three caste groups also worked as labourers, the labouring groups consisted primarily of the dominant castes, the Shudras (now officially part of the Other Backward Castes [OBC]), and the untouchables.

Against this backdrop, I examine to what extent caste-based occupational norms persisted in large-scale modern manufacturing industries in urban areas. I use information from the British colonial census from

Bombay; Deshpande, et al., *Labour Flexibility*; Van Wersch, *The 1982–83 Bombay Textile Strike*; Zachariah, "Bombay Migration Study".

1872 to 1941; and secondary data published by various organisations and scholars to cover the period between 1940 and the 1980s. Survey data on 924 of Mumbai's former mill workers' households, which I gathered in 2009, is used to understand occupational patterns during industrial closures. I use qualitative evidence gathered over fourteen months, from 2008 to 2009, including several periodic visits between December 2010 and January 2014. As for the qualitative data, eighty in-depth interviews were conducted among Mumbai's former mill workers who had lost their jobs in the late 1990s. In addition, semi-structured interviews were conducted with major trade union leaders and government officials. Besides, informal discussions were carried out with political activists, social workers, and others engaged in various ways with the issues of Mumbai's mill workers.

I argue that occupational choices in modern manufacturing industries were influenced by caste-based notions of occupational (in)flexibility and (im)mobility. In varying proportions, the socially superior castes, the dominant castes, and the OBCs moved between the least desirable to the most prestigious jobs in textile mills. On the other hand, untouchables were actively prohibited from entering the most prestigious jobs, restricting the majority of them to work in the least desirable occupations.

I also argue that the weakening of caste-based occupational norms was more prominent among non-untouchable castes. However, here too the socially superior and dominant castes cornered a larger share. A large proportion of untouchables (Dalits) were restricted to the least desirable occupations, suggesting immobility for them. Meanwhile, dominant castes and OBCs also worked with the untouchables in the least desirable jobs, indicating flexibility in their occupational choices.

Caste, Occupations, and Modern Industry

Large-scale statistical data gathered over regular intervals is crucial for analysing the role of caste in modern industrial occupations. The data for the Bombay textile mills comes from the census of India by the British colonial state between 1872 and 1941 and various Labour Commission reports. Regarding academic work, Pradhan's (1938) study on the untouchable workers of Mumbai does have *jati*-specific information about mill workers, but the sample is limited to various untouchable castes. For the year 1940, the information comes from the Bombay Mill Owners Association Survey of 37,639 workers in nineteen textile mills in 1940. While the 1955 BMOA Survey gathered information on the religion, gender, language, and regional origin of individual workers, it discontinued the data collection on castes.[7] Where data on caste was gathered, it was never analysed with respect to occupations. Patel's (1963) study on the Ratnagiri labour migrants, which has *jati*-specific information on 500 mill workers, is one such example.

The third trend is that of scholars who gathered information on caste and occupations but did not examine the relationships.[8] But of course other scholars were able to access the raw survey data and conduct analyses. For instance, Holmstrom's work uses data from Deshpande's 1979 study.[9] Similarly, Hemalata Dandekar's (1986) data is available on the Inter-university Consortium for Political and Social Research (ICPSR) website.[10] To the best of my knowledge, my 2009 survey among former mill workers is the only large-sample effort to collect data on caste besides the other categories mentioned in the 1940 BMOA Survey. Of course, by this time all the textile mills had closed. There is a gap of six decades, making it challenging to explain the shifts in the social composition of the textile workforce throughout the twentieth century. Keeping these limitations in mind, I use secondary sources.

The Beginnings of Industrialisation, 1870s–1890s

Caste has historically played a vital role in shaping the livelihood choices of individuals and groups in the countryside. Subcastes (groups), *not individuals*, were allocated occupations in the village political economy.

[7] Gokhale, *The Bombay Cotton Mill Worker*, p. 13.

[8] Deshpande, "The Bombay Labour Market"; Joshi, "Socio-Economic Condition of Women"; Dandekar, *Men to Bombay*.

[9] Holmstrom, *Industry and Inequality*, p. 238.

[10] It is a unit within the Institute for Social Research at the University of Michigan. Dandekar, *Men to Bombay*.

It was left to the subcastes to assign work to individuals in their groups. As mentioned earlier, economic rights were reduced as one moved down the caste ladder. In the village political economy, there was little or no monetary exchange for services performed by members of each subcaste. Rather than individuals, subcaste groups received compensation for services they offered to the village. Untouchables received meagre compensation in kind and, in most cases, were at the mercy of caste-Hindus.

Scholars have copiously documented labour migration to cities as having occurred within caste, kinship, and village networks.[11] Caste, religion, gender, and language have been deployed to gain access to scarce employment and new entrepreneurial opportunities. Labour intermediaries, known as jobbers, were entrusted with extensive powers to recruit, allocate work inside textile mills, and discipline labourers.[12] However, very little attention is paid to the fact that the urban industrial context treated the *individual* as a unit for monetary compensation, representing a significant departure from the rural socio-economic structure. The socially superior castes, the dominant castes, and the OBCs were the earliest migrants to urban areas and took advantage of the work available in modern factories, such as the textile mills in Mumbai. As the industry expanded, the Marathas deployed their dominant caste position to corner the largest share of best-paid weaving jobs. Untouchables were late entrants to modern urban manufacturing industries because of their bonded ties in the villages and the migration cost of moving to the cities.

The first textile mill in Bombay city was started in 1856. However, very little is known about the number of workers employed in the mill.[13] By 1864, about 6557 mill workers were employed in ten textile mills.[14] The 1872 Census of India recorded the caste, gender, religion, and races of people engaged in wide-ranging occupations. In total, 11,465 workers were employed in ten spinning and weaving mills in Bombay. Male workers constituted 67 per cent of the total workforce and female

[11] Chandavarkar, *The Origins of Industrial Capitalism*, p. 168.
[12] Ibid.
[13] Mehta, *The Cotton Mills of India*, p. 17.
[14] Morris, *The Emergence of an Industrial Labor Force in India*, p. 213.

workers 33 per cent. For those engaged in the Spinning and Weaving departments, their information on caste, gender, religion, and race was recorded. Secondly, in most cases several *jatis* (subcastes) have been clubbed into broader categories. Muslim male and female workers dominated the Weaving department, which had a higher social status than the Spinning department. Of the total male weavers, 86.7 per cent were Muslims, merely 12.6 per cent Hindu of Other Castes (HOC), and 0.4 per cent Dalits. Among women weavers, 77.8 per cent were Muslims, 21.8 per cent HOC, and merely 0.4 per cent Dalits. In contrast, among male workers in the Spinning department 65 per cent were HOC, 29 per cent Muslims, and 4 per cent Dalits. Among women spinners, 53 per cent were Muslims and 46 per cent HOC.[15] Even in the occupations classified as "Weavers, Spinners, Cleaners of Cotton Goods, Thread and Tape" there were 49 per cent Muslims, 49 per cent HOC, and 0.6 per cent Dalits.[16]

The overall trends from 1872 indicate the dominance of Muslims (both male and female) in the weaving section, indicating mill owners' preference for hiring Muslims as weavers. It has been widely documented that Julaha-Ansari Muslims' traditional caste-based occupation was weaving. Therefore, it is very likely that the Muslims reported in the census were Julaha-Ansaris. The absence of disaggregated data among the HOC makes it challenging to know whether caste played any role in acquiring weaving jobs. In any case, the proportion of HOC weavers is extremely low compared to their Muslim counterparts. Dalit men had a negligible presence, and the absence of their female counterparts suggests an extremely low level of migration to work in the factories at the beginning of industrialisation.

By 1881, there were thirty spinning and weaving mills.[17] The total number of workers now reached about 37,000 which was also accompanied by a significant change in the social composition of the workforce.[18] For the first time, the 1881 census recorded separate figures for male and female workers among Brahmins, Bhatias, Lingayats, and Jains.

[15] *Census of the City of Bombay, 1872*, p. 143.
[16] *Census of the City of Bombay, 1873*, p. 145.
[17] *Census of the City and Island of Bombay, 1883*, p. 184.
[18] Ibid., p. 184.

The number of Muslim workers increased from 6391 to 9635. In contrast, the number of HOCs increased phenomenally from about 4856 to 27,356. Among the male workers in Cotton Spinners, Cleaners and Weavers by "Hand", Muslims constituted about 88 per cent and HOC about 12 per cent. Among female workers in the same department, Muslim women accounted for 77 per cent and HOC women 22 per cent. In contrast, among male workers in the "Steam" section, 86 per cent of the jobs were taken by HOCs, Muslims constituted about 9 per cent, and the Dalit share was merely 2.5 per cent. Among women workers in the "Steam" section, HOCs cornered 85 per cent of the jobs, 13 per cent were taken by Muslims, and merely 1.8 by Dalit women.

In the "Unspecified" category, while HOC men held 66 per cent of the jobs, Muslim men constituted 28 per cent of the workforce. HOC women held 81 per cent, and Muslim women held about 15 per cent of the total employment. Dalit men's and women's share was 1.2 per cent and 3.1 per cent, respectively.

Thus, Muslims remained dominant in the processes carried out by the "Hand" department. In the rest of the departments, the HOC dominated the workforce. The phenomenal increase in the share of HOC was due to the 1870s famine-induced migration to urban areas. The staggering increase in the number of non-Brahmin migrants saw the opening of the Jotirao Phule-led non-Brahmin movement's Satya Shodhak Samaj (SSS) branch in Mumbai in 1874.[19] Narayan Meghaji Lokhande, a prominent non-Brahmin leader, took over the reins of the SSS unit in Mumbai. The 1880s saw a further expansion of textile mills, and in 1884 Lokhande formed the Bombay Mill Hands Association (BMHA), the first labour organisation in India. Lokhande raised workers' issues and participated in negotiations with mill owners and the colonial state.

The most powerful legacy of the SSS for labour mobilisation has been the Satyashodhaki *jalsa*, which included *powada* (ballad), *kirtan* (devotional music), and *abhang*s (verses). In Mumbai, across political ideologies, *jalsa*s remained central to labour mobilisation throughout

---

[19] Jotirao Phule founded the Satya Shodhak Samaj in 1873 in Pune to challenge Brahmin caste hegemony and the oppression it perpetuated. See O'Hanlon, *Caste, Conflict, and Ideology*, p. 247; Omvedt, *Cultural Revolt*, p. 152.

the twentieth century. The introduction of the Factory Act of 1881 prohibited the employment of children under seven – thus effectively banning child labour. From the 1890s onwards, we don't have much information about the social background of mill workers. However, there are reports of mill workers organising strikes. Social tensions, too, had come to the fore by 1893, which saw the first Hindu–Muslim riots in Mumbai. Lokhande played a crucial role in containing the riots.

The Textile Boom Period, 1910s–1940s

The beginning of the twentieth century saw a massive expansion in textile mills. While the censuses of India from 1911 to 1931 provide caste-specific information about textile workers, they do not give evidence on labourers in the various departments. In 1911 there were about 89,000 textile mill workers. The proportion of Brahmins remained negligible and the dominant caste – Maratha men and women – occupied the largest proportion of jobs. For instance, of the total male textile workers, Marathas cornered 71 per cent of the employment, Dalits 9 per cent, and Muslims 2.5 per cent. Among the OBCs, the proportion of Bhandari men in the workforce was 4.5 per cent, Kunbi 3.3 per cent, and Vani 2.3 per cent. As for women mill workers, Maratha women occupied 68 per cent of the jobs, Dalits 13 per cent (Chambhar-Mochi 5.3 per cent and Dhed-Mahar 7.7 per cent), Bhandari 5 per cent, Kunbi 3.2 per cent, and Muslim women merely 0.8 per cent. The 1911 census figures reveal the absolute hegemony of the Maratha caste in the textile industry.

The two world wars resulted in a major boom for the textile industry, which saw a massive increase in mill workers. By 1921, the number of mill workers had gone up to 218,185. Of these, 79 per cent were male and 21 per cent were female. According to the 1921 census, "59.9 per cent of the jobbers came from the Maratha and allied castes, 22.2 per cent from the Kolis and backward classes and 9.1 per cent from the Muslims."[20] Since jobbers relied on their caste, kinship, and village networks for recruitment, it is not surprising to find this reflected in the

---

[20] Newman, *Workers and Unions*, p. 53.

social composition of the workforce. While the proportion of Marathas remained the highest, it was now 35 per cent. Followed by Marathas, Dalit men accounted for 13 per cent, and Muslims 9 per cent. Among the OBCs, Kunbi men had a share of 5 per cent, and Bhandari men 2.9 per cent. Among women mill workers, Maratha women's proportion was 51 per cent. Followed by them, Dalit women's share was 28 per cent, OBC women 7 per cent (Kunbi 4 per cent and Bhandari 3 per cent), and Muslim women 1.8 per cent. The expansion of the workforce also saw newer groups consolidating their position. Brahmin workers saw a significant increase in the workforce, occupying 6.8 per cent of the total positions. Thus, during the boom period Marathas retained their dominance, even as other groups made their presence felt in the workforce.

The 1920s was a boom period for the textile industry. It was also a period of intense political mobilisation by all groups. The Communist Party was formed in 1925, and the Muslim League, the Rashtriya Swayamsevak Sangh, the Socialists, the Moderates, and anti-caste groups had a notable presence in Bombay. Dalits were successfully mobilised under Dr B.R. Ambedkar's leadership. The political consolidation of Dalits saw them challenging caste-based restrictions on their entry into the most desirable weaving departments. In the weaving process, "each time a weft bobbin required replacement, the yarn had to be sucked onto the shuttle."[21] The Marathas argued that this put them at risk of being polluted, and under this pretext closed the door against Mahars (the Dalit community in Maharashtra).

The Mahars successfully articulated their exclusion from weaving jobs during the famous 1928 strike. Ambedkar threatened the Communist unions by saying that if Dalits' right to work in all mill departments was not recognised, he would "dissuade the Depressed Classes [Dalits] from taking part in the strike."[22] The Communist leadership reluctantly accepted this and placed it among seventeen demands presented to the mill owners. However, the mill owners snubbed the Communists by arguing that if the exclusion of Dalits from the Weaving

---

[21] Chandavarkar, *The Origins of Industrial Capitalism*, p. 224.
[22] Ambedkar, *Dr Babasaheb Ambedkar: Writings and Speeches*, vol. 2, p. 474.

department "was an injustice, they certainly were not responsible for it."[23]

Following the 1928 strike, Ambedkar organised training for Dalit weavers through the "130 people [that] were brought in from Berar region."[24] At this the Marathas went on strike at various places. They also resisted the Bombay Millowners Association's recruitment of Dalits in Weaving departments. Later, the mill owners gave up such initiatives when experienced Maratha weavers returned to work and complained that Dalits "lacked the necessary skills and aptitude for weaving."[25]

Maratha resistance to the entry of Mahars into the Weaving department is hardly surprising, as this was the best-paid and the most desirable and prestigious textile-industry occupation. However, what is remarkable is that Mahars were able to stake a claim for the most desirable jobs that dominant-caste Marathas and Julaha-Ansari Muslims had cornered in the urban industrial context. Such claims by Dalits were impossible in the village political economy, where they had limited access to land ownership and were compelled to take up menial, heavy manual, and stigmatised occupations. The major difference in the urban industrial context was that Marathas resorted to strikes and non-cooperation to resist the entry of Mahars in the Weaving section. In rural settings, such claims by Dalits would have resulted in them facing social ostracism and, in some cases, extreme forms of physical violence. In the post-1950s period Mahars in rural areas gave up degrading and humiliating work as part of their conversion to Buddhism. Such action resulted in violence against the Mahars by non-untouchables.

The proportion of Dalit mill workers within the total workforce doubled between 1911 and 1931. In addition to mills, the Dalits had an overwhelming presence in the municipal corporation, hospitals, dockyards, and miscellaneous industries. Together, they played a crucial role in shaping the initial years of organised Dalit politics and participated in movements led by Ambedkar.[26]

While Maratha men staunchly opposed the entry of Mahars into the

[23] Ibid.
[24] *Bahishkrit Bharat*, 15 November 1929.
[25] Chandavarkar, *The Origins of Industrial Capitalism*, pp. 427–8.
[26] Pol, "From the Margins".

Weaving department, they did not resist the employment of Julaha-Ansari Muslim workers. The failure of Marathas in this respect was rooted in the fact that mill owners preferred Julaha-Ansari workers for their traditional weaving skills. In fact, mill owners entrusted Muslim workers with the "fancy and jacquard loom work".[27] It is precisely for this reason, as Chandavarkar noted, that Julaha-Ansaris not only "appropriated important areas of control over their labour," but could also refuse to work night shifts. Furthermore, Muslim weavers' "average earnings were reputed to exceed those of their Hindu counterparts."[28] However, it is also important to note that, as the industry expanded, Marathas took over the largest share of weaving jobs and Muslim weavers were concentrated in large numbers in specific mills in central Mumbai.

The data from the 1931 census shows the numbers for Kunbis and Marathas together. The Marathas had persuaded the Kunbis to report themselves as Marathas to the census authorities. The Kunbis saw this as an opportunity for upward social mobility. This explains the nature of the data available. Among male workers, 42.4 per cent were Kunbi-Marathas, 11 per cent Marathas, and 0.3 per cent Kunbis. Dalit men accounted for 17 per cent, Bhandari men 3 per cent, and Muslim men about 13 per cent. Likewise, among women mill workers Maratha-Kunbis had a share of 68 per cent, Maratha women 9 per cent, and Kunbis 0.2 per cent. Dalit women accounted for 14.5 per cent, and Muslim women merely 0.6 per cent.

The 1940 survey carried out by the BMOA remains the principal reference for scholars examining the social composition of the Bombay textile workforce.[29] It shows that the share of Maratha men among the male workforce was 52 per cent.[30] Following this category were North Indians (Brahmins, Rajputs, and Thakurs), who constituted 14 per cent, Dalits 12 per cent, Muslims 5 per cent, Kunbis 4 per cent, and Bhandaris 3 per cent. Muslim men constituted 5 per cent of the total mill workforce in 1940.[31] I will begin with the Ring department, which rep-

---

[27] Shah, "Labour Recruitment", p. 183.
[28] Chandavarkar, *The Origins of Industrial Capitalism*, p. 320.
[29] Gokhale, *The Bombay Cotton Mill Worker*, p. 116.
[30] Ibid.
[31] Ibid., p. 15.

resents the least desirable occupation, and end with the Weaving department, which represents the most desirable, prestigious and highest-paid job.

The Ring department accounted for 22 per cent of the workforce. Of the total workers in the Ring department, the share of Marathas was 42 per cent, and that of Dalits 40 per cent. Among Maratha men, merely 17 per cent worked in the Ring department, contrasting with Dalits – among whom 73 per cent worked here. In the case of women mill workers, merely 4 per cent worked in the Ring department. Of the total women in the Ring department, 78 per cent were Dalit, 16 per cent Maratha, and 2 per cent Muslim. Among Dalit women, about 13 per cent worked in the Ring department; among Muslim women, it was 7 per cent, and among Maratha women, it was merely 1 per cent.[32] It is, therefore, not surprising that jobs in the Ring department were associated with Dalits.

While Dalits may have been primarily concentrated in the Ring and Spinning departments in the 1940s, this was *not* the case from the beginning of industrialisation. Until the 1880s, the HOCs, who included the Marathas and OBC castes, worked in the Ring and Spinning departments. Back then, Dalits had a negligible presence in the textile mills. The increase in cloth production opened up job opportunities in the Weaving section. As Morris stated, this subsequently increased the wages of the weavers. This development indicates the movement of Marathas and the OBCs from the least desirable to the most desirable weaving jobs.[33]

The change in the production process opened up opportunities for Dalits in Ring and Spinning. Working in these departments already had a low status because of the low wages: here, workers earned half, or a quarter, of the income of weavers.[34] While a section of the Marathas and OBCs also worked in this department, Dalits were particularly vulnerable because of other factors: for instance, they did not have farmlands to rely on during long-drawn industrial actions, which their

[32] Pradhan's findings also concur with this information; of the total Dalits employed in the textile mills, 83 per cent worked in the ring department. Pradhan, *Untouchable Workers*, p. 55.

[33] Morris, *The Emergence of an Industrial Labor Force,* p. 67.

[34] *Bahishkrit Bharat*, 3 May 1929.

non-Dalit counterparts had. To add to their miseries, grain-shop dealers did not extend credit to Dalits, especially during prolonged strikes.[35] The only way Dalit workers, both men and women, could participate in a strike was by taking loans from Pathans – which had life-threatening consequences. By contrast, Maratha workers received support from grain-shop owners during strike periods. Marathas and OBCs working alongside Dalits is a sign of flexibility and mobility in their occupational choices. However, the Dalit concentration here was out of restrictions imposed on them. It is also important to remember that until the early 1980s, even the least desirable textile jobs, being part of the organised sector, were the most protected and best-paid in the country.

The Mixing to Speed Frame departments constituted about 16 per cent of the workforce. Of the total workers in this department, North Indian men (Brahmin, Rajput, and Thakur) occupied 47 per cent of the jobs, Maratha men 32 per cent, Dalit men 8 per cent, Kunbi men 4 per cent, and Muslim men 3 per cent. While among the North Indian men 54 per cent worked in the said departments, Maratha men were merely 10 per cent. Among women, 1.4 per cent worked here. Of the total women here, 30 per cent were Maratha, 31 per cent Dalit, 6 per cent Muslim, 5 per cent Kunbi, and 5 per cent North Indian. Thus, North Indian men and Marathas dominated the Mixing to Speed Frame departments. Besides them, OBCs, Muslims and Dalits also had a marginal presence.

The Engineering, Mechanic, Watch and Ward accounted for 7 per cent of the textile workforce. Of the total workers here, the share of Maratha men was 40 per cent, North Indian men 14 per cent, Dalit men 11 per cent, and Muslim men 11 per cent. Within each group, while 4–7 per cent worked here, among Muslims it was 14 per cent. In both the departments discussed, there was a mixed caste workforce with the domination of North Indians in Mixing to Speed Frame, and of Marathas in Engineering, Mechanic, Watch and Ward. The presence of Muslims may have had to do with mechanical jobs, in which they seem to have become indispensable. Dalit men, too, had a marginal presence, most probably as security guards.

The Winding and Reeling department accounted for 15 per cent of

35 Ibid.

the total male and female workforce in 1940.[36] In this department the
share of women mill workers was 94 per cent, and that of male workers
merely 6 per cent. Of the total women workers in the Winding and Reeling departments, the proportion of Maratha women was 56 per cent,
Dalit women 21 per cent, Kunbi women 7 per cent, Bhandari women
5 per cent, and Muslim women 1 per cent. Among Maratha, Kunbi,
and Bhandari women, more than 92 per cent worked in the Winding and
Reeling departments; among Dalit women, the proportion was about
74 per cent, and among Muslim women 54 per cent. While Maratha
and Dalit women dominated the Winding and Reeling department,
they also had a notable presence in other textile departments. OBC
women had a marginal presence too.

The Weaving department was unique because it accounted for
39 per cent of the workforce in 1940. It was also the most desirable,
highest paid, well respected, and sought after job in the textile industry.
According to the 1921 census, out of the 30,000 weavers, Marathas
(and allied castes) cornered 61.7 per cent of the jobs.[37] According to
the BMOA 1940 Survey, of the total male weavers, 67 per cent were
Marathas, 7 per cent Muslims, 6 per cent North Indians, 4 per cent
Kunbis, 3 per cent Bhandaris, and 0.6 per cent Dalits. The distribution
of male weavers within each caste group is also telling. Over 50 per cent
of the Marathas worked in the Weaving department. Among Muslims
52 per cent, Bhandaris 50 per cent, Kunbis 44 per cent, North Indians 17 per cent, and Dalits merely 2 per cent worked in the Weaving
department.[38] Thus, among Marathas, Muslims, and Bhandaris, more
than half worked as weavers. Dalit men had a negligible presence in the
Weaving department, and North Indian men showed a lower presence
than the rest of the groups. Of the women workers, merely 0.2 per cent
worked in the Weaving department. Among women, it was Marathas,
Dalits, and Muslims who worked here. The Marathas worked alongside
OBCs, North Indian Brahmins, Rajputs, and Thakurs, and Muslims in
Weaving departments. However, the Marathas expressed militant opposition to the entry of Dalits into weaving jobs by invoking the caste
norms of "purity" and "pollution".

[36] Gokhale, *The Bombay Cotton Mill Worker*, p. 116.
[37] Newman, *Workers and Unions*, p. 42.
[38] Gokhale, *The Bombay Cotton Mill Worker*, p. 116.

Textile Decline, 1950s–1990s

From the late 1940s on, other textile sectors challenged the organised textile industry with technological innovations and competition. In some cases, this resulted in a gradual reduction of the workforce in the textile mills. In 1950, India adopted a new constitution that delegitimised the traditional caste-based framework of governance. It also banned the practice of untouchability. Also, successive legislations for the organised manufacturing sector meant that textile mill workers, even the ones in the least desirable occupations, had access to social security provisions and were the best-paid workers in the country.

The BMOA 1955 Survey shows a massive decline in women workers in Winding and Reeling – from 16 per cent in 1940 to 7 per cent in 1955.[39] Jobs in Winding and Reeling declined from 15 per cent in 1940 to 8 per cent in 1955. The most striking trend was a massive reduction in the overall share of women workers – from 94 per cent in 1940 to 65 per cent in 1955. By contrast, there was a phenomenal increase in male workers – from 6 per cent to 35 per cent.

By 1955, the proportion of Muslim male workers had decreased from 5 per cent in 1940 to 3 per cent of the total male workforce. Muslim women constituted merely 1 per cent of the total women's workforce in 1940, and their proportion fell to 0.6 per cent in 1955. The proportion of Muslims in the Winding and Reeling department decreased drastically from 6.5 per cent to 2.2 per cent, whereas the proportion of Hindus increased from 90 to 96 per cent. The overall proportion of jobs in Engineering, Mechanic, Watch and Ward in 1955 was 7 per cent – the same as in 1940. Here, the share of Muslim men decreased considerably, from 11 per cent to 4.7 per cent, whereas the proportion of Hindus increased from 77 per cent to 91 per cent.[40]

There was a marginal decline in weaving jobs, from 39 per cent in 1940 to 35 per cent in 1955. The drop in weavers also saw a fall in the proportion of Muslim weavers, from 7 per cent in 1940 to 5 per cent in 1955. On the other hand, the proportion of Hindu weavers increased from 91 per cent to 94 per cent in 1955. There are no caste-wise figures for 1955. However, given the fact that Marathas, Kunbis, Bhandaris,

[39] Ibid., p. 7.
[40] Ibid., p. 15.

and North Indian Brahmins, Rajputs, and Thakurs occupied these jobs, it is very likely that they took over these jobs from Muslims. The decline of Muslims in the textile mills could be attributed to the Hindu–Muslim riots that broke out on the eve of Independence, followed by Partition. Ironically, the Muslim mill workers of Mumbai, mainly the Julaha-Ansaris, supported the All-India Momin Conference, which was opposed to Partition and yet bore the brunt of Partition's consequences. The process of Muslim exclusion continued after Independence.

In the 1960s, as jobs became scarcer, upper-caste mill workers, especially the Marathas, managed to hold on to their jobs, but others did not. The Marathas now excluded Muslim weavers by deploying the notion of "pollution".[41] However, the alibi of pollution in the case of Muslims was fundamentally different from the caste notion of purity-pollution that Marathas used to exclude Dalits from the weaving departments. In the case of Muslims, the roots of "pollution", I have argued elsewhere, can be understood through the negative emotion called *karahiyat* among non-Muslims.[42] *Karahiyat* has several negative connotations – such as aversion, nausea, disgust, detestation, dislike, disdain, loathing, abhorrence, antipathy, disagreeableness, and hideousness. Muslims sense the feeling of *karahiyat* among non-Muslims during their everyday interactions in the social, economic, political, and cultural spheres. The sources of *karahiyat* are rooted in beef-eating, the Partition of India, and the perception of Muslim-dominated areas as spaces of illegal activities, crime, and prostitution. The Marathas exploited these feelings of *karahiyat* because of the arrival of technologically advanced weaving machines which challenged Julaha-Ansari workers' traditional claim to skilled weaving work.

By the mid 1970s cloth production was gradually transferred to Bhiwandi in the outskirts of Bombay, resulting in the reduction of jobs.[43] The decline in job opportunities was accompanied by explicit

[41] Hansen, *Wages of Violence*, p. 163.

[42] For a detailed discussion on the concept of *karahiyat*, see Mhaskar, "Ghettoisation of Economic Choices", pp. 29–37.

[43] Bhiwandi, where mill owners subcontracted their work, saw a phenomenal growth from 18,000 looms in 1963 to 48,000 in 1975.

anti-Muslim recruitment policies by some of the textile mill managements.[44] For the 1990s period, qualitative evidence suggests that during the 1992–3 anti-Muslim pogroms in Mumbai, Muslim workers were often unable to report for work over long periods and consequently faced dismissal.[45]

For the late 1970s period, we have data provided by Holmstrom.[46] Although the sample size is small, patterns can be noted. This data suggests that, of the total weavers, Marathas occupied 45 per cent, Kshatriya (probably Rajput or Thakur) claimed 16 per cent, North Indian Brahmins 3 per cent, Muslims 5 per cent, and Dalits 5 per cent. While Marathas retained their dominant position in the Weaving department, their proportion declined from 67 per cent in 1940 to 61 per cent in 1979. The decline in the share of Marathas can be attributed to Kunbis *not* reporting as Marathas. More importantly, however, as Dandekar's study of Sugao village notes, the decline of workers in mills was mainly due to Marathas diversifying into other well-paid jobs in Mumbai, such as in the police and military, as well as taking up clerical and white-collar jobs.[47] Following the Marathas, Padmashali weavers accounted for about 11 per cent, a significant increase considering their proportion was 5 per cent in 1940.

The Dalit proportion also seems to have increased from 0.6 per cent to 5 per cent. The increase in Dalits could have been due to biased sampling and initiatives from the Social Welfare Department's affirmative action policies. In the early 1970s, under pressure from Dalit Panthers the government tried to "extend fair placement opportunities" to Dalits through its Social Welfare Department. Only the government-owned

[44] Interview with Hussain Dalwai: this socialist labour organiser told me that in the 1970s he confronted the Khatau mill management for putting out an explicit notice stating that Muslims would not be hired.

[45] During the pogroms, Shiv Sainiks became aggressive, and occasionally violent, towards the Muslim mill workers. In many factories, members of the Shiv Sena union threatened Muslim workers, and where the latter protested, physical force was used. Date and Fernandez, "Workers' Insecurity", *The Times of India*, 1993. Date, "Workers Bear Brunt", *The Times of India*, 1992.

[46] Holmstrom, *Industry and Inequality*, p. 238.

[47] Dandekar, *Men to Bombay*, p. 295.

Jupiter Textile Mill responded positively to the initiative. The state's attempts worked to a certain extent, and Deshpande's 1979 survey does indicate this change.[48] However, despite the ban on untouchability, caste-Hindus (non-untouchables) successfully resisted the recruitment of Dalits as weavers.[49] This shows how caste-based occupational norms shaped employment choices in the most desirable jobs. The share of Muslim weavers was 5 per cent, matching their proportion in 1955. However, the earlier discussion shows that, already in the 1960s and 1970s, Muslims were excluded from the textile mills' weaving departments. Therefore, it is possible that some biased sampling may have happened in the case of Muslims.

According to the 1983 study on remittances,[50] weavers constituted 25 per cent of the total workforce, indicating a decline in cloth production. The Ring department saw a marginal decline, and jobs in Engineering nearly doubled. Watch and Ward, too, saw an increase. In the early 1980s, mill workers went on an eighteen-month-long strike, which also saw the transfer of production to Bhiwandi's power looms. After the strike ended in 1983, 91,251 workers lost their jobs.[51] There is no statistical information on which caste and religious groups had to bear the brunt of lay-offs. Ethnographic data gathered in 2009 shows us that, during the 1982–3 strike, the Century Textile Mill in the Worli area recruited many North Indian Brahmins as strike-breakers. On the other hand, it was evident from fieldwork in Madanpura that a large number of Muslim workers lost their jobs after the strike.

Textile Mill Closures, 2006

By 2006, nearly all the textile mills had closed. My survey was conducted in 2009, among 1037 Mumbai's former mill workers. Of these, 924 lived in the city after losing their jobs and 113 returned to their village. For this essay I only use data from city-based former mill workers. The survey is biased towards women, Dalits, and Muslims, as random sam-

[48] Holmstrom, *Industry and Inequality*, p. 238.

[49] Purandare, "Untouchability in City Mills".

[50] TINTWF & TAILS, "Urban Rural Transfers", p. 39.

[51] From my field visits to Bhiwandi it had become clear to me that mill workers did not relocate from Mumbai.

pling would not have captured the required numbers to examine the patterns. Of the total male and female workforce, 24 per cent worked in the Weaving department, 22 per cent in the Winding and Reeling departments, 14 per cent in the Mixing to Speed Frame departments, 8 per cent in the Engineering Mechanic, Watch and Ward department, and 8 per cent in the Ring department. Besides the BMOA classification, I have included information on three departments wherein 10 per cent worked in the Folding department, 9 per cent worked in the Dyeing and Processing department, and 5 per cent in the Canteen, Store and Administration departments. Regarding gender division in the workforce, male workers constituted 97 per cent of the total, and female workers 3 per cent.

Of the total male workers in the Ring department, 56 per cent were Marathas, 18 per cent OBC, and 16 per cent Dalits. Among Marathas, 13 per cent worked in the Ring department in 2006, compared to 17 per cent in 1940. Among Kunbi and Bhandari men, the proportion decreased from 20 per cent to 7 per cent, and 8 per cent to 3 per cent, respectively; similarly Muslims, whose proportion shows a decline from 8 per cent to 5 per cent. A significant decline is visible in the proportion of Dalit men: while 73 per cent worked in the Ring-Spinning department in 1940, their proportion came down drastically to 12 per cent when the mills closed. Among women mill workers, only Dalit women worked in the Ring department. Of the total Dalit women, about a quarter worked in the Ring department. Job scarcity must have led Marathas and OBCs to expand their presence at the cost of Dalits, even in the least desirable occupations.

In the Mixing to Speed Frame departments, Maratha men cornered 42 per cent of the jobs. Followed by them, Brahmins (predominantly North Indians) and Dalits each occupied 16 per cent of the employment. Kunbi men accounted for about 5 per cent, and Bhandari, Nhavi, Yadav, and Agri each accounted for 2 per cent, respectively. Nomadic Tribes Gawali had a share of 4 per cent, while Muslim men had merely 1 per cent share. There were no women workers in this department. Among Maratha men, while in 1940 there were 10 per cent, their proportion in 2009 increased to 17 per cent. There was also a substantial increase among Dalit men – from 10 per cent in 1940 to 28 per cent in 2006. The proportion among Kunbi men saw a marginal decline from 17 per cent to 16 per cent. Among the rest of the groups, there was a decline. For instance, of the total North Indians, 54 per cent worked in the said departments in 1940, their proportion coming down to 14 per cent in 2006. Similarly, among Muslims 7 per cent worked in 1940, and their proportion came down to 1 per cent. Among Bhandaris, the proportion came down from 6 per cent to 4 per cent. Thus, Marathas switched to Mixing and Speed Frame as jobs in other departments declined. Dalits, too, managed to gain some jobs in this department.

In the Engineering, Mechanic, Watch and Ward departments, Marathas took away 39 per cent of the jobs – the largest share for any sub-caste. About 10 per cent of Dalits held jobs, among whom 5 per cent were taken by neo-Buddhists/Mahars and 1 per cent by Chamars/Charmakars. Among OBCs, Bhandari men accounted for 5 per cent, while Kunbi and Teli each had a share of 4 per cent. Sutar, Vani, and Yadav each occupied 3 per cent of the jobs, and Agri men had 7 per cent of the positions. The Muslim share was 4 per cent, and Brahmins occupied 3 per cent of the employment. Once again, there were no women in this department.

Among Marathas, Dalits, North Indians, Kunbis, and Bhandaris, their proportion increased in the Engineering, Mechanic, Watch and Ward departments. Among Maratha men, the proportion increased from 5 per cent in 1940 to 10 per cent in 2009. Dalits' share increased from 6 per cent to 9 per cent. The share among North Indians increased marginally from 7 per cent to 8 per cent. Among Kunbi and Bhandari men, their proportion increased from 5 to 7 per cent and 3 to 6 per cent, respectively. Only among Muslims is the decline starkly visible – from 14 per cent to 7 per cent. Thus, except for Muslims, each group increased its share in the Engineering, Mechanic, Watch and Ward departments.

Among various caste and religious groups, about 1–3 per cent of men worked in the Winding and Reeling department in 1940. The 2009 data shows that, except for Muslims, there was a substantial increase in the proportion of male workers in the Winding and Reeling department. Across caste and communities, the proportion of men increased between 18 and 34 per cent. In the Winding and Reeling departments, the share of Maratha men was 33 per cent. Following them,

Bhandari men occupied 13 per cent of jobs, while Kunbi, Teli, Agri, and Vani accounted for 9 per cent, 4 per cent, 6 per cent, and 3 per cent, respectively. Other OBCs, such as Nhavi and Sutar, had a share of 1 per cent. Dalits' proportion in this department was 9 per cent. Brahmins occupied 4 per cent of jobs, while the Muslim share was merely 1 per cent.

The overall share of women fell to 2 per cent by the early 1980s. As with Dalits and Muslims, the 2009 survey is biased towards women workers. Among women workers, 87 per cent worked in the Winding and Reeling department. The following is the caste-wise division within women in this department: Maratha women, 33 per cent; Kunbi women, 11 per cent; Bhandari women, 7 per cent. Sutar, Agri, and Vani women constituted 4 per cent, 7 per cent, and 4 per cent respectively. Dalit women accounted for 22 per cent.

There has been an overall decline in the number of weaving jobs. In 1940, nearly 40 per cent of the workforce was made up of weavers. By 1979 this had declined to 29 per cent; when the mills closed in 2006, their percentage decreased further – to 25 per cent.

The decline in weaving jobs is also reflected in the reduced share within each caste and community. There are notable exceptions. The Padmashalis (a weaver caste) increased from 5 per cent in 1940 to 31 per cent in 2006. Maratha men cornered 30 per cent of the jobs. Followed by them, there were 4 per cent Bhandari men, and 2 per cent each of Teli, Sutar, and Vani men. North Indian Brahmin men accounted for 3 per cent. Muslim weavers' share was 9 per cent. The Dalit share was 5 per cent. Once again, none of the women in my survey reported working in the Weaving department.

The Dalit proportion saw a marginal increase. As noted earlier, there is a slight over-representation of Dalits because of biased sampling. Another reason could be the implementation of affirmative action policies in the late 1970s by government-owned textile mills. A few private mills, too, hired Dalit weavers, which was a matter of surprise in Dalit households.[52] Dalit weaver informants told me that Marathas did not co-operate with them. As a result, they had to learn to operate the machines on their own or had to join one of the "upper-caste lobbies".

---

[52] Interview with a Dalit ex-millworker from the Swadeshi Textile Mills.

The decline of Marathas in the weaving department is phenomenal – from 67 per cent in 1940 to 30 per cent in 2006. This could be explained by the return migration of Marathas to their villages, which may have resulted in their low participation in my survey. The historic 1982–3 strike was also a factor. Marathas from western Maharashtra participated in the strike, and some of them may have lost their jobs when the mills reopened in 1984.[53] These factors may have also increased the proportion of Padmashalis.

The overall proportion of Muslims in the Weaving department increased marginally. Like Dalits, the patterns showing for Muslims could be due to a sampling bias. As noted earlier, Muslims lost jobs since the late 1940s.

Qualitative evidence throws some light on the marginalisation of Muslims. One of my Maratha caste respondents from the Hindustan Mills, where Muslims constituted about 50 per cent of the total workforce till 1979, claimed that Rashtriya Mill Mazdoor Sangh (RMMS) followed a deliberate policy of not recruiting Muslims.[54] As a result, when the Hindustan Mills closed at the beginning of the twenty-first century, the proportion of Muslims had dropped to 10 per cent.

~

This essay has examined the relationship between caste and occupations in modern textile mills. I have sought to demonstrate how caste-based occupational norms shaped occupational choices in modern manufacturing industries in Mumbai city. I have argued that occupational choices in modern manufacturing industries were influenced by caste-based notions of occupational (in)flexibility and (im)mobility. Marathas and OBCs began with the least desirable occupation (ring and spinning) and later moved to the most desirable occupation (weaving). As jobs became scarcer, the Marathas and OBCs expanded their presence in the least desirable occupation. While the Marathas dominated most textile mill departments, they worked alongside the OBCs, North Indians (Brahmins, Rajputs, and Thakurs), and Muslims. While one might treat this as a sign of the weakening of caste, it

[53] Interviews with ex-mill workers in Kolhapur and Satara districts.

[54] The RMMS was the officially recognised union in the textile industry.

must be remembered that this flexibility was largely among the non-untouchable castes.

Dalits were predominantly concentrated in the least desirable (ring and spinning) jobs and were actively prohibited from working in the most desirable occupation (weaving). Even after independent India's constitution banned untouchability, the non-untouchable castes were able to resist the recruitment of Dalits. Dalits also had a marginal presence in other departments. However, job scarcity saw them losing their foothold even in the least desirable jobs.

Despite Dalit concentration in low-paid and least desirable jobs, their coming into the modern workforce was a remarkable departure from their situation in the rural political economy. In the mills, Dalits earned monetary compensation for their labour. This aspect was especially crucial for Dalits, who were paid in kind for their services and were, in most cases, at the mercy of caste-Hindus. Most importantly, they were able to mobilise politically in urban settings.

Muslims, especially Julaha-Ansaris, enjoyed preferential treatment in the weaving section due to their caste-based weaving skills. However, the shrinking of jobs and technological transformation saw Muslims lose their claim over skilled weaving jobs. The presence of anti-Muslim sentiment, together with the introduction of technologically advanced weaving looms, saw Marathas push out Muslims from weaving jobs.

To conclude, caste norms of mobility and immobility remained at the heart of occupational choices in the modern manufacturing industry. Caste enabled socially superior castes, dominant castes, and OBCs to flexibly move between the least desirable and most desirable jobs. On the other hand, caste restricted Dalits to the least desirable jobs and excluded them from working in the most desirable occupations.

Table 1.1: Caste of Male Mill Workers by Departments,
Row Percentage 2009

	Morning to Speed Frame	Ring	Winding and Reeling	Weaving Shed	Dyeing and Processing	Folding	Engineering, Maintenance, Watch & Ward	Canteen, Hosiery & Store	N
Brahmin	23	2	16	14	19	7	5	14	43
Maratha	17	13	18	21	7	11	10	4	314
Miscellaneous High Caste Hindus	22	0	28	22	17	6	6	0	18
Kunbi	16	7	34	14	16	5	7	2	44
Bhandari	4	3	34	12	16	19	6	4	67
Teli	0	5	35	25	5	10	15	5	20
Nhavi	38	0	13	25	0	13	0	13	8
Sutar	10	0	20	50	0	0	20	0	10
Yadav	19	6	25	6	19	6	13	6	16
Agri	7	3	34	0	17	14	17	7	29
Vani	18	0	23	18	0	9	9	23	22
Miscellaneous OBC	8	12	24	22	6	12	12	6	51
Padmashali	0	0	2	84	2	6	1	4	81
Buddhist/ Mahar	29	15	9	15	6	12	12	3	34
Charmakar	30	11	24	16	8	3	3	5	37
Miscellaneous Dalits	19	13	19	6	13	6	19	6	16
Gawali	28	17	28	0	6	11	6	6	18
Miscellaneous Nomadic Tribes	17	8	17	17	17	17	8	0	12
Julaha	0	0	0	100	0	0	0	0	4
Bagwan	0	0	0	0	0	100	0	0	1
Muslims No Caste Reported	0	20	0	40	20	0	20	0	5
High Caste Muslims	3	3	3	42	32	6	6	3	31
Not Reported	25	0	8	17	17	8	17	8	12
Average	15	8	20	25	10	10	9	5	893

Source: Author's calculation: Mhaskar, Mumbai's Ex-millworkers' Household Survey Data, 2009.

Table 1.2:   Caste of Male Mill Workers by Departments,
Column Percentage 2009

	Morning to Speed Frame	Ring	Winding and Reeling	Weaving Shed	Dyeing and Processing	Folding	Engineering, Maintenance, Watch & Ward	Canteen, Hosiery & Store
Brahmin	8	1	4	3	9	3	3	14
Maratha	42	56	33	30	24	38	39	25
Miscellaneous High Caste Hindus	3	0	3	2	3	1	1	0
Kunbi	5	4	9	3	8	2	4	2
Bhandari	2	3	13	4	13	15	5	7
Teli	0	1	4	2	1	2	4	2
Nhavi	2	0	1	1	0	1	0	2
Sutar	1	0	1	2	0	0	3	0
Yadav	2	1	2	0	3	1	3	2
Agri	2	1	6	0	6	5	7	5
Vani	3	0	3	2	0	2	3	11
Miscellaneous OBC	3	3	7	5	3	7	8	7
Padmashali	0	0	1	31	2	6	1	7
Buddhist/Mahar	8	7	2	2	2	5	5	2
Charmakar	8	6	5	3	3	1	1	5
Miscellaneous Dalits	2	3	2	0	2	1	4	2
Gawali	4	4	3	0	1	2	1	2
Miscellaneous	2	1	1	1	2	2	1	0
Julaha Nomadic Tribes	0	0	0	2	0	0	0	0
Bagwan	0	0	0	0	0	1	0	0
Muslims No Caste Reported	0	1	0	1	1	0	1	0
High Caste Muslims	1	1	1	6	11	2	3	2
Not Reported	2	0	1	1	2	1	3	2
N	130	72	175	222	87	87	76	44

Source: Author's calculation: Mhaskar, Mumbai's Ex-millworkers' Household
Survey Data, 2009.

Table 1.3: Caste of Female Mill Workers by Departments,
Column Percentage 2009

	Ring	Winding and Reeling	Folding	Canteen, Hosiery, & Store	Average
Maratha	–	33	100	–	35
Kunbi	–	11	–	–	10
Bhandari	–	7	–	100	10
Sutar	–	4	–	–	3
Agri	–	7	–	–	6
Vani	–	4	–	–	3
Miscellaneous OBC	–	7	–	–	6
Padmashali	–	4	–	–	3
Buddhist/Mahar	100	11	–	–	13
Charmakar	–	11	–	–	10
N	1	27	2	1	31

Source: Author's calculation: Mhaskar, Mumbai's Ex-millworkers' Household Survey Data, 2009.

References

Ambedkar, B.R., *Dr Babasaheb Ambedkar: Writings and Speeches, Volume 2* (New Delhi: Dr Ambedkar Foundation, Ministry of Social Justice & Empowerment, Govt of India, 2014).

Burnett-Hurst, Alexander Robert, *Labour and Housing in Bombay: A Study in the Economic Conditions of the Wage-earning Classes in Bombay* (London: P.S. King, 1925).

Census of the City and Island of Bombay, Taken on the 17th of February 1881 by T. S. Weir, Surgeon-Major, Health Officer, Acting Municipal Commissioner (Bombay: Times of India Steam Press, 1883).

Census of the City of Bombay, Taken on 21st February 1872 (Bombay: Education Society's Press, Byculla, 1873).

Chandavarkar, Rajnarayan, *Imperial Power and Popular Politics: Class, Resistance and the State in India, c. 1850–1950* (Cambridge: Cambridge University Press, 1998).

Chandavarkar, Rajnarayan, *The Origins of Industrial Capitalism in India: Business Strategies and the Working Classes in Bombay, 1900–1940* (Cambridge: Cambridge University Press, 1994).

Cholia, R.P., *Dock Labourers in Bombay* (London, New York, Calcutta: Longmans, Green and Co., 1941).

Dandekar, Hemalata C., *Men to Bombay, Women at Home: Urban Influence on Sugao Village, Deccan Maharashtra, India, 1942–1982* (Ann Arbor, Mich.: Center for South and Southeast Asian Studies, University of Michigan, 1986).

Dandekar, V.M., and M.M. Jagtap, *Maharashtrachi Gramin Samajrachna* (Pune: Gokhale Institute of Economic Research, 1957).

Date, Vidyadhar, "Workers Bear Brunt of City Riots", *The Times of India*, 13 December 1992.

Date, Vidyadhar, and Clarence Fernandez, "Workers' Insecurity Leads to Poor Attendance, *The Times of India*, 21 January 1993.

Davis, Kingsley, *The Population of India and Pakistan, by Kingsley Davis*, With a Foreword by Frank W. Notestein (Princeton: Princeton University Press, 1951).

Deshpande, Lalit K., *Segmentation of Labour Market: A Case Study of Bombay* (Pune: Gokhale Institute of Politics and Economics, 1985).

Deshpande, Lalit K., "The Bombay Labour Market", Mimeo, Bombay: Department of Economics. University of Bombay, 1979.

Deshpande, Prachi, "Caste as Maratha: Social Categories, Colonial Policy and Identity in Early Twentieth-century Maharashtra", *Indian Economic & Social History Review*, vol. 41, no. 1, 2004, doi: 10.1177/001946460 404100102.

Deshpande, Sudha, Guy Standing, and L.K. Deshpande, *Labour Flexibility in a Third World Metropolis: A Case Study of Bombay*, 1st edn (New Delhi: Indian Society of Labour Economics / Commonwealth Publishers, 1998).

Fernandes, Leela, *Producing Workers: The Politics of Gender, Class, and Culture in the Calcutta Jute Mills* (Philadelphia, Pa.: University of Pennsylvania Press, 1997).

Gokhale, R.G., *The Bombay Cotton Mill Worker* (Bombay: Millowners' Association, 1957).

Hansen, Thomas Blom, *Wages of Violence: Naming and Identity in Postcolonial Bombay* (Princeton, N.J. and Oxford: Princeton University Press, 2001).

Holmstrom, Mark, *Industry and Inequality: The Social Anthropology of Indian Labour* (Cambridge: Cambridge University Press, 1984).

James, Ralph C., "Discrimination Against Women in Bombay Textiles", *Industrial and Labor Relations Review*, vol. 2, 1962.

Joshi, Heather, and Vijay Joshi, *Surplus Labour and the City: A Study of Bombay* (Delhi: Oxford University Press, 1976).

Joshi, Malati Madhav, "Socio-Economic Condition of Women Working in Cotton Textile Mills in Greater Bombay" (PhD Thesis, SNDT Women's University, Bombay, 1981).

Kadam, Manohar, *Narayan Meghaji Lokhande: Bharatiya Kamgar Chalvaliiche Janak*, 3rd edn (Bombay: Mahatma Jotirao Phule Samata Pratishthan and Akshar Prakashan, 2002).

Khairmode, C.B., *Dr Bhimrao Ramji Ambedkar Charitra, Khand Tisra* (Pune: Sugawa, 1990).

Mehta, S.D., *The Cotton Mills of India, 1854 to 1954* (Bombay: The Textile Association, India, 1954).

Mhaskar, Sumeet, "Ghettoisation of Economic Choices in a Global City: A Case Study of Mumbai", *Economic and Political Weekly*, vol. 53, no. 29, 2018.

Mhaskar, Sumeet, "Mumbai's Ex-millworkers' Household Survey Data: A Sample of 1037 Households" (Oxford: Department of Sociology, University of Oxford, 2009).

Morris, Morris David, *The Emergence of an Industrial Labor Force in India: A Study of the Bombay Cotton Mills, 1854–1947* (Berkeley: University of California Press, 1965).

Newman, Richard, *Workers and Unions in Bombay, 1918–1929: A Study of Organisation in the Cotton Mills* (Canberra: Australian National University, 1981).

O'Hanlon, Rosalind, *Caste, Conflict, and Ideology: Mahatma Jotirao Phule and Low Caste Protest in Nineteenth-century Western India* (1985; rpntd Ranikhet: Permanent Black, 2016).

Omvedt, Gail, *Building the Ambedkar Revolution: Sambhaji Tukaram Gaikwad and the Konkan Dalits* (Mumbai: Bhashya Prakashan, 2011).

Omvedt, Gail, *Cultural Revolt in a Colonial Society: The Non-Brahman Movement in Western India* (New Delhi: Manohar Publishers, 2011).

Padki, M.B., "Outmigration from a Konkan Village to Bombay", *Arth Vijnana*, vol. 6, no. 1, 1964.

Panini, M.N., "The Political Economy of Caste", in M.N. Srinivas, ed., *Caste – Its Twentieth Century Avatar* (New Delhi: Viking, 1996).

Papola, T.S., *Small Establishments in an Indian Metropolis: A Study on Employment and Labour Marketing in Bombay* (Ahmedabad: Indian Institute of Management Ahmedabad, 1976).

Patel, Kunj M., *Rural Labour in Industrial Bombay* (Bombay: Popular Prakashan and Bombay University, 1963).

Pol, Prabodhan, "From the Margins to Mainstream: Dalit Journalistic Writings in Maharashtra, 1920–56" (PhD Thesis, Jawaharlal Nehru University, New Delhi, 2015).

Pradhan, Gopinath Ramchandra, *Untouchable Workers of Bombay City* (Bombay: Karnatak Publishing House, 1938).

Purandare, B.M., "Untouchability in City Mills", *The Times of India*, 25 November 1973.

Rutnagur, S.M., ed., *Bombay Industries: The Cotton Mills. A Review of the Progress of the Textile Industry in Bombay from 1850 to 1926 and the Present Constitution, Management and Financial Position of the Spinning and Weaving Factories* (Bombay: Indian Textile Journal, 1927).

Savara, Mira, *Changing Trends in Women's Employment: A Case Study of the Textile Industry in Bombay* (Bombay: Himalaya Publishing House, 1986).

Shah, M.N., "Labour Recruitment and Turnover in the Textile Industry of Bombay" (PhD Thesis, University of Bombay, 1941).

Srinivas, M.N., "Social Anthropology and the Study of Rural and Urban Societies", *The Economic Weekly Annual*, vol. 11, nos 4–5–6, 1959.

Suradkar, Santosh, "Mukti Kon Pathe? Caste and Class in Ambedkar's Struggle", *Economic and Political Weekly*, vol. 52, no. 49, 2017.

Suradkar, Santosh, "The Anti-Khoti Movement in the Konkan, c. 1920–1949", *NLI Research Studies Series, V.V. Giri National Labour Institute*, no. 106, 2013.

TAILS (The Ambekar Institute for Labour Studies), "Education of Workers' Children: Report on an Enquiry into the Problems Experienced by Textile Workers in Bombay (Bombay: The Ambedkar Institute for Labour Studies, 1979).

TINTWF (The Indian National Textile Workers Federation), and TAILS (The Ambekar Institute for Labour Studies), "Urban Rural Transfers and Balance: A Sample Survey of Textile Workers in Greater Bombay" (Bombay: The Ambekar Institute for Labour Studies, 1983).

Van Wersch, Hub, *The 1982–83 Bombay Textile Strike and the Unmaking of a Labourers' City* (New Delhi: Speaking Tiger, 2019).

Zachariah, K.C., "Bombay Migration Study: A Pilot Analysis of Migration to an Asian Metropolis", *Demography*, vol. 3, no. 2, 1966.

Zelliot, Eleanor, *Ambedkar's World: The Making of Babasaheb and the Dalit Movement* (New Delhi: Navayana, 2013).

Acknowledgements

An earlier version of this essay was presented at the "History Research Group" meeting held in the Summer of 2022 at the Centre for Modern Indian Studies, University of Göttingen. I would like to thank the participants for their critical engagement. All errors are mine.

10

The Anti-Caste Hermeneutic

Iyothee Thassar and the Tamil Buddhist Past

DICKENS LEONARD

OREGROUNDING THE works of the anti-caste Tamil intellectual Pandithar Iyothee Thassar (1845–1914), this essay evaluates his writings on the history of India as a textuality against caste and Brahminism. Treating his work as a discussion on a community that remembers the Buddha, I seek to show that his narratives belong to a longer history of specific figurations of the Buddha. Within this corpus, it would be correct to view Thassar's reading as an anti-caste hermeneutic that is distinct. The figure of the Buddha, in Thassar's treatment of the past, appears relatively different from those that were perpetuated by the British discovery of, and/or the "desi" (nativist) response to, the caste question. Thass perhaps inaugurates and constitutes a millennial anti-caste reading as creative opposition in the historiography against caste. His Buddhism withdraws its religious relationship with caste and Brahminism; moreover, it differentiates itself from any provenance sanctified by caste-centred discourses – which it views as falsehood. His works sought to conceive and construct a community against caste in the vernaculars (Tamil as well as many others), in both global and local contexts, and by way of a highly scholarly as well as creative engagement with Buddhism and the Tamil literary archive. In the colonial and nationalist context of India in the nineteenth century, Thass' interpretive *imaginaire* of the history of India – entitled *Indhira Dhesa Sarithiram* – can be viewed

274

as a pedagogical activity that establishes a sense of belonging not only to the world community but also to one's own vernacular communities.

Anti-Caste Interpretations
of Temporality

Time in Tamil has three different meanings: (a) Samayam –religion (epochal); (b) Kaalam – period; and (c) Neram – moment. The imports of these are very meaningful, and one can argue that anti-caste thought in India uses interpretation as a tool to reconfigure notions of space and time as open, creative, and resistant. Together they inaugurate and constitute a millennial anti-caste Samayam, Kaalam, and Neram as creative opposition, as a history conceived against caste. This has relevance, because of its shape as resistance, for the rampant violence and humiliation that has been institutionalised to oppress body and mind in India.

The various studies on caste that exist can be designated as three different kinds of theorisation – constructionist, essentialist, and collaborationist. This taxonomy serves as a backdrop in the present study of heterogeneous and continuous Dalit efforts to create religion, history, and writing in the domain of early-twentieth-century knowledge production, i.e. writing and thought against caste by Dalits for an emancipatory practice.

One can argue that works that have contributed to the modern anti-caste tradition of thought in India have used interpretation as a tool to reconfigure the past through alternative notions of space and time – and thus of community – that are casteless and therefore open, creative, and resistant. In an ethical-ontological direction, intellectuals like Jotirao Phule and Iyothee Thass – to whose anti-caste thought and writing this essay is devoted – question the philosophical suppositions of a caste society through what, I propose, can be seen as a deconstructive understanding of community; and that they thereby open out an essential way to the possibility of a casteless community. They reconstitute community by questioning the logic of immunity in ways that invite us to consider any ethico-ontological community as being obliged to engage with the violence of caste in order to then construct anti-caste values. Their works open up the chance of a politics to emerge that caste has always already foreclosed.[1]

The Tamil intellectual Iyotheethassa Pandithar, or more commonly Pandit Iyothee Thass (1845–1914), strenuously opposed the caste order and developed anti-caste ideas through his interventions as a major political leader, intellectual, activist, and practitioner of Siddha medicine. He was born in the Parayar community, which has been among those most oppressed through the caste system and been treated as untouchable. He contested the category Parayar – anglicised as Pariah, and serving ever since as a metaphor of exclusion in general – and floated alternative, open identities such as Poorva Bouddhar (Ancient Buddhist), Jaadhipedhamatra Tamizhar/Dravidar (Casteless Tamils/Dravidians), and Tamil Bouddhar (Tamil Buddhist). At the time of the 1881 British-India census, Thass' appeal was that the Panchamas (ex-untouchables) were not Hindus, and so must be recorded in the census as original Tamils – Adi Tamizhar.[2] He played a formative role in the Tamil and anti-caste public sphere, running a magazine, *Tamizhan* (*T* 1907–14), which revived interest in Buddhism as an anti-caste religion.[3] In many ways a precursor to towering anti-caste figures like Periyar E.V. Ramasamy (1879–1973) and Babasaheb Dr B.R. Ambedkar (1891–1956), Thass was the first to develop an anti-caste discourse by espousing and writing on Buddhism. His works sought to conceive and construct a local-global community against caste by way of a highly scholarly as well as creative engagement in the vernacular with Buddhism. His life, work, and legacy have regrettably remained neglected by historians until recently.[4]

[1] This anti-caste hermeneutic of civilisation provides ethico-ontological insights that are comparable to the efforts made by later philosophers – such as Maurice Blanchot and especially Jean-Luc Nancy – to conceive community as based on the thought of Being as "compearance", i.e. life as "finite being presenting 'together,' and severally": Nancy, *The Inoperative Community*.

[2] Aloysius, *Iyothee Thassar and Tamil Buddhist Movement*, p. 69.

[3] Thass' quotations from the *Tamizhan* archives, including those cited in Gowthaman, *Ka. Iyotheethassarin Aaivugal*, and from Iyotheethaasa Pandithar's *Indhirar Dhesa Sarithiram* (2010), have been translated into English by me. The references from the *Tamizhan* archives are taken from Aloysius' three edited volumes, *Iyothee Thassar Cinthanaikal*, and are cited as *T*.

[4] Likewise, many such figures seem to have worked in ways similar to Thass

In the words of contemporary philosophical discussions on community, it can be said that Thass inaugurated a millennial anti-caste *communitas* as creative historiography against caste *immunitas*; particularly as a casteless community that withdraws from caste and Brahminism. Increasingly, recent works on Thass have thus reclaimed his incisive contributions as social emancipation against Brahminism;[5] as native thought, culture, and civilisation;[6] and as anticaste feminism and memory of castelessness.[7]

Gulamgiri (1873) and *Indhirar Dhesa* (1912)

Gulamgiri (Slavery) is a cult text in anti-caste history. Published in 1873 by Jotirao Phule, the well-known reformer, activist, and thinker from western India, it worked as a kind of manifesto that conceptualised the Indian form of slavery. It evaluated the British–Indian confrontation and collaboration as well as laid a sly, if not sarcastic, rationale of historical thinking, a new social outlook, and a very creative polemic against "Arya-Bhatt" exploitation and the Brahminic myth. The Aryan migration theory is turned inside out in the earlier parts of the text where Phule, in a conversation between Jotiba and Dhondiba, reminds his readers of "Bali-Rajya" and "truth seekers"; the latter part works as a critique of elite-led nationalism and Brahminical interpretations of history while foregrounding an alternative ethical universal religion (Sarvajanik Satyadharma). It is at once a remembrance and a reconstruction of "a modern form" of community and belonging.[8]

---

during the same period in the vernacular regions. Narayana Guru (1856–1928) from Kerala, Bhima Bhoi (1850–1895) in Orissa, Poikkayil Yohannan (1878–1939) in Kerala, and a little earlier Jotirao Phule (1827–1890) in Maharashtra created a hermeneutic of anti-caste communitas in their writings.

[5] Aloysius, *Iyothee Thassa and Tamil Buddhist Movement*.

[6] Dharmaraj, *Iyothee Thassar*.

[7] Ayyathurai, "Living Buddhism"; idem, "Colonialism, Caste, and Gender".

[8] Phule's *Gulamgiri* (Slavery, 1873) reinterprets Hindu mythological tales via deconstruction and prepares the ground for building a historical counter-narrative of India. For a systematic study of Phule's movement, see O'Hanlon, *Caste, Conflict and Ideology*.

Indhirar Dhesa Sarithiram (History of the Indhirar Country; henceforth *Sarithiram*), which was published fifty years after Phule's *Gulamgiri*, is Thass' attempt to reconstruct a Buddhist history of India in sixty-
five parts. It was serialised in the journal *Tamizhan* from August 1910 to
November 1911 and published as a book in 1912, with a second edition in 1957 and a republication in 1999 by the Dalit Sahitya Academy.
The word *sarithiram* means history. Thass' text is a reconstructive social history which counters, politically and culturally, the established
"story of caste". It builds on oral folk narratives that emphasise not only
an enmity in practice against Brahminical discourses, but also claims spatial and temporal precedence against all things Brahminical and Hindu.
Thass presents a narrative of the Indian subcontinent as originally a Buddhist country. He begins the text with a question: Wasn't there a saying,
"Paarapaanukku moopan paraiyan kaelpaarillamar keelsaathi aanan"
(The Parayar is elder than the Brahmin, as no one listened to him he became low caste).[9] The Parayar (the "untouchable" outcaste) is generally
degraded and exteriorised in relation to the ritually superior Brahmin
(the "top-of-the-twice-born" caste). However, Thass interrogates another
story here: Why is there folklore about the Parayar preceding the Brah-
min/Aryan? The question pushes him to consider the history of a civilisational opposition and enmity between the original Buddhists – who he
believes were later degraded as Parayars – and deceptive Brahmins. The
first part of the *Sarithiram* functions as a political template of Buddhist
historical materialism which prefigures Thass' examination, in later
parts of the series, of several matters: the arrival of the Aryans, the emergence of their Saivism and Vaishnavism, the destruction of Buddhist
kings such as Nandan and Iranyan, the radical opposition of lay Buddhists to pseudo-Brahmins, the ascendancy of the caste manual *Manu
Dharma Smriti* and the way it dehumanised Indian society.

Thass treats history as a researching of the past through an ethico-
ontological pedagogy. His Preface states that his intent in publishing
Sarithiram was "to explain and to remove problems" (*vilakudhal . . . allala-
ineekudhal*) of stories taught as history. In his reading, the stories established as history are relevant only in order for him to reconstruct a

[9] *T*, vol. 1, p. 26.

counter-story. He urges historical research and the rejection of everything else (*sarithira aaraichi ininri sagalavatraiyum usaava vendugiren*).[10] The Tamil word *vilakudhal* stands for both interpretation and explanation. It is instructive to read this practice of research in the light of Ricoeur's hermeneutic phenomenology, where understanding and explanation are treated as an ontological aspect of interpretation. This method seeks to "bring into language an experience, a way of living in and of being-in-the-world."[11] Through his seminal works, Ricoeur argues that the attempt to structure time using language, in history as well as in fiction, fulfils a narrative function that ultimately leads back to the question of self. The interrelation of understanding and explanation is, thus, described as an ability to reconstruct the internal dynamic of the text, and to restore its ability to project itself outside in the representation of a world that one could inhabit. Hence interpretation, for Ricoeur, is a dialectic of understanding and explanation at the level of sense immanent in the text. Discourse never exists for its own sake and for its own glory; it seeks, in all its uses, to bring into language an experience, "a way of living in and of being-in-the-world" which precedes it and which demands to be said.[12]

Thus, Thass treats history (*sarithiram*) as pedagogy to lay claim over civilisational memory against Brahminism and casteism in the early twentieth century. He creates a hermeneutic of castelessness to explore the reserves of Tamil language and literature by using them for his specific counter-interpretation. Caste experience is described as the civilisational violence that came with the Aryans from a world outside. Although *mlechha* – a Sanskrit term and part of the Brahminical discourse – refers to barbarian outsiders and others who are distinguished from the Aryas (Vedic religionists), Thass creatively inverts the term: he coins the term Arya Mlechha as a derogatory name for the Aryan invaders who brought in caste. This is done to indicate the uncouth and incomprehensible

---

[10] *Sarithirangalai aaraichi seiyavendumae andri karpanaa kadhaigalai alla . . . sarithira aaraichi ininri sagalavatraiyum usaava vendugiren* (Research just history, not fantasy stories . . . and research nothing but history). See *T*, vol. I, p. 573.

[11] Ricoeur, "On Interpretation", p. 154.

[12] Ibid.

speech of foreigners as well as their unfamiliar and deceptive casteist behaviour as Vesha Brahmanas. Thass floats a narrative of ancient Indians
(Indhira Desathor) as originally comprising several casteless communities. He thus inaugurates a creative hermeneutic of thought against
caste which claims a civilisational memory through Poorva (early) Buddhism from within the Tamil language.

It is imperative to understand Thass as someone who de-institutes
prevailing history and, against settled ideas, constructs a genealogy of
loss due to civilisational violence, thereby constituting a new *Sarithiram*
in Tamil. This also reflects Bergunder's argument that "Dalit anti-Brahminical groups reinterpreted the Aryan-migration theories" by bringing
up their own resources against Brahminical hegemony during the colonial period.[13] By this argument subaltern resistance is possible through
anti-Brahminical reinterpretations of the Aryan migration theory,
especially by the active inversion of dominant discourses. Bergunder
states that these resistances have been socially relevant. Hence, though
the Orientalist theories of the nineteenth century feed into identity-
shaping discourses about Indian pre-history, the intent of subaltern reinterpretations was not the same as that of the Orientalists and the Hindu revivalists. They did not just contest pasts, they invariably produced
anti-caste social imaginaries as civilisational memory. In other words,
the anti-caste intellectuals who took to Buddhism subtracted caste subjectivity to understand the self as a "chain of alterations". Thus, scholars
such as Figueira evaluate the textual links that bind Enlightenment and
Orientalist discourses with the formation of collusive authority and national self-esteem in the construction of the Aryan myth as an aspect of
civilisational identity.[14] On the other hand Omvedt discusses and com-
pares the "social vision" of anti-caste intellectuals in nineteenth- and
twentieth-century India as the genealogy of a longer and deeper resistance against caste for a sense of utopian belonging.[15] In the works of
these scholars caste is not understood as a thing in itself; it is a no-thing,
a violent relationship. Hence, they insist on a transformation of this relationship into a "sense of being" towards the world.

[13] Bergunder, "Contested Past".
[14] Figueira, *Aryans, Jews, Brahmins*.
[15] Omvedt, *Seeking Begumpura*.

Four such themes seem to preoccupy such practice. First, they delimit the practice of history; second, naming is argued as a casteless act; third, caste is identified as deception; and fourth, discourses upholding caste involve a clear abduction of language. It does not stop with these four elements, but a civilisational memory and hermeneutic of castelessness is "exscribed" against an ongoing conscription and inscription of caste in the history of India.

A Comparative Textualising of History

In reconstructing the history of Buddhism through Tamil print, Thass works with concepts and myths in his language to liberate meaning from a limited history – his historical research is conducted through a dispersal of meaning in Tamil. For instance, independent India was additionally given the Sanskritic name "Bharat" at the insistence of Hindu nationalists, but he gives a different explanation for why India is called *barathagandam* – the continent of Bharat. He states that *Indhiram ennum mozhi aindhiram enum mozhiyin thiribaam*, i.e. India, the word, is a derivation of the word *aindhiram*, denoting the five senses while also a name for the Buddha.[16] The Buddha – in Tamil "Aindhirar" – was also called Varadhar, which is a derivative of the word *barathar*, since he preached *ara-"varam"*, or a gift-giving of the ethical treatise, to his followers.[17] The land was called North and South Bharat, where Varadhar's ethical treatise was preached across lands that spoke at least twenty languages – including Chinese, Sinhala, Konkani, Tulu – alongside Sanskrit, Pali, and Dravida (Tamil). This interpretation treats the Indian nation as the geography of an action principle via which the ways preached by the Buddha are practised.

[16] Pandithar, *Indhirar Dhesa Sarithiram*, p. 5.

[17] In Tamil *aram* means ethics and *varam* means gift or boon. In Hindu mythology, boons are generally received from God for persistent penance by mortal individuals. However, Thass' interpretive implication here is that a pedagogy of ethics is remembered as a gift to the world through a Buddhist hagiography of India, where the land is memorialised by the gift-giver of ethics; the Varadhar as the Bharathar as the Aindhirar as the Indhirar (the Buddha) through a creative referential etymology.

There are two aspects to this historical reconstruction. The first is to resist the general reading of a given story; and the second is to constitute an alternative cosmology. Names and etymologies were especially used to redefine the geography of a practice, and to counter the fundamental meaning that was attached to locate caste as the space of India. Phule too works this out in a very flexible and sarcastic way in his narrative on the memory of "Bali Rajya", which presents an interesting unravelling of the time of natives. This period is represented as a flurry of conquests: of Brahma over Aryaloka, Matsya over Shankasur, Keetcha and Varaha over Hiranyakashipu, Narasimha over Prahlada, and Vamana over Baliraja – this being the longest discourse in the dialogue.

This subverted story of India is an act of delimitation as well as limitation. Thass rejects the claim that India is caste-Hindu in its content. His exercise is neither an anthropological nor a sociological enquiry; it is a highly charged textual communication. By reconstructing Buddhism he constitutes a new textual imaginary in his nineteenth-century milieu and for the succeeding generations which saw the emergence of a major anti-Brahminical movement in Tamil Nadu. Thass' practice of history also thus subverts the idea of institutional history – or rather, it deinstitutes the definition of space and time as a quantifiable reference to construct a nation. He constitutes his Indhirar Dhesam (India) by situating thought-practice as history. The limitation consists in the way he sets up his alternative "history research" in Tamil by accessing a variety of resources in at least four different languages – Tamil, Sanskrit, Pali, and English. He develops a referential and descriptive prose register which shares space with poetry, compendiums, and epic narratives that are then transcribed into journalistic print space. Through this en-textualisation he creates a space for a knowledge-practice that is published and disseminated as Tamil prose within a limited linguistic boundary. By this limitation Thass creates an alternative history through reading and referencing sources that contend with authorised versions of history and historical practice, especially those with a Sanskrit and Aryan orientation. His counter-narrative thereby competes with the other powerful contemporary hermeneutics of caste – of the colonial census and the upper-caste discursive and political manoeuvres that it generated, and of missionaries such as the Christian, Vaishnavaite, and Vellala Saivaite variety.

Thass' methodology, then, is also an attempt to democratise power and practise it in his own way in order to claim an alterity. Projecting as default the Buddhist location of his resources, he argues that castelessness is Buddhist and hence pre-dates and resists Brahminism. However, this should not be mistaken for an attempt to recreate history through a linguistic (Tamil), or cultural (Vedic), or temporal (ancient) basis for defining India. Rather, it is a definition of India as a domain which was and should again become anti-caste. His sources delimit the spatial definition of the idea of nation while going beyond it to reconstruct it as a community identified by anti-caste practice. They reveal to Thass the idea of India as *against* something, and describe it – pre-empting Ambedkar and others – as a historical conflict against Brahminism. Hence this delimiting as well as limiting practice of history is a novel attempt to describe who Indians are: for them, interestingly, it is all those who are outside and against caste-time.

Naming Casteless Spaces in Time

In contrast to thinking of a casteless time, as in Phule, Thass explores castelessness as an action-oriented principle where ethics conceives and orients truth. He thereby creates a textuality of castelessness in *Sarithiram*. For instance, he calls the embodied being *than-mei*, i.e. self-truth. According to the Buddhist ethos, the person who realise a true sense of his being attains enlightenment. This is the assertion of an anti-caste position which is based on the possibility of individual and personal enrichment, an expansion of knowledge-seeking and giving, and the adoption of a civilisational view of life. This way of life also, in the past, produced epistemic texts in law, philosophy, numbers, medicine, literature, grammar and art. These textual embodiments were produced and practised in spaces known as viharas. Thass states that knowledge produced in these spaces, primarily as self-truth, is shared as a gift and a debt through kindness and compassion to the Other.[18] Action, Knowledge, Being, and Truth were linked in such a view of life.

[18] Pandithar, *Indhirar Dhesa Sarithiram*, p. 35.

Unlike Brahminism's mischievous dichotomisation of the spiritual-inner-pure and the material-outer-impure, Thass conceives a steady flow and continuity of the inner and outer, of the particular and the universal, of the singular-as-plural. Caste is in this way negated as a sacral inner space of secrecy in Indian civilisation. The assertion that everything had to be shared as a gift and an obligation is the alterity that makes for the recovery of a true civilisational ideal along which a community may forge ethical practice. According to Thass, the way of the Buddha was in practice largely an experience-based episteme. Some upper-caste individuals – including Gandhi, Vivekananda, and other proponents of "Hindu" religion – claimed caste as a civilisation sanctioned through divine sanitation and the immunisation of elites; conversely, Thass reclaims a pre-caste lifeworld as an ethical civilisation which counters the self-centred life that stigmatises and exploits others.

Thass considers the land itself as fundamentally divided into five spaces (*ainthinaigal*), or eco-zones. These are: sea (*neidhal*); plains (*marudham*); forests (*mullai*); mountains (*kurinji*); and desert (*palai*). Contradicting caste-based discourses and practices asserting various human occupations as inherited and enforced, Thass reinterprets work-related identities as spatially connected to each eco-zone. He thereby argues that knowledge (*putthi*, an equivalent of *techné*) is experientially produced through work related to each zone. For instance, he suggests that the name Shudras derives from the term *soosthiram* – meaning technical know-how. The Shudras, he claims, possess knowledge of water-sharing and working on the land. This work-related knowledge contributes to linking the five landscapes, and identity is the product of people's ability to link eco-zones with each other. The Shudras were therefore people who worked the soil and served people with water and food and linked those eco-zones. Because eco-zones sustained a specific economy, work-names, such as those in the varna stratification, were originally identified within eco-zones across languages – in Pali, Sanskrit, and Tamil. The Indhirar Dhesam of Thass' interpretation was a Buddhist casteless space comprising these five eco-zones that cut across multilingual zones.[19]

[19] Ibid., p. 9.

Thass states that "naming" becomes a crucial act in these spaces as they reflect an appropriateness and relationship to their eco-zone, work, action, character, and life. Naming is shown as having been a casteless act, and names carried validity. They were not dispensed as a sign or symbol of humiliation. Different people achieved their different names by creating their identity through their action. For instance, he suggests that the terms for farmer – *usavar, uzhavazhar*, and *vellalar* – were given as work identities to people, denoting the work they did rather than the identity they were born with.[20]

The notions of love and kindness are upheld in Thass' understanding of space and action, while conciliation (*sama*), gift (*dhaana*), rupture (*bedha*), and force (*thandam*) seem to have been the governing factors in Indhirar space.[21] An eclectic and Buddhist unitary space seems to emerge by linking the Buddha to the rulers of the country, namely Vimbasarsan, Udhaiyanan, Kalakoodan, Asokan, Chandraguptan, Nandan, and so on. But Thass also argues that personages such as Asoka and Nandan create a dialectical notion of space as *dhesam* in which people are encouraged to live an ethical life.[22] Ethics, Thass confirms, orients communication and relationships in Indhirar Dhesam.

Sathi, the Tamil word for caste, is itself reinterpreted by Thass as an ethical orientation towards life as action and achievement. The term is seen to be derived from the word *sadhithal*, to achieve. Thass argues that *sathi* can only mean the achievement of a language. One can equip, access, and use a language such as Tamil, Telugu, Kannada, Marathi, Sanskrit, or Pali, and that would be one's *sathi* – one's own achievement. *Sathi*, in an action-achievement mode of life, would mean that a person is a Tamil *sathi*, a Kannada *sathi*, or a Marathi *sathi*.[23] The terms for hierarchical stratification in the varna theory – such as Brahmin, Kshatriya, Vaishya, and Shudra – are each reinterpreted as sharing within Buddhism the same meaning across three different languages – Pali, Sanskrit, and Tamil. Thus, Arahat, Brahmin, and Andhanar are used for enlightened teachers; Arayan, Kshatriya, and Arasan for rulers; Vyapari,

---

[20] Ibid., p. 13.

[21] Ibid.

[22] Ibid., pp. 13–14.

[23] Ibid., p. 37.

Vaishya, and Vaaniyan for business people; and Soosthirar, Shudra, and Soothirar for farmers. In each case the three terms are nominally equivalent in Pali, Sanskrit, and Tamil respectively; they are work-related names based on personal achievements. In Thass' argument the *mlech-has* misinterpreted such terms into meaninglessness and deployed them as self-protection for a ritualised sanctioning of divinity, via *varna shrama dharma*, against those they subjugated.[24]

The meaning of the name Asoka, the Buddhist king of the Maurya Empire, is explored by Thass to link it to the basic principle of the ethical religion promoted in *Sarithiram*. Asoka is treated as the primal figure who spread the Dhamma (ethic) through peace, non-violence, and in written form across the subcontinent. Asoka, the name, is reinterpreted as A-Soka, i.e. one who negates suffering to spread peace and joy across space.[25] The topography of the country is recreated within a narrative of Buddhist belonging and civilisational remembrance. Similarly, Thass treats all the Tamil (Dravidian) kings in succession – from Pandyas, Cholas, and Cheras – as Buddhists who built viharas and cities such as Maduraipuram (Madurai), Kanchipuram, Thirisirapuram (Trichy), Mavalipuram (Mahabalipuram), and Chidambarapuram (Chidambaram). *Puram* (space) is identified as a domain of knowledge production and dissemination, not of ritual authority. It is identified by its contribution to Dravidian civilisation, such as via language and its scholarship in literature, grammar, mathematics, and medicine.[26] Thass thus takes recourse to the idea of a Tamil ancestry in assertively reclaiming a casteless location which produced a region-specific anti-caste civilisation in the vernacular. He claims language itself as a critically open space for a casteless past.

Caste and Deception

In Thass, the meaning of *mlechhas* becomes Vesha Brahmanas or Aryans, thus inverting the Brahminical usage of *mlechha* for foreigners and untouchables. He interprets the entry of the Aryans as that of an

[24] Ibid., pp. 40–1.
[25] Ibid., p. 14.
[26] Ibid., p. 15.

enclosed and dehumanising way of life into Indhirar space. He asserts this claim by reference to the Indo-Aryan migration theory, much like other anti-caste intellectuals such as Phule. Thass believes that those who call themselves Brahmins were immigrants into the subcontinent from Persia. They possessed a fairer skin tone, a different culture and dietary customs, and worshipped fire with sacrifices. He also particularises them as a group which secluded menstruating women for seven days. He deploys figures such as Nandan the king and Ashvaghosha the Buddhist monk within his narrative to argue that deception was the Aryan method of acquiring an unethical status – a *vesha*, that which is unreal – in a country where indigenous casteless groups lived a life of truth. He suggests that *vesha*, which was scrupulously imitated, stole the Buddhist way of life, ultimately destroying and violating the basic principles of life in Indhirar Dhesam.[27] He also termed Vesha Brahmanas *akkaraiyorothor*, i.e. people from the other side, who practised deception and made people deceitful.

On the face of it, it might seem that Thass uncritically borrows from Orientalist research that had proposed an Aryan in-migration theory, but he himself claims to take his instances from Tamil sources such as *Mungulai Nool* by Sendhanrivagara Devar and *Pingalai Nool* by Mandala Purudan.[28] Thass is also distinguishable from others insofar as he takes references from *Soolamani* and *Naradhiya Sangath Thelivu* to imply that Brahminism is constitutively deceptive and that the caste-Hindu way of life is one which is alienating – it makes people foreigners to their own self.[29] Instead of creating spaces that were open and active, the space constituted by caste located people in order to lock them into a socially immovable fixity. He condemns this *mlechha* way of life as deceptive, self-centred, fake, and truthless.

He sees an Aryan as a person who sacrifices another's life to the fire in order to protect himself. His life is neither constituted by equality

[27] Ibid., pp. 25–7.

[28] Ibid., pp. 21–2.

[29] Thass' research and thoughts were largely based on literature, history, and ethics in the Tamil language. Texts, such as these in the Tamil language, were used as an embodiment of thought and practice against caste. Thass interprets this Tamil archive (largely manuscripts) as intellectual tools for an anti-caste religion.

of action nor by an ethical life shaped as gift-giving and obligatory debt to the Other. Mostly what mattered within caste were material things and property. For Thass, by contrast, ethical actions mattered more than material goods; hence, communication becomes the origin of community sociality. A constant exposure to the self outside, and a constant sharing with others marks the Poorva Buddhist claim for civilisation against *mlechha* Brahminism. This casteless political state of Poorva Buddhism signifies a civilisational community predisposed to sharing and conscious of its constitutive, communicative experience. Caste is considered anti-Buddhist and therefore anti-civilisational since it is the most anti-social, anti-communicative, and anti-communal of relationships.

Thass twists the meanings of Vedas, which according to him, were meaninglessly ritualised by Brahminism. By re-terming *vedham* as *bedham*, he makes his anti-Brahminism clear. The *tiribedhavaakiyam* (the three Vedas), he claims, were originally Buddhist ethical texts. They were understood as utterance-based knowledge books within Buddhism. These were meaninglessly copied by the Vesha Brahmanas and called *vedhavaakiyam* for material gain. Copying texts while distorting their relevance and context were unethical acts done to make money. He sees them as the signatures of *mlechha* worship in scholarship.[30]

The Tamil terms *paapan* and *paapathi* (Brahmins), denoting those whom Thass had redesignated Vesha Brahmanas, are explained as names originally referring to those who "look after" or "follow" the Dhamma, i.e. Poorva Buddhists. These terms, he says, had been used deceitfully by the *mlechha*s in order to hollow out their actual meaning and practice, leaving only the outer form but not the inner content of the life they were intended to denote. Earlier, only those who stayed in the sangha and practised the Dhamma towards enlightenment were called *paapan* (*paar* is "to See"; therefore "Seer"). A sense of loss and a cry towards a civilisational memory seem to structure Thass' narrative since *paapar* and *paapini* are defined by this story of stealth – of *mlechha* life entwined in self-aggrandisement instead of anything virtuous. In this story the Buddha is created afresh as an exemplar of Indhirar Dhesam against the *arya mlechha*.

[30] Ibid., p. 136.

In this war over names, Thass claims that even the term Brahmin belongs to Poorva Buddhism. He explains that this Sanskrit word shares its meaning with the Tamil "Andhanar" and the Pali "Arahat". These were Buddha-like figures who had no connection with oppression and bondage, and only those who could love everyone and everything without discrimination could be called by these words. However, according to Thass Andhanars were one in a million. They lived a life of kindness, peace, empathy, and detachment, following the Buddha as ideal, whereas Vesha Brahmanas practised deceit and self-aggrandisement as a way of life; and when they imitated the Buddhist way of life, they did so only to destroy and violate it.[31]

In Thass' account Buddhist practices such as the distribution of *aval prasadham* (milk-mixed rice-flakes) within the viharas, as well as Upanayana (the thread worn around the body), Viradham (fasting), and eighteen kinds of *yagas* (offerings) were fundamentally practices that represented insistence on ethical action and right conduct.[32] The *mlechha*s, he claims, took over these practices and ruined them: self-interest and self-protection instead of love and compassion, the promotion of wealth and consumption instead of charity and help, greed and the accumulation of power instead of wisdom and insight – these were made the basis of daily life and practice. A life of pleasure was created within gargantuan structures to destroy what was *poorva*. The honest practice of communitas was converted into an institution of deceptive immunitas.

Caste and Abduction

For Thass, words are neither meaningless nor empty ritual utterances.[33] They are meant for communication – they are the very basis of a community. Therefore it is necessary in his way of thinking for a complete discourse on civilisational violence to be mapped wherein a memory preceding caste is posited as an originary sociality. He describes the Brahminical masking (*vesham*) of truth as a violence against the land itself: *kaarunyamatrapusippu, perasaimikkaviruppu* (an action-oriented

---

[31] Ibid., pp. 24–5.
[32] Ibid., pp. 28–33.
[33] Ibid., p. 56.

thought and life of the country was violated and converted into a com-
passion-less consumption and self-desire-driven caste society).[34] Thass
says that *mlechha*s who took on the role of Brahmins branded those
who protested and opposed this life of caste – the Poorva Buddhists –
as untouchables and Parayars.[35] A life of elite laziness built on their
exploitation of others was promoted through the framework of caste.[36]
Molestation, over-consumption, and promiscuity were spread through
Vesha Brahminism.[37]

He suggests that many names, words, concepts, icons, and symbols that were genuinely Buddhist in content and form were "abduct-
ed" and violated through all this deception. For example, whereas the
Buddha was *sangha harar* – leading to *sankarar, sangha dharmar*, and
sangha mitrar, these being names given to the Buddha for instituting the
idea of a commune through his sangha – the Vesha Brahmans adapted
it to throw the populace into servitude.[38] Even the concept of Shiva, he
claims, was created from the Buddha – the physical attributes of the
Buddha were used for a mythic figure of Shiva, and Vesha Brahmanism
thrived by creating a new cult around *vibuthi* (ashes).[39] Yoga too was
used for Saivism, he claims. And where earlier there were no offerings of
food or money, or prayers for salvation, or rituals as such, this new sect
by the Vesha Brahmans created wealth and power in the name of Saivism. Where the Poorva Buddhists claimed salvation through effort with
an immediate Other, Vesha Brahmans countered it through offerings
and sacrifice to a transcendental Other.[40] Hence Brahminism is seen
as an otherworldly falsehood characterised by its incorporation of fire
worship, ritual offerings to fire, and Siva Aalayangal (Shiva temples).

Similarly, for Thass the god Krishnan is *kiruteenan*, a Buddhist
king. He states that *kiruteenan* as a figure is known in the *mullai* (forest) region as *manivannan* and *karudavaaganan* – Buddhist names.

---

[34] Ibid., p. 53.
[35] Ibid., p. 43.
[36] Ibid., p. 44.
[37] Ibid., p. 45.
[38] Ibid., p. 48.
[39] Ibid., pp. 48–9.
[40] Ibid., p. 50.

This figure was systematically abused by the *mlechha*s through their historically unverifiable *krishnaleela* story to make money and deceive the masses.[41]

Every name becomes an opportunity in Thass for an interpretive reclamation of a Buddhist ethics within a hermeneutic wherein the figures are shown as subsequently Brahminised and Hinduised, which is to say made unethical. In Thass' counter-narrative they were in fact de-Buddhised, and his attempt is to re-Buddhise by deploying Tamil sources.

Mythic figures such as Sambhavar and Nandanar, who were treated as untouchables within Hinduism, appear as Buddhist intellectuals within *Sarithiram*. They question the falsehood and deceptions of the so-called Brahmanas. Even as they exposed the trickeries of fraudsters, Brahminism branded them as untouchables and finished them treasonously.[42] The *mlechha*s invented new names to demean and defame their opponents. Words such as *para-naai* and *para-parundhu* (Paraya dog and Paraya owl) were appropriated and made abuses.[43]

Other than Nandan, Ashvaghosha the Buddhist monk too is a character within Thass' narrative. He exposes the *mlechha* life of falsehood, accusing *arya mlechha*s as *agnanigal* (anti-thinkers/intellectuals).[44] Thass' Ashvaghosha rejects the *mlechha* worship of fire and animal sacrifice.

The Vesha Brahmanas forced caste into the achieved languages (*sathi*) of the region. Poorva Buddhists became untouchable because they lost their value for names and *sathi* became frozen and ossified as *jathi* (caste), paving the way for a discourse on high and low castes. Thus, Nyaya Alakar (just measurer) became a caste name, Nayakar. Those who doubled (*iratippul irettiyar*) their income and did good business became a caste called Reddiyar (Reddy). Other working class names such as *chettuvaipavar* (one who keeps bunds) became the caste name Chettiyar. The Vesha Brahmanas named themselves *achari*, *appa*, and

---

[41] Ibid., pp. 123–7.
[42] Ibid., p. 58.
[43] Ibid., p. 59.
[44] Ibid., pp. 67–8.

rao, as in Gunda Achari/Appa/Rao, Beema Achari/Appa/Rao, and Thima Achari/Appa/Rao.[45] And *sann-aalar* – those who did all the six tasks of a Buddhist properly – became *sandalar* (*chandala*, outcastes). Kodun Thamizh, or Malayalam-speaking Nyayar (just people) were called Thiyar (dangerous people) by the Vesha Brahmanas; Thass claims that those rebuked as Thiyar were originally Buddhist scholars who had spoken against the Vesha Nayars that had taken up Brahminism.

Civilisational Memory and the Buddhist Hermeneutic

In the last part of the *Sarithiram* Thass presents various Hindu myths and stories to counter-interpret them and create a dialectical herme-neutic. His interpretation deploys an egalitarian vocabulary and pitches it against the Brahminism that claims superiority, despising others as lowly, deceiving them, and depriving them of the basic values of life: here his effort resembles Phule's.[46] Thass says that through the deifica-tion of statues, seeds, and dung ash, Buddhism was completely de-stroyed – but not before redeploying itself as Saivaite in the South and Vaishnavite in the North of Indhirar Dhesam.[47] Vinayaga as the elephant-faced god is an example of a story in *Sarithiram* challenging deification and exposing it as a way of money-making and hyper-con-sumption. Thass argues that gods were created in order for Vesha Brah-mans to run religious shops. It was none other than the Buddha who was called the *nayagar* (the leader or the chief), and he redeploys the word *vinayagar* as *sabha-nayagar* and *gana-nayagar*, meaning the leader of the community (*sangha/sabha*), a term which has come to mean *vi-nayagar*. The elephant-faced god was a spin-off.[48]

Similarly, he examines the stories of other deities such as Meenakshi Amman, Hiranyakashipu, Vinayaka, Garuda, Krishnan, and Vishnu, all of which he counter-reads to connect them to the figure or trope of the Buddha. Meenakshi Amman (whose temple at Madurai is inter-nationally famous) is re-narrated as a rich woman whom the *mlechha*s

[45] Ibid. p. 97.
[46] Ibid., p. 114.
[47] Ibid., pp. 101–12.
[48] Ibid., pp. 122–3.

deceived, grabbing her wealth to build a temple in her name but only to feed themselves.[49] The king Nandan is in *Sarithiram* immolated, being deceived by the *mlechhas*. This figure, prominent as an untouchable saint within Saivism, is completely reconfigured by Thass in the voice of Ashvaghosha.[50] In this retelling, Nandan's empire and his palace were taken over by the *mlechhas* in Tanjore. This story is narrated as one of defeat over the *samanamunivargal* (Samanas or Sramanas, forest ascetics who were against Brahmanas) in Tanjore, where Saivaites killed Buddhists and Jains by deceitful means and converted those defeated into untouchables.[51] Thass' counter-narrative historicises defeat as deceit.

Vishnu's statues were often originally Buddha's statues – in fact, recent archaeological findings have reconfirmed this fact.[52] Many such statues, Thass claims, were used to create a pantheon of gods for the Hindus.[53] History was not created; rather, false stories were spread among the illiterate indigenous masses by Arya Vesha Brahmanas. This affected the truth-seekers, the Poorva Buddhists, for they were branded untouchables and the meanings of their names – Chandala, Thiya, and Paraya – were violated for eternity, more or less.[54] This resulted in the closing down of *arappalligal* (ethical schools), which came to promote laziness and ignorance.[55] In *Sarithiram* the practice of caste is heinous because it entails not just violence but also inaction and thoughtlessness.

In his Hiranyakashipu and Prahlada retellings, Hiranya is a Buddhist king who questioned the Vesha Brahmanas; he was murdered by a Brahmin wearing a lion mask (*singhavesham*) and not by a *narasimham* (man-lion). Thass' hermeneutic also poses a fundamental question to Brahminism: how is it possible for a god concept to murder? "Does a God kill people, and if it has to use deception, is it God at all?"[56]

---

[49] Ibid., p. 27.
[50] Ibid., pp. 88–9.
[51] Ibid., pp. 90–2.
[52] Monius, *Imagining a Place*; Sekhar, "A Broken Padmasana".
[53] Pandithar, *Indhirar Dhesa Sarithiram*, p. 127.
[54] Ibid., p. 128.
[55] Ibid., p. 129.
[56] Ibid., p. 109.

Tamil Buddhism Against
Anti-Knowledge

Thass' largest endeavour was the attempt to claim the reserves of language and ethics through the possibilities offered by the public sphere – i.e. through the production of knowledge, books, journals, and interpretations in print which would disseminate a casteless Buddhist legacy and counter what he called anti-knowledge. In this view, no texts which foregrounded communication and community were written by the *mlechha*s – they had obstructed the sharing of language and knowledge by emphasising Sanskrit as a "pure" and sacred language and proscribing it for the other castes. Vesha Brahmana texts had in essence celebrated fire worship whereas Poorva Buddhist texts had emulated the sangha stories.[57] I would argue, following Thass, that the former forcibly immunised the word through fire whereas the latter communised the word through sangha (community). Accordingly, in this dialectical hermeneutic, self-protection and self-centredness marked the Brahminical immunitas, whereas gift and debt as action-based ethics marked the Buddhist communitas.

For both Phule and Thass, the *Manusmriti* and the *Manu Dharma Shastra* of the Vesha Brahmanas was anti-knowledge. For both, these texts were opposed to a long list of knowledge seekers, teachers, and writers of Buddhism. They were unjust and unethical texts – *aneedhinool* and *adhanmanool*.[58] Though he saw the *Manu Dharma Shastra* as a "thoughtless" text,[59] its caste prescriptions were potent as a weapon. As against this weaponry, Thass lists many Siddhars – practitioners of the Siddha tradition upheld by Thass as enlightened teachers and therefore Buddhists – who had written against Vesha Brahmanism through an

---

[57] Ibid., p. 135.

[58] Ibid., pp. 138–41.

[59] *Manusmriti*, or the *Laws of Manu* (also called the *Manu Dharma Shastra*), is considered one of the supplementary arms of traditional Vedic life amongst Hindus, sanctioning sacrality to caste. It is one of the standard books in the Hindu canon and considered part of "revealed scripture". It comprises 2684 verses divided into twelve chapters which present the norms of domestic, social, and religious life in India under Brahmin influence. This work has had a long-lasting ideological as well as existential influence in the practice of caste which continues into present times.

alternative textual legacy. These were Pambaati Siddhar, Siva Vaakiyar, Patinathar, Thayumanavar, Sambavanar, Kaduvelli Siddhar, Agape Siddhar, Idaikattu Siddhar, and Kuthambai Siddhar.[60] These Buddhists, he says, lived as a casteless community in a space called *cheri* – where everyone stayed together. This is the very opposite of the contemporary meaning of the word denoting an outcaste ghetto or slum. *Cheri* was, as figured by Thass, a space of castelessness, where Vesha Brahmanas were rejected for false caste rituals, false Vedic sacrifices, false epics, *smriti*s, *sivalingam*s, and false religious shops.

Thass does not limit the experience of caste as civilisational violence to the practice of untouchability. Rather, he claims that a narrative of some people as "backward" or "depressed classes" was much promoted during colonial times and was equally devoid of civilisational claims.[61] These were not backward or depressed people, for they were the Poorva Buddhists who had been destroyed or lowered in status. They were not allowed in the *oor* (village, homeland). They had no access to potable water, no clean clothes, they had been rendered unapproachable and untouchable, which was the equivalent of social and cultural annihilation.[62] At the zenith of this civilisational violence, Poorva Buddhists remained untouchable, uncrossable, unseeable, unhearable, unapproachable, and outside the domain of all communication. They had been pushed outside time and space.

Conclusion

Thass' treatise on history is an interpretive pedagogy which communicates castelessness as the original habit that defines an Indian. *Indhirar Dhesam* is a creative hermeneutic against the violence of caste *immunitas*

[60] Pandithar, *Indhirar Dhesa Sarithiram*, pp. 148–9.

[61] "Depressed Classes" was a statist categorisation of the erstwhile untouchables and backward classes as scheduled for ameliorative benefits within India during the British Raj. The term was coined after many civic protests by the oppressed castes. Today the erstwhile Depressed Classes of British India, in the context of the increased contemporary demand for caste enumeration, are generally understood as being those communities that benefit from reservation quotas and representation within a dwindling public sphere and diminishing state-supported social welfare.

[62] Pandithar, *Indhirar Dhesa Sarithiram*, p. 150.

which reconstructs a space where *vithai, buthi, eegai,* and *sanmarkam* (knowledge, compassion, right conduct, and action) determine the identity of people and history. As these very practices had been made depressed, Thass laments that the land was also made depressed and identified by falsehood and trickeries in the name of caste and false religion.[63] Thass' history is not only a hermeneutic of rejecting Brahminical domination, but also simultaneously a reconstruction of Buddhist egalitarianism. His interpretive exercise provides an ideological and historical understanding of the condition of "being broken" – which is the meaning of the word Dalit. It is a text in which, for generations of people who were demoted to untouchable status, Buddhism is not alien, nor alienated from the idea of India. Rather, Thass refamiliarises it for us by positioning it within the culture of the Tamil people, even while inspiring them to wage a civilisational battle against caste. Towards this end he rejects terms such as Depressed Classes, Untouchables, and Panchamas, all of which carry the stigma and memory of enforced and inherited inferiority.[64] This worked as a sharp indictment of nationalist reformers of his time, particularly of those who advocated depressed class uplift for their own selfish ends. Instead, as a Buddhist himself, Thass called on his readers to involve themselves in efforts aimed at resurrecting an originary sociality as community in *Sarithiram*. Through its insurrectionary reversal of the dominant view of caste-Hindu history and its prophetic call for a caste-free future, Thass' *Sarithiram* voices a monumental civilisational claim.

It should be noted that Thass' notion of a casteless community, while affirming an affiliation with a Dravidian and Tamil cultural past, emphasises the establishment of a communitarian society that would include the whole world, not only Dravidians. This is because Thass' writing is informed by the claim that communication lies at the origin of the community: it is the originary sociality of communication, as against caste, which is the antithesis of communication because it "excommunicates".

Phule's and Thass' anti-caste hermeneutic foregrounds exposure to an outside by a sharing with others of all the limits and borders

[63] Ibid., p. 152.
[64] Ibid., p. 153.

of finite beings. In Thass' articulation, Tamil Buddhism seeks to be a community disposed to sharing, not closings and enclosures. I have here suggested the similarity of Jotirao Phule and Iyothee Thass, two modern anti-caste thinkers who preceded and foreshadowed Ambedkar and Periyar. In the colonial and nationalist context of the nineteenth century in the Indian subcontinent, the *imaginaire* (also dialectic) of their historical reconceptions of India in *Gulamgiri* (Slavery, 1873) and *Indhira Dhesa Sarithiram* (History of India, 1914), can be read as a pedagogy that advises belonging to a world community and simultaneously to one's own vernacular community outside a caste-immunised space.

References

Aloysius, G., "Caste In and Above History", *Sociological Bulletin*, vol. 48, nos 1–2, 1999.

Aloysius, G., *Dalit-Subaltern Emergence in Religio-Cultural Subjectivity* (New Delhi: Critical Quest, 2007).

Aloysius, G., ed., *Iyothee Thassar Cinthanaikal* (Thoughts of Iyothee Thassar), 2 vols (Palayamkottai: Folklore Resources and Research Center, St Xavier's College, 1999).

Aloysius, G., ed., *Iyothee Thassar Cinthanaikal* (Thoughts of Iyothee Thassar), vol. 3 (Palayamkottai: Folklore Resources and Research Center, St Xavier's College, 2003).

Aloysius, G., *Iyothee Thassar and Tamil Buddhist Movement: Religion as Emancipatory Movement* (New Delhi: Critical Quest, 2015).

Aloysius, G., *Religion as Emancipatory Identity: A Buddhist Movement among the Tamils under Colonialism* (New Delhi: New Age International, 1998).

Aloysius, G., "Transcendence in Modern Tamil Buddhism: A Note on the Liberative in Popular Religious Perceptions", in Surendra Jondhale and Johannes Beltz, eds, *Reconstructing the World: B.R. Ambedkar and Buddhism in India* (New Delhi: Oxford University Press, 2004).

Aloysius, G., "Vicissitudes of Subaltern Self-Identification: A Reading of Tamizhan", in Michael Bergunder, *et al.*, *Ritual, Caste, and Religion in Colonial South India* (Halle: Neue HallescheBerichte 9, 2010).

Ayyathurai, Gajendran, "Colonialism, Caste, and Gender: The Emergence of Critical Caste Feminism in Modern South India", *Journal of Women's History*, vol. 33, no. 3, 2021.

Ayyathurai, Gajendran, "Foundations of Anti-Caste Consciousness: Pandit Iyothee Thass, Tamil Buddhism and the Marginalized in South India", unpublished PhD thesis, Columbia University, New York, 2011.

Ayyathurai, Gajendran, "Living Buddhism: Migration, Memory, and Castelessness in South India", *History and Anthropology*, 2020: https://doi.org/ 10.1080/ 02757206.2020.1854751.

Balasubramaniam, J., "Migration of the Oppressed and Adi Dravida Identity Construction Through Print", *Contemporary Voice of Dalit*, vol. 8, no. 2, 2016.

Balasubramaniam, J., *Suriyodhayam Mudhal Udhaya Sooryan Varai: Dalith Idhalgal, 1869–1943* (From Suriyodhayam to Udhaya Sooryan: Dalit Journals, 1869–1943; Nagercoil: Kalachuvadu, 2017).

Bandyopadhyay, Sekhar, *Caste, Protest and Identity in Colonial India: The Namasudras of Bengal, 1872–1947* (Delhi: Manohar, 1997).

Basu, Raj Sekhar, *Nandanar's Children: The Paraiyan's Tryst with Destiny, Tamil Nadu 1850–1956* (New Delhi: Sage, 2011).

Benjamin, Walter, "Theses on the Philosophy of History", in Hannah Arendt, ed., *Illuminations*, trans. Harry Zohn (New York: Schocken, 1969).

Bergunder, Michael, "Contested Past: Anti-Brahmanical and Hindu Nationalist Reconstructions of Indian Pre-History", *Historiographia Linguistia*, vol. 31, no. 1, 2004.

Bhargava, Rajeev, ed., *Secularism and Its Critics* (New Delhi: Oxford University Press, 1998).

Blanchot, Maurice, *The Unavowable Community*, trans. Pierre Jorris (Barrytown: Station Hill, 1988).

Chandra, Bipan, *Freedom Struggle* (New Delhi: National Book Trust of India, 1972).

Chatterjee, Partha, *Nationalist Thought and the Colonial World: A Derivative Discourse?* (London: Zed Books, 1986).

Chatterjee, Partha, *The Nation and Its Fragments: Colonial and Postcolonial Histories* (Princeton: Princeton University Press, 1993).

Chatterjee, Partha, *The Politics of the Governed: Reflections on Popular Politics in Most of the World* (New Delhi: Permanent Black, 2004).

Dalit Panthers' Manifesto (Bombay, 1973).

Dharmaraj, T., *Iyothee Thassar: Paarpanar Mudhal Parayar Varai* (Iyothee Thassar: From Seer [Brahmin] to Utterer [Parayar]; Chennai: Kizhakku Pathipagam, 2019).

Dirks, Nicholas, *Castes of Mind: Colonialism and the Making of Modern India* (New Delhi: Permanent Black, 2003).

Esposito, Roberto, *Communitas*, trans. Timothy Campbell (Stanford: Stanford University Press, 2009).

Figueira, Dorothy M., *Aryans, Jews, Brahmins: Theorizing Authority through Myths of Identity* (Albany: SUNY, 2002).

Gaon, Stella, "Communities in Question: Sociality and Solidarity in Nancy and Blanchot", *Journal for Cultural Research*, vol. 9, no. 4, October 2005.

Guru, Gopal, ed., *Humiliation: Claims and Context* (New Delhi: Oxford University Press, 2009).

Guru, Gopal, "The Idea of India: 'Derivative', 'Desi' and Beyond", *Economic and Political Weekly*, vol. 46, no. 37, 10 September 2011.

Guru, Gopal, and Sundar Sarukkai, eds, *The Cracked Mirror* (New Delhi: Oxford University Press, 2012).

Guha, Ranajit, *An Indian Historiography of India: A Nineteenth Century Agenda and Its Implications* (Calcutta: K.P. Bagchi, 1988).

Gowthaman, Raj, *Ka. Iyotheethassarin Aaivugal* (K. Iyotheethassar's Research; Nagercoil: Kalachuvadu, 2004).

Jangam, Chinnaiah, *Dalits and the Making of Modern India* (New Delhi: Oxford University Press, 2017).

Kaviraj, Sudipta, "The Imaginary Institution of India", in Partha Chatterjee and Gyanendra Pandey, eds, *Subaltern Studies VII: Writings in South Asian History and Society* (Delhi: Oxford University Press, 1992).

Leonard, Dickens, "Casteless Tamils and Early Print Public Sphere: Remembering Iyothee Thass (1845–1914)", *South Asia Research*, vol. 41, no. 3, 2021.

Little, Adrian, *The Politics of Community: Theory and Practice* (Edinburgh: Edinburgh University Press, 2002).

Mohan, P. Sanal, *Modernity of Slavery: Struggles Against Caste Inequality in Colonial Kerala* (New Delhi: Oxford University Press, 2015).

Monius, Anne, *Imagining a Place for Buddhism: Literary Culture and Religious Community in Tamil-Speaking South India* (New Delhi: Navayana, 2009).

Nancy, Jean-Luc, *Being Singular Plural*, trans. Robert D. Richardson and Anne E. O'Byrne (Stanford: Stanford University Press, 2000).

Nancy, Jean-Luc, "Corpus", in Juliet Flower MacCannell and Laura Zakarin, eds, *Thinking Bodies*, trans. Claudette Sartiliot (California: Stanford University Press, 1994).

Nancy, Jean-Luc, *The Inoperative Community*, ed. Peter Connor, trans. Peter Connor, *et al.* (Minneapolis and London: University of Minnesota Press, 1991).

Narayan, Badri, *Women Heroes and Dalit Assertion in North India* (New Delhi: Sage, 2006).

O'Hanlon, Rosalind, *Caste, Conflict and Ideology: Mahatma Jotirao Phule and Low Caste Protest in Nineteenth Century Western India* (1985; rpntd Ranikhet: Permanent Black, 2010).

Omvedt, Gail, *Dalits and the Democratic Revolution* (New Delhi: Sage Publications, 1994).

Omvedt, Gail, *Seeking Begumpura: The Social Visions of Anticaste Intellectuals* (New Delhi: Navayana, 2008).

Oppert, Gustav Solomon, *On the Original Inhabitants of Bharatvarsh or India* (Westminster: Archibald Constable & Co., 1893).

Pandithar, Iyothee Thassa [Thass], *Indhira Dhesa Sarithiram* (History of Indhirar Country) (1912; rpntd Chennai: Tamil Kudiarasu Publication, 2010).

Prakash, Gyan, *Bonded Histories* (Cambridge: Cambridge University Press, 1990).

Prashad,Vijay, *Untouchable Freedom: A Social History of a Dalit Community* (New Delhi: Oxford University Press, 1999).

Raj, Jayaseelan, "Post-colonial Caste, Ambedkar, and the Politics of Counter-narrative", *History and Anthropology*, 2022, https://doi.org/10.1080/02 757206.2022.2096021.

Rao, Anupama, *The Caste Question: Dalits and the Politics of Modern India* (Ranikhet: Permanent Black, 2010).

Rawat, Ramnarayan, *Reconsidering Untouchability* (Bloomington: Indiana University Press, 2011).

Rawat, Ramnarayan, and K. Satyanarayana, eds, *Dalit Studies* (Durham: Duke University Press, 2016).

Ricoeur, Paul, "On Interpretation", in *Philosophy in France Today*, ed. Alan Montefiore (Cambridge: Cambridge University Press, 1983).

Ricoeur, Paul, *The Conflict of Interpretations*, ed. Don Ihde, trans. Kathleen McLaughlin (London & New York: Continuum, 2005).

Sarkar, Sumit, *Writing Social History* (New Delhi: Oxford University Press, 1998).

Seal, Anil, *The Emergence of Indian Nationalism* (New Delhi: Cambridge University Press, 1971).

Sekhar, Ajay, "A Broken Padmasana: The Fissured Buddha of Pattanam", 2012, https://ajaysekher.net/ 2012/11/02/broken-padmasana-pattanam-buddha-returns/, accessed 26 Dec. 2021.

Viswanath, Rupa, *The Pariah Problem: Caste, Religion, and the Social in Modern India* (New York: Columbia University Press, 2014).

Viswanathan, Gauri, *Outside the Fold: Conversion, Modernity and Belief* (New Delhi: Oxford University Press, 2001).

Waghmore, Suryakant, *Civility Against Caste: Dalit Politics and Citizenship in Western India* (New Delhi: Sage, 2013).

Wakankar, Milind, *Subalternity and Religion: The Pre-history of Dalit Empowerment in South Asia* (New York: Routledge, 2010).

Zelliot, Eleanor, *From Untouchable to Dalit* (New Delhi: Manohar, 1992).

Notes on Contributors

ANUPAMA is an Assistant Professor, Department of History, M.M. Mahila Mahavidyalaya, Veer Kunwar Singh University, Ara, Bihar. She did her BA in History at Lady Sriram College, University of Delhi, and a PhD from the Centre for Historical Studies, Jawaharlal Nehru University, New Delhi. Her research and teaching interests relate to caste, visual culture, gender history, and history of dress. She is completing a book manuscript, "Caste, Class, and Clothing in Northern India in the Early-Twentieth Century".

CHAKALI CHANDRA SEKHAR is Lecturer, Department of English, SRR and CVR Government Degree College, Vijayawada, Andhra Pradesh. He is working on a book provisionally entitled "Empowering the Marginalized in Colonial India: The Conversion of Telugu Dalits and their Social Journey in Rayalaseema (1850–1930)". He is also working on colonial Christian print and Christian periodicals in Telugu.

DICKENS LEONARD is Assistant Professor of Literature in the Department of Humanities and Social Sciences at the Indian Institute of Technology Delhi. His PhD (2017) in Comparative Literature from the University of Hyderabad was on the nineteenth-century Tamil intellectual Iyothee Thass and Tamil Buddhism.

JESTIN T. VARGHESE did his PhD from the School of Social Sciences, Mahatma Gandhi University, Kottayam, Kerala. He is part of the research team of the Kerala Maritime Communities Project of the IUCSSRE, Mahatma Gandhi University, in collaboration with the University of Pennsylvania. He also teaches at the Department of Social Work, De Paul Institute of Science and Technology, Angamali, Kerala.

K. SATYANARAYANA is Professor, Department of Cultural Studies, EFL University, Hyderabad. He has co-edited *No Alphabet in Sight*

(2011), *Steel Nibs Are Sprouting* (2013), *Dalit Studies* (2016), *Dalit Text* (2020), and *Concealing Caste* (2023). He is interested in questions of dignity and equality in Indian literary cultures, intellectual traditions, and cultural practices. He is working on a book provisionally entitled "The Protagonist in Dalit Literature".

KOONAL DUGGAL is a researcher and tutor in Social Anthropology, School of Social and Political Science, University of Edinburgh. He was a postdoctoral research fellow in the Leverhulme Trust-funded project *Gurus, Anti-gurus and Media in North India* (2019–22). He is co-editor of *Gurus and Media: Sound, Image, Machine, Text and the Digital* (UCL Press, 2023). He is working on a book on deras, gurus, caste, and media politics in contemporary Punjab.

LUCINDA RAMBERG is Associate Professor of Anthropology and Feminist, Gender, and Sexuality Studies at Cornell University. Her essay in this volume is drawn from a manuscript in progress, "'We Were Always Buddhist': Dalit Conversion and Sexual Modernity".

P. SANAL MOHAN is a retired professor at the Mahatma Gandhi University and currently a Visiting Fellow at the Inter-University Centre for Social Science Research and Extension at Mahatma Gandhi University. Kottayam, Kerala. India. He has researched and published on caste, slavery, and Christianity in Kerala and presently working on a book project, "Global Christianity and the Transformation of Dalits in Colonial and Postcolonial Kerala".

RAMNARAYAN S. RAWAT is Associate Professor of History at the University of Delaware, USA. He has published on caste and inequality in South Asian history. His next book is provisionally entitled "The Language of Liberalism: The Lost History of the Dalit Public Sphere in Late Colonial India".

SHARIKA THIRANAGAMA is Associate Professor of Anthropology at Stanford University. She has written extensively on Sri Lanka and India. Her essay in the present volume is drawn from her forthcoming book project tentatively titled "The Monster in Your Path: The Private Life of Caste in India".

SUMEET MHASKAR is Professor of Sociology at the Jindal School of Government and Public Policy, O.P. Jindal Global University, Sonipat. His essay in the present volume is part of a larger project, *Technical Change and Occupational Choices in the Modern Indian Industry, c. 1870s–2006: A Study of Mumbai's Cotton Textile Mills.*

Index

www.ingramcontent.com/pod-product-compliance
Lightning Source LLC
Chambersburg PA
CBHW021126270326
41929CB00009B/1061